HELMUTH VON MOLTKE

Helmuth von Moltke

A LEADER AGAINST HITLER

by

MICHAEL BALFOUR

Professor of European History
in the University of East Anglia

and

JULIAN FRISBY

MACMILLAN

SBN 333 14030 3

Library of Congress catalog card number 72–86789

Published by
MACMILLAN LONDON LIMITED
London and Basingstoke
Associated companies in New York Toronto
Dublin Melbourne Johannesburg and Madras

Printed in Great Britain by
RICHARD CLAY (THE CHAUCER PRESS) LTD,
Bungay, Suffolk

Contents

List of Illustrations

Between pages 148 and 149

1. HELMUTH IN 1931
   Although Helmuth brought Fräulein Schneefuss to Kreisau to make a picture of him as a present for his parents, he declared that he was too busy to sit inactive while she drew, so that this charcoal sketch had to be made while he was working at his desk.
2. THE SCHLOSS
3. THE BERGHAUS
   Helmuth had this picture with him in Ravensbrück.
4. HELMUTH'S PARENTS
5[a] DOROTHY AND FREYA
 [b] HELMUTH AND CASPAR, 1938
6. FREYA 1946
7. HELMUTH AT HIS TRIAL
   Freisler on the left
8. LETTER OF 16 November 1941
   Actual size

Preface

THIS book has been written because its authors believe that only in a continuous narrative, which not merely introduces at the proper chronological points the material already published but also draws upon the considerable amount of unpublished material, can the character of Helmuth von Moltke be properly appreciated.

Chief among the unpublished (or partially published) documents are the 1,600 letters which he wrote to his wife Freya between 1929 and 1945. Out of these, which besides being difficult to decipher are often concerned with trivial and ephemeral matters, she has selected 580 for transcription as being of wider and lasting interest; of these 425 date from the war period. To our regret, however, we have found ourselves unable to reproduce anything like all of these. For few of the letters can be properly appreciated without a knowledge of the private and public background against which they were written. It was clearly essential for us to sketch the private background, while if we had taken the public one for granted we should have narrowed appreciably the circle of those who could through the book come to know the man. Even as things are, we have run to a greater length than we intended and are in danger of producing an inappropriate memorial to someone who valued brevity.

Our first and incomparably our biggest debt of gratitude is to Freya Gräfin von Moltke, particularly for placing at our disposal her knowledge and memories as well as the letters and other material which she has preserved with such faithful care. Both in writing the book and in regular contacts throughout the years since 1945 we have been privileged to observe how her lively interest and involvement in the present have at no time overshadowed her awareness of the past or prevented her, while retaining a profound fidelity to Helmuth, from viewing him and his activities objectively. We feel an obligation to make this remarkable personal achievement known.

Our second major obligation is to Dr Ger van Roon who has done so much to collect information about Helmuth and his friends and has generously put his knowledge and archives at our disposal. We intend this book to be regarded as complementary to rather than as a substitute for his. He has looked at the group as a whole and has documented the evolution of their ideas; we have been primarily concerned to give a picture of the man we knew.

We are also indebted to many members of Helmuth's family and, among persons mentioned in the book, to Professor Dr Fritz Christiansen-Weniger, Sir John Foster, Dr Eugen Gerstenmaier, the Hon. Alexander Kirk, Dr Harald Poelchau, Professor Dr Wilhelm Wengler and Marion Gräfin Yorck von Wartenburg. Grizel Balfour has given us invaluable help as typist and index-maker, beside holding a watching brief for the general reader. The number of other people who have assisted us is so great that we hope they will accept an expression of gratitude which is no less sincere for being collective.

The book has been written as a joint enterprise to which J.F. has contributed his intimate knowledge of the Moltke family and M.B. his wider acquaintance with the history of the time. Primary responsibility for the views expressed accordingly varies with the subject but neither contributor is in disagreement with anything in the book. Where we have had occasion to refer to parts which one or the other of us has played in the story, we have identified the person concerned by initials, since it would have been inappropriate to use the first person either singular or plural and we felt it incongruous to use our own names. Freya von Moltke has read the entire text and as far as her knowledge goes (which is saying a good deal) believes it to be factually accurate. We have not asked her to endorse all our judgments but we have no reason to think that any of them make her unhappy.

MICHAEL BALFOUR

JULIAN FRISBY

1 February 1972

Authors' Note

UNLESS otherwise specified, all Helmuth's letters were addressed to Freya. In reproducing his letters, italics have been used where he himself wrote the passage or words in English. In such cases, his own punctuation has been retained.

Unless otherwise stated, the references to Dr van Roon's book are to the English edition: *German Resistance to Hitler: Count von Moltke and the Kreisau Circle* (1971).

Abbreviations

AA	Auswärtiges Amt = Foreign Office
AHA	Allgemeines Heeresamt = General Army Office
AWA	Allgemeines Wehrmachtamt = General Office of the Armed Forces
COS	Chief of Staff
GOC	General Officer Commanding
HWK	Handelskrieg und Wirtschaftliche Kampfmassnahmen = Trade War and Measures for Economic Warfare
IfZ	Institut für Zeitgeschichte (Contemporary History) Munich
IMT	International Military Tribunal Nuremberg
OKH	Oberkommando des Heeres = High Command of the Army
OKW	Oberkommando der Wehrmacht = High Command of the Armed Forces
PoW	Prisoner-of-war
RSHA	Reichssicherheitshauptamt = Head Office for State Security
SD	Sicherheitsdienst = Security Service
VfZ	*Vierteljahreshefte für Zeitgeschichte* = Quarterly Journal of Contemporary History

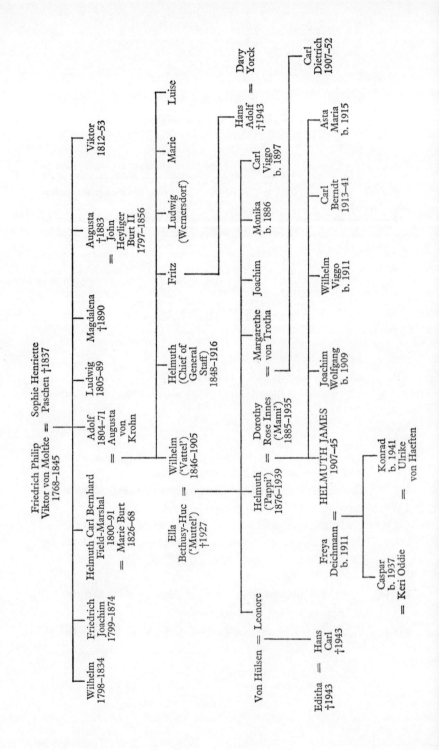

1 The Moltke Family

WHEN on 22 September 1942 Helmuth von Moltke had supper in Oslo with leaders of the Norwegian Resistance, the main dish, in a meal which he found 'fit for a prince', was grouse.* This, as he jokingly wrote to his wife, was 'very tactful' because his hosts had – unwittingly – involved him in consuming his family crest. For the Moltkes, like grouse, came from Northern Europe and there is scarcely a country in Scandinavia or along the Baltic shores where they have not been active. Helmuth sometimes attributed this dispersion to their habit of choosing the losing side in political disputes, and needing in consequence to change domicile quickly.

The earliest known ancestor was a Matheus Moltke whose name figures among a list of knights instituted in 1264 by Henry the Lion at Schwerin in Mecklenburg, recently conquered from the heathen Slavs. Until the end of the eighteenth century, descendants continued to own estates in that Duchy. Two notable Moltkes were Margarethe, who in the fifteenth century married Christian Nielsen Vasa, thus becoming the ancestress of the Kings of Sweden down to Charles XII, and Nicholas, who in 1692 was beheaded on the walls of Hanover for conspiracy.

Joachim Christof Moltke (1602–65) fought with Gustavus Adolphus and then lived in Mecklenburg and Holstein. His grandson Otto Friedrich distinguished himself in the Saxon Service, and his great-grandson Friedrich Casimir Siegfried in the Austrian. The last-named was remarkable for his ability to crush twelve pewter plates into a roll at one squeeze and for the generation of thirteen children. Such philoprogenitiveness, however, proved a mixed blessing because he left his estate between them and the only way of sharing out the heritage was to sell the land and divide up the proceeds.

The seventh son of Friedrich Casimir Siegfried (1768–1845) found employment as a volunteer in the Prussian army, as did five of his brothers. In 1796 he resigned and for some years found it hard to settle, even with his creditors. But in 1805 he fetched up, in company with Henriette Paschen of Lübeck whom he had married in 1797, at the farm of Augustenhof in Holstein. As historians of the nineteenth century are only too well aware, that province then belonged to the Danish

* Probably the 'willow' grouse as the red variety is peculiar to the British Isles.

crown, and accordingly he had to become a Danish subject and join the Danish Militia/*Landwehr*. In due course he rose to the rank of lieutenant-general but while doing so parted not only with his property but, for all practical purposes, with his wife. As the third and most distinguished of their sons once wrote to his mother, 'If only my father could rent and manage a farm! But the worst of it is that the mischief is not so much in his ill-luck as in himself.'

The same son, on being asked in later life how he could keep going for so long without food, replied, 'I went hungry for twenty-one years in my youth.' Helmuth Carl Bernhard was born in 1800 at Parchim in Mecklenburg and judiciously given his first name as a compliment to the uncle who commanded the local garrison. Having originally at the age of nineteen joined the Danish army, he thought to better himself (and thereby his family) by transferring to the Prussian in 1822. Eleven years later, he procured an appointment to the General Staff, still a small and select body whose creation a few years earlier is a landmark in military history. In 1835, already a captain, he went to Constantinople and while there was seconded to the Turks as a military adviser. He did not come back for four years and on his return felt secure enough to marry. The bride's grandfather was an Englishman, John Heyliger Burt, who had made money in the West Indies and set up as a country gentleman in Staffordshire. His son, of the same name, coming of age shortly after the father's death, let the estate to tenants and went off to visit an English friend who had married a German and was living near Kiel. John Heyliger Burt II fell in love with a relation of his hostess but only got his prospective mother-in-law's consent to the marriage on condition that he and his wife lived in Germany. Their children, of whom Marie the Field-Marshal's wife was the youngest, never therefore lived in England and there is no record of them even visiting that country although they presumably had British nationality. Burt's first wife died after ten years and he then married in 1834 the Field-Marshal's younger sister Auguste.[1] Marie Burt was accordingly marrying, at the age of sixteen, a man twenty-six years older than herself who was into the bargain her step-uncle. All the evidence, however, is that they were a singularly happy pair, though the fact that they were childless is of material importance for this book.

There is no need to give further details here of a career which belongs to history. But, since the Field-Marshal's example and inheritance were important influences on his great-grand-nephew, a few words about them are called for. The world regards him as a soldier but he once said that, if he had not felt compelled to join the army as the quickest way of supporting his family, he would have chosen an academic career. Except for a few skirmishes which he observed in Turkey, he was sixty-four before he heard a shot fired in battle and his victories owed more to his brain than to his right arm. In October 1935 the then Chief of the General Staff, General Beck, when lecturing in the presence of Hitler, pointedly praised the Field-Marshal for preferring cautious evaluation to bold adventuring (*das grundliche Wägen vor dem kühnen Wagen*).

He read widely in modern European literature and the classics (though he was not beyond confusing Persephone with Eurydice and Hephaestus with Poseidon). He published essays on such topics as the political relations between Belgium and Holland 1579–1831 and the points to be considered in choosing routes for railways, as well as a short story called 'The Two Friends'. He won the highest Prussian decoration, *Pour le Mérite,* not for his exploits in the field but at an unusually young age for topography. He knew Europe intimately and some of his letters advising his brothers on how to travel and where to stay are as good as any guide book. He used pencil and paint-brush to considerable effect and was a keen botanist and gardener. He listened avidly to music, especially Bach, Mozart and Beethoven, but liked to tell the story of the Roman countess who said, 'We Wagnerians resemble drunkards. They know they will end in destruction yet drink all the same.'

Some weeks before his marriage his future wife told him she knew well that the Moltkes were quiet and reserved. Indeed the common saying about him was that he could be silent in seven languages (German, Danish, French, Italian, English, Russian and Turkish – to which he later added Spanish). According to a family story, he and his brother were once travelling from Berlin to Silesia (probably going second class) and were in the local train on the last lap of their five-hour journey before the brother broke the silence by pointing out of the window and saying, 'Look, a hare' – to which the Field-Marshal replied, 'Chatterbox!' But the fact that such a story was told in the family suggests that foibles were being exaggerated, and a connection recorded that 'only very occasionally was there any justification in the family circle for referring to him as "*der Grosse Schweiger*". He could chat with my wife and my grown-up children for hours on end and his mild and friendly expression when he devoted himself to playing with the younger generation was enchanting to see.'

The truth seems to have been twofold. Prussia grew great by making limited resources go a long way and, as in Scotland, there was a tradition of thrift and caution among all ranks from the King downwards. The Field-Marshal himself had known poverty at first-hand and even after he had become comfortably off wrote that 'the abominable habit of economy sticks so firmly that it is difficult to get rid of'. But in addition part of the secret of his success – as of his longevity – was that he was essentially a simple personality who did not give himself airs or boss other people about. 'Strict with himself, he was indulgent to others, a benevolent superior, a kind master.' 'He esteemed work of whatever kind, whether it were the creative activity of the intellect or physical exertion.' After he had established himself, he was generous not only to members of his family but also to others in need, though he preferred to do his charity by stealth. Yet hand in hand with generosity went a stark doctrine of self-help.

> Poverty and distress are necessary elements in the scheme of life – what would become of the whole social system if this stern necessity did not force man to think and work?

The story goes that a distinguished English philosopher, on being asked how he managed to change from day to full evening dress and pass the night in apparent comfort in spite of arriving without visible luggage, replied, 'Underneath, underneath.' Much the same was true of the Field-Marshal who always travelled light. On one occasion the niece who after his sister's death kept house for him went to spend the week-end with some relatives. Her host, welcoming her on arrival, noticed in the background a slim, slightly bent figure with a big black hat whom at first he took for some young artist she had brought along. However it revealed itself as the Field-Marshal who, although by then in his eighties had accompanied her 'as a surprise'. Under his light overcoat he proved to be wearing a dress-coat with the Cross of the Order of St John. 'Forgive this get-up,' he said 'but I have to attend the meeting of the Order in Breslau and full dress is obligatory.' His other decorations were in his pockets together with goodness knows what else, for he had brought only what he stood up in. The next day he was persuaded by his host to borrow one of the latter's jackets. In the afternoon he was taken for a drive and it came on to rain. When his hostess wished to have the hood of the carriage raised he mischievously remarked, 'Please don't go to the trouble. This isn't my coat.'

His political views illustrate a central question of German history in the nineteenth century. For, though he owed much of his success to exploiting the Industrial Revolution for purposes of war, he was neither able nor anxious to admit the consequences which that process was bound to have in terms of government. In 1848 he referred to 'the shriekers in Frankfurt' and wrote that 'the better sort of the nation are silent, the scum come to the top and govern'.

> Whatever happens I do not think that the worst of all enemies, democracy, has much chance of success with us.
>
> All these demonstrations prove nothing or very little. Only a small number of persons attend them and always the same ones.

In 1865 his view was that 'assemblies are the mere tools of individual intriguers and a useless or dangerous plaything'. Two years later he was of the opinion that 'the masses are blind and woe to the State and society where they obtain supremacy'.

On German unification he saw eye to eye with Bismarck. 'A strong Prussian government and then German unity can be achieved by Prussia' (1848). 'The passion of the Germans for separation, observed by Tacitus, necessitates decision by force of arms' (May 1866). 'A [German] union cannot be effected by persuasion; we shall have to fight for it sooner or later' (1868). But they were not always in agreement. For the Field-Marshal believed firmly that war was something which should be left to the technicians and in a series of celebrated conflicts opposed the efforts of the chancellor to subordinate the course of campaigns to considerations of international politics.[2]

He died as he had lived, in his ninety-first year at the end of an active day and after making a grand slam at whist (a game in which his enjoyment often outran his skill). He was having the piano played to him when he collapsed and all was over in a few moments. Fifty years later to the day his great-grand-nephew finished the first draft of his proposals for the reconstruction of Germany after the overthrow of National Socialism.

2 Kreisau

A M I D the troubles of 1848, the Field-Marshal had written to his favourite brother Adolf:

> My cherished idea is that by degrees we should gather together on an estate somewhere or other, where each of us should contribute in capital or working power whatever he could bring. I would prefer this possession to be on the beloved soil of Germany.

This wish he was at last able to gratify when the King in recognition for his services in 1866 granted him 200,000 talers (£30,000 at the prices then current).* As a lieutenant he had been stationed at Frankfurt-on-the-Oder and from there had explored the mountains on the border between Prussian Silesia and Austrian Bohemia (the lands of the Sudeten Germans). He acquired not merely a familiarity with the region which stood him in good stead in 1866 but also an affection for the Silesian meadows and hills. Towards the beginning of 1868 he bought for 245,000 talers the three neighbouring estates of Kreisau,† Nieder-Gräditz and Wierischau, about 1,000 acres in all (and thus a relatively modest estate by East Elbian standards where they ran up to 45,000 acres).

There was already a house at Kreisau but the Field-Marshal set out at once to improve both it and its surroundings. The two people whom he most wanted to enjoy it had little opportunity to do so. For his wife Marie died on Christmas Eve 1868 and his brother Adolf on 7 April 1871. Marie lay in a specially built mausoleum on a hill a little way from the house, and there in due course her husband's body also came to rest. Other members of the family were buried close by.

* As a further reward, he was made a count in 1871. The title was among the relatively few in Germany which passed by primogeniture alone. The position about succession to such titles after the formal abolition of all titles in 1919 is open to argument, as is the extent to which anyone not in the direct line of descent was thereafter entitled to call himself count. The subject of this book was generally addressed as count and on occasion described himself in the same way. But he laid no stress on his rank and for that reason the title is not emphasised here.

† A law passed in 1930 required most German place-names beginning with C to change to K. But, for simplicity, the form 'Kreisau' has been used throughout this book except in quotations from pre-1930 documents.

A trust was set up to manage the property. For in 1868 Kreisau as a unit was entailed on the sons of the Field-Marshal's brothers and sisters in order of seniority, and was in fact inherited by Wilhelm, the eldest son of Adolf, known in the family as 'Vattel'. Only part of the purchase money was handed over immediately and 100,000 talers remaining from the royal grant, along with 56,000 talers which the Field-Marshal had saved independently, were used as trust funds to provide interest payments on the remaining mortgage as well as to meet other legacies and grants and act as general backing for the estate. By the time of the Field-Marshal's death his careful husbandry had created a situation enabling the trust to buy another estate at Wernersdorf near Zobten. This was leased to Wilhelm's younger brother Ludwig and after his death (unmarried) to his nephew Hans Adolf who finally bought it outright in 1942. All that prudence could suggest was thus done to secure the future well-being of the family and protect its property from any incompetent members. The only failure was to foresee the need to protect it – and the nation – from incompetent political leaders!

Even before his wife's death the Field-Marshal had claimed to be 'longing for the quiet life of Creisau. I should much prefer to be there while the trees are in blossom than to sit in the stuffy atmosphere of Parliament.' He once told a visitor that 'it is never too late to do a good work. I began to plant these trees shortly before my seventieth year and I am now sitting in their shade.' When the same visitor expressed admiration, the old man replied that 'it has all been done of set purpose for I laid out all the roads and transplanted many of the trees'.

What was there about Kreisau to arouse such affection, for, as will be seen, the feeling was not confined to the Moltke who bought it? The answer lies in amenity rather than drama; it was not a question of classical or romantic loveliness but rather the simple and placid charm of a friend. The place and its owners were in fact in harmony.

Kreisau lies some 800 feet above the sea in gently undulating country, thirty miles west of what used to be called Breslau and four south-east of a small town fortified by Frederick the Great and known till 1945 as Schweidnitz. Between Kreisau and Breslau lies the long-extinct volcano of the Zobten, some 2,400 feet high, the last mountain of any size before the great plain stretching to the Urals. To the south-west runs the long wall of the Eulengebirge with the Hohe Eule, 3,400 feet, opposite the main front of the house and some fifteen miles away. This is the outer northward-facing bastion of the whole complex of high ground which forms the Czech frontier. Kreisau thus lies among foothills but enjoys a prospect of mountains.

Kreisau village is long and narrow, lining the sides of a road which the third Moltke owner tarred so as to provide his residence with a more stylish approach than the previous dirt-track (and also one more easily negotiated in winter). This road runs from the station, at which through trains only took to stopping after the Kaiser had alighted there for the Field-Marshal's funeral. It passes to the north of the Schloss and continues through Gräditz to join the main road. This follows the line of the old trade route along which the towns were said to be strung out like pearls, so that Schweidnitz is a convenient day's journey by cart from Reichenbach, the next halting-place to the south. The village, with a population of 400, contains a small Catholic church, a school, two inns and a post-office. The Lutheran church was in Gräditz. Wierischau, the third part of the estate, lies beyond the railway to the south.

The estate is watered by the little river Peile, which was a persistent source of worry through its tendency to flood in spring but which in summer was little more than a stream meandering through meadows and between banks vividly yellow with rudbeckias. In the 1930s the Nazis established a Labour Camp at Gräditz and for several summers a hoard of young conscripts strained and sweated to iron out the curves of the river, substituting a channel of uniform width along a broad and graceless arc. This did more to reduce the charm than to remove the floods and would have prevented the Field-Marshal from recognising the 'Park' to which he devoted so much attention. But the word Park can be misleading; there was little of Capability Brown, still less of Le Nôtre, in Kreisau. By 1930 the need to bring all the available farmland into use had reduced the Park to the grassy tract through which the Peile flowed, the only traces of landscaping being the conifers screening the railway and several fine specimen trees, mainly spruce, which appeared to have been planted haphazard. Originally there had been a flower garden next to the Hof with fine borders and lawns and a greenhouse containing vines and Maréchal Niel roses. Behind was a large vegetable garden, also with a greenhouse. Later, however, as much as could be cultivated was given over to vegetables and the rest left to go wild. The last traces of former glories were four fine specimens of magnolia soulangeana at the central intersection of the main paths and a rather derelict tennis court, the only outdoor game for which, according to his mother, Helmuth ever had any taste.

The German word 'Schloss' is usually translated 'castle' but 'hall' would better convey the scale and style of the Kreisau house. The façade was plain, large windows regularly spaced in walls faced with rough-cast, the whole washed a pale khaki-colour under a slate roof. In the 1890s Wilhelm von Moltke's sociable wife (Muttel) had had the building lengthened by projections added at either end and heightened by an extra storey to provide more guest-rooms. The house faces south-west towards the mountains but has no view of them, partly because it stands too low, partly because the Field-Marshal planted a thick belt of spruce to shut out the railway. It has the river to its back and the 'Hof', or Great Farmyard, in front. Both gave out at various seasons peculiar odours which are for many people who came to Kreisau intimately connected with their memories of the place.

The front door of the Schloss gave into a large rectangular entrance hall, at the left end of which double doors led into the dining-room with elaborate rococo decorations in gold and white. In one corner stood a notable baroque confection which enshrined a leaden basin; this constituted the font at which members of the family were baptised. At the far end and at right angles was the Field-Marshal's study, sparsely and simply furnished; out of this opened the closet in which he had slept, with the stand on which each night he put his wig. On the other side of the hall was the library, also used as a breakfast-room, and the room which Dorothy von Moltke used as her bedroom, and in which Helmuth was born on 11 March 1907. The floor below, the real ground floor of the house, contained kitchens, still rooms, servants' quarters, laundry and the like.

Standing at a little distance on a rise to the east of the Schloss, at right angles to it and the railway, was the Hill House (Berghaus). This is of importance because the family moved into it in 1928 as an economy measure, and much preferred it to the more pretentious Schloss. The house itself was at first glance scarcely to be distinguished from those occupied by local small-holders, especially on the western face which it turned towards the world. This was plain to starkness – a white wall sparsely and haphazardly fenestrated with those small apertures designed to admit light without heat to such places as larders and 'offices'. But the garden side was a different matter. Helmuth liked to tell a story that a former owner of the estate had a nephew who went bankrupt. The uncle gave him money to build a house but insisted on it being modest. The uncle, however, was crippled and therefore had to judge by what he could see from his windows!

Though entirely without pretensions, the rear of the Berghaus yet had an air. The windows were large, tall, regularly spaced, each with a framework of ornamental plaster. There was also a wide verandah with a flat roof. It was as high as the house and had the proportions of a large living-room. Here in summer the life of the family was lived, meals eaten, books read, bridge played, discussions held. Although the Berghaus did not give the impression of a large house, it provided on its two upper floors sufficient bedrooms for the whole family, two guests and staff. These, however, being under the pitch of the roof, were low and narrow.

But the great advantage of the Berghaus was that, being higher than the Schloss, it had a fine view of the hills. The garden, originally sloping with the natural lie of the ground, was reconstructed by the sons in 1931 so as to provide a wide grassy terrace in front of the house with flowers round its edges. There were also on the lawn a pair of large thuyas and, round the corner, a splendid acacia from which Helmuth used genially to say he would be hanged when the revolution occurred.

From the point of view of agricultural economics, the Kreisau estate was not only on the small side but uneven in quality of soil. It was run as a mixed farm, the pleasant kind which is going out of fashion. About a quarter was meadows and woodland, the rest grew potatoes, flax, peas, rape-seed and sugar-beet (a chancy crop). All the grains were produced and particularly summer barley for the brewers. About sixty head of milking cows were kept, along with their offspring. About ten sows produced young pigs and a hundred were as a rule fattened for slaughter. During the war a herd of sheep was acquired. There were eight teams of horses for working the fields. Eventually two tractors were introduced, along with a modern threshing machine, two silos and a blower for the hay. Some sixty people were employed all the year round, with additional help at peak times. By the time the war came, the turnover was about 120,000 *Reichsmarks* (£6,000), the tax value RM500,000 and the income obtained – in good years – RM30,000. Thus it could be a going concern, provided only that it was well managed.

3 James Rose Innes and His Daughter

W I L H E L M von Moltke, who presided at Kreisau from his uncle's death in 1891 until his own in 1905, rose to the rank of lieutenant-general. The family said that if he had not offended the Kaiser, the post of Chief of the General Staff might have gone to him rather than to his younger brother Helmuth. He was sometimes called 'the dwarf violin-ist' – a somewhat perverse description because, although he certainly played well on the Steiner which the Field-Marshal had given him, he stood over six feet high (as did his three brothers, one of his sons, three of his grandsons and four of his great-grandsons). He married in 1874 Countess Ella Bethusy-Huc, whose mother was a talented singer. Although her family is said to have been French in origin, they had lived in Silesia for some time and the father was a Free Conservative deputy in the *Reichstag* from 1871 to 1880. The daughter was a vivacious and attractive but rather easy-going person inclined to think that she had done enough for the five children born between 1875 and 1886 by bringing them into the world as Moltkes. Even the arrival of another son in 1897 did not keep her from being bored by the long summers in Kreisau.

Accordingly she put into the paper a notice saying that a noble family living in the country was anxious to take in paying guests – a course of action regarded at that time as highly unorthodox. The only qualification required of the visitors was the capacity to play bridge. This advertisement was seen and answered by a South African lady who had come to Europe and Germany with her eighteen-year-old daughter to complete the latter's education. The answer was accepted and mother and daughter came to Kreisau. As the newcomers appeared for dinner on the day of their arrival, Muttel must have felt that her initiative had been rewarded. For she was incorrigibly superstitious and had recently heard from a fortune-teller that good luck would come to Kreisau with a girl from across the sea wearing a white dress and a blue necklace. The family still possess the chain of turquoise native beads which Dorothy Rose Innes was wearing with a white dress that first evening.

Sir James Rose Innes, Dorothy's father, was descended from Thomas Innes of Muiryfold in Banffshire, whose great grandson James (1799–1873) emigrated to the Cape of Good Hope sixteen years after its acquisition by Britain in 1806, to become in due course Professor of Mathematics and superintendent-general of the Cape education system. He and his descendants took 'Rose' as an additional given name (in distinction from the descendants of Thomas Innes' daughter Elizabeth who married James Rose of Gask, Aberdeenshire, and founded a family with the hyphenated name of Rose-Innes).

Sir James himself was born in 1855 and married on 18 October 1881 Jessie Dods Pringle, who came of a farming family which had also emigrated from Scotland, having secured land in South Africa thanks to the friendship of one of its members with Walter Scott. Of Jessie's father, William Pringle of Lynedoch, the story went that in some skirmish with natives he was lying on the ground, his old-fashioned long-barrelled pistol having misfired, in imminent danger of having a spear thrust through his chest. As a young neighbour galloped up to his rescue, the victim remained sufficiently unperturbed to advise him, 'Steady, Willie, take your time.'*

Sir James was educated in South Africa and had quick success at the Cape Bar. He was a member of parliament from 1884 to 1902 and in 1890 became for three years Attorney-General under Rhodes, whom he later described as a contradictory personality and considered to have infected Cape public life with a harmful virus. In 1900 he rather un-willingly assumed the same post in the cabinet of his uncle-by-marriage J. G. Sprigg whom he did not admire and whose policies he generally opposed. In 1902 he became Chief Justice of the Transvaal, and in 1910 moved to the Supreme Court of South Africa of which he was Chief Justice from 1914 to 1927.

It was said in 1898 that 'he was a progressive when it was not popular to be one' while in August 1900 Milner wrote to Chamberlain that

> Innes ... is steeped in the old doctrine that you must always give way to the Dutch. But he has an essentially honest mind. The 'lie in the soul' can effect no lodgment in his clear intellect and absolutely sincere nature.[1]

Another South African once said, 'There goes Rose Innes. He is so straight that he is bent backwards.'

These characteristics were not without their disadvantages. Professor Harrison Wright, who is editing a volume of Sir James's letters, has written that

> he insisted on principles on occasion beyond the point of political practicability. He was reluctant to compromise even when he per-

---

* This story and various other details in the present chapter and the next are drawn from Sir James's autobiography, published after his death in 1949 – a book which is characteristically reticent on personal matters.

ceived that such a compromise might actually be more productive of his goals than rigid adherence to principle. He had not in fact a temperament to match the rough and tumble needs of party politics. Although frequently invited or urged to take positions of power, he drew back from the kinds of commitments that were involved, from the limitations that would necessarily be placed on his freedom of action, from threats to his moral integrity that might arise.[2]

On South Africa's major problem, his views were as firm as they were in the long run destined to futility. He wrote in his *Autobiography* that 'Justice and sympathy are the only sure foundations on which a (successful) native policy can rest.' Speaking in 1905 he said, 'We look forward to a union of races in this country. They were meant to be joined together and no body of men will in the long run keep them asunder.' 'The part of Statesmanship is not to stress racial differences but to emphasise the interests which exist in common.' Two years after his retirement and in connection with the 1929 Election, Sir James helped to found an Association which argued that, if the franchise was to be limited, the limit should be based on something other than colour. Smuts considered that this line was a 'godsend' to the Nationalists in winning them a clear majority.[3] Sir James put the arguments for his view in a speech during the campaign:

> In a comparatively short time we shall have to deal with a great body of natives whose education has enabled them to appreciate the value of the political status denied them and has stimulated their determination to obtain it and they will be embittered by the grievances, economic and administrative, which are bound to accumulate when one section of the people is deprived of those voting rights which its fellow-citizens enjoy. Is it seriously contemplated to repress those aspirations and to hold this aggrieved and angry multitude down by force?

The strength and at the same time the weakness of his position is shown in his assertion that 'force is no solvent of human problems'. This is only half the truth. It assumes that all human problems are capable of solution by agreement. It assumes also that, if force is used to impose a solution offensive to a minority's ideas of humanity and justice, that solution is bound to fail. But these assumptions are unproven, perhaps unprovable. There is unfortunately justification for thinking that, where two groups in a single society are each inspired by deeply held but incompatible beliefs, agreement may not be possible and that, if the stronger is then able to impose its solution ruthlessly for a sustained period, the result can be as permanent as anything in human affairs. But this does not lessen the need for minorities to fight and fight again for their beliefs. For, if it remains true that they are not bound to prevail, there are plenty of historical examples to show that they may do so – provided only that they fight. For Liberalism to be backed by force may threaten its ability to remain liberal. Yet for it not to be backed by force may threaten its ability to exist. Perhaps it was some awareness of the tension in events between power and ideals which was responsible for the deep strain of melancholy and pessimism which at times overcame Sir James, as though he knew that human beings were incapable of maintaining the standards which he set for himself. He was fated, like his grandson, to spend much of his time moving against the stream.

There were many qualities which he shared with the Field-Marshal. Both were men of the highest personal integrity who believed in hard work, self-discipline and restraint. Both were reticent men with feelings of strong affection for their near relations who, so far from wearing their hearts on their sleeves, went some way to disguise the fact that they possessed such organs at all. The Field-Marshal had a vein of ironic humour and of Sir James it was said that he indulged in the art of good-natured badinage with a lightness of touch which never failed to raise a smile even on the face of the victim. But it is a remarkable sign of the triumph of environment over temperament that two people in so many ways alike should have had such different attitudes to the political rights of the individual in society. Moreover while Sir James asked (after the war of 1914–18) 'Can we wonder at the condonation of political crime while we extol and glorify the legalised murder of war?' the Field-Marshal described the idea of perpetual peace as a 'not very pleasant dream'.[4]

These were the two traditions which were brought together when Dorothy Rose Innes married on 18 October 1905 Wilhelm von Moltke's eldest son Helmuth. The match goes to show how strong and mysterious the mutual affection of the two sexes can be. Dorothy was the only child of James and Jessie Rose Innes and between her and her parents there was a deep reciprocal affection, although they were originally averse to having a child. She could hardly have dealt them a heavier blow than by marrying into an alien country so far from home. Indeed they insisted on a year's delay and at one stage it looked as though the affair might peter out. Then, after he had succeeded to Kreisau on his father's death, the suitor learnt that Dorothy and her mother were about to leave London for South Africa. He hurried over and all was settled; his sister who came with him described how 'a dull pale young woman was overnight transformed into a beauty'.

For many people, including his parents-in-law but excluding his own immediate family, the bridegroom's qualities did not lie near the surface. His parents had tended to spoil him as their eldest son and a

delicate child, but at the same time neglected to give him a proper
education. This had the effect of making him somewhat preoccupied
with himself. Although his wife's letters warmly praise his hard work,
energy, unruffled courage in difficult times and unfailing kindness, his
management of his estate showed him to have inherited something of
the practical ineffectiveness of his great-grandfather. His eldest son
described him as 'easy-going, good-natured and when he chose full of
consideration for others. But at other times he would insist on pursuing
some objective which he chose to regard as important without paying
attention to the interests of anyone else, including his wife.' He possessed a fine baritone voice and of an evening at Kreisau would sing
Schubert, Brahms and Strauss to an appreciative audience.

He had become a convinced Christian Scientist as a young man
owing to the help which the practice of the doctrine had given in curing
an illness. His wife adopted his belief (as did his sister Margarethe von
Trotha) and together with Frau Ulla Oldenbourg they translated into
German Mary Baker Eddy's *Science and Health*. But they did not
impose their beliefs on their children for whom Dorothy was quite
prepared on occasion to call in doctors.

Coming to Kreisau as the lady of the house, she stepped into the
shoes of a strongly extroverted if somewhat superficial character who
had given the place the reputation of a large and hospitable mansion
where life was gay and stimulating. It was the central meeting place for
the family, all of whose members possessed and exercised the right to
come and go as they pleased. Even in the more difficult days after 1918
they seldom sat down to table less than fourteen and often the number
was nearer twenty. This was no easy inheritance, especially as her knowledge of German was at the outset far from perfect. But she gradually
succeeded in winning all hearts, including those of the elder generation.
Her South African experience in mediating between two cultures of
course stood her in good stead. Things did not just go on as they had
done; the atmosphere became richer and more sincere. People came to
the house not simply because it was pleasant and amusing but because it
radiated a humane concern for others.

This influence was not confined to the Schloss. Her mother had distinguished herself in work for women and Dorothy did the same. In the
year after her marriage, she used some of her own money to enlarge the
kindergarten which the Field-Marshal had founded alongside the village
school. In 1909 she brought in as village nurse a deaconess whose personality had impressed her and who for the next thirty-six years was to
be the trusted and loved stand-by of the community in health as well as
sickness. When war broke out, the Countess immediately decided that
her place was with the people of her adoption rather than of her birth
and made herself into the prop and stay of the village women instead of

a cause of offence. All this was not done easily, for she afterwards admitted to her children that in the early years she had often felt isolated and perplexed in a way which her husband found almost impossible to comprehend. Though she did much to smooth the more abrupt sides of his nature, he made life difficult for her in some respects. But she resolutely refused to make scenes and studiously tried to keep knowledge of her difficulties from her parents; she was rewarded by the devotion of her children and daughter-in-law.

Five years after her marriage, she put her point of view in one of the letters which she wrote weekly to her parents:

> Driving home from Conradswaldau last night in the clear calm moonlight (do you remember what Matthew Arnold wrote about the stars, that we must 'be as they'?) I was thinking how different in many ways my married and unmarried years are and I could not help being thankful that I have had so much rich experience of several sides of life, several points of view, several sorts of ideals, for it has enriched me very much. As a rule one lives and dies in one circle, it may be a large and beautiful one but it is nevertheless *one*, whereas I have learned to know two circles and taking the best from both – or at least trying to – I have formed my own. After nearly five years in this new circle I still feel that this is my place, that I have work to do (this sounds conceited but it is not, for I know too well that each has a work which it is *his* to accomplish) and therefore is it any wonder that I am happy? But it certainly was a strange business that the Fates should have chosen me to fill this place.

To appreciate the full difficulties of her position, one needs to remember that circumstances had combined to produce, first in Prussia and then throughout Germany, a society with an outlook very different from that of Anglo-Saxon Liberalism. Its leaders were suspicious of people who might try to introduce English ways, as Queen Victoria's daughter the Crown Princess Frederick had found to her cost, and such people had to face both lack of sympathy and disappointment.

In person Countess Dorothy was above middle-height though not outstandingly tall. In middle age she put on weight but this did not prevent a village woman from saying, '*Unsere Frau Gräfin wird jedes Jahr schöner.*' Dark hair cut short and simply brushed; dark eyes glowing with love – there really is no other word – understanding and compassion; an olive skin; a light voice; a smile which never seemed far away even when she was serious. Her mother, looking round during a family dinner, once said in her emphatic carrying voice, 'Dorothy, you have ruined the Moltke nose!' but she brought in compensation beautiful hands, small, well shaped and surprisingly white. Yet no catalogue of features, however detailed or faithful, can convey the glowing warmth and comfort of her nature, to which the years added experience, understanding and the ripeness brought by suffering. Of the many things both tangible and intangible which she gave to her children none was more important than the sense of security based on love and understanding.

The effect of mixing strains is often hard to foresee. The inculcation of loyalty to two discrepant cultures can easily prevent a child from developing an integrated personality, as was apparent in Kaiser Wilhelm II. The eldest child of Helmuth and Dorothy, Helmuth James Ludwig Eugen Heinrich, successfully concealed from his friends the possession of all his Christian names after the first two, but these indicated unmistakably the dual nature of his inheritance. It may well help to explain the undoubted complexity of his character. Neither background was suited to making life easy for him in the epoch into which he was born. But the rational outlook and humanitarian instincts, the passion for freedom, decency and justice which his mother inherited from her father and passed on to him in full measure were to prove at one and the same time his greatest source of strength and also his doom.

4 Early Life

O N E of the first things which Helmuth James did on being put into prison in January 1944 was to write down for his young sons a description of his own boyhood at Kreisau. Passages from this have been drawn on already; the next few pages depend on it even more.

His first memories were not of the Schloss but of the Berghaus where a favourite great-aunt and her companion had a genius for making people feel welcome. He once stumped the household by asking why grace was only said before the mid-day meal, to which no better answer was forthcoming than 'because there's less to eat in the evening'. This silenced him for the moment but made him laugh later on.

A brother Joachim Wolfgang ('Jowo') was born in 1909, another Wilhelm Viggo ('Willo') in 1911, a third Carl Berndt in 1913 and finally a sister Asta Maria in 1915. The three elder boys all grew up tall and dark – Helmuth at 2 metres did not far outstrip his brothers. Carl Berndt, however, was of ordinary height, blond and blue-eyed. Lacking the intellectual gifts and interests of the others, he was the family's one athlete and was endowed with the Bethusy-Huc high spirits. The only daughter inherited so much physically from her mother that at no stage could she have been anyone else's child.

In 1913 the three elder boys were taken to Southampton, Willo travelling in a washing-basket. There they met their parents who were returning from America and the whole party proceeded to South Africa. The Cape at this stage only left behind vague memories, of fishermen and a lighthouse and his grandparents' vintage car, of a peculiar kind of red fish and being overtaken by the tide. But, on Helmuth's two later visits, he was to keep encountering scenes and corners which were familiar.

When he came back, his memories of Kreisau were of rides on his pony through the meadows and along the drives, escorting carriages or as one of a cavalcade, of playing in the sandpit and of helping with the hay. The greatest excitement came in the autumn of 1913 when, to celebrate the centenary of the battle of Leipzig, big manœuvres were held in Silesia. Helmuth was entranced by riding all day among the troops and still more by coming across an observation balloon.

Every winter the family went to Berlin, since the Count was a member of the Prussian House of Peers. Their original house was taken over in 1910 to make room for government offices and thereafter they rented a house in the Grunewald near the Halensee. Helmuth remembered his father going off to the war in 1914, with all the household lined up on the steps. The Count embraced his wife, got into his grey Mercedes, drove away; and with that the war, as far as the family were concerned, had set in. For the duration no English was spoken with the result that, fluent though Helmuth became in its use in later life, he was never without a faint accent and made occasional mistakes. Soon afterwards he was taken to a debate in the House of Peers and on to dinner with great-uncle Helmuth and his wife Liza who were still living in their personal apartment in the great red-brick headquarters of the general staff near the *Reichstag*. When the ill-fated Chief of Staff* came in, his great-nephew called out 'Uncle Helmuth, when are we going to win the war?' Whatever the answer may have been it led the younger Helmuth to realise for the first time that Germany could – and indeed even would – lose the war. Thereafter no amount of excitement over victories or books about heroes were able to efface this awareness.

By then lessons had already begun, first from the village schoolmaster in private, then from a governess who paid more attention to poetry than to reading, writing or arithmetic. At Easter 1916 he entered the bottom form of the Schweidnitz Grammar/High School/*Gymnasium*, and as this rendered the gaps in his knowledge painfully obvious a new governess was installed to help with his prep, by which means he worked his way painfully through the fifth and into the fourth form. He had to drive himself to the town in a trap with a dapple-grey horse. As a rule the journey only needed some twenty minutes, but he did the harnessing and unharnessing in Schweidnitz himself and in bad weather things were less pleasant; once in the snows of 1916/17 the four-mile trip took three hours.

This was the infamous winter in which the staple of German diet was turnips. Conditions were in general better in the country than in towns with the result that Kreisau soon became as full of children as it was to be in the Second War. In particular Helmuth's four cousins, the von Trothas, lived there, of whom the eldest Carl Dietrich was almost exactly his own age.

Soon after the war ended news arrived through the Red Cross that the Rose Innes grandparents were coming to Holland and authorisation was obtained for Countess Dorothy, her five children, the governess and a maid to meet them there.

When they got to their hotel in Scheveningen the manager advised

---

* General von Moltke was in fact replaced as chief of staff by General von Falkenhayn on 14 September 1914 but Supreme Headquarters were no longer in Berlin, so that the von Moltkes would not have had to shift house immediately.

them to begin by only eating half-portions because the Germans who failed to take this precaution suffered from bad indigestion. Sir James recorded that

> they were all rather fine-drawn: the blockade had left its mark upon them. The children were peaked and sallow and their mother declared that she never wanted to look at mangold-wurzels or potatoes again.

They were in Holland for over two months. What Helmuth remembered was playing on the beach, taking trips by train and above all the day when the ban on whipped cream was lifted and they were able to celebrate Willo's birthday by eating it with chocolate in Leiden. But Sir James no doubt made sure that his grandson saw the pictures by Franz Hals which he mentioned in his own memoirs and the statue of Grotius at Delft to which his interest in Romano-Dutch law (as that of South Africa) made him pay special attention.

They came back to Germany shortly after the signing of the Treaty of Versailles, which Sir James – like his fellow-countryman Smuts – condemned for its severity.

They arrived home to a scene of confusion. One of the fundamental causes both of the war and of the German refusal to consider a compromise peace had been the unreadiness of the ruling classes in the Empire to adapt themselves to the aspirations of the many whose living standards had been raised by industrialisation. These same classes now refused, for the most part, to accept the verdict of the war or the consequences of defeat and denounced as traitors those republican politicians who reluctantly decided that, as the generals declared themselves unable to resist the Allies, the terms of peace must be accepted. Thus Germany, which had still not completely recovered from the division created at the Reformation, was divided again and the Republic started under a tremendous handicap. Helmuth's parents had met President Wilson's assistant Colonel House in the United States and were as a result reluctant to join in the general chorus of criticism against America; this led to the first of several family quarrels over politics.

In Silesia particular points of controversy were not merely the loss of the province of Posen in the north to Poland and of the Teschen district in the south-east to Czechoslovakia but even more the proposal to hand over the whole of Upper Silesia to the Poles. One of the few concessions which the German delegation, with the help of Lloyd George, managed to secure at Versailles was the postponement of this transfer until after a plebiscite. From the beginning of 1920 until after the poll in March 1921 the province was administered and order kept by an Inter-Allied Commission and Force. The voting went in favour of Germany in the proportion of 3 to 2 but the Poles came out on top in the south-east corner where most of the industry and coal-mining lay. In October 1921 the League of Nations finally drew through this tightly knit district a line which satisfied neither side and which, although it lasted until 1939, was a powerful stimulant to German nationalism in the province.

At two stages during the long-drawn-out process, Poles sought to precipitate a decision by resort to force and, in view of the Versailles limitation on the size of the German army, irregular units or *Freikorps* were organised to oppose them. Helmuth's uncle Carl Viggo and his first cousin Hans Carl von Hülsen served in these, while his father's first cousin Hans Adolf von Moltke of Wernersdorf, who was in the diplomatic service, belonged to the German liaison mission with the Inter-Allied Commission. (He was succeeded in this capacity by a Westphalian Catholic lawyer called Paulus van Husen who thus came across Helmuth for the first time.)

For six months Helmuth's only schooling had been a few weeks at a German institution in Holland where the chief emphasis was on boxing and wrestling, so that when he got back to Schweidnitz, he found himself far behind. Convinced that he would not get moved up, he made himself so sick with anxiety that he was able to plead illness and stay away on the day the results were announced. His relief was great when Jowo came home and reported that the headmaster, after going through all the other names, had ultimately added 'and provisionally, in view of his long absence, Helmuth von Moltke'. Thereafter things got better and by 1922 he had worked his way into the Upper Second.

Probably as valuable as his book-learning was the activity which went on at home. There was a magic lantern and round games, while his father often read aloud in the evening, or the family read plays with the parts assigned to various members. There were also charades and amateur theatricals every winter in which all generations joined. Part I of *Faust*, *Hamlet* and Molière were in the repertoire. Helmuth himself had no confidence in his acting ability and steadily refused to take a part, concentrating instead on stage-management and lighting.

But he had developed such an absorption in Kreisau that he could not bear to go away from it even to Schweidnitz. His parents decided that this was unhealthy and would end in his becoming a country bumpkin. Accordingly in the autumn of 1922 when he was fifteen and a half, they sent him away to a boarding-school on the Ammersee in Bavaria. From prison he looked back upon this as the point at which his childhood ended –

that lovely time which seems to me golden in retrospect, an in-

B

exhaustible source of memories on which one draws with affectionate delight and of scenes which I will always treasure as home.

This was hardly an auspicious way in which to approach new surroundings, and the experiment was not a success. The institution was supposed to be inspired by something akin to the English 'public school spirit', which Helmuth, who did not take to many of his classmates, considered to be empty hypocrisy. With a few like-minded companions, he set himself to oppose it and managed to get on the School Council with this end in view. This made him so unpopular that he and another boy were given a separate room near the headmaster's study. The school assembly decided to send them to Coventry for a fortnight, whereupon his supporters, about ten in number, retaliated by doing the same to everyone else. This led to the majority breaking into his room and beating him up. Rather to their disappointment, he refused to offer any resistance and his ear-drum was damaged. He used the incident as an argument to make the management allow the ten nonconformists to live for the rest of the school year in the house of the only master for whom they had any use and merely to join the other boys for lessons. Among the ten was Carl Deichmann, the son of a leading Cologne banker and destined to become his brother-in-law.

His father, on hearing of his troubles, sent him a map of Germany and asked him to mark where he wanted to go to school next. He elected to go for two years to a *Gymnasium* in Potsdam, as being near Berlin; he lodged with Baron von Mirbach, whose wife was a sister of Hans Adolf von Moltke. French was much talked in their household so that when Helmuth had to deliver a lecture as part of his '*Abitur*' (leaving examination), he was able to begin by asking whether he should speak in German, English or French. Among the other boys was Kaiser Wilhelm's grandson Prince Louis Ferdinand of Prussia who later wrote that Helmuth had a genius for doing his prep after the lesson had begun.

> He could talk very effectively and spiced his remarks with witty anecdotes which amused the masters. Although they must have noticed that he had no respect for them, and may have suspected that he knew more than they did, they appreciated his intelligence ... I used to cycle home with him and liked him for his lively and rather cynical manner which at times made him seem almost supercilious.[1]

All the same they retained (the more formal) '*Sie*' in talking to one another instead of (the more intimate) '*Du*'. This, however, was not due to pride on the part of the Prince, who stood on little ceremony with his companions, but to Helmuth's disapproval of Hohenzollerns on principle. When about this time he was taken, through another connection, to visit the old gentleman at Doorn, his interview did not last long because when the Kaiser asked, 'What was your father's regiment?' he got the cheeky reply, 'No idea, Your Majesty.'

Helmuth always had a great capacity for absorbing quickly the essential facts of a subject and his exposition in his *Abitur* of the relationship between Napoleon and England was so brilliant that, although the Socialist Government of Prussia had appointed an examiner prejudiced against the aristocracy, he passed without more ado. His school work thus sat fairly lightly on his shoulders and he contrived to spend much of his time in Berlin where he found employment by acting as interpreter for journalists on the *Christian Science Monitor* and other foreign papers. One of his occupations was to take them to the theatre and explain the plots of the plays – this was the great era of the Republican stage. The association with people of their wide experience, coming when it did, had an important influence on his thinking. He began to propagate the kind of views which many people thought inappropriate for a Moltke and which were long afterwards to make him strike a Bavarian friend as 'an extraordinary type of Prussian'.* He was unfavourably impressed by the way in which each political party abused all the others and insisted that it alone was capable of setting things right.

> This period had a great effect on me by convincing me that everybody was wrong which I discovered by advocating each view in turn. I doubt whether there was a single Party which I didn't at some stage support.

This certainly included the Communists – there exists a photograph of him taken about this time at Kreisau holding up a hammer and sickle and he had the reputation of a Communist in Schweidnitz.[2] But views do not have to be very radical to produce such a reputation in a country town and there was an element of bravado about his attitude; he was open-eyed to the evil inherent in Communist methods.

When in 1925 he took his *Abitur*, he had to write an account of his life till then. He put down that he had 'received his education in the absence of his teachers'. He was no doubt right in thinking that his education had not produced in him the effect which its official designers intended. When taken in conjunction with the great influence of his mother (and the proportionately smaller influence of his father), this meant that he had not been conditioned in anything like the same degree as his contemporaries to the standards and outlook of the society in which he was to live. That society was the product of past historical situations, in the middle ages on the eastern marshes, in seventeenth- and eighteenth-century Prussia and in world politics after 1871. In each

* Below, p. 328.

of these situations, the leaders of the society had adopted aims (repelling the Slavs, making Prussia a European power, making Germany a World Power) which almost if not quite exceeded the physical resources in men and materials available to realise them. The only hope of success had lain in concentrating those resources on the major aims and preventing them from being dissipated on minor ones. This resulted in heavy stress being laid not only on thrift and courage but also on discipline, obedience, determination and self-sacrifice. In such an atmosphere authoritarian tendencies flourish and there was to be found a large number of authoritarian personalities (as well as other personalities who, though not naturally authoritarian, were anxious to conform to the pattern and overcompensated in their desire to do so). In a society of this kind, a liberally minded individualist, such as Helmuth, is bound to find life uncomfortable.

5 Two Important Influences

T H E R E then arose the question of a profession. For, much as Helmuth loved the country, he did not want to spend his life as a farmer. The army, in which so many of his family had served, would have had no appeal to him even if the Versailles limitation on its size had not made entry difficult. He therefore decided on the legal course which in Germany, as in so many other countries except Britain, was and indeed is the standard training for those wanting to enter public life; in Helmuth's case the goal was definitely politics.

At the outset he signed on as an undergraduate in Breslau because in the summer of 1925 his South African grandparents were in Europe and he wanted to be free to spend as much time as possible with them both at Kreisau and motoring through Germany. His cousin Carl Dietrich von Trotha was already a student there and he came across (without getting to know intimately) the son of another Silesian landowner, Count Peter Yorck von Wartenburg, who was two and a half years his senior. He attended a course given by a lecturer/*Privatdozent* called Hans Peters on 'Administrative Problems of Modern Industry'. Either at Breslau, or at Berlin, to which he moved in 1926, Helmuth studied both social history and political science and even managed to spend two terms looking into the functions of the Press. He took his studies seriously – a number of letters from himself and his mother during the next few years say how hard he is working. But he looked on knowledge primarily as an aid to action rather than as something to be valued for its own sake; he never even started to work for a doctorate and could not be described as a learned man. The result was that his acquaintance with the classics of political thought remained a little perfunctory, and when during the war he started to think things out from basic principles he found his knowledge inadequate to the task.

Soon after he got to Berlin, he went like many other students to a canteen run for them in the former palace of the Kaiser by a certain Dr Eugenia Schwarzwald. A Jewess from Czernowitz in the Bukowina, she had found her way to Zürich at the beginning of the century and had there been one of the first women in Europe to become a doctor of philosophy. In due course she moved to Vienna, although Zürich is said to have always remained her spiritual home and thither she returned to die as a refugee in 1940. About 1903 she was asked to look after a school as a stop-gap, discovered her vocation and a year or so later set up a progressive co-educational establishment in Vienna. Egon Wellesz* taught music, Kokoschka† art – until the Ministry insisted on his being dismissed for lack of formal qualifications. (When the Frau Doctor protested that he was a genius, she was told that the Education Laws made no provision for such a category.)

The Frau Doctor was short and stoutish. Countess Dorothy described her as

> clever, enthusiastic, a great talker, full of fun and go, doing and showering kindness on everyone she meets, helping wherever she sees a need, something of an autocrat but most lovable. A pacifist of course

also a socialist and a free-thinker. A medical doctor in Zürich is said to have told her that she was incapable of bearing children and she accordingly resolved to make her pupils into her children. On the one hand she believed in allowing people to do what they liked; on the other, she liked to gather people round her and throw herself into their concerns with intensity. By telling them that they were beautiful or clever, she often made them so – but sometimes left them dissatisfied for life.[1]

Her protégés were not confined to her pupils; all sorts of people came to consult her. Carl Deichmann's brother Hans, who had gone to Vienna to study and was taken to her house by a friend, said he learnt more by sitting in her waiting-room than by any number of university lectures. Her husband, small and lame, had risen to a high post in the Austrian Ministry of Finance and played a leading part in the stabilisation of the schilling after 1922. He refused an invitation to become president of the National Bank on the ground that so prominent a post ought not to be held by a Jew, and became instead president of the Anglo-Austrian Bank. Kokoschka painted his portrait several times – but never apparently his wife's. Detached and witty, and more universally liked than his wife, he provided the money which paid for a house designed by Adolf Loos‡ in the Josephstädterstrasse and a summer holiday home in a converted hotel on the Grundlsee in Styria. This was the setting in which they gathered round them a circle which included such people as Gottfried Benn, Bert Brecht, Egon Friedell, Hans Kelsen the international lawyer, Karl Kraus, Karin Michaelis, Arnold

---

* Wellesz, Egon (b. 1885), Professor of Musical History at Vienna. Moved to Oxford, 1938.

† Kokoschka, Oskar (b. 1886), expressionist painter of Austrian birth. Moved to England, 1938.

‡ Loos, Adolf (1870–1933), architect, mainly in Vienna. Maintained ornament to be a crime.

Schönberg, Rudolf Serkin the pianist, Helen Weigel and Carl Zuckmayer.*

After the war the Schwarzwalds organised several country homes for needy children, and three soup kitchens in Vienna. The canteen in the Berlin palace was modelled on these and first opened during the inflation of 1923. The Frau Doctor kept an eye on it whenever she visited the city and it was thus that Helmuth met her. She urged him to come and study in Vienna; he went there on a number of visits and took some courses (under Verdross,† for example, though not under Kelsen whom he only met socially). Frau Schwarzwald made much of him, talked of him as a future chancellor and sought to turn him into one of her intimate disciples. She never quite succeeded in doing so, for he had an ultimate reserve which it was very difficult to penetrate, especially when he did not want that to happen. His reticence spurred her to greater efforts, which were of no avail; he remained, for example, a person to whom she used 'Sie' rather than 'Du'. For all that, her readiness to accept new ideas and refusal to revere conventions had a considerable effect on him.

Another person whom she befriended was the American journalist Dorothy Thompson, at the time when her first marriage to the Hungarian Josef Bard was breaking down. Miss Thompson moved on to Berlin where on 9 July 1927 she invited Countess Dorothy and 'her wonderful son' to a birthday dinner.[2] Among the other guests was the novelist Sinclair Lewis, author of *Main Street* and *Babbitt* who, although meeting his hostess for the first time, promptly invited her to marry him. Indeed Helmuth played a somewhat catalytic part in that stormy union for when it was breaking down she wrote that 'it has never been the same since he [S.L.] sneered at Helmuth von Moltke'.[3] All the same, Helmuth cannot have altogether regretted his acquaintance with Lewis who was a brilliant and irreverent talker. And it was to Helmuth in the summer of 1942 that Dorothy Thompson was addressing herself

---

* Benn, Gottfried (1886–1956), poet, novelist, essayist. Worked as a doctor in Berlin. Brecht, Bertold (1898–1956), dramatist, moved abroad 1933, returned to East Berlin 1948. Friedell, Egon (1878–1936), actor, critic, essayist, historian of culture in Vienna. Committed suicide on arrival of Nazis. Kelsen, Hans (b. 1881), Professor of Law successively in Vienna, Cologne, Geneva and Berkeley. Judge of Austrian Supreme Court till 1930. Kraus, Karl (1874–1936), writer, critic, satirist, editor of periodical *Die Fackel*. Michaelis, Karin (1872–1950), novelist, born in Denmark. Friend of Brecht. Schönberg, Arnold (1874–1951), musician, exponent of twelve-tone notation. Serkin, Rudolf (b. 1903), learned composition under Schönberg. Emigrated from Austria to the United States in 1939. Weigel, Helen (1900–71), actress, married Bertold Brecht 1928 and created the leading female roles in many of his plays. Zuckmayer, Carl (b. 1896), dramatist, lived in Germany, Austria, America and Switzerland. Wrote *The Captain of Köpenick*, *The Devil's General*, etc.

† Verdross, Alfred (b. 1890), Professor of Law in Vienna from 1924.

when she wrote her broadcasts to Germany under the title 'Listen Hans', though if he had heard them (as he did not) he might not have recognised himself from the way he was described. Through her Helmuth also met Edgar Mowrer, Berlin correspondent of the *Chicago Daily News*, and his wife Lilian. To Dorothy Thompson and Edgar Mowrer must go a major share of credit for realising the danger which National Socialism meant to the world and for alerting American opinion to it.

For some time Helmuth had been concerned about economic affairs in Silesia, particularly in the textile and mining areas round Waldenburg due west of Kreisau. Even in the short economic summer of the Weimar Republic, conditions here left a lot to be desired. The situation was similar to that in Britain's 'distressed areas' where whole districts depended on basic industries which were ceasing to be competitive. Helmuth got to know Dr Ohle, the energetic young Socialist who was *Landrat** of Waldenburg, and at Easter 1927 worked for a few weeks in his office to gain experience. He also brought down some of his foreign journalist friends to see for themselves. Karin Michaelis in particular wrote a series of articles in the Viennese *Neue Freie Presse*. His cousin Carl Dietrich von Trotha was also deeply interested in the problem along with some of his fellow-students at Breslau, one of whom, Horst von Einsiedel, later wrote:

> One day a cousin of C.D.'s came on the scene. A man who made me feel very inferior the first time I met him. Nearly two years younger than me, only just twenty, he knew from the Kaiser and Hindenburg downwards all the politicians of Europe like Löbe and Loucheur.† He was colossally clever and sophisticated, efficient and really impressive. Naturally he talked to everyone in a rather man-of-the-world sort of way, which was perhaps his limitation. But as he made no claims to anything, this did no harm. This Count M had a plan to bring into existence a large-scale rescue operation for the Waldenburg area.[4]

---

* There is no British equivalent of the Prussian *Landrat* who was at one and the same time the senior central official in a *Kreis*, a unit rather smaller than a county, and also the chairman of the county council, usually with an acknowledged political allegiance. The holders of these posts were the backbone of the Prussian administrative system.

† Löbe, Paul (1875–1967), a native of Silesia, SPD Deputy, Speaker of the *Reichstag* 1920–32, represented Berlin in *Bundestag* after 1949. Loucheur, Louis (1872–1931), was a French Radical Socialist Deputy who several times held office between 1919 and 1930. It is not known how Helmuth met him or Hindenburg. In 1928 he met at a dinner party the French politician Édouard Herriot (1872–1957), who had come to Berlin to get material for a book on Beethoven.

The three young men turned for advice to Eugen Rosenstock, then professor of the History of Law at Breslau and a man of thirty-nine, whom Helmuth had already got to know during his studies at the university. His is one of those adventurous minds which refuse to respect the frontiers of academic disciplines so that it is misleading to label him philosopher, theologian, historian, economist, sociologist, jurist, philologist or educationalist. For he has a claim to all these titles, being, as he once put it, 'an impure thinker'. But encyclopaedic knowledge is securely yoked to common sense and a mischievous humour, which have been ripened by experience and humanity into a deep wisdom. In 1918 he had realised not merely that Germany had lost the war and Europe her predominant position in the world but also that Germany would be dependent for her future welfare on the good-will of her neighbours. For some years he devoted himself to work in adult education in the hope of getting these facts more widely recognised. But he knew it was an almost hopeless task and foretold, as early as 1919, that the Germans, out of unwillingness to accept their situation, would turn towards a dictatorship which was both radical and nationalist at the same time. He asserted that the task of responsible Germans would be to survive this tyranny and, while doing so, to lay the foundations for what might come after. He taught his pupils to think of history in terms of long cycles, in which the shape of tomorrow was decided by yester-day so that the real task and opportunity of today is to think about the day after tomorrow.

Eugen (who was Jewish) left Germany for America immediately his prophecy of Nazi rule was realised, and thus passed fairly soon out of Helmuth's life. But he was important not merely in providing another stimulus to independent thinking, and one which was Christian (in an unorthodox way) rather than Marxist. His emphasis on the need to take long views sank thoroughly in, as did his diagnosis of what was wrong with Germany and the world. He maintained that the Industrial Revolution had taken place at a speed which precluded a gradual adjustment between the arrangements best suited for human needs and those best calculated to maximise profit. Thus the harmony of pre-industrial society had been shattered without anything being put in its place.

As has been said, Germany in the 1920s was a deeply divided country. The ruling and possessing classes had shown scant sympathy for the aspiration of the workers. But this was partly because the Social Democratic Party, which provided the political channel through which those aspirations were expressed, had adopted as its creed the doctrines of Marx, who was indeed one of its founding fathers. It was thus committed – in theory – to both revolution and atheism. The alarm which this fact engendered among the opponents of Socialism was such as to blind them to the consistent way in which the Social Democratic leaders, at all the crucial moments of German history, had chosen the path of prudence, caution and patriotism. This disregard was made easier by the existence of a noisy left wing who habitually denounced the leadership for failing to live up to its principles and who after 1919 had constituted themselves into the Russian-directed Communist Party.

Prior to 1914 German Socialism had been a political outcast. Even after it won more seats in the 1912 elections than any other party, it was regarded in a characteristic phrase as 'regierungsunfähig' – inadmissible to any share in the government (except at local levels). Although after 1919 the Socialists provided one of the main piers on which the Republic rested, they were represented in the cabinet for only a small part of the Republic's duration and the suspicion against them was slow to fade. The Socialists replied to this treatment by building up a self-contained world of their own, with organisations providing not just for the political activities but also for the information, education, welfare, culture and recreation of their members – in other words, from cradle to grave. Mistrust was answered with mistrust; nothing good could come out of capitalism. In addition, as Eugen Rosenstock emphasised, work under modern conditions gave the employee neither security nor satisfaction. A man could take little pride in an article to which he had only contributed a single component: he could feel no affection for surroundings which were drab and associated with monotony.

Religion provided no effective bridge across this chasm, not merely because the atheism of the Socialists drove the churches into reaction but because ever since the 1555 Peace of Augsburg (cujus regio ejus religio) the churches had depended for their existence on one or other of the German states. Germany lacked that tradition of religious nonconformity which played so influential a part in the history of British radicalism, although small groups of unorthodox religious socialists (with whom Eugen had links) were trying to remedy this very lack. Education did equally little to provide a bridge. Facilities for giving technical training to the working-class child were as good as anywhere in the world but scholarships to support him (let alone her) at the university were few and far between. The undergraduates were not only almost exclusively middle-class but a large proportion of them were imbued with the authoritarian inclinations of their class. This tendency was stimulated by the failure of the Weimar Republic to provide enough openings for the middle classes, particularly in the professions; the artistic excitement of the time had little appeal to a majority which was conventionally philistine. Helmuth once told Dorothy Thompson that 'the students are the worst class in Germany'.[5]

But Germany had a third social group, which had vanished in Britain, in the shape of the peasants, or small independent farmers owning and tilling a smallish holding with little help from outside the family. Bismarck's protective tariffs had sheltered these people against the competition of cheap food from overseas but had not been able to screen them from the effects of a large-scale market economy in which producer had lost contact with consumer. Whereas the industrial worker sought protection by allowing himself to be absorbed in the mass of his fellows, finding strength in unity, and had no attachment to any particular locality, the peasant farmer remained an individualist, to whom the ancestral plot meant everything. He ate his bread in the sweat of his brow and of the brows of his wife and children. The stream of development was flowing against such an existence, which can only be made to yield a livelihood comparable to that of the city-dweller by pumping in capital and enlarging the unit. But such changes have disruptive effects on rural society and most peasants, unable to do either, regarded industry and workers and middle-men and towns, and the modern world as a whole, with suspicion – which was a main reason why many of them were ready to vote National Socialist.

Eugen and his disciples believed that, for German democracy to stand any chance of success, a sense of community must be generated between the three groups of workers, students and peasants. This may at first sight seem to resemble a Nazi aim, but there was an essential difference. The patriot with the authoritarian personality is outraged that members of his own nation should think differently on matters which he regards as vital or refuse to recognise the values and loyalties which to him are sacred. He seeks to overcome this heresy by generating a wave of emotion which sweeps away all those whose convictions are too weakly rooted to resist, and by using force or public disapproval to silence the individuals and organisations who stick to their convictions. A movement of this kind will of course have a creed, because it is impossible for any leader to communicate aims without using words. But the creed is not usually one capable of standing up to rational analysis and the public will therefore be discouraged or prevented from using their critical faculties. The authoritarian seeks to smother differences, whereas the liberal knows that they are bound to exist. He seeks to order society in such a way that they can be brought to the surface, discussed and overcome. He seeks to convince the mind by argument rather than to intimidate or to sweep people off their feet by appeals to narrow feelings and interests. He believes that freedom to say and do what one likes will not extinguish readiness to compromise and that the process of mutual criticism will not erode the readiness for mutual understanding. The man who deliberately sets out to build a consensus by democratic means has a hard task but it is one which must be undertaken if a society is to be both durable and free.

This was the approach underlying the Silesian *Arbeitslager* or Work

Camps. There already existed in Silesia (and throughout Germany) a body called the *Jungmannschaft*, which consisted largely of students who held aloof from the aristocratic student corps, were anxious to see changes in society and sought links with the workers. They had opened in 1926 a centre called the Boberhaus at Löwenberg, in the foothills some fifty miles north-west of Kreisau. This was used for conferences of various kinds, particularly with Germans living in Poland and other parts of Eastern Europe. When on 18 September 1927 Eugen Rosen-stock came to lunch at Kreisau with another Breslau professor, Schultze-Gävernitz, and Dr Peters, it was decided to use this as the scene of a work camp in the following spring and another meeting was sub-sequently held at the Boberhaus itself from 27 to 30 October to work out details.[6]

The first camp was held from 14 March to 1 April 1928. Some hundred young men attended, drawn from workers, students and peas-ants in roughly equal numbers. They were invited by a letter signed by Helmuth, Einsiedel and the secretary of the *Jungmannschaft*. Every morning, after a lecture given by Eugen Rosenstock, they went off in detachments for four hours' hard manual labour – building walls, sawing wood, gardening, clearing waste ground. After a lunch-time break the same groups met for discussions, which at the first camp centred round the question 'Under what conditions can a sound form of life be devel-oped in German industry?' The evening was devoted to games, singing and acting. Intrinsic to the idea of the whole operation was the three-fold origin of the participants and the threefold way in which they spent their time. The latter aspect seems to have been more of a new depar-ture than the former.

About two-thirds of the way through the proceedings, some seventy leading personalities of Silesia – professors, officials, clergy, land-owners, industrialists and trade unionists – were brought to the camp, told about the main views which had found expression there and given a chance of contributing to the debate. The younger generation were intended to gain, both from the camp as a whole and from their contact with the influential, a clearer idea of how they fitted into a modern society, of the points of view of other groups in it and of the things which had to be considered in seeking solutions to its problems.

Two further camps were held in the same place in March 1929 and March 1930. The second was centred on the question of the flight from the land, the third on that of problems posed to the younger generation (and particularly students) by the continual shifts in the professions. The second camp was handicapped by the problem of finding enough jobs to work at manually, the third diversified by the presence of twenty-nine girls, drawn from the same social groups as the men.

Helmuth's main contribution lay in getting the camps going. In

September 1927 he went to Berlin for four days on business connected with them; this was probably the time when at Rosenstock's prompting he called on Dr Heinrich Brüning, then a back-bench deputy in the Catholic Centre Party with Waldenburg in his electoral area, and persuaded him to get a government grant for the project. Helmuth spent his twenty-first birthday in March 1928 driving his parents' Opel through deep snow on a mission connected with Waldenburg. But ten days later he wrote to his grandparents:

I'm going to take one department only and get free of the rest because I can't do it all. It is a pity because I certainly do better at the head of the whole work than at the head of one department and I really fear that my successor will not be able to do as much work as I have done in the beginning.

He went to the whole of the first camp and his parents came for the central week-end; his mother told the grandparents that they ought to have seen him scraping carrots in the kitchen. In the 1929 camp he took no part at all because of preoccupation with his law work; his name does not occur in the book which Rosenstock and Trotha published about the camps, except for the remarks by Einsiedel already quoted. Helmuth had become interested in them primarily as an alleviation of the problems of Waldenburg but, before he had done, he had undoubtedly absorbed some of Eugen Rosenstock's wider ideas.

The camps attracted a good deal of attention. Similar events were organised in Brandenburg, Swabia, Baden and Schleswig-Holstein while Rolf Gardiner,* who had been at the second, organised camps in England at Springhead and Cleveland. In 1940 Eugen Rosenstock ran something similar at Camp William James in Vermont to train leaders for the Civilian Conservation Corps. Brüning as Chancellor instituted a voluntary labour service in 1931, and this led to the compulsory National Socialist Labour Service. But in these the original purpose of the operation evaporated, for neither made any attempt to balance its intake from different social groups, and once compulsion is used the chances of carrying conviction by rational argument dwindle.

Yet the task of persuading young workers, students and peasants to come to the camps voluntarily proved an uphill one and Helmuth's withdrawal was due not only to lack of time but also to loss of illusions. Many workers suspected a venture which was not initiated by their own sort and involved people with aristocratic names (although no titles were used in the camps). Some were reluctant to do anything which might take the heat out of the class struggle; others could not get leave of absence or afford loss of wages. The student corporation in Breslau University refused to have anything to do with the scheme, saying that

* Gardiner, Rolf (1904–71), Dorset landowner and conservationist.

they could not see the point of it and suspected ulterior motives. The peasants were afraid of feeling fish out of water in an intellectual atmosphere and often could not be spared from work on the farm just after the snow had melted. As the economic situation got worse and unemployment rose, antagonisms deepened and financial help became harder to get. The two to three hundred people who passed through the Silesian camps represented so small a proportion of the population that the failure to hold a fourth camp, due partly to the collapse of the whole Boberhaus organisation, may not have mattered much. What was more serious were the implications for Germany of the breakdown of even such a modest attempt at bridging social divisions. For a country deeply divided within itself can seldom be politically or economically effective so that, if voluntary measures to heal the differences are unsuccessful, impatience with the government's ineffectiveness is likely to make more people listen to those who call for more drastic methods.

Perhaps the most important result of the camps in the long run was that they brought together for the first time a number of people who did not believe that drastic methods would afford a better cure. Helmuth and Eugen Rosenstock, Carl Dietrich von Trotha and Horst von Einsiedel have already been mentioned. Adolf Reichwein, an educational pioneer who was at that time personal assistant to Carl Becker,* was one of the teachers in the first camp and Fritz Christiansen-Weniger,† then a professor at Breslau, held a similar post in the second. Hans Peters attended the original meeting in October 1927. Peter Yorck and Otto von der Gablentz,‡ read papers. Theodor Steltzer§ was involved in the Schleswig-Holstein camp. We shall later find all these applying on a wider scale the ideas which underlay the Waldenburg experiment.

* Becker, Carl H. (1876–1933), orientalist, professor in Heidelberg, Hamburg, Bonn and Berlin, non-party Prussian Minister of Culture 1921 and 1925–30. Educational reformer.
† Christiansen-Weniger, Fritz (b. 1897), student and professor at Breslau, Agricultural Adviser to Turkish government 1928–9, 1931–40. Head of Agricultural Institute at Pulany, Poland, 1940–5. Head of Agricultural Institutes in West Germany 1945–54. Agricultural Attaché German Embassy Ankara, with responsibility for Middle East in general, 1954–62.
‡ Gablentz, Otto von der (1898–1972), wounded in First World War, studied law and political science in Berlin and Freiburg, follower of religious socialism of Paul Tillich, worked in *Reich* Statistical Office and Chemical Section of Economic Ministry; since the war a Professor of Political Science at the University of Berlin.
§ Below, p. 161.

6 Crisis at Kreisau: Marriage

DURING the summer of 1928, Helmuth's grandfather expressed some concern lest the variety of irons which he had in the fire should lead to his professional studies being neglected. Helmuth replied in a long letter of 6 September, which gave a picture of his recent doings and future plans.

After the work-camp, he had taken a party of American journalists to Upper Silesia where he had investigated the situation of the German minority.* He criticised them for allowing themselves to be run from Berlin (as were Henlein and the Sudeten Germans to do ten years later). He then went to stay with the young Prince of Pless† at his family Schloss in the same area. His next stop was at Zagreb where he had an introduction through the Schwarzwalds to the Croat peasant leader Radić and consulted him about the problem of enabling small farmers to earn a decent livelihood. When a month later Radić was assassinated, Helmuth thought it *'the greatest possible loss for Europe'*.

From Zagreb he went to Heidelberg *'to bring about a connection between Heidelberg intellectual spirit and our western problems, really needing a lot of spirit and intellect'*. He also called on the Baden politician Willy Hellpach in connection with a supplement which he had been commissioned to write on 'The New Germany' for an American paper. Hellpach was a prominent member of the Democratic Party which represented the most enlightened non-Socialist non-Catholic views of the time (with a marked Jewish element); its supporters included Helmuth's parents. Its difficulties and steady decline epitomised the problems of the Republic.

After Heidelberg came a stay with the Schwarzwalds on the Grundlsee,‡ from which he made a trip to Marienbad and spent three days talking to Becker, 'one of the finest men in Germany'.§ As his mother explained

---

* It was probably on this trip that he met Hans Lukaschek (1885–1960) who was mayor of the town of Hindenburg and in the following year became *Oberpräsident* of the province (an *Oberpräsident* is the senior representative of the central government in the area who at the same time presides over the provincial council).

† Hans Heinrich XVI, Prince of Pless, son of Prince Hans Heinrich XIV and Daisy Cornwallis-West, b. 1900, succeeded father 1938.

‡ Above, p. 26.   § Above, p. 34.

He gets his wonderful opportunities partly because of himself but also partly because of his name and the fact that so few of the aristocracy are willing to take a part in the future of republican Germany.

Back at Kreisau, he settled down to prepare for the qualifying examination as *Referendar* (the first step in the legal profession. This examination, conducted by the state, serves in the case of many Germans as a substitute for the university examination for a bachelor's degree which does not exist in Germany.). This, thanks to effective cramming, he passed in Breslau in the spring of 1929. Thereafter, as he explained to his grandfather, he wanted to learn Polish and some Balkan languages.

> *I believe that Silesia and Vienna are the two centres from which Germany and Europe can really take a serious interest in the East and the Balcan [sic]. I believe the whole European crisis between west and east and the German crisis between west and east and the agrarian crisis in the whole of Europe's east spring from the same root and it is our duty to work on this problem. To work on this problem is of course no profession but I think before you go in for your profession in Eastern Germany you ought to know something of these things. So I want first to learn the languages.*

In July or August 1929 he proposed to accept an invitation from the Polish Government for a visit to that country, and next go via the Grundlsee through the Balkans to Athens. Thence he proposed to travel to South Africa in acceptance of an invitation from Sir James and thereafter return home in the spring of 1930 by way of England.

His mother seems to have guessed that this letter might be badly received, for two days later she wrote to her father:

> Helmuth tells me that he has written you a long letter about his future plans. Don't be too horrified at their bulk, half or none of them probably won't come off [they didn't!] but like me he enjoys making plans.

She failed, however, to prevent him from being considered an opinionated young man – a view which must have percolated to Kreisau, for on 12 November Helmuth wrote a long defence of his position.

> *What is 'Concentration'? I feel I am bound firstly to Europe secondly to Germany, thirdly to East Germany, fourthly to the land. 'I feel bound' means that I feel responsible, the degree of responsibility weakening with the widening of the circle. Now the intensity of the feeling of responsibility is overwhelming on the side of the agricultural European East. I have the certain feeling that this is my*

real job. On the other side I am studying law.... But law is not my life.... I am sure that my life is not the law but politics.... You can only solve political problems by spreading out on everything.... I believe that the minute I concentrate on one of the parts of the problem I will become an 'expert' and that as soon as you are an 'expert', you die away for political work.

He was in fact in considerable uncertainty as to what he should make of his life. In May 1929 he explained to his grandfather that he had three choices. One was to go into Germany's chemical giant, I.G. Farben, which he felt he would be unable to endure. The second was to work as Edgar Mowrer's assistant, which would not by itself bring in enough to live on, but only take up half his time. The third was to go to New York to work for the *New York Evening Post*. He had no sooner decided on the last course than he was advised on all sides that it was a bad moment to leave a Germany where important things were about to happen. As he would have arrived in New York just at the moment when the Wall Street Crash started the world on the road to depression and war, the advice was hardly well judged though its effects proved far-reaching. Instead Helmuth decided to join the Statistical Department of a big Berlin bank. This meant working without pay for six months and giving up for the moment a visit to South Africa, but was expected to provide valuable experience.

But his uncertainties were not confined to employment. At times he was prone, like his grandfather, to fits of depression in which he saw in the darkest colours the outlook for Europe, Germany, his family and himself. He then considered decay to have gone so far, and disaster to be so certain, as to make any serious constructive work futile and the assumption of responsibilities like marriage foolhardy. But in the following summer two developments occurred which in the long term were to have a decisive and beneficial effect upon his career and character.

First of all he met at the Grundlsee in August Freya Deichmann, whose brothers Carl and Hans he already knew and who had come under the wing of a suspicious mother to see an establishment about which their accounts had whetted her curiosity. For the time being there was no thought of marriage. Freya was only eighteen and had still to take her *Abitur*; her family had not discovered how little the Moltkes fitted their picture of East German landowners, and were therefore undeserving of the deep aversion which they (in common with many Rhinelanders) felt for that caste; Helmuth was fond of declaring that he would never marry. The only immediate development was the starting of a correspondence without which this book would have been infinitely the poorer. But it took a year – and another visit to Grundlsee – before they were addressing one another in the second person singular, while the first letter, dating from October, was an almost unbroken catalogue of disaster. One of his friends had been drowned, another had been killed in an accident and at Kreisau the death of the manager had brought to a head a situation which had been deteriorating for a long time.

The main causes of trouble numbered four. In the first place the arrangements made by the Field-Marshal, and particularly the entail* had proved too inflexible for post-war conditions; agreement could not be obtained quickly enough to take advantage of situations which changed rapidly. In 1927 the entail was finally broken but the advantages which it was hoped to gain had mostly disappeared. Secondly, much of the capital fund built up by the Field-Marshal had been invested in bonds which became worthless during the inflation. Moreover, the Trust was not empowered to provide capital for the estate which was consequently left without enough for working purposes. Nieder-Gräditz had to be let in order to raise the money for running Kreisau itself.

Thirdly, a number of misjudgments were made by the Count. He, like most of the rest of his family, but unlike his wife, was slow to recognise that they had come down in the world and must draw in their horns.

Lastly, there was a run of bad luck. A barn full of corn burnt down in the early twenties. When in 1926 the lease of Nieder-Gräditz was wound up, the stock was not only bought back at too high a price but the cereal crop was ruined by a hailstorm a few days after it had been taken over and proved to have been underinsured. An attempt to sell Wierischau in 1928 was frustrated by a fall in property values. The Count spent much of the next year in Berlin working as a Christian Science practitioner, which may have been the reason why, when the estate manager had a stroke in the spring, it was not detected. During the next six months this man overordered materials and made contracts to supply larger quantities of produce than were available; when he died from a second stroke, his accounts were found to be in complete confusion. The estate, reckoned to be worth RM866,000 (£43,000) was in debt to the tune of RM700,000 (£35,000). The creditors, of which the chief was the *Allgemeine Kredit Anstalt*, threatened to foreclose. To make matters worse the Count lost his nerve. He realised that Helmuth was much better fitted than himself to cope with the situation. His commitments in Berlin made it impossible for him to give Kreisau the constant attention without which it could not possibly be rescued. Countess Dorothy, as it happened, was on a visit to South Africa.

Helmuth agreed to give up his work at the bank and take over for a year, on condition that his father kept away for the next few months

* Above, p. 7.

until the people on the estate and in the neighbourhood had got used to taking orders from him. He was given full legal powers of action on 14 October and set himself at once to discover what the situation really was. For some days all the surprises were unpleasant and he told Freya that it was like being chained to a bed on which other people were piling feather mattresses '– or anything else that takes away one's breath but not one's consciousness'. He was alone; he had no training in agriculture or in business management. By driving himself to the point of breakdown and by saying to himself at the worst moments that 'everything ends sometime', he began to sort things out and to evolve a plan which on 25 November he discussed with the creditors.

> The worst thing about it is that all the details hang together; if one won't work, the whole breaks down. The best part is that it is a job which calls for all one's abilities and which keeps one's hands full.

The strongest point in Helmuth's position was that many other estates were in a bad way and it would be hard to find a buyer for Kreisau except at a giveaway price.* There were good prospects of the estate earning enough to service the long-term debts but not the short-term ones. He therefore suggested turning it into a company with himself left in control as agent for the creditors, who would be allowed to install a manager of their own choosing. The family would get no money out of it for twenty years; their only gain was that they would keep their home. The proposal was accepted, partly because nobody could suggest anything better but largely because Helmuth's handling of the situation had inspired a belief that he was as likely as anyone to run the estate successfully. He had kept cool enough to threaten that, if his proposition was turned down, he would precipitate matters by starting proceedings for bankruptcy.

> *22 November 1929*
> I am in Breslau to deal with the people here. Things are going better than I expected but it is a strain on the nerves. I have finally adopted the attitude that I am indifferent about the outcome and am not going to stop the creditors if they insist on being silly. But when every conversation begins with 'Your proposal is ludicrous and unacceptable,' the pose of disinterestedness takes a lot of keeping up, as one knows all the time how much is at stake not merely for us but for a lot of people who depend on us. Yesterday I got desperate at times. For I am all by myself. Everybody says to me, 'I can't help you. You get on much better on your own.' And flattering as that is, it makes the responsibility ten, or even a hundred times as great.

---

* Most of the other landowners met the crisis by demanding radical remedies from the government rather than by overhauling their own balance-sheets. Here, as in so much else, Helmuth was untypical of his class.

Thus, when his mother got home on 20 December, there seemed to be a ray of hope. Then for a moment it seemed to disappear.

28 December

It was one of the nicest Christmases I have spent and certainly unique in its background. On the 23rd our chief creditor declared that the scheme wouldn't do as it was and I must improve my offer if I wanted to count on his support. As I had told him a month before that my offer was the umost I could make, I was naturally surprised. ... I at once rang the head-office of this creditor in Leipzig and said I would call on them on the 24th. On the evening of 23rd, it became clear that I couldn't get away because I still had so much to get through here.

The 24th saw the great battle. At 8 in the morning I rang everyone up and told them I must be able to get in touch with them throughout the day. Then I went to the Official Receiver and told him that I might very possibly start proceedings in a few days. ... I worked solidly till 6 in the evening on getting ready for the bankruptcy, went through all the agreements I had reached to make sure they were valid, checked that they could be executed in the event of bankruptcy and in places revised them. ... I got home at 6 and then we had the pleasantest, gayest and most peaceful Christmas I have ever known, talking till 1 in the morning.

The 25th was madly strenuous because I had to work through everything I had done here since 12 October, with enough related papers to fill a book, in order to make sure that a defensible case could be based on them. For one mistake could cost a lot of money to a lot of innocent people.

... I got to Leipzig on the 26th [in company with his father, as his mother's letters reveal] where I talked for four hours on end to the head office of my chief creditor, in the course of which it came out that the Breslau representative clearly wanted to ruin us since he had reported things all wrong. The people at the head office by contrast were intelligent, broad-minded and judicious. And that was very pleasant. So once more I have the tiniest ground for hoping that I can in spite of everything put matters right again.

All the same, prospects for the family were dismal. Countess Dorothy had £200 a year from her parents and the Field-Marshal's trust paid another £200. They were allowed to draw food from the farm to the value of £175. On this the entire family had to live, with the exception of the Count (who supported himself by his own earnings in Berlin) and Jowo, then studying art-history on money provided by the grandparents (who behaved with great but prudent generosity throughout). All luxuries like cars had to be given up. In 1930 silver, jewellery and furniture (including the Lenbach portraits) had to be sold for what they would fetch (which was not much) so that the creditors could be paid what they had been promised. The *Reich* was induced to buy the Field-Marshal's papers and other relics connected with him; many of these remained in the Schloss on condition that some of its rooms were opened to the public. The shooting was let. If paying guests were taken, the cash which they provided was now as important as the amusement. J.F. was one of the first to come.*

Through all these troubles, Countess Dorothy never quailed or grew bitter or flagged in her determination to make the sacrifices needed to save Kreisau. She had been the first to see the direction in which things were going and had opposed some of her husband's steps. During the 1920s she often said, 'Oh! how I hate running the place on an over-draft!' Perhaps she found it a relief to be rid of the pretence and know the worst. The experience certainly brought her and her son closer together than ever.

This was all the more noteworthy because Helmuth was not drawn to Christian Science. He had been christened and confirmed as a Lutheran and remembered long arguments with the local pastor before the latter ceremony. For some time thereafter he used to go with his parents to the Christian Science church in Schweidnitz but gradually gave this up. As acting Lord of the Manor Helmuth was responsible for maintaining the fabric of both the Evangelical and the Catholic churches on the estate and in the years immediately after 1929 his inability to provide all that was expected led to occasional criticism. On the whole relations with the clergy were good but the Berghaus should not be thought of as a place where, with the exception of the parents, conventional piety was noticeable. Churchgoing was the exception rather than the rule.

In March an important step forward was made.

8 March 1930

I am in such a good temper, so much above myself that I wish you were here. Today I've seen for certain that I shall be able to resolve the unpleasantest part of this business. I simply must tell you about it so that if I bore you, you must forgive me.

In the spring of last year the manager sold plots of land to small peasants, took the money from them and spent it. Now when land is sold, the rule is that ownership does not pass to the purchaser until the plot is struck off the register of the vendor's holdings. This can only be done with the consent of the mortgagers who will only give that consent if some of the money owing to them is paid.

Now it is usual to devote the money received from the purchaser

---

* See Preface, page x above. Where the authors refer to parts which one or other played in the story, they have identified the person concerned by initials.

to satisfying the claims of the mortgagees. But the manager had spent all the money and when I got here in October it looked as though the peasants were bound to lose their money. At any rate the mortgagers were demanding thirty-five thousand marks.

By endless negotiating, by adjusting the register, by shifting mortgages from one page of the register to another and by all the devices I could think of, I have succeeded in bringing down the amount of hard cash needed to pay off the mortgagers to seven thousand marks and that I can find.

You can have no idea what that means to me, for what is going to happen even if everything else goes wrong is that small peasants aren't going to lose the money which they handed over on the strength of our good name.

I can hardly write, I am trembling all over for joy. If this hadn't come off, an entire villageful of peasants would have been plunged into debt and impoverished.

He was due to meet Freya at the Schwarzwalds' in Vienna in April but at a crucial moment found himself kept in bed by a broken ankle.

24 March

The result of my long lie is naturally that I have got dimwitted and regard myself as a superfluous limb on the body of mankind, a feeling which is only marginally counteracted by the fact that a pitch-black, mild gentle damp spring night is pouring in through the open window and the undrawn curtains.

The prospects for my getting away become worse every day. Objectively the difficulties have increased because I have been wrongly informed: subjectively they have grown enormously because my two assistants here [the manager and a book-keeper] who are very assiduous declare that they cannot get their share of the work done. The result naturally is that they are very timid – or, as they put it, careful – and leave to me anything involving responsibility. As fresh initiatives are needed every day when things have gone as badly off the rails as here, I have more to do than ever and can less than ever afford to go away. It may be just a matter of atmosphere, a feeling which the chaps have when they see the blades of corn starting to come up out of the ground. But just for the moment the machine is creaking far more than in the months when I was in charge by myself. . . .

I know perfectly well it would make more sense for me to leave things here to look after themselves and head straight for Cologne. But I just can't. Do you know how Luther begins his sermon 'On a Christian Man's Freedom'? 'A Christian man is a free lord over all things and subject to nobody – a Christian man is a dutiful servant of all things and subject to everybody.' It is the same in all connections: one is free as long as one doesn't forget that one is only a servant. I am free not to forget for an instant that what I do here is completely unimportant.

He did get away, however, only to find things in confusion when he came back.

19 April

It is really astonishing what has been achieved in my absence. All the accounts for the last week are faulty and have now got to be revised. And so gradually black has become dark grey and dark grey, light grey. One is conscious of an enormous satisfaction if one can reduce chaos to some sort of order.

Soon afterwards Freya came with Hans on her first visit to Kreisau which was very successful. The summer brought a calmer mood, though there were still problems to be tackled.

15 June

People here – that is to say my family and my fellow-workers – keep on being astonished that I am so relaxed and content and unperturbed just when everything seems to be going wrong. My two closest colleagues in particular are pained that I don't share their concern. I shall never succeed in making clear to them that with me concern is already a thing of the past by the time the reason for it begins to be obvious. Besides I have learnt such a lot in this last half year, particularly that one must never get alarmed when things go wrong but learn to live through it.

22 June

My calendar says 'The first day of summer' and 'Always be Punctual'. I apply both to the first of August [when he was to meet Freya at Grundlsee] and will do my utmost to comply. I warned my two colleagues today that I was thinking of going on holiday in just over a month. They nearly fell off their chairs and said it was out of the question for me to go away before the books were made up – to which I replied that by then the books would have to be made up. They gave a faint and meditative smile.

The difficult days lie ahead for I have got to discuss dismissing people and giving them notice. Anyone who sees my proposals will abuse me roundly. I am proposing to cut between ten and fifteen thousand marks off the pay-bill. That is terrible because it is all to be done by bits and pieces. Every one of our sixty contracts is going to be revised and for the worse. I am therefore in the lowest of spirits because it is thoroughly unpleasant to have to carry out the capitalist system against one's convictions.

Franz Josef Furtwängler, a Social Democrat who first met Helmuth about this time described him, after the war, as having considered large landed estates, including his own, to have become morally and politically indefensible.[1] This may be too sweeping but there is no doubt that he took the established order in no sense for granted.

At the end of June, having failed to get a Rhodes Scholarship for which he had applied, he started on the next stage of legal training, which consists of practical experience in various types of legal work. At first he had to go to Reichenbach on most days of the week; later he transferred to Schweidnitz.

29 June

I have now been a *Referendar* for a week. It is pretty difficult because the work can't be done in less than 6 hours a day. As I have hitherto been working for 12 to 13 hours a day, the sum now adds up to 18 or 19. Surprisingly enough, that can be compressed to 14 by working more intensively. But even that is quite enough.

6 July

Every morning I spend in Reichenbach. On Monday afternoon I went to a meeting on a neighbouring estate, on Tuesday afternoon I was in Schweidnitz, on Wednesday afternoon in Upper Silesia, on Thursday afternoon in Lower Silesia. On Friday the Juvenile Court goes on sitting till 6, on Saturday I must draw up 6 judgments. I deal with my post between 6 and 8 in the morning and 8 and 9 in the evening. I have to discuss the accounts at 9 on every evening this week, preparing for the discussions in the train. The real work gets done later in the evening and on Sunday.

Yet what made his head spin was the thought that in a month's time they might be lying peacefully somewhere in a meadow beside the Grundlsee! A hint of what they discussed in that Arcadian setting is given in a letter written after his return.

27 August

As regards the claims which I should make on life, that has been the main question of the last few months and I haven't come to any conclusion, or rather I haven't stuck to any conclusion. Before I went to the Grundlsee, or rather before I stayed at the Grundlsee with you [Here the second person singular is used for the first time], I was absolutely determined not to make any claims on life. If anyone had offered me five pounds pocket money and a place somewhere in the country, I'd have gladly promised not to do anything else or go anywhere else ever again. I didn't of course reach that conclusion out of modesty but because I didn't think the game was worth the candle. You've shaken my faith in this principle – that's all I can say for the moment.

3 October

I am very pleased with life chiefly because the work I am now doing is something quite new: building up, rationalising, financing new projects, creating the legal conditions in which one can carry on business as one thinks best. Whereas my job so far was to look for a way through what appeared to be a solid wall, to discover the one course which was possible, it is now much more a question of choosing the best out of a variety of possible courses.

After this a gap of over six months occurs in the record, providing a convenient opportunity to say a little about the kind of person that Helmuth was, though for a full picture this book needs to be read as a whole. As he himself said at the end of his life,* his was a complicated character and for it no single label will suffice. On the one hand he had a decided taste for society, provided it was interesting – 'the only thing he finds dull,' said his mother, 'is chatter, I mean social chatter.' Moreover he liked his company mixed. 'How pleasant,' he once remarked, 'to meet some women after being all day with men.'

He has sometimes been described as witty, but (apart from the question of whether this is the best way to translate the German word 'witzig') the description could mislead. While he could be very funny, it was not by producing a string of epigrams. Mrs Mowrer is nearer the mark in referring to his 'impish' sense of humour, as when she met him in Berlin holding a balloon on a string and asked, 'Why the decoration?' 'I've just been to the *Reich* Chancellery!' He liked to tease people, particularly those of whom he was fond, and had a keen sense of the ludicrous, the incongruous and the bogus. To amuse and interest his audience, he tended to present life dramatically, as many letters in this book illustrate. The practice inevitably leads to exaggeration, a fault of which his grandfather thought him guilty. Indeed he himself admitted that exaggeration was not at all times pardonable and asked Freya to tell him when she thought he was indulging in it.

Yet on the other hand he seldom revealed his inner self or thoughts. It is remarkable how many people, even among those who at some stage worked closely with him, have said, on being asked for reminiscences, that they never felt on terms of close intimacy. As has been seen, people who were well entitled to address him as *'Du'* forebore from being so familiar. 'Younger people,' wrote his mother, 'are often rather

* Below, p. 324.

overawed by him.' Of course, both the conditions of the time, particularly after 1933, and the early age at which responsibilities fell on him made for reticence. But one cannot resist a suspicion that Helmuth found it congenial. His very small, though neat, handwriting seems to symbolise this. After war broke out, the two English godfathers of his son discovered their mutual existence for the first time. Although he must on several occasions have travelled straight from the house of the one to that of the other, it hardly occurred to him to tell people things which he did not think they needed to know.

It has been said that Goerdeler trusted everybody and Adenauer nobody. Applying the same yardstick, one might say that Helmuth overestimated the capacities of those whom he liked and too easily dismissed the capacities of those whom he did not like. His judgment, in other words, was capable of being affected by his feelings. But this is a natural tendency in youth, while it is the mark of a leader to expect of his associates a higher standard than comes naturally to them. If he was an idealist, it was more in the sense of having the highest principles himself than of assuming that most other people shared them. His mother told Sir James that

> I often find very strong traces of you in him. He is less balanced in judgment than you, has got more of his father's impetuosity but it is often as if you were speaking when it is a question of ethics or a matter of right versus opportunism.

He took a close and almost fatherly interest in the younger members of his family and other people junior to himself who had problems.

While he had an extremely good intellect, he was not in the normal sense of the word an intellectual. Without being a Philistine, he had no particular artistic or creative gifts.* His abilities were practical rather than speculative. He could analyse soundly and fast, pick up the essence of any question in a short time and deploy accurately the relevant facts. This made him a good lawyer, with a grasp of principle and a care for detail. With his interest in people, it should have made him a first-class administrator if large-scale responsibility had ever come his way. But he was better at the impromptu argument than at the set speech (though this may have been a matter of practice). He was also prone to the clever man's fault of supposing that, because he has seen something to be self-evident and drawn appropriate conclusions, everyone else will have done so too. He was, as a result, capable of making wrong estimates about the time a trend would take to develop or the support which a proposition might receive.

---

* He gave shelter and work in 1941 to the expressionist painter Karl Schmidt-Rottluff – but this seems to have been due more to a community of political views than of aesthetic tastes.

By instinct as well as practice, he became extremely good at organising his time – if he had not been, he would never have got through as much as he did. This showed itself in the smallest details. At one period of his life, he professed to file one of his nails every day so as to average out the time taken to cover the lot. At another, he used to carry one brief-case under each arm, with the contents divided into urgent and less urgent! Wally Deuel remembered him as personifying 'grace under pressure' while his mother wrote that she could not remember ever having seen him ruffled, much less angry or nervy.

The pejorative senses which have come to be associated with the word 'aristocrat' make it dangerously misleading to use the term in connection with somebody who certainly did not claim unjustified privileges or seek to bolster up a system which he believed to be doomed. Yet in two ways he was aristocratic in the best sense of the word. Although his inclination and his penury combined to make his tastes simple, he liked what he did have to be of the best. And it came naturally to him to lead, to accept responsibility, to take initiatives. He did not use his position to impose himself or get pleasure out of being important. He took it for granted that the ends he was interested in were worth while and that it was accordingly his duty to use in furthering them the opportunities which had been given him. In a society where the 'leadership principle'/*Führerprinzip* was being debased, he provided an example of its true character.

In Freya Helmuth found his ideal counterpart and his good fortune in meeting and marrying her deserves to be emphasised. In character, ways and even looks she so well fitted into the Moltke pattern that at first strangers sometimes took her for a daughter of the house rather than a daughter-in-law. This was partly due to her birth in one of the most enlightened areas of Germany. Thanks to a long line of Rhineland ancestors, thanks in particular to her own mother, Freya had grown up and been allowed to develop in a genuinely liberal tradition. It thus came naturally to her to share in full the almost idealistic political and social standards of Countess Dorothy and her children – later her relationship with Sir James was characteristically one of great mutual warmth and affection – but she also possessed qualities which Helmuth lacked and which, being complementary to his own, proved of great benefit and support to him in times of need. 'She is a delightful creature,' wrote her mother-in-law, 'and just the right wife for Helmuth, being full of strength and optimism.' Her gaiety, spontaneity and zest for life proved unquenchable. She bubbled over with fun and appreciative response to whatever might be going forward. 'When Freya stops talking,' her father-in-law once said, 'she stops living.'

These, however, were not the responses of a shallow or frivolous personality. Freya obtained the degree of Doctor of Law from Berlin

University in 1935 – when strangers erroneously addressed Helmuth as
'Herr Doctor', as sometimes happened, he delighted to point out that
the doctorate was held on the distaff side of the family. She also
possessed in depth the moral, intellectual and emotional endowments
necessary to bring her unscathed and unembittered through so much
strain and sorrow. From the outset Helmuth made clear to her the
mortal risks involved in the course he proposed to take and in the
conviction that it was right she accepted them without flinching.

In June 1931 he spent a week with Freya at her Rhineland home,
during which marriage seemed as remote as ever. He then went to see
the Frau Doctor, who had been an ardent advocate of the match and
urged him to forget his hesitations over marrying at all. A practical
consideration which played some part, at any rate in influencing the
timing of the wedding, was his mother's intended visit to South Africa
for the first half of 1932. If they married before she left, Freya would
be able to look after the Berghaus in her absence. Countess Dorothy
was at first inclined to argue that one could not marry without anything
to live on. Helmuth was in the course of putting the estate back on its
feet but he would not get any income from it in the foreseeable future,
or earn anything as a *Referendar*. He countered by pointing out that
both he and Freya would have to live on something even if they didn't
marry, and supposing that they could manage to do so separately there
should be no reason why they could not do so together. Warm support
for the idea came from his father who suggested the date of 18 October,
the wedding anniversary of the parents and the golden wedding day of
the grandparents.

Helmuth approached the event in his own way.

27 July 1931
I have suddenly got afraid that you expect too much from me. . . .
'Marriage' is such a high-sounding word which calls up a grandiose
idea – at the very least, a more settled way of life. Dear Freya, will
you . . . be content for us to be just two students who would rather
live together than alone?

13 September
My idea is this – you fix the wedding whenever it suits you. And
to deprive the occasion of all excitement, we won't go off in an
express on a honeymoon but will remain your Mother's guests for
four or five days. . . . Please tell your Mother, so as to knock the
bottom out of any festive ideas she may have in connection with us,
that I have handed my dinner-jacket and morning-coat on to Willo
and they are both already at the tailor's being altered and I don't
intend to get any more!

17 September

As regards the wedding, I don't mind what happens so long as nobody turns up!

Things did not, however, work out quite as expected. Not merely was Helmuth induced to buy a new suit (from his favourite Viennese tailor Prix)* but he and Freya did go off for a honeymoon in the normal way. This, however, was not to last long. For the wedding was held in unhappy circumstances. On the Moltke side, only Helmuth's parents and Willo could afford to attend, while the Deichmann finances were in an even more critical condition. During the boom, the family banking firm had over-invested in industry so that the economic depression caused its ruin. The wedding reception was the last event in the family home before it was sold. They had intended to be content with a civil ceremony but, out of respect for the family, agreed at a late stage to a church service. Freya's father was already in bed with pneumonia and when they reached Zürich, they were called back by telegram because of his death.

* Many people assumed that Helmuth bought his clothes in England but in fact he only once had a suit made in London and that was not a success.

7 The Nazi Menace

THE failure of the Deichmann bank was only one example of the economic disaster which overwhelmed Germany in these years and brought about the collapse of the Weimar Republic. In March 1930 the last Socialist Chancellor (prior to Willy Brandt) resigned. He was succeeded by Brüning who, lacking a firm parliamentary majority, took to governing by presidential decree – indeed President Hindenburg had appointed him on the understanding that he would do so. When in July a majority of M.P.s challenged this course, Brüning dissolved the *Reichstag*; the elections of September sensationally strengthened the National Socialists and Communists but weakened the Socialist and middle-class parties. Thereafter the majority (composed of Socialists, Democrats and Catholics) tolerated Brüning's method of government by decree, which enabled him to weather the economic storms of 1931. What undermined him was his need to get the President's signature for the decrees; in May 1932 the old gentleman was persuaded to refuse this and Brüning saw no alternative to resignation. He was replaced by von Papen, who had virtually no backing in the *Reichstag* at all and could not gain one in spite of holding two elections. In November 1932 Papen was ousted in favour of General von Schleicher and retaliated by conspiring with the National Socialists who were worried by a recent loss of ground. This led to the appointment of Hitler as Chancellor on 30 January 1933, with Papen as Vice-Chancellor and only two other acknowledged Nazis in a cabinet of twelve. What most people failed to realise was that, once the Nazis had got a foot in the door, they would stop at nothing in pushing it right open and, once installed in the house, could only be evicted by force.

Helmuth's parents supported Brüning; his mother wrote in December 1930 that 'the Opposition, especially on the right, make me boil with rage'. He himself, however, criticised the introduction of government by decree and from the first took a serious view of the Nazi menace. In February 1931 he went with Dorothy Thompson to discuss economics with Gregor Strasser and Gottfried Feder, two of the less orthodox members of the Nazi left-wing with whom Hitler soon afterwards broke for fear of frightening off industrial support. 'It is like discussing astronomy with someone who believes that the sun is not the centre of our system but, say, Saturn.' Later he wrote to Freya:

16 July 1931

I must admit to drawing an aesthetic satisfaction from these stormy days. This alarms me by making me realise how little responsibility I feel for Germany any more. But thus far it isn't serious. It has hardly any repercussions on our own affairs. For the time being we have to pay a slightly higher rate of interest but as at the moment we have not drawn much credit, the effect is small. On the other hand we have been very liquid for the last six weeks and are taking the opportunity to buy cows cheap while nobody has any money.

In April 1932 Hindenburg's term of office expired and, although he was eighty-four, he allowed himself to be put up for re-election as the only candidate likely to stop Hitler from getting in. Helmuth had no use for Hindenburg (an attitude which the latter went far to justify by abandoning Brüning immediately after the election) and decided to vote for the Communist Thälmann. Not only was this a highly unusual thing for a Prussian aristocrat to do but he was advised that there was nobody else at all in Kreisau who would do it (although there had been four Communist votes in the village in 1928) so that the way he had balloted would quickly become common knowledge; he took the hint and advantage of a legal provision which allowed him to vote elsewhere. About the same time he wrote to his grandfather that

I really long for decisions which are based on solid fundaments and therefore I am rereading the parliamentary work in the first German Imperial Constitution/Reichsverfassung in 1848.

Two months later his mother told her parents that it was 'chilly weather for people with liberal standpoints'.

The Weimar Republic, like the Kaiser's Empire, consisted of a number of states among which Prussia (subdivided into sixteen provinces) was larger than all the rest put together. For a long time the Prussian government had been dominated by the Social Democrats but in July 1932 the Federal Government under Papen turned them out on the pretext that they were not showing enough anti-Communist zeal. The Prussian Ministers, led by Carl Severing (1875–1952) as Minister of the Interior, yielded to force, refrained from calling a general strike and contented themselves with bringing an action against the Federal Government for breaking the constitution. They were much criticised both at the time and afterwards for being too tame. But they would have had army, police and civil service against them and they judged that, with unemployment high, the workers would be reluctant to strike for fear of losing their jobs. As Countess Dorothy wrote:

The opposition have no money and of course half its adherents are men who may be desperate, poor wretches, but have been underfed for years which doesn't make for courage.

In September she explained that

> there is no opposition to all this because there is no money to finance active opposition or even the propaganda for it and the people are so tired by years of strain and worry while those who have a billet prefer to keep quiet so as to run no risks.

In October Helmuth went to Leipzig to report for Edgar Mowrer the hearing of the Prussian case before the *Reich* Constitutional Court. Though the judges did not wholly reject the Prussian Government's view, they gave little practical help. Helmuth wrote to his grandparents that

> *the principle that was fought about was, whether the state in his actions has only to submit to power or to law and justice and the constitution too. It is a bad sign for the German feeling for law that a thing like the Reich's sudden invasion of Prussia should have been possible ... but at any rate it is a good sign for German scientific law-work that the most important professors of Germany have joined the case of Prussia by their free-will and without any payment, while the Reich has only found three professors whose name nobody has known before.*

Hans Peters, who had taught Helmuth at Breslau,* was at Leipzig on behalf of Centre Party members of the Prussian Parliament, so that their paths crossed again.

Helmuth and Freya had by this time moved to Berlin and were living in a minute flat in the Bendlerstrasse; Countess Dorothy also came to Berlin to be with her husband, leaving a caretaker in the Berghaus. Helmuth worked at the Prussian Appeal Court/*Kammergericht* and with the law firm of Koch-Weser and Karlebach,† so as to complete the remaining pieces of practical work needed for him to qualify as a lawyer. On the infamous 30 January their old friend Dr Ohle happened to come to lunch. He expressed the view, widely current at the time, that the holding of power would show up the inability of Hitler to deal with the situation so that his government would last no longer than its predecessors. The sooner the Nazis were in power, the sooner they would be out of it again; there was nothing to be gained by postponing the episode. Helmuth disputed this with the passion of despair. He regarded Hitler's appointment as a catastrophe of the first magnitude.‡

---

* Above, p. 25.

† Koch-Weser, Dr Edgar (1875–1944), belonged to the Democratic Party, helped to draft the Weimar Constitution, was Minister of the Interior 1919–21, Minister of Justice 1928–9. As a half-Jew emigrated to Brazil 1933. Helmuth worked mostly with Dr Karlebach who, being a Jew, emigrated in 1933.

‡ Dr Ohle as a socialist was driven out of the Civil Service, found refuge as a manager on an estate but died before the outbreak of war.

As F. J. Furtwängler later wrote:

> This gifted lawyer saw more clearly than any politician that the millions of unemployed portended a revolution and the spectre of war. In the unemployed workers, the young graduates turned out on the streets, the peasants up to their eyes in debt and the bankrupt businessmen, he already discerned the end of established society with all its consequences in the shape of world revolution.[1]

His mother may well have been reflecting his views when she wrote in July that 'we are in the middle of a revolution quite as important as and in many ways similar to the Russian revolution'. Several people at Kreisau later remembered how he had said from the start, 'Voting for Hitler means voting for war.'

In February, according to his mother, he found at Kreisau that the whole village was for the Nazis because the price of pigs had risen. The estate manager put in by the creditors, Herr Zeumer, though a sensible and capable man, had been taken in by Nazi propaganda and joined the party before it came to power. This, however, proved more of an advantage than the reverse because Helmuth and he had established an excellent working relationship based on mutual respect. Moreover, like many early Nazis, he shed some of his illusions as time went on and the net result was that he stood between the Moltkes and the local party bosses. Whenever the flying of flags was ordered, he displayed a small swastika on his own house, but none was ever hung out at the Berghaus or Schloss and no trouble resulted. In November 1934 Helmuth wrote that the relationship with the village was getting better, though in Wierischau the atmosphere was thoroughly bad. Earlier in that year, however, when he and Freya were in South Africa, his mother thought it wise to go through his books and destroy those which might have proved compromising if anyone had searched the house.

Compromise was not otherwise a word which figured in his relations with the Nazis. When in early September extreme pressure by Goebbels induced the *Chicago Daily News* to withdraw Edgar Mowrer, the author of 'Germany Puts the Clock Back', from Berlin for his unfavourable reporting, Helmuth was one of the few Germans who showed up at the station to see him off.[2] When Mowrer's permanent replacement Wallace Deuel arrived later in the year, Helmuth made friends and invited him to Kreisau. Fearing that too close an association with a foreign and anti-Nazi correspondent might be risky for a German, Deuel found one excuse after another for refusing. Before long, Helmuth detected an ulterior motive behind the excuses and asked what it was. On Deuel coming clean, he said:

> I had occasion to go through some old family papers the other day and I found, as I had rather suspected, that the Moltkes have been on

c

the losing side of virtually every violent civil upheaval for several generations and one or other of the men of the family usually lost his head as a result. The same thing will probably happen this time too. But there are a number of us and I have taken steps to see that some will survive. Meanwhile I propose to associate with whom I choose.

The prop and stay of the Berghaus from 1927 till her death in June 1939 was the cook Frau Maerkert called, as is usual in East German households, Mamsell (though there was little trace of French *chic* about her). A short woman, almost as stout as she was tall, her hair drawn straight into a tight bun, dressed mostly in dark blue with stripes, and wearing lace-up boots in which she rocked rather than walked, she had a shrewd humorous kindly face, was a tireless worker with no mercy for slackers and held fast to her opinions with the innate independence of the peasant. Her kitchen window overlooked the front door. After Hitler's advent to power Helmuth, who eschewed to the utmost the official Nazi greeting, was wont to call to her 'Heil Maerkert' whenever he returned to the house. To this Mamsell, who had conceived a high respect and affection for him, would reply 'Heil Moltke'.

He continued with his legal training through 1933, although the Nazis brought in regulations virtually closing the judicial career, to which that training often led,* against anyone who did not openly support them. 'Helmuth has lost all relish for his work at the Supreme Court,' wrote his mother in May, 'since even there righteous judgment, as the Bible says, is no longer judged. And he and Freya with hundreds of other law students say: what's the good of studying something that becomes more obsolete each month?' In a letter written soon afterwards to Karin Michaelis† Helmuth himself said:

7 March

I may well give up the law for the time being. The old jurisprudence, which I have learnt and which is inspired by the concept of abstract justice and humanity, is today only of historical interest because no matter how things develop in Germany there is absolutely no chance of bringing back these old ways of establishing what is just. Although they have been tested and reinforced over the centuries, such drastic inroads have now been made in them that it would take decades to unearth them again from under the débris.

He became qualified to take the examination for the post of *Assessor* towards the end of the year and planned to leave with Freya for South Africa immediately afterwards. But a complication arose. The Nazis

* In Germany, as in many other countries, judicial posts, instead of being filled by people previously practising as advocates, constitute a career service.
† Above, p. 27.

set up training camps in which all *Referendars* were required to take a six-week indoctrination course before they could be admitted to the *Assessor*'s examination. Could he get a place in such a camp soon enough to take the examination without forfeiting the passage which he had booked for 13 February? After some nerve-racking weeks, he made it – by the skin of his teeth. He only got the mark of 'Satisfactory' in the examination, the ostensible reasons being that he had such an indecipherable hand-writing (which was true) and so little practical knowledge (which was not). On the boat he sent to his friend Helli Weigel* a lively account of proceedings at the camp.

7 March

The camp was as such things are except that the troop of 58 men to which I was posted was particularly nice, so that in the whole time there wasn't a single fight and there were never more than a few drunks, which is unique for any camp. Our training consisted of field sports in the morning which were very elementary and in which we were treated far too gently for us to get any real benefit. What we ought really to have done you know very well. In the afternoons we had an hour's sport and then theoretical training, singing and lessons in world affairs. The singing was particularly comic because I, as the right hand man [because of his height], had to give the note. I had driven myself silly learning up first lines from the old familiar songs, to make sure these were all we used [i.e. to keep out any with Nazi associations]. The theoretical training was very interesting because I learnt a lot of all sorts of things which I should never have come across otherwise.

The lessons in world affairs, by contrast, were a first-class joke. The sort of thing that happened was as follows. We were informed that the medieval Emperors were traitors to the blood of the German people in that instead of satisfying the instinctive urge to colonise the east, they went south. That could only be attributed to racial adulteration of the imperial stock, for, as the instructor rhetorically asked, what true German had ever felt a call to the south? Up shot four hands, one of them mine, followed by at least forty of the fifty-eight. We said we regarded ourselves as completely Aryan – had we not had a lecture on the previous day about the pedigree of Field-Marshal Moltke, which entitled me to give evidence in defence of the German Emperors. The man was knocked completely off his balance.

After this splendid initial success we went over to the attack in a lecture about the Jews, and fell on the assertion that Spengler had deliberately skated over the role of the Jews in his book *Decisive Years*, so as to increase its circulation. The oldest of us, who had

* Above, p. 27.

commanded a battery during the war and was thus above challenge, got up and declared that his respect for Spengler was far too great for it to be affected by such a remark on the part of an Assessor Timmermann (loud applause!) and if Spengler had considered the Jewish question to be without historical significance, that carried more weight with him than did Assessor Timmermann saying the opposite (loud applause!).

Thereupon instruction in world affairs was abandoned and a reading period substituted, in which we were to study the Nazi Party programme and *Mein Kampf*. The programme complete with explanations was finished off in two hours and the only bit of *Mein Kampf* which we read was the section on German policy towards the east which in view of the Treaty with Poland* seemed a bit out of date. We then said we'd all read it once and couldn't possibly do it twice and so decided that I should get a gramophone and that in the reading period we should play Bach, Brahms and Beethoven. And that was what happened. During the reading period we all lay motionless on our beds and played a complete symphony, with usually a short piece as well. Before long we stopped being alone but had visitors from all the other rooms. So it was a notable spiritual triumph.

For the rest we ran things quite democratically. Every afternoon we took a vote about what was to be done and as a result got the best results. Those among us who stood for the Leadership principle never spotted what they were doing. In addition I demanded unanimity before I brought along the gramophone on the ground that we didn't want anyone to be quiet who didn't want to be so of his own free will, and this unanimity was immediately forthcoming.

One more thing. Once when I woke at night I heard a lot of drunks from another troop singing on the square. And what do you think they were singing? The Internationale.

A newspaper cutting which has been preserved by chance reveals that the camp was inspected by an Under-Secretary from the Ministry of Justice called Roland Freisler.

In South Africa the love and respect which Sir James and Lady Rose Innes had won caused many doors to be open to their grandchildren, starting with those of Lord Clarendon the Governor-General and General Smuts (who had previously read and approved Helmuth's supplement on 'The New Germany'†). At first they stayed at the Cape with the grandparents. Here old misgivings by Sir James as to his grandson's cocksureness and diffuseness of purpose proved not entirely to have

---

* In January 1934 Germany and Poland signed a non-aggression pact to last ten years.
† Above, p. 35.

died away, so that it was with Freya that he established the more intimate and tender relationship. Helmuth on the other hand had long responded positively to his grandmother's resolution, optimism and zest for life. Her qualities of firmness, uprightness and efficiency were just such as would appeal to him and their mutual love and admiration influenced him deeply. Other friends whom they made were Dr Petronella van Heerden and Jean van der Poel, who took them on a trip to the east parts of Cape Province. Later they bought a car of their own and went up-country visiting relatives and staying with the Patrick Duncans in Pretoria.* In such enlightened company they experienced the magnanimity of South Africa without its narrowness (apartheid was then the gospel of a small group with little power) and came to look on it as a second home. The only thing which marred the visit was an accident in which Helmuth fell and concussed himself badly, but without lasting results.

They started back to Europe in October, stopping in England on the way. Here again Helmuth's connections brought him into more exalted circles than would normally have been accessible to a young German of twenty-seven. They included Gilbert Murray, E. M. Forster, Eileen Power the historian, Sir William Beveridge and Sir Alfred Hopkinson of Manchester University. Others, like Lionel Curtis,† Lionel Hichens,‡ Percy Molteno§ and Lady Bower,‖ had a more obvious link with South Africa.

Meanwhile his mother had written on 9 September, 'It is a mad world that Helmuth and Freya are coming back to and one that will distress them profoundly.'

* Duncan, Sir Patrick (1870–1943), b. Scotland, educated Oxford, came to South Africa with Milner, practised as lawyer, M.P. 1910–36, Minister under Smuts and Hertzog, Governor-General 1937–43.
† Below, pp. 67–9.
‡ Hichens, Lionel (1874–1940), treasurer in Johannesburg under Milner 1902–7; chairman of Cammell Laird 1910–40; killed in the 'Blitz'.
§ Molteno, Percy A. (1861–1937), son of Sir J. C. Molteno, first Prime Minister of Cape Colony; Liberal M.P. for Dumfriesshire 1906–18; shipping magnate; benefactor.
‖ Widow of Sir Graham Bower, Imperial Secretary to the British High Commissioner to South Africa 1884–97.

8 Life and Death in Nazi Germany
1934–5

ON the boat to South Africa Helmuth had taken advantage of the freedom to write not only to Karin Michaelis and Helli Weigel but also to a third member of the Schwarzwald group, Maria Lazar, who was living like the others in Sweden. He made a frivolous attempt at a sociological sketch of the Third Reich which can be instructively compared with the much profounder and more serious picture drawn by him nine years later.* The superficial jocularity, however, masked not only anxiety about the future course of German society but also uncertainty about his own position as a landowner with a famous name.

> I really wanted to write you a letter about the people in Germany who aren't persecuted. They are the people whose patriotism is beyond question, who are above having socialist inclinations and who are for all that not outspoken monarchists. You will have already gathered from the description that I belong to this group, though there seems to be some doubt as to whether we shouldn't be reckoned monarchists.
>
> Anyhow, apart from all these negative criteria, a very important precondition for a tolerable life in Germany is not to have joined the Party in the years '32 and '33. The order of precedence goes something like this. At the bottom come the moderately well-off Jews who still have something to lose (Intellectuals and Pacifists haven't counted for a long time). Second the poor Jews, thirdly those who became Party members in '32 and '33, fourth those Aryans who, although they didn't actually join the Party then, now run after it; fifthly the very rich Jews from whom one can't take anything away without creating havoc and who have no intention of surrendering anything willingly (this includes the members of the Berlin Trading Bank who refuse to go to the *Reichsbank* so that Herr Schacht has to put himself to the trouble of visiting them); sixthly the Party members, with the exception of those in category three above and of Number 7,† seventhly those unchallengeably Aryan‡ people whose

---

* Below, pp. 215–24.
† Hitler held membership card Number 7 in the Nationalist Socialist German Workers Party (NSDAP) which had been founded as the German Workers

patriotism is above, and socialist leanings are below, suspicion and who haven't joined the Party; and eighthly the Führer, Number 7. With the seventh group I forgot that control over means of production is essential though being in debt doesn't matter. I count myself – or rather am counted – among the sevens. That means that to begin with one is free of the following obligations: one doesn't have to believe the Führer is infallible, one can think that a different system of government would be desirable; one has no need to read papers or go to the theatre; one doesn't need to attend meetings or instruction courses; one doesn't have to make big contributions to Winter Aid but only pays what one is assessed at; one doesn't have to pay other subscriptions to the Party, to one's professional organisation, to the Labour Front, to impecunious comrades in Austria or anything of that sort.

By contrast one has the following advantages: one can express a dissenting opinion without worrying, for the worst that people will think is that one is a bit injudicious, not that one is lacking in character; one is much sought after, for the Party has no other way of swelling its ranks except winning over those who still keep aloof; as a result one gets complimentary tickets to the shows to which one is invited, while the honourable Party members have to sit at the back; one need never use the Hitler salute – the idea seems gradually to be taking root that the proletariat use the Hitler salute while the well-bred man says 'Good morning'.

It only remains to define the kinds of people who belong to this privileged caste: the senior Catholic clergy and the lower Catholic clergy in south and west Germany; the Protestant clergy in the Pastors' Emergency League; the large landowners; a few Catholic professors in each faculty; a few private bankers and big industrialists, though the latter are few and far between; and finally a few independent people who have inherited famous names or made their own names well known.

In truth, however, all in Helmuth's seventh class, i.e. those Germans who were neither Jews, Socialists nor Nazis and possessed a source of income independent of the government, found themselves increasingly faced by an unpleasant choice. One possibility for them was to emi-

---

Party by Anton Drexler in January 1919, nine months before its future leader heard about and joined it.
‡ Certain Nazis had at one stage asserted that the Rose Innes family was Jewish with a view to sequestrating the Moltke estates. Documents from South Africa and the Lyon office in Edinburgh were invoked to refute this. The danger was, however, reduced when the group in question were liquidated on 30 June 1934.

grate. But to do so involved not only the problem of finding a livelihood and building up a fresh position in an alien land. It also meant cutting themselves off from friends and relations and from their inherited environment of which they might well be fond. Yet more than that, it meant deserting their country and their fellow-countrymen in a time of need. After all, it was not practical politics for everyone who disliked the Nazis to emigrate. Opinions might differ as to how long the brown tyranny would last but few outside the movement thought that it would be permanent. When it disappeared, much would depend on the right people being ready with plans for rebuilding. But the confidence of the German people would not be easily given to those who had looked on from outside instead of sharing the dark days within.

Yet how were those who remained inside the country to exist? On the one hand they could shut themselves into an ivory tower, perhaps in a university or a profession or in business, getting on with their technical job and keeping as far as possible out of politics. But this 'inner emigration' had its difficulties. For one thing a number of posts which in Britain and America were (and mostly still are) private are in Germany official. Teachers, clergymen and most lawyers are civil servants; admission to their ranks, and certainly promotion, depended on conforming and often on joining the Party. Some degree of compromise with the régime, some amount of infection from its monopoly of propaganda, was almost inevitable. Moreover a more or less silent detachment from something one abhors is not an easy stance for anyone of spirit. Sooner or later one was likely to find oneself in trouble and, if the object of remaining in Germany was to survive, what was to be gained by that? Great causes may be made by their martyrs – but until 1945 the only martyrs of whom the German people heard were those invented by Nazi propaganda.

On the other hand one could try to organise opposition. In 1934 this still appeared to have some prospects. Helmuth's letter was written before the 'Night of the Long Knives' on 30 June in which Hitler took the dispensing of punishment into his own hands instead of leaving it to the deservedly respected German legal system. After that display of ruthlessness, it was less easy to be jocular or to expect an early collapse of the régime. But even then the security forces had not fully established their grip. Most persons prominently connected with socialism, communism, the trade unions and the like had been rounded up (unless they had fled the country) and were either dead, in 'preventive custody' or closely supervised. All forms of communication were watched and spies were active. But the habits of liberty established under the Republic, imperfect though they were, took time to break down and there were limits to the resources available for repression. Both the Protestant and Catholic churches were resisting, with some signs of success, the attempts to co-ordinate them, while a considerable amount of quiet opposition was being organised among the working classes. A case could still be made out for staying in the country, avoiding compromise as far as possible, keeping in touch with friends who were known to be like-minded, discreet and trustworthy, taking every opportunity which offered of unobtrusively frustrating the government's intentions or helping people in trouble, and waiting to see how the situation developed. As late as July 1934, a shrewd (and Jewish) observer like (Herr) Dr Schwarzwald was in favour of 'good people' doing this, where they could. There would always be room for argument as to whether the amount which could be achieved in this way offset the drawbacks. But the situation was one in which no solution was indisputably the 'right' one; each individual had to make up his or her mind according to circumstances and character.

The Moltke family exemplified most of the various solutions. Helmuth and Freya never thought seriously of staying in South Africa in 1934 nor, at this stage, of emigrating. He was too tied to Kreisau and felt too much responsibility for it and for his family. His brother Jowo, who was just putting his foot on the bottom rung of the ladder leading to Art Gallery Director, found that he had no chance of keeping it there unless he joined either the Brown shirts or the Party; for a time late in 1933 he chose the former as the lesser of two evils. Helmuth took great pains to see that the next brother Willo, who was becoming an architect, appreciated the principles which were at stake and encouraged him to emigrate, so that one member at least of the family would have a chance of surviving outside Germany. Willo did a spell of work in London in 1937-8, later moved to Sweden and thence (with difficulty, during the war) to the United States, returning to Germany after the end of the war as an American officer. The youngest son Carl Berndt showed more sympathy for the Nazis than any of his brothers; Helmuth did not allow this to affect their relationship but arranged for him to go on a long trip to South Africa whence he returned with much modified views. Among the cousins, Hans Adolf served as German Ambassador in Warsaw from 1931 to 1939 and was then asked to go to Madrid. When he raised objections, he was told to choose between Madrid and a concentration camp.[1]

Freya now started work on her doctorate and spent some time in Berlin about it; Helmuth had to wrestle with new complications over the estate.

In November 1931 his mother had written to Sir James:

A new emergency decree has been issued giving a certain body of men called the *Osthilfe* [Eastern Aid] the power to suspend or reduce the payment of debts owed by Eastern agriculturalists to their creditors. The *Landbund* etc. is jubilant but all sensible people shake their heads for, unless it is very wisely and restrainedly administered (and even then), it means practically that the creditors have no legal protection at all and that all commitments are invalid or in danger of becoming so. For us personally this may prove extremely useful but it isn't right and undermines all right feeling about obligations and of course destroys confidence. Your legal mind will be horrified and so is Helmuth's.

The Countess' forebodings about administration were realised and threats supposedly made by Brüning, and then by Schleicher, of a public inquiry into irregularities are said to have contributed to their downfalls. Under the Nazis the scheme was revised and extended as part of a grandiose agricultural programme. Helmuth was compelled to join in and provided with a loan which enabled him to pay off all the private creditors but brought him under the control of the Provincial Office in Breslau. They tried to impose a plan for paying off the public loan which involved selling Nieder-Gräditz and Wierischau. They also foiled for a time a move of Helmuth's to exploit the Field-Marshal's connection by getting the estate declared an 'heirloom property'/*Erbhof* under new legislation, leaving him in no doubt that they would be more amenable to all his wishes if he would change his attitude to the régime. After a long struggle, in the course of which he bearded the local peasant leader in the Schweidnitz office – or as he preferred to call it Chief Robbers Den/*Haupträuberhöhle* – he got his way.

The episode had the benefit of cementing more firmly than ever his relationship with Zeumer whose personal loyalty and professional interest had been in conflict with his political allegiance and who as a result felt uncomfortable about the obstruction and prejudice which Helmuth had encountered. In 1935, with the new loan negotiated, the creditors lost their right to have their own manager but Zeumer remained to work directly for the Moltkes, a clear testimonial to the skill with which he had been handled. His new employer increasingly left to him the executive part of the farming but kept a firm grip on policy-making. Nor did detail become beneath his notice.

15 May 1935

I keep on finding slips in the book-keeping.... That is very time-consuming because it usually takes a long search to discover the mistakes which for the most part only concern details. But I must not let them go past. Yesterday I discovered an error of a farthing and let it go. Two pages later came the same mistake again, but this time multiplied by 28. When I added the whole thing together it had cost us 25/– since last August and would have gone on doing the same every year. I had to spend an hour and a half on the job. The girl must get used to being absolutely accurate – otherwise she will cost us a fortune.

The results justified the method. One of Helmuth's advisers calculated that, during the first seven years of his management, he had made an annual average profit of 50,000 marks, since the total of debt had been reduced by 350,000 marks. As a result there was a good prospect of paying off the only remaining loan within the foreseeable future. Whereas in 1929 Helmuth had written that the family would get nothing from the estate for twenty years, now it was again yielding a small income. This was of material importance since the possibility of retaining any reasonable degree of spiritual independence in the Third *Reich* was bound up, as Helmuth explained to his Swedish correspondent, with control over a means of production and the livelihood which this provided. But this was not the only way in which his work on the estate helped Helmuth. The success which he achieved demonstrated beyond possibility of doubt his powers of management and must have given him considerable confidence in his practical ability. This made all the more frustrating the improbability of finding in Nazi Germany a wider stage on which to deploy them.

At one time during this period, he was living on his own in the Berghaus and being looked after by Mamsell. Cooking was not the latter's strongest point and Freya must have been worried as to whether he was getting enough to eat. (A doctor to whom Frau Schwarzwald sent him in Vienna in 1923 said he was perfectly sound but weighed 20 lb too little for his great height.) His letters are full of gastronomic details. 'Chervil soup with goose-eggs; flan with rhubarb and salad; sorrel soup with devilled eggs and baked apples; asparagus soup, mashed potatoes with onions and white sauce, apple slices. You see, I live like a prince.' Some princes might have demurred but Helmuth, as has been said, had simple tastes. He was sensible enough to prefer country cooking when it was good but to notice when it was bad. On one of his journeys during the war, he gave special marks to a breakfast he had taken with the Jesuits in Freiburg; what he relished about it particularly was the apple jelly! A tea in Oslo was made 'heavenly' by interesting biscuits, or, rather, the biscuits themselves were not interesting so much as the strong flavour of the jam spread on them. He neither drank nor smoked, not because of any Christian Science principles as some supposed but because the tastes did not appeal to him. Such self-restraint fitted in with his dark clothes, plain white shirt and habitual black tie. In spite of all his zest for life, he had an austere side corresponding to the melancholy strain in his character which sometimes made him critical of those whom he thought over-indulgent.

But a shadow was destined to fall suddenly on Kreisau and the

Moltke family. Soon after Countess Dorothy got back from South Africa, while her mother (who had accompanied her) was taking a cure in the Black Forest, she went with her husband on a trip to north-east Germany. She had been having bad headaches but treatment from a Christian Science healer in Schweidnitz had alleviated them. Suddenly while she was staying with relatives at Balfranz in Pomerania she became seriously ill and on 11 June died at the age of fifty-one; the cause was believed to have been a brain tumour. Nearly forty years later one of her sons could speak of her death as a 'catastrophe' and it was one which, if possible, hit Helmuth harder than some of her other children since he had at that time no firm belief in an after-life.[2] But for her herself it was arguably a fortunate hour. For she had lived to see her children grown up and the home which she so much loved retrieved for them. She died without knowing the catastrophes which were to fall on Germany, on Helmuth and on Kreisau.

Freya had already more than once run the Berghaus during Countess Dorothy's visits to her parents in South Africa and was therefore able on the latter's death to follow without interruption in her footsteps. Two factors greatly contributed to the continued management of the house without noticeable change of tempo. The first was that Mamsell continued to serve the Moltkes until her death in 1939. The second was that the whole new style of living imposed on Countess Dorothy by the crisis of 1928-9 – albeit most readily accepted by her – was in its simplicity and absence of fuss thoroughly congenial to Helmuth and Freya, as also to the brothers and sister. It was said locally that the Moltkes lived more simply than their peasants. Adam von Trott was to write to his wife in 1943, 'You must come to see for yourself how they live here, simply yet generously, joyfully and actively.'[3]

Thus Kreisau continued to play a central role in the hearts and minds of the immediate members of the family and the Berghaus remained to them their home. The only changes were in the amount of general entertaining done and the character of the guests. Certain social obligations as well as friendships with her own generation had accompanied Countess Dorothy from the Schloss to the Berghaus. With her death the friendships naturally faded and the opportunity also occurred to let slip such ties as still remained to Silesian society. Relations with the village remained close but guests were chosen less on the basis of whom one ought to invite than of whom one wanted to see. The reaction was reflected in a local saying that if the Moltkes needed to buy a trouser-button they would go to Berlin for it.

9 A Lifeline to England
1935–8

THE changing character of life at Kreisau helps to explain why Helmuth, after spending a fortnight on his own at the Berghaus in November 1934, wrote to Freya that the idea of permanently existing there seemed so absurd as to make him unable to think how he could have contemplated it. But this conclusion ruled out one possible answer to the problem of how to make life tolerable in Hitler's Germany; he could not do so by withdrawing to his farm. He therefore began to look for other solutions and in the following autumn started to practise law privately in Berlin in conjunction with an older man called Karl von Lewinsky.* Two considerations led him to specialise in international law. Most of the German experts in this field had been Jews and had therefore had to cease work, so that there was a shortage of qualified advisers at a time when the need for advice, particularly from would-be emigrants, was growing. To go on with, this field would fit in well with his wider objective of building up a position outside Germany as well as one inside.

As has been said, he had stopped in England on his way back from South Africa.† Then in March–April 1935, before his mother's death, he paid a fortnight's visit to Basle (for the Bank of International Settlements), Berne, Geneva, Paris (where he met the Mowrers), the Hague, London and Oxford. He visited the League of Nations and the Permanent Court of Justice to explore the possibilities of employment in them. His impressions were not on the whole encouraging.

Geneva   31 March 1935

There are a number of well-read people in the League Secretariat but nobody with any personality. Bureaucrats abound but men of weight are lacking. What is worst is that everyone regards himself as his country's representative rather than as the League's official. His behaviour in the Secretariat is so designed as to ensure that his government will give him a good post as soon as he leaves. Most

---

* Lewinsky, Karl von (b. 1873), served in German diplomatic service; 1922, German representative on German-American Mixed Commission; 1925–31, Consul-General in New York. After 1946, head of Institute for Public Law and International Law.
† Above, p. 57.

members of the Secretariat belong to their country's diplomatic service and look on their time with the League as just another posting. ... This personnel policy is quite enough to explain the League's failure. The only neutrals and really international officials are those Germans, Russians and Italians who are not Nazis, Communists or Fascists and have broken their links with their home governments without leaving the Secretariat....

The present position of the League is about as bad as can be. People here seem to take a big European war in the foreseeable future for granted. One international jurist said in the discussion after a lecture, 'Geneva is Mount Ararat and the flood waters are rising all around. The only justification for optimism in the whole affair is that even though the ark cannot prevent the flood, a number of people have taken up station in the ark who are doing all they can to create conditions under which effective dams can be built once the flood is over.'

One thing anyhow is clear to me: the significance of the League as an organisation based on the idea of law and operating according to legal principles is by the very nature of things slight because the legal principles don't exist or rather aren't accepted as authoritative. At the present moment therefore the Hague Court is much more important than the League and most important of all perhaps are the Courts of Arbitration.

In the Hague he attended a session in which the Court pronounced judgment on a case between Greece and Albania, and met the German and Dutch judges as well as the Swedish secretary of the Court, Ake Hammarskjöld, who impressed him considerably. Hammarskjöld had been told by the German judge of Helmuth's problem and was able to appreciate it because a young German assistant of his, Berthold von Stauffenberg, had a year previously been forced to give up his position with the Court and go back to Berlin. (Nobody is likely to have mentioned that Stauffenberg had a brother called Claus or Hammarskjöld a brother called Dag.) Hammarskjöld's suggestion was that Helmuth should study the work of Britain's Judicial Committee of the Privy Council from the standpoint of international law. He argued that the British wanted the Judicial Committee to be regarded as part of their national legal system so that no Englishman would ever examine its *inter*national side; that thus far no foreigner had paid any attention to its activities; and that the position of the Hague Court in international law must gradually be assimilated to that of the Judicial Committee so as to make any study of major interest to the court. Helmuth wrote to Freya that this might prove his 'Columbus' egg', i.e. the starting-point of an enterprise which would lead him far afield.

This, however, was not to be because in London he was persuaded – perhaps by Sir Alfred Hopkinson – to apply for admission to the Inner Temple and start reading for the English bar. This scheme had two great advantages. In the first place he was required to eat a fixed number of dinners in the Temple, which gave him a cast-iron excuse for coming to England at frequent intervals; at least seventeen visits can be traced during the next five years. In the second place a qualification as an English barrister might put him in a position to earn a living outside Germany. The chief snag was that both the admission and the travelling (always by train) were expensive, whereas currency regulations made it difficult to take money out of Germany. Here, however, the sterling payments which his grandparents continued to make after their daughter's death eased the situation.

He had already met Lionel Curtis during his earlier visit and now the acquaintance deepened. Curtis, then in his sixties, had been, along with Philip Kerr, Patrick Duncan, Geoffrey Dawson and R. H. Brand,* one of the group of young Oxford graduates whom Lord Milner had gathered round him in South Africa during and after the Boer War. There he had become a friend and admirer of the Rose Innes parents and of Dorothy, who all commended Helmuth to him. Curtis, who married late in life, had no sons and took a truly paternal interest in a young man whose character and abilities impressed him deeply.

Milner, who left South Africa in 1905, was convinced that the restoration of self-government to the various states by the Liberal government in 1907 was a grave mistake which in the long run would enable the Boers to wipe out the effects of the British victory (as it has done). Those members of his 'kindergarten' who stayed behind after he went home agreed with him but decided that, as the step could not be reversed, the predominance of British over Boer interests would best be served by the early formation of a union government for the whole country. Exhaustive discussions between them led to the drafting of a joint document which they persuaded Lord Selborne (Milner's successor as High Commissioner) to issue under his own name. Curtis then published what purported to be 'an objective study of the facts' leading

---

* Kerr, Philip H. (1882–1940), after service with Milner, private secretary to Lloyd George 1916–21; Secretary to Rhodes Trustees 1925–39; succeeded as Marquis of Lothian 1930; Ambassador to the United States 1939–40.

Dawson, Geoffrey (1874–1944), original name Robinson, after service with Milner, editor *Johannesburg Star* 1905–10, *The Times* 1912–19, 1923–41, *Round Table* 1914–44.

Brand, R. H. (1878–1963), after service with Milner, director Lazard Bros till 1960; director of *The Times* till 1959; head of British Food Mission, Washington, 1941–4; representative of H.M. Treasury in Washington, 1944–6. Made a baron, 1946.

Duncan, Patrick, see p. 57.

to the desired conclusion. A society to press for union was next formed, and Curtis devoted great energy to getting branches started all over the country.

There were a number of forces working for union but the group flattered themselves that they were largely responsible for the speed with which it was achieved. Turning their attention from South Africa to the British Empire as a whole, and inspired by a biography which F. S. Oliver at that moment published of the American Founding Father Alexander Hamilton, they grew convinced that the Empire could not last unless it was turned into a federation. Returning to England and extracting finance from the Rhodes Trustees (who included several of themselves), they applied to the new objective the methods which were supposed to have achieved the old. They met at regular intervals, usually in London but sometimes in a country-house at the week-end. Membership of the group was flexible; it had no rigid organisation, or qualification for admission. The immediate object of the meetings was to produce a quarterly journal, *The Round Table*, a name soon applied to the group itself. Each number set out to include articles about current conditions in each of the main Dominions where they sought to establish groups like their own for the supply of contributions and the conduct of propaganda. Curtis was given the job of travelling round the Empire to stimulate these groups and to collect material for another objective study of the facts, again pointing unmistakably to the desired conclusions. The targets of the Round Table were the politicians, businessmen, dons and journalists throughout the Empire who influenced opinion and thus policy. So far from belonging to any particular party, the members of the group followed Milner in affecting to despise party politicians and to seek friends in all sections of the ruling classes.*

The plans took longer to work out than had been expected and during the war the Dominions gained so much autonomy that even enthusiasts for the 'Organic Connection' of a federal constitution saw it to have become unattainable. The Round Table fell back instead on the solution of voluntary association between free and equal units which they had previously (under the influence of Oliver) rejected as inadequate. Curtis claimed to be able to point to a spot where during a walk in the countryside he hit on the idea of using the title 'British Commonwealth of Nations'.[1]

He also engaged in devising schemes to satisfy the demands of Ireland and India for autonomy without disrupting the Empire; the constitution of the Irish Free State and the 1935 Government of India Act were to some extent the fruits of his ingenuity. Experience in the

* For the influence of Round Table methods on the Kreisau Circle, see below, p. 188.

British delegation to the 1919 Peace Conference convinced him that the intrusion of 'public opinion' into diplomacy was going to be disastrous unless it grew better informed, which led him to initiate the Royal Institute of International Affairs as a centre for providing the information. In the later 1930s he became increasingly concerned with the problem of world order, convinced that war could only be eliminated if, using the Commonwealth as a starting-point, the various states were brought into some sort of 'organic relationship' based upon the 'infinite duty of each to all'. He elaborated these ideas against the background of world history in a three-volume work with the challenging title of *Civitas Dei* published between 1934 and 1937.

Curtis had the face and voice of a prophet, which was the nickname given him by Lothian's younger brother. He was neither a deep thinker nor an exact scholar (he got 3rd classes in both parts of his Oxford classical course 'Mods' and 'Greats'). But what he saw, he saw clearly and pursued with single-minded intensity of purpose. He has been accused of using history as propaganda and of being incapable of objectivity about any matter in which he was deeply involved.[2] But the dividing line between exposition and persuasion is notoriously hard to draw and, if like many of us he sometimes chose his facts to suit his conclusions, he would have been horrified to be told that he was being dishonest. There can be no denying that the problems with which he concerned himself are of great and continuing concern to humanity, and if the solutions which he offered (in the two main cases as second-bests) proved ineffectual it is because the forces and interests working against them had deeper roots than he realised.

One of the curiosities of British society at the time was that Curtis managed to achieve what he did without having any official position. Indeed the Round Table as a whole preferred (perhaps of necessity) having friends in high places to being in such places themselves. He persuaded people to listen to him by virtue of his personality and his pertinacity, which proved more effective in small matters (like the regulation of ribbon-development) than in big ones. Four members of his group had been elected to fellowships at All Souls College Oxford before going to South Africa and in 1924 they were able to get the same privilege conferred on him, so that it is hard to say whether he owed his fellowship to his influence or his influence to his fellowship.

During the years from 1935 to 1939 the fellows of All Souls included Lord Halifax,* Sir John Simon† and Geoffrey Dawson of *The Times*. By taking Helmuth to dine in college as his guest, generally at the weekend, Curtis gave him access to such people, as well as to a number of

* Halifax, Lord (1881–1959), Foreign Secretary 1938–40.
† Simon, Sir John (1873–1954), Foreign Secretary 1931–5, Home Secretary 1935–7, Chancellor of Exchequer 1937–40.

distinguished lawyers. When one considers that among Curtis's close friends were also Lords Lothian and Astor,* the paradox emerges that Helmuth was coming into contact with some of the chief upholders of the appeasement policy (though All Souls had a number of firm opponents of that policy, led by A. L. Rowse). Seeing how impervious they remained to the objections raised against that policy by people of greater authority and experience, Helmuth's failure to exert any influence on them is not to be wondered at, even though, on one of his early visits, he wrote that 'I have driven some very important points into some equally important heads.' They for their part, perhaps because they would have talked with care in front of a foreigner, did not convey to him any great sense of the practical strategic and economic considerations which underlay that policy and provided the best excuse for it. What is noteworthy is that Lionel Curtis never became an enthusiastic advocate of appeasement, as on his past record and connections might have been expected: another major war involving Britain was likely to interfere with his hopes for Britain and a federal world as seriously as the first one interfered with his hopes for a federal Empire.

Unfortunately few records of Helmuth's discussions on this subject have survived.† The principal one is a description which he sent to Curtis of a ten-minute conversation between himself and Lord Lothian in July 1935. In the previous January Lothian (who was incidentally a Christian Scientist) had had an interview with Hitler and thereafter written two articles in *The Times* asserting that Hitler genuinely desired peace. Lothian now denied the existence of such a thing as international law; the situation between nations was one of anarchy. Helmuth argued that there were unwritten international rules. He suggested that this was borne out by the war of 1914–18

> *which to a certain extent was a war of sanctions by allied powers against one who had broken the unwritten laws or better unwritten customs of international behaviour, probably on wrong evidence on the side of the Allied Powers* [sic]

Lothian repeated the view, widespread at the time, that Hitler's rise to power was chiefly due to the post-war policy of Britain and France towards Germany, particularly in the Versailles Treaty (where he had himself been inadvertently responsible for the so-called 'War-Guilt' clause)[3] and the 1923 occupation of the Ruhr. Helmuth replied that in

* Astor, Waldorf 2nd Viscount (1879–1952) husband of Nancy Viscountess Astor, M.P. Chairman of *Observer* and of Royal Institute of International Affairs, owner of Cliveden.

† No evidence is forthcoming to support the story that he had an interview with Neville Chamberlain. It seems inconceivable that, if he had done so, he would never have mentioned it to Freya.

his opinion the influence of this had been greatly exaggerated, though it was often exploited by Germans as a convenient excuse. He did not believe it was possible for a German to accept Lothian's view that, as time went on, the wilder men among the Nazis would disappear. Lothian maintained that a policy of concessions would help to modify Nazi behaviour. This Helmuth described as a fallacy; it was misleading to believe that, by giving in to threats of war, one made the authors of those threats less inclined to repeat them. Summing up the talk Helmuth wrote to Curtis:

> *I fear that his policy will be successful in England ... I fear that it will prove to be misleading for Germany; it will induce our government to believe that we can count on the English neutrality while in truth, should a European war break out, England would fight on the side of France; this possibility of misleading others is what I fear most about the English policy of keeping the balance: England is not really an arbiter but the party to the struggle, but its lack of rigid policy is what induces Germans to believe that she is an arbiter.*

Another person whom Helmuth met at All Souls was Bishop Headlam of Gloucester (1862–1947) who was chairman of the Church of England Council on Foreign Relations and has been described as 'the leading Christian apologist in Britain for the German government'.[4] They discussed the position of the German Protestant Churches and in November 1935 Helmuth sent him a message through his chaplain urging him to be ready to protest against what was going to happen to the German church.

> The present lull is only temporary. Various measures hostile to the church, including the strict censorship of its papers, are intended in the near future. Still more drastic action can be expected in 1937 after the Olympic Games are over.

A week later Headlam wrote to his antithesis, Bishop Bell of Chichester (President of the Universal Christian Council of 'Life and Work'), saying he believed Heckel* gave a truer account than Moltke. 'Moltke seems to me to be a bitter opponent of the whole Hitler régime and to be determined to keep up the Church feud because he thinks, rightly, that it will injure National Socialism.' In view of Helmuth's religious beliefs (or lack of them) at the time, the comment was not unfair even though the judgment was to prove mistaken.[5]

By November 1937 Helmuth could write to his grandparents that 'I have more friends now in London than I have in Berlin.' Some were

---

* Heckel, Bishop Theodor (1894–1967), head of the Foreign Relations Department of the German Protestant churches.

friends from earlier times. Some were Jews and other anti-Nazi Germans, including Brüning himself and many whom Helmuth had helped to get out of the country. Some he met through Curtis and All Souls like John Foster, Con O'Neill (posted in 1938 to the Berlin Embassy, only to resign after Munich), M.B. (who as a result of an introduction from Curtis went with his wife to stay at Kreisau in August 1936 and who later introduced Helmuth to his cousin Henry Brooke, then on the staff of the Conservative Research Department).*

One first meeting which did improbably enough occur in England was with Adam von Trott zu Solz to whom early in March 1937 A. L. Rowse introduced him by the fireside in All Souls. Mr Rowse's account of the occasion[6] is much to Helmuth's advantage, though the statement that 'dark and glittering, he looked like a sword' might have applied almost as well to Adam. Superficially the two Germans had much in common. Both were handsome men, standing well over six feet, both sons of landowners, with a deep affection for the country estates on which they had been brought up. Both were lawyers, both had Anglo-Saxon blood on their mother's side, both convinced anti-Nazis. They shared many English friends. Yet at the same time there were considerable differences. Adam's love for the good things of life would have been likely to upset Helmuth's streak of asceticism, just as the talkativeness of the one would have jarred the reticence of the other. Adam can fairly be called an intellectual and had written a book about Hegel; there is no evidence that Helmuth ever read a page of that philosopher and, though he could not have gone through a German education without picking up something about the dialectic, it is unlikely to have appealed to him. Mrs Mowrer tells a story of his interrupting an abstruse discussion on the absolute with the remark, 'What do you mean by saying that there's nothing absolutely bad. There's bad grammar and bad eggs.'

But in 1937 there was a deeper division between them. During the visit to Oxford in which they met, Adam spoke strongly in favour of appeasement[7] whereas Helmuth's interview with Lothian shows how strongly he opposed it. Adam's attitude arose from his attempt to reconcile his loyalty to what he considered the true German traditions with his repugnance for the Nazi flouting of law and morality. Helmuth was already accustomed to think in international terms, regarded the national state as an anachronism and was thus almost devoid – some

---

* Brooke, Henry (b. 1903), M.P. (Con.) for Lewisham 1938–45; Leader of Opposition L.C.C. 1945–52; M.P. (Con.) for Hampstead 1950–66; Financial Secretary to Treasury 1954–7; Minister of Housing 1957–61; Chief Secretary to the Treasury 1961–2; Home Secretary 1962–4. Made a Life Peer 1966. M.B. met Curtis only on two other occasions (in 1942 and 1946) besides the one which led to this introduction and was never privileged to work for the 'Round Table'.

people would say, too devoid – of conventional patriotism. There is therefore no cause for surprise that the two men did not become firm friends until the circumstances of wartime gave them an end in common and led them to work closely together in its pursuit.

10 Hitler Offends the Army

1938

T H E problem of how and where to live did not prove to be one of those which, if left alone, answer themselves. Having decided that he could not exist permanently at Kreisau, Helmuth did not take long to discover that he could not permanently endure Berlin. By the autumn of 1935 he was writing to Freya that 'dozing in the train I suddenly realised that I wouldn't mind in the least if I had to part company with Lewinsky to-morrow'.

At the time of the Olympic Games in August 1936 (when, as on other state occasions, he and his partner refused to hang flags from the windows of their office in the Unter den Linden) he wrote:

> Berlin is frightful. A solid mass of people are pushing their way down the Unter den Linden to look at the decorations. And what people! I never knew that the likes of them existed. Probably these are the people who are National Socialists because I don't know them either!

Although Lewinsky gave him some interesting cases to handle, most of the work was of a depressing character. For it was largely connected with easing the lot of Jews and other victims of Nazi tyranny and helping some of them to get out of the country. 'It is hard to spend so much time contemplating the sufferings of other people.'

Yet when he and Freya went on a second but shorter visit to South Africa from December 1936 to February 1937, which proved the last time they saw Sir James,* they still felt too tied to Germany to consider leaving it. Another major deterrent was the problem of how to earn a living outside, at any rate until Helmuth had qualified as a barrister (although in 1937 he was told by a solicitor in Messrs Slaughter & May that, in the experience of the firm, advice was hard to obtain in London on matters involving conflict between the legal systems of different countries).

After they got back, a new factor was introduced into the situation when Freya found herself pregnant and gave birth on 2 November 1937 to a son Helmuth Caspar. Helmuth himself had shown as little enthusiasm for the idea of being a father as he originally did for the idea of marriage. He had too many misgivings about the future of the world and the ability of his family to manage their affairs in it. The know-

*Lady Rose Innes came to Germany in the spring of 1938.

ledge that a child was on the way threw him into a state of great tension. But, as soon as it became a person instead of a prospect, his humanity and interest in people got the upper hand. Indeed parenthood, like matrimony, did much to soften him and draw him into the world. He was delighted when his mother-in-law's gardener invested the boy with the incorrect title of '*Barönchen*' and promptly adopted it. A year later he wrote, 'Today is the baron's first birthday and accordingly a day to wish you happiness. Your spouse is enchanted to see how well the baron becomes you.' But the new arrival was undoubtedly a complicating factor in deciding what to do for the future.

A further complication was provided by Helmuth's father. The difficulties in Countess Dorothy's relations with her husband had receded during her last years, and she had spent much time with him in Berlin, as lengthy visits by him to Kreisau had become a source of possible embarrassment once he had handed over to Helmuth responsibility for the estate. Her death left him solitary. Helmuth and Freya had tried to alleviate this, sharing a flat with him in the city for a year in 1935–6 and pressing him to make visits to the Berghaus. But close proximity between generations is not always the best way of maintaining good relations. His other children were also grown up and out in the world so that, perhaps inevitably, he began to feel lonely. Plans were made for him to live with his widowed sisters but in 1937, before these came to fruition, he suddenly decided to marry again. This was a decision which his children could understand in principle, and over which they would have been unlikely to make difficulties if the person chosen had been at all congenial. She was one of his pupils as a teacher of Christian Science and was, as Helmuth put it, 'divorced, with a son of eleven, lame, penniless and comes from Memel'. When the Count proposed to bring her to the Berghaus for Christmas Helmuth felt constrained to say that this was a festival which all the children particularly associated with their mother and that her successor would not be welcome. In their exchanges on this subject the Count accused Helmuth of having stolen the other children from him, a charge which Helmuth, in view of the way in which responsibility had been laid upon him, found extremely painful.

Unwelcome also was the need to provide for the lady – quickly dubbed 'Pensioner Annie' – out of Kreisau funds. It was hardly with such a result in view that Helmuth had battled to get the estate clear of debt. A pre-marriage settlement made the best of the situation, but the family's forebodings were realised when the Count's health deteriorated and he died in March 1939, leaving his widow for them to support. The terms of the settlement were honoured until Kreisau was lost in 1945.

All this while Helmuth was increasing his circle of acquaintances in Berlin and becoming as a result well informed as to what was happening behind the scenes. This was demonstrated in the events which followed the attendance of Hitler and Göring at the wedding of the Minister of Defence, General von Blomberg, on 12 January 1938. Almost immediately afterwards rumours began to circulate about the bride's past, and before long police reports were brought to light. Göring seems to have known the facts all along but Hitler professed at any rate to have been duped and to be extremely angry. Blomberg was made to offer his resignation on 4 February. But simultaneously accusations of homosexuality began to circulate about his natural successor the army's commander-in-chief, General von Fritsch. These were based on evidence provided some two years earlier by a man who was serving a sentence for blackmail and in fact applied to a much more junior officer called Frisch. Although Hitler had previously ordered the evidence to be disregarded, he now chose to treat it as true and, without giving Fritsch a chance to vindicate himself, called for his resignation as well. The Führer then disappointed Göring's hopes of becoming Defence Minister (and incidentally subordinating the army to the upstart air force) by taking over the post himself. In a further reshuffle Ribbentrop succeeded Baron von Neurath as Foreign Minister while Funk, a notorious homosexual, succeeded Schacht as Minister of Economics. Hitler then distracted attention by annexing Austria and thus evaded the demands of the senior generals for a public rehabilitation of Fritsch.

Immediately after the seizure of Austria Helmuth wrote to M.B. explaining that he could not at the moment come to London but would welcome it if one of his English friends could come to Berlin. M.B. therefore went to Berlin and Kreisau from 23 to 27 March and was then told not merely the story of Blomberg's marriage (which was common knowledge) but also that of the plot against Fritsch. M.B., being quite certain that Helmuth would not have gone to such trouble to give this information unless he had been satisfied about its validity, did not question him about his sources. On returning to London M.B. wrote a report and gave copies to people whom he knew to be likely to pass them to Downing Street and to the Foreign Office. Unfortunately all copies seem to have disappeared and it is impossible to be sure whether Helmuth knew of Göring's complicity in Blomberg's marriage.[1]

What Helmuth could hardly have known (though it would not have surprised him in the least) was that Hitler's main reason for eliminating Blomberg and Fritsch were the doubts which these generals had expressed (in varying degrees!) about the plans for Germany's forceful aggrandisement sketched by the Führer at a secret conference in the previous November. And, although Helmuth clearly recognised that an important turning-point had been reached, neither he nor anyone else realised the full implications – for to do so would have required not just insight but second sight.

In the first place Hitler at this point took the conduct of strategy into his own hands and this, after four years of brilliant successes, was to prove the undoing of Germany. But secondly from this point onwards he began to part company with the army and many of the circles associated with the army. The army leaders had never had much use for the Weimar Republic and some of them (notably General von Schleicher) had played a leading part in engineering its downfall and the accession of Hitler. They had, moreover, welcomed his foreign programme in its early years because it consisted in doing all the things which most Germans had wished to see happen ever since 1919 – defiance of the League of Nations, rearmament, reoccupation of the Rhineland. It is true that the next items on the programme – the reunion with Austria and with the German-speaking districts of Czechoslovakia and the elimination of the Polish Corridor – completed this process of annulling the Treaty of Versailles. But the speed at which Hitler proposed to move involved risks which the generals thought excessive. To carry out his plans, he had to put himself in a position where he could disregard their advice and, having done so and having disregarded it with success, he continued the practice after that advice became well founded.

This considerably altered the internal situation in Germany. In the years 1935–7 the security services had been making opposition increasingly difficult. Most of the socialist groups* had been infiltrated and their leaders imprisoned; many workers remained hostile but were able to do little beyond keep in touch with one another and make the leadership afraid of insisting on too big a production effort.[2] Among Protestants the acquittal of Martin Niemöller late in 1937, though it looked like a victory, was in fact a Pyrrhic one. Not only was he immediately put back into a concentration camp but a succession of administrative and financial measures, unobtrusive when regarded one by one but cumulatively crippling, was introduced to force the pastors into subservience. Much the same happened with the Catholic Church after the successful promulgation of the Papal encyclical 'With deep anxiety' in March 1937. Henceforward the only place where there seemed to be a chance of organising anything systematic in the shape of opposition was inside institutions capable of protecting themselves and accordingly it was into these that those who felt keenly against the régime gravitated. One such was the AA (=*Auswärtiges Amt*/Foreign Office) which, after Ribbentrop's appointment, was literally split into two, with the Minister and his personal staff in a new building and the career diplomats under the State Secretary Ernst von Weizsäcker† in the old one, each group trying to frustrate the other.

* Above, p. 61.

† Weizsäcker, Ernst von (1882–1951), Minister in Oslo and Berne, 1931–6, State Secretary 1938–43, Ambassador to the Vatican 1943–5, condemned at

By far the most important of these institutions, however, was the army because not only was the army essential to Hitler's plans but it had weapons which it could use to defend itself and, if its leaders chose, turn against him. The spreading inside the army after the Blomberg–Fritsch crisis of a view of Hitler as a menace to Germany was therefore a major development. But this was not all. Blomberg, whose subservience to Hitler had earned him the nickname of 'rubber lion', had largely discredited himself by his marriage. But Fritsch was a much-respected officer and the way in which he had been disposed of, coupled with the refusal to rehabilitate him when the sordid details of the frame-up leaked out, caused deep resentment. Many officers had been prepared to tolerate the Nazis and overlook their methods because of what they were thought to be doing for Germany. Once they were thought to be 'doing for Germany' in a different sense, this toleration waned. The treatment of the churches and the fact that many officers were practising Christians assisted the tendency. Some consciences even became reconciled to the fact that plotting against the Führer meant breaking the oath of loyalty into which he had rushed the armed forces on Hindenburg's death in August 1934.

The army opposition built up rapidly during the summer of 1938 in the face of Hitler's plans for an attack on Czechoslovakia. It concentrated round General Beck, the Chief of the Army General Staff.* It

---

Nuremberg in 1949 to seven years' imprisonment, but released in 1950. A German State Secretary is roughly equivalent to a British Permanent Secretary but in the absence of junior ministers has rather more political functions.

* The following table may help the reader:

MINISTER OF DEFENCE	ARMY C-in-C (OKH)	ARMY CHIEF OF STAFF
VON SCHLEICHER 1 June '32–30 Jan '33	VON HAMMERSTEIN Oct '30–Feb '34	BECK Oct '33–Aug '38
VON BLOMBERG 30 Jan '33–4 Feb '38	VON FRITSCH Feb '34–4 Feb '38	HALDER Sept '38–Sept '42
HITLER 4 Feb '38–30 April '45	VON BRAUCHITSCH February '38–19 Dec '41	ZEITZLER Sept '42–July '44
	HITLER 19 Dec '41–30 April '45	GUDERIAN July '44–March '45.
		KREBS March–May '45

On becoming his own Minister of Defence, Hitler set up a Defence Staff (OKW) intended to be responsible for co-ordinating all three services. The head of this from its institution till Germany's defeat was General KEITEL, with General JODL in charge of its main branch. But, after Hitler took over the command of the army, he issued orders about the Russian campaign direct to the OKH so that operations in that theatre ceased to be properly co-ordinated with operations elsewhere.

found support from Weizsäcker and other AA officials. An alternative civil régime was planned under the aegis of Karl Goerdeler (1884–1945), a tireless if tactless member of the former German Nationalist Party whose disapproval of Nazi militancy had led him to resign from the post of Price Commissioner just as his disapproval of anti-semitism had led him to resign that of Lord Mayor of Leipzig. The conspirators calculated that an attack on Czechoslovakia would bring Europe to the verge of a war which Germany could not win. This external crisis would provide them with the justification for removing Hitler.

Helmuth's involvement in these plans was, at most, marginal. In May 1938 General Halder, who in October succeeded Beck as Chief of Staff, visited the Field-Marshal's grave in the course of a staff exercise and talked to Helmuth for an hour but only in general terms.[3] Thereafter they came in touch through a lawyer-friend of Halder's called Etscheit but there is no evidence that this occurred in 1938. Hans Lukaschek, who had been dismissed in May 1933 from his post as Oberpräsident of Upper Silesia* and thereafter practised as a lawyer in Breslau, declared after the war that Helmuth called on him between June and August to tell him of the conspiracy and of the need for persons of experience to act together so as to decide what should happen next.[4] Even if Lukaschek's memory did not mislead him into attributing to this conversation details which really belonged later, the story does not prove any close knowledge on Helmuth's part and the absence of other evidence makes it questionable.

Helmuth certainly resembled the conspirators in having his attention directed outside Germany in 1938, particularly towards England. But he had reasons of his own for this. Closer acquaintance had done nothing to reconcile him to Berlin. At the beginning of the year, he told Freya that he found the city loathsome. Every day made him more certain that he was right in trying to reduce the amount of his work there to the lowest level consistent with solvency.

> If in three or four years' time things aren't working out in London, I shall withdraw completely to Kreisau and become a country bumpkin by your side. What goes on here is only a *stop-gap*.

One of the results of the Nazi seizure of Austria was to break up the Schwarzwald circle, several of whose members committed suicide. At the end of April and again in May he went to Vienna 'where things look pretty bleak for our friends'. In between these visits, he met the Frau Doctor in Copenhagen and was depressed at the prospect which the future held for her. Probably this was the time to which the story relates of two of his Jewish clients disappearing. He succeeded in tracing them to Gestapo headquarters in Vienna but not beyond. He there-

* Above, p. 35.

fore decided to visit those headquarters and make inquiries. Everyone said that he was crazy and would only get himself into trouble, but he persevered, obtained the information which he sought and was as a result able to proceed with the case.

In May 1938 he decided to part company with Lewinsky, who said to him, 'Get out of this odd country, you will never be able to make good in it. The pity is that I am too old to go.' Instead he took from 1 July a room in the office of another lawyer called Leverkuehn,* who for a few months in 1934–5 had had Adam von Trott as an assistant.

On 2 August Helmuth wrote:

> I can't stand the inanity of this existence much longer. Wouldn't it be better to be done with the false values and the pretences here and live extremely humbly in some place where one isn't continually under pressure to conform? I have the feeling that I would far far rather starve in a free land than go on trying to keep up appearances here. For that is what we are all doing. We let ourselves be a façade to cover up the atrocities which go on continually and the only reason for it is that we are left alone for a relatively long time before it's our turn to be got at. I've just no more stomach for it.

On the following day, after a sleepless night, he sketched out the possibilities. It was better for all concerned if Freya and Caspar stayed at the Berghaus as long as possible because then they could live on the money which they could not take out of Germany, while he himself would have greater freedom of movement abroad and could come back to Kreisau now and then for a rest. He doubted being able to earn enough as a lawyer abroad for them to be able to afford life in a city. Basically it would be much more appropriate and pleasant for them to live more or less as farmers in the southern hemisphere. He did not, however, want to give up the law altogether but somehow or other to use it as an asset. In case he were to leave Germany Freya must be able to support herself and Caspar by her own endeavours since anything else was too starry-eyed. He therefore suggested that she should cut herself sufficiently loose from the Kreisau household for her to take on agricultural training in Schweidnitz or Breslau.

One thing, however, emerged clearly from all these speculations. It was of the utmost importance for him to get his English qualification. He was unwilling to let threats of war deter him from achieving this at the earliest possible moment.

* Leverkuehn, Paul M. A. (b. 1893), studied at Edinburgh. In N. Persia 1915–16. Member of Anglo-German Mixed Arbitration Tribunal and German–U.S. Mixed Claims Commission 1923–6. German Property Commissioner in Washington 1928–30. Lawyer in Berlin after 1933. Consul in Tabriz March 1940–Jan 1941. *Abwehr* Representative in Istanbul July '41–spring '44. Lawyer in Hamburg after 1945. Died before 1964.

11 The Munich Crisis

HELMUTH passed his qualifying bar examination in October 1937 and his Part I in May 1938. At the beginning of the following October he presented himself for the finals, for which some people (though admittedly not the most able) allow themselves two years. He had to read 7,000 pages and write ninety-five short essays in a month. To improve his chances, he came over to London about 12 August and remained there almost continuously until the examination, working twelve hours a day and living in Lionel Curtis' flat near St James's Square. Curtis himself was in New Zealand and at Oxford the Long Vacation was at its zenith. Helmuth therefore was able to realise his intention of being left very much to himself, though he usually went down to the country at the week-end to stay with one friend or another.* It thus came about that he was out of Germany, and virtually dependent for his information on the newspapers, when the Munich crisis came to a head. This makes it hard to believe that he was much involved in any plots against Hitler, but it also means that the passages in his letters which are interesting are those showing his own reactions or his assessment of British opinion.

In the previous March he had commented on the debate in the Commons after the invasion of Austria:

> Only Churchill rises above mediocrity, and among opposition leaders, who go almost without mention in *The Times*, perhaps Henderson and Alexander. What I would really like to see would be a letter in *The Times* which simply said, '*Would not a cryptic saying meet the position: if you will not cross the Rubicon, you will destroy a great empire?*'

The saying was possibly more cryptic than Helmuth intended for he had combined Julius Caesar crossing the Rubicon in 49 B.C. with the advice given by the oracle to King Croesus of Lydia five hundred years earlier! All the same, the clash of judgment between Helmuth and the advocates of appeasement could hardly have been put more clearly, for it was part of their argument that 'crossing the Rubicon' (i.e. incurring the risk of war by making commitments in Europe) was the very thing

* He also met at this time Baron Hans Christoph von Stauffenberg who was working in the German Embassy and had an English wife.

that was likely to precipitate the undoing of the Commonwealth. On 16
June 1937 after the Commonwealth Conference, the Commonwealth
Secretary had reported to the Cabinet that the Commonwealth Prime
Ministers had been inclined 'to look rather more critically at British
involvement in Europe than His Majesty's government cared to'.[1]

Before a short visit to England in May Helmuth wrote:

> I have the feeling that a fundamental change has taken place.
> More and more I get the impression that England and France are
> inclined to force a show-down in the immediate future which will
> lead to a resounding victory for them or to war. Whether Czecho-
> slovakia constitutes a suitable occasion for war seems to me doubtful.

During this visit the first scare of an invasion of Czechoslovakia took
place and he was impressed by the apparent readiness to fight. He must,
however, have been given cause to think during the following week-end
when at Bob Brand's house near Rugby he met Robin Barrington-
Ward* of *The Times* and the American airman Colonel Lindbergh.
Lindbergh had just been subjected to high-pressure salesmanship by the
German air force and gave an alarming account of its superiority to the
British and French.[2]

By August the stage was being set for the final battle of nerves:

26 August

The atmosphere is no longer one of nervous anxiety as in May and
June but rather one of knowledge that storms lie ahead and that one
must hold to one's course through them without batting an eyelid.

9 September

It was rumoured today that Beck, the chief of staff, had resigned.†

13 September

The crisis seems to be upon us and the Cabinet appears to be more
nearly unanimous today than yesterday. The reactions to the Führer's speech [on the previous evening at the end of the Nuremberg
party rally] is thoroughly hostile which surprises me. I had expected
that it would succeed in winning over a section of English opinion.

About this time Helmuth wrote to his grandparents that:

> *Hitler will try to split the English people on the issue involved. His
> whole technique is over and over again to avoid fighting and to avoid*

---

* Barrington-Ward, R. W. (1891–1948), assistant editor of *The Times*, 1927–
34, deputy editor 1934–41, editor 1941–8.
† He had ceased to perform his duties on 18 August but allowed Hitler to
keep the fact quiet. The first public report of the resignation to appear seems
to have been that in the *News Chronicle* for 15 September. The formal resignation was not submitted till 19 October.

*an issue. The long cabinet meeting here today is not a good indica-
tion as it tends to show, that the Cabinet are not really united and of
one mind.*

14 September
Do as I can, I find it impossible to see how we can allow ourselves
to go to war on this issue since, if we wait, most of what we could
gain will fall into our lap. I think some Englishmen find my conviction that peace will be maintained a little provocative.

15 September
[The day of Chamberlain's arrival at Berchtesgaden]
Events here are enormously instructive. In the course of a few days
the government has succeeded in arousing among the public, with a
diminishing number of exceptions, the will to fight and I have
watched the process with fascination. If war were to break out, it
would be fought here with enthusiasm from the start.... It now looks
as though it will all blow over. It is noteworthy that, excited as I
have been at watching the way a people have been united by delay
and patience, I have never seriously believed in war.

17 September
It is a curious country and the more one sees the more impressive
is its simplicity and the ingenious and complex way in which this is
secured. Once again I have learnt a lot in these weeks.

18 September
Now that the English have told the Führer face-to-face that they
will fight if anything happens, I do not think we will fight. I do not
think we have any intention of committing suicide ... I hold the view
that Chamberlain is only trying to win over to his side the people
who are still hesitating. I do not believe that a compromise is going
to be arranged just at the moment and if everyone who is involved
keeps his head, the trouble will blow over.

19 September
One is only a looker-on but that is nerve-racking enough because
the principles which are ultimately at stake are the ones which make
life in Europe tolerable. If they get thrown overboard, one will have
to get out as quickly as possible ... I cannot believe that Chamberlain is seriously considering a partition of Czechoslovakia and if he
is, I am not sure it would not cause his fall.

20 September
The day was dominated by the resounding defeat of the French
and the English, for which there is no adequate explanation. [This

must refer to the publication of the proposed terms of settlement which Chamberlain had accepted at Berchtesgaden.]

One gets the impression that everybody feels ashamed of having once again left in the lurch a small nation which one had promised to back up and that the very fact of things having been allowed to come to this pass is a reason for deep embarrassment. On top of that is the feeling that this won't be the end of humiliations but that policies will have to be changed in other matters too. One cannot overlook what this decision is going to mean for internal politics in the two countries. One has the impression that the outcome will be the fall of the present governments. In comparison with the feeling of shame, the feeling of relief that there is no longer any immediate danger of war hardly weighs at all.

21 September
[On the eve of Chamberlain's visit to Bad Godesberg]
This is a remarkable country. Its infinite variety becomes clear to one in times like these. Over the past weeks the numerous strands of opinion have gradually woven themselves into a pattern which has now dissolved again but into different components. Everyone has a new point of view, nobody has stuck obdurately to his original opinion and, irrespective of what the immediate and long-term consequences of these events may be for the world, everyone has emerged the richer for having gone through the strain together – even those people who are disillusioned and embittered. It must be a great pleasure to govern a country like this and to keep on deriving new incentives from the way in which agreement is continually finding new issues to focus round. That was Baldwin's gift.

26 September
As always, I regard it as insane to believe that England and Germany will be at war by the end of the week. It seems to me that the Führer will only embark on war if he can keep it isolated and as, by all one hears, Chamberlain has told him that England will fight, I can't see how anything can happen.... There is little sense in working when one feels so on edge.

In my view it is wrong to lose one's head over all this talk of war and rush out of the country. In the last resort, the more that individuals can keep calm and cool and collected, the greater the chances of nothing happening.

27 September
Yesterday I allowed myself to be carried away by the stupid newspapers and worked badly. With so little time to spare, I can't afford that so now I just read the papers in bed, with excellent results.

30 September
[The day after the Munich Conference]
The feeling here today is one of immense relief. Even though people had come to terms with what was impending and were facing it with steady determination, the news that it was not going to be necessary came to everybody as a release. I think it is immaterial what Chamberlain brings back, for anything will be welcome. All the same, the determination and commitment of the entire population was a remarkable demonstration.

1 October
A new epoch is opening here unless a miracle occurs and, although the inhabitants of this country still don't realise it, we are certainly going to look at such things with new eyes. What I have experienced certainly wasn't the last flickerings of the old, but I don't think it will ever again come so close to getting the better of the new. Behind the façade of old and honourable institutions the social structure of this country is going to change just as much as it has done in Germany.

On 5 October he wrote a somewhat alarmist letter to his grandmother.

In England a violent antisemitic propaganda has started; all the Beaverbrook papers have taken up the campaign and are publishing daily some extract from Herr Hitler's Mein Kampf, and already today one can notice the signs, that Fascism is in the ascendant here; I have really noticed it most when I had lunch with John Martin and a few of his firm's people in the City. They are all very unpolitically-minded men but the way in which they pleaded for a strengthening of the administrative machinery and of the power of the executive, the obvious pleasure which they took in the fact, that Chamberlain has succeeded to govern without taking Parliamentary opinion into consideration, all that shows clearly which way the stream is running and if there is not a very strong reaction very soon, England is for fascism; the consequences of this, though it will certainly appear in very decent forms and under the cloak of unchanged principles, are too awful to be thought out.

5 October (to Freya)
It would be a miracle if I got up to pass level with what I wrote in the exam. I put down what I believed to be right but at best it was no more than *intelligent guesswork*.

Yet he did pass and thereby testified to his capacity for absorbing a lot of information in an extremely short time. The pity was that he was to have so little chance of putting his knowledge to the uses which he had intended.

D

12 The Last Months of Peace

THE German opponents of Hitler had set considerable store by his first real international clash. In order to make sure of overcoming Czech resistance, the German general staff only felt able to leave eight divisions on the western front. If the French had decided to renounce an essentially defensive strategy based on the Maginot line and gone over to the attack, the position of the Germans would have been precarious. General Gamelin described their western defences as being *de la marmalade*. Moreover many people, in the light of history, did not believe that Germany could withstand a war on two fronts if Britain were among her enemies. For these reasons the conspirators in Berlin had planned to arrest (and if necessary shoot) Hitler and his immediate associates as soon as he gave the order to attack Czechoslovakia. If on the other hand he had backed down on finding that the French and British really were going to fight, he would have suffered a major loss of face which might have undermined his whole position.

Opinions seem likely to go on differing for some time as to what all the various parties concerned would really have done if it had come to the crunch. As things were, news of Chamberlain's visit to Berchtesgaden and of the Munich Conference arrived at the two crucial moments when the conspirators in Berlin claim to have been on the point of acting. Hitler proved to have divined the situation better than any of his opponents and it may well be that, if he had not done so from an early stage, he would never have allowed himself to get into the corner in which some of them fancied him to be trapped. But they could not help feeling that, if only the British had stood firm, and had encouraged rather than discouraged a similar attitude on the part of the French, the Third Reich would have been at or near its end. (What would have happened thereafter is another question.) They therefore felt let down and dejected.

When Helmuth got back to Germany and found this attitude prevalent, he had much sympathy with it. During a later visit he wrote on 20 November a long post-mortem analysis to Curtis. After praising the steadiness and unanimity of the English people, much as he had done in writing to Freya from London, he went on

> *You know what happened and you know that the leadership of the government was found lacking and that the government was not*

worthy of the people they were called upon to lead. It was a remarkable spectacle, that a whole nation should have been united by a government on one issue, and that at the decisive moment the government abandoned the people they had united and led them the other way. ... Well, I suppose nothing else could be done in these days, although the whole story is not yet known, and the mistakes of the government were made in the earlier part of the year and not in the last days. ...

I went back to Germany with the gravest apprehension for the future of Europe as a whole. If this continent came under the domination of the Nazis for any length of time the sort of civilisation which has been built in centuries and which is founded in its last resort on Christianity and the Classics would go and we do not know, what would emerge instead. But whatever would emerge it would be different from that to which we had been educated and for which we had to stand. From the first day when I was back in Germany I noticed that the radical group in the party had gained the upper hand and that terrible internal developments were to be expected. So I had an enormously busy time preparing for the worst, and especially getting Jews out of the country. Perhaps a week before the murder of vom Rath the party-organs foreshadowed ghettoes and confiscation of property, and under normal circumstances the way from the daily newspapers to the official gazette would have taken 3 to 6 months. But of course the murder precipitated events and things happened which are now known to all the world.

The last passage refers to the murder in Paris on 7 November of a junior official in the German Embassy. The murderer was a young Jew whose parents had just been driven out of Germany into Poland (where their treatment was not much less brutal). Goebbels used the pretext to order the smashing and plundering of Jewish shops and synagogues, so that the episode has become known as the 'Plate-glass Night'/*Kristallnacht*. The Jewish community was finally excluded from almost all economic activities. Many Jews decided to leave the country (although many did not) but were only allowed until the end of the month to get the formalities completed. Multifarious complications cropped up and it is hardly surprising that on 12 December Helmuth admitted to feeling the effects of his exertions over the past few weeks.

During the winter of 1938–9 he seems gradually to have been building up contacts with old friends like Horst von Einsiedel (now working in the chemicals branch of the Economics Ministry) and Adolf Reichwein. On 30 November he went to supper with Arnold von Borsig, whose family had a well-known engineering firm in Berlin and who had once been a pupil of Eugen Rosenstock. There he found 'a former leader of the Reichsbanner' [the republican attempt to answer the Nazi Storm troops] called Haubach. According to Carl Zuckmayer,[1] Helmuth had met Haubach as long ago as 1927 at Zuckmayer's house near Salzburg, along with a friend called Carlo Mierendorff, and both of them had also known the Schwarzwalds. But, if this was so, Helmuth does not seem to have remembered it. He also renewed his acquaintance with Otto von der Gablentz* (a friend and colleague of Einsiedel's), while he had regular meetings with Eduard Waetjen, an industrial lawyer with an American mother, who was a friend of Carl Deichmann. At these meetings they chose two subjects to talk about, so as to avoid becoming discursive and getting nowhere; favourite topics were German–U.S. relations and the reorganisation of German society after the Third Reich had ended.

Discussions about such topics led on so naturally to the activities in which Helmuth engaged during the war that it is tempting to treat them as the beginning of the 'Kreisau Circle'. This is a matter on which a balanced judgment is not easy, partly for lack of firm information. Historians have such a tendency to magnify origins that a certain scepticism is prudent and some evidence is open to challenge. On the other hand the documents which have survived from 1940 show clearly that something had been happening previously. Probably the question 'When did it all start?' is not one that is any more susceptible of a precise answer than the question 'Who belonged to the Kreisau Circle?'† It was natural for intelligent opponents of the régime to discuss among themselves many matters about the present and future of Germany and Europe. Helmuth was no exception. At the start such discussions are unlikely to have had any more constructive purpose than is usual in such cases. But they may well have received a stimulus from the discovery in the course of, or after, the Munich crisis that, if Hitler had been overthrown, the various groups involved had no clear or agreed ideas as to what should be set up instead (except that it must be unlike the Weimar Republic). By the outbreak of war Helmuth seems already to have realised how important it would be for a group to be ready with clear plans to take over when Hitler fell. But exactly when he formed this idea or how early he decided to do anything practical about it is something which he may not have realised at the time and certainly is impossible for us to decide in retrospect. His action in the Fritsch crisis‡ shows that he had put himself in a position to get reliable inside information, but it does not follow that he was taking any active part in planning action.

There still exist, however, four memoranda with the date 1939 (but no month) marked on them in his unmistakable writing. They are:

* Above, p. 34. † Below, p. 188.
‡ Above, p. 76.

The small communities (8 pages)
Working plan on scale and limits of self-administration (7 pages)
Remarks on the theory of self-administration (6 pages)
Remarks on higher education (4 pages).

The opening paragraph of the first document merits quotation, in that it echoes the ideas underlying the Waldenburg camps and looks forward to the later plans for a post-war world.

I start from the premise that it is intolerable from the point of view of European society if the individual is isolated and only brought into politics through a community which is already large-scale. Isolation leads to mass society. In such circumstances single individuals, when combined, merely form part of a mass. In face of the large-scale community of the state, the only person who can really have a proper share of responsibility is somebody who takes some share of responsibility in a smaller-scale community. Otherwise the governed come to feel that they have no lot or part in events, while the governing classes come to feel that they are not answerable to anybody. Such a development may be acceptable for Russia or Asiatic countries; it cannot provide the basis for a European society....

In pursuit of his profession, Helmuth agreed in November to go into partnership with Leverkuehn, although this meant compromising himself and exposing himself to possible future pressure by joining the 'National Socialist League of Jurists'. But he wanted to be sure, for the purposes of his plans regarding Germany, that his rear was covered. He was becoming increasingly convinced that he might have to leave Germany for reasons which he explained to Lionel Curtis on 15 February during a trip to London.

I leave today for Germany and I must say that I have never left with a more pessimistic view about the future of Western Europe to which I belong. At the same time I simply cannot see where I can do anything useful and constructive. It seems to me that now it is not a question of how to continue until the Caesarian régimes fall but really how to preserve the rest of Western Europe from falling either a prey to those régimes or developing such régimes themselves. The paralysis which has befallen this country simply stares one into the face [sic] at every turn. At the same time everything has been done during the last year to strengthen and stabilise my dear Führer and Chancellor: he has thereby been enabled to clear the whole of Germany from any possible inimical movement. Where there was a chance for a change a year ago there is nothing now. A change of régime is therefore dependent upon a weakening of the hold through exhaustion; and there is no reason to expect this to happen during our lifetime.

As regards my own personal affairs I see my position as follows: my work in Berlin must come to an end. It is torturing me because in my profession one cannot help aiding those whose spirit is governing this country. But it is also not safe for me to continue as I have done, because I will not be allowed to sit on the fence indefinitely and keep my passport, my permits to foreign exchange, etc.

There are two possible ways in front of me. I can return to Kreisau and live there the life of a tiller of the soil with all the amenities and drawbacks of country life and with the absolute certainty, that never in my life will I be able to do anything useful, i.e. anything assisting those to whom I really belong.

The other possibility is to come to England and try my luck at the Bar. The chances of success are one to 99. But even if I should succeed this would only be a very small advance on living at Kreisau. The only real advance would lie in the chance of giving Caspar an education, which he could not get here in Germany. What really attracts me is not this vague gambling chance at the Bar but the possibility that I might be useful in defending and perhaps restating the European creed versus the Caesarian creed: in short the attraction really lies in being on the right side.

But, you see, what has troubled me this time is that I do not know whether I would be wanted. This spirit of frustration, defeatism, paralysis which has spread rapidly during the last few months in this country, and which was not apparent in August and September is so well known to me. It is the spirit which reigned in Germany from 1930 to 1933. If this is so you will soon start to lose good people and you will certainly not require any foreigners however well-intentioned.

This is the problem that vexes me and has brought me again to doubt whether it is not better for me to be buried alive at Kreisau. On the other hand I cannot help feeling that it is my bounden duty to try to be on the right side whatever difficulties, unpleasantness and sacrifices this may entail. I cannot simply say, that as the chances of an immediate or near change in Germany have vanished, I can retire. So you see I am at cross-purposes with myself, and this complication is added to the complications imposed from outside.

Of course I would like to wait another year. But I am unable to do so. I will soon be drafted into the army and will thereafter be controlled by the S.A. Passport regulations are being tightened up and it is already difficult for anybody who has not got a very strong reason to travel to get a passport. Undoubtedly the visits of foreigners to

Germans in Germany will soon be scrutinised and the isolation of every individual German from foreign contacts will be carried to great lengths.

Curtis replied by calling Helmuth's attention to a speech in which Goebbels deprecated the talk of war and to an offer by Hitler to guarantee the independence of Holland.[2] Helmuth's answer was in effect 'Beware the Ides of March' and punctually on that date the rump of Czechoslovakia was occupied. He had by that time gone back to Germany and thus did not experience the violent reaction of British public opinion, already stirred to frustrated indignation by the *Kristallnacht*. Had he done so, he might have been persuaded that he had overestimated the defeatism in February just as he had overestimated the unity in September.

During the intervening summer Helmuth arranged to take a room in the chambers of Sir Donald Somervell (then Attorney-General) and Mr (now Sir John) Foster, the Fellow of All Souls and international lawyer whom he had known since 1935; he even ordered the furniture. When he came with Freya on their last visit to England in June, they told their friends of their intention to spend a considerable amount of the following winter in London. He also wrote on 25 June from that city a long description of his position to his grandfather.

Work in Berlin is highly unsatisfactory. Not in volume, mind you, but in quality. The courts have practically ceased to function for all big cases, and Chancery work has been reduced by the uncertainty of the law, which makes every arrangement entered into of doubtful value. Long-term business with foreign countries, in which I had specialised has practically come to a standstill. The work coming in is of a kind which is derogatory of one's mind as well as one's conscience. It is concerned with negotiations with the various ministries controlling the country, one is expected to be able to bribe, to establish connexions with influential officers of the state or the party; this is the result of a system of government which has placed into the hands of officials of every grade the power to give decisions which turn success into failure or otherwise and which are not given as quasi-judicial decisions but which are given on grounds of expediency, uncontrolled and uncontrollable by any impartial person, open to influences of various and dubious kinds. I need not enlarge on this subject. No person with self-respect could agree to act under such conditions unless he is forced to do so under the stress of making a living coute que coute ... I only handle the few, the very few cases where law is still the most important determinant, and I still do the drafting of documents concerned with international investment, in-

*ternational wills or settlements and international export–import
business. As regards all this drafting work I am not bound to Berlin
at all, as work of that kind comes in from all parts of Europe, and
is usually work given me in Brussels or Cologne or Breslau or Vienna.
... In both lines of the work in my Berlin Office I will make sufficient money to enable me to carry on the Berghaus Haushalt and
to pay all my German expenses and taxes.*

*The state of the profession in Germany has of course not come
about with one step, but has gradually developed or better deteriorated into the present state. Precisely because I foresaw this deteri-
oration I started working for my Bar examinations in Berlin, and
started building up firm connexions with the big firms of solicitors in
London doing international business. Now I believe to be sufficiently
rooted in London to try to do some work there. My authorities have
given me a sufficiently wide permit to allow me to keep a good
proportion of the money made in London here and therefore I hope
to be able to make a living here, which will enable me to divide my
time between London and Kreisau. That of course is only the ultimate goal, if all goes well. At the beginning I will have to keep in
touch with work in Berlin to a certain extent so as to maintain an
open door there for me in case of failure in London. The work I am
proposing to do in London is of three kinds, (a) I hope to get some
work of drafting contracts on international business and family
affairs; there is no reason why solicitor-firms who have sent me
chancery-work to Berlin should not be prepared to send it to me in
London; for work of this kind I have already got a retainer for two
years from one firm at £150 a year. (b) a certain part of my work
done at Berlin will come my way also in London; it will perhaps
come in at the Berlin office but will simply be sent to me in London,
and instead of paying me in Berlin they will pay me in London. (c)
The third type of work is research work for the University of
London; I have been given a grant for a special research on international law of £200 for two years....* I believe therefore that that
is as good as it can be under present circumstances and that as prospects in Germany are as black as they are it would be folly not to try
to make a start in London.*

These plans were not, however, destined to be realised, for the outbreak of war found Helmuth still in Germany. Superficially, this was
due to his misreading of the situation, for letters which he wrote to
England at the end of July show him once again convinced that there

---

* This may have been connected with a comparative study of the German and
English Law of Inheritance which he at one time proposed to undertake jointly
with John Foster.

would be no war. Perhaps the factor for which he, like so many other people, failed to allow was the Soviet–German Pact. On 24 August, three days after the news broke, he wrote to M.B. that *'I am bound in here just now, as tightly as possible, because I have entangled myself in the process of freeing myself for the autumn plans.'* (The autumn plans were those for moving to England and the entanglements the arrangements and authorisations needed to make the move possible.) The same letter contained an appeal for help in containing the antagonisms which the war would cause.

These days shatter many hopes but I trust we will be able to start again later. We have to make a start and I hope you will consider it your duty to keep as many people as possible in a balance,* where matters can be discussed later.

* Presumably 'in a balanced frame of mind towards Germany'.

13 The *Abwehr*

H E L M U T H had gone to Berlin on 21 August with a view to finding a job which, if war did break out, would protect him from being called up as a soldier.[1] Within a fortnight he had succeeded in getting posted as a War Administrative Counsellor/*Kriegsverwaltungsrat* to the Foreign Countries Division of the *Abwehr* in the Supreme Command of the Armed Forces (OKW). As early as 11 August officers of the *Abwehr*, realising that in the event of hostilities they would need to strengthen their arrangements for getting advice about international law, had started negotiations with the 'Institute for Foreign Public Law and the Law of Nations' which was part of the Society for the Promotion of Knowledge founded in 1911 by Kaiser Wilhelm II (and which still exists though rechristened after Max Planck). Helmuth had had dealings with the Institute in the course of his legal activities and had written articles about Commonwealth law for their journal: he was now recommended to the *Abwehr* by the Institute's director Professor Viktor Bruns. No doubt the name of Moltke helped to make him acceptable to the soldiers. Bruns, who was getting on in years, did not himself join the *Abwehr* but his deputy Ernst Martin Schmitz was given a position parallel to Helmuth.

The attraction of this appointment was fourfold. It gave Helmuth an official justification for keeping in touch with the world outside Germany and with Britain in particular. Throughout the war, he read *The Times* and *Hansard* regularly. It also allowed him a chance of doing what he could to see that Germany, in her conduct of the war, was kept to the rules of international law. Although he never wore uniform and was distinctly averse to being ordered about by other people, he became in effect a member of the armed forces and so obtained their protection against the party. For example, the personal file of anyone posted to the *Abwehr* was transferred to its archives from those of the police. Finally he was convinced that the war would bring about the downfall of the Nazi party and, at the outset, that it would not take long to do so. He thought it vital for there to be inside the administrative machine men who would be able to see that the work of rebuilding after the catastrophe followed sound lines. He believed that the OKW represented a position from which it should prove possible to exert influence at the crucial moment. He cannot have imagined that the people with whom he would be working were convinced supporters of Hitler, since if he had done he would have tried to get sent somewhere else. But he certainly did not fully grasp that he was in fact going into the nerve-centre of the group seeking to deprive Hitler of power, an organisation which General Jodl in his trial at Nuremberg was to describe as a 'Nest of Conspirators'/*Verschwörernest*.

The word *Abwehr* means 'protection' or 'warding off' and the name was given to the Military Intelligence Department of the German army in 1921 when any term having the smallest connotation of aggressive-ness invited Allied suspicion. Starting with six officers, the unit grew in size once rearmament got under way and became known as the Foreign Information and Protection Group/*Amtsgruppe Auslandnachrichten und Abwehr* in the Ministry of Defence. In 1935 a naval officer, Rear-Admiral Wilhelm Canaris, was appointed as its head. There was a further reorganisation when the OKW was set up after the crisis of February 1938* and the unit was incorporated in it as an 'Office for Foreign Countries and Protection/*Amt Ausland/Abwehr*. As such it was divided into three main parts – the Foreign Countries Division/*Abteilung*, later *Amtsgruppe Ausland*, of which Rear-Admiral Leopold Bürkner† was in charge from July 1938 until 1945; Division Z respon-sible for personnel, finance and administration under Colonel Hans Oster;‡ and the three divisions of the *Abwehr* proper, responsible respectively for the procurement of intelligence, for sabotage/subver-sion, and for counter-intelligence.

The Foreign Countries Division, to which Helmuth was attached, was largely engaged in liaison between the AA and OKW, interpreting each side's point of view to the other. In the course of this work it engaged in a good deal of evaluation of the secret intelligence material which the three *Abwehr* divisions collected and of such other material (largely open) as it collected for itself. Officially evaluation of this material was the function of the three services and of the AA but this left not only Canaris but also Keitel, as head of the department co-ordinating all the services, without evaluations of their own. Bürkner's division thus seems to have been one of the few places in the whole German machine where a clear view could be had of the war as a whole. The division consisted of seven branches of which Number VI, under Lt-Colonel Tafel, was concerned with international law; this branch in turn was subdivided into seven sections of which Helmuth initially led that responsible for questions concerned with economic warfare. The whole group was accommodated in 1939 in the OKW building, with

* Above, p. 78.
† Bürkner, Rear-Admiral Leopold (b. 1894), had served as a naval attaché. Made the technical preparations for the 1935 Anglo-German Naval Treaty.
‡ Oster (1887–1945) also acted as Canaris's Chief-of-Staff.

one entrance on the Tirpitz-Ufer and another in the Bendler-Strasse,* to the south of the Tiergarten in Central Berlin. Fortunately for Helmuth his brother-in-law Carl Deichmann had a mews flat in the Derfflingerstrasse some 600 yards away and there he mainly lived until both house and office were bombed in 1943. He was thus able to go home at lunch-time when many of his most vital meetings took place.

Canaris (1887–1945) was often called 'the little Greek' but in fact his family are believed to have come from Lombardy and, although they had been established in Germany for several generations, he looked like a native of the Mediterranean and spent much of his time there. One of his subordinates said that 'the Admiral may not be much to look at but he's got what it takes in the top storey'. Civilised, astute, versatile, profoundly pessimistic and withal enigmatic (as the head of any Secret Service must be!), he knew far too much about what the Nazis were doing to stomach what he regarded as brash stupidity and recognised as inhuman brutality. If his efforts to get rid of them had ever relaxed, he would have been kept up to the mark by Oster, by Oster's right-hand man Hans von Dohnanyi† or by his liaison officer with the OKW Colonel Helmuth Groscurth (1898–1943). Elsewhere in the chain of command Bürkner, though by no means a Nazi, was not inclined to look for trouble (he succeeded in evading both arrest by the Nazis and trial by the Allies!) but Tafel, a relative of the Bonhoeffers, had taken Jews under his personal protection on the 'Plate-glass Night'‡ and was quick to protest about SS atrocities in Poland. Helmuth was thus lucky in his surroundings but the *Abwehr* leaders were also lucky in their recruit. Canaris was as anxious as anyone to use international law as a check on Nazi excesses; he now had the resourceful and determined technical expert who could show him how, if at all, it could be done. They were alike in their principles, their pessimism, their ability to think fast and their dislike of prolixity.

Anyone inclined to feel surprise that the opposition to Hitler should have had one of its chief centres in the German Secret Service must remember that the Third *Reich* was a very peculiar place. Its character was such that after 1938 much the best prospect of offering and organising opposition to its excesses was from inside. The disadvantage of this solution was, of course, that, to avoid suspicion, those who practised it had outwardly at any rate to give satisfaction in the conduct of their

---

* Now Reichpietzufer and Stauffenbergstrasse.

† Dohnanyi, Hans von (b. 1902), son of Hungarian composer. State Prosecutor in Hamburg 1931. Personal assistant to Franz Gürtner Minister of Justice 1932–8, removed by Roland Freisler as anti-Nazi 1938. Judge of Supreme Court Leipzig 1938–9. Posted to *Abwehr* at outbreak of war. Married to sister of Dietrich Bonhoeffer while his own sister was married to Bonhoeffer's elder brother Karl Friedrich.

‡ Above, p. 87.

duties and thus assume a certain degree of complicity for the acts of the régime. Moreover it would be a mistake to regard these men as dedicated liberals. They mostly had a conservative and nationalist background, though they nearly all of them were or grew into being committed Christians. What motivated them was both revulsion at the cruelty and alarm at the potential damage to Germany.

Few or none of these people thought of their acts as being of historical significance. One close associate of Oster who has survived, Hans Berndt Gisevius, has commented[2] that in their activities they never regarded themselves as a 'Resistance'/*Widerstand* or indeed used the word. Conditions in Germany itself were so unlike conditions in countries occupied by Germany (particularly in the attitude of the mass of the population to anti-Nazi activities) that it was out of the question to expect Hitler's German opponents to undertake the same kind of activities as were engaged in by the French, Polish and other 'resistance' movements; by calling premature attention to themselves, they would have put paid to their chances of striking at the decisive moment. On the other hand, the term 'opposition' suggests something far too constitutional – and therefore in Nazi Germany impracticable – for which reason the German word *Widerstand* will be used in the remainder of this book. To carry out their basic objective of removing Hitler from power – whether by a *coup d'état/Staatsstreich* or by assassination/*Attentat* – they needed one of two things, access to his person or command of armed force. Neither was easy to obtain, for the Führer appeared less and less in public and only persons having business with him were admitted to his presence, while staff-officers in organisations like the *Abwehr* do not command troops. It was for these reasons that they devoted so much of their energies to trying to secure the support of commanding officers, although even then there was doubt whether the rank-and-file would obey orders as long as Hitler lived. Helmuth could offer little help in either respect and that is why he played no great part in the various plans.

The secrecy which naturally cloaks intelligence operations was, of course, of great assistance to the *Abwehr* members of the *Widerstand*. But they were not able to conceal their attitudes altogether. The Nazi creed called for all activities of the state and society to be co-ordinated with and absorbed into the movement. Naturally the party had its own intelligence service, and one with something denied to the *Abwehr*, an executive arm in the shape of the Secret State Police/*GEheime STAats POlizei*. As its name implies, this was originally a state rather than a party force, like the Criminal Police/*KRIminal POlizei* who were led by another crypto-conspirator in the person of Arthur Nebe. But in 1936 both had been amalgamated with the party's own Security Service/*Sicherheitsdienst* SD. From September 1939 onwards the whole machine was directed from the Security Head Office/*Reichssicher-heitshauptamt* RSHA under Reinhard Heydrich reporting to Himmler as head of the SS and Chief of Police for the whole of Germany.

Heydrich and his men naturally cast envious eyes on the *Abwehr* but the generals were too well aware of the importance of good intelligence to allow themselves to become dependent on somebody else for it and until 1944 they were strong enough to protect Canaris. In the autumn of 1936, however, a division of functions, generally known as 'The Ten Commandments', was agreed on by which the *Abwehr* was left supreme in the military field and the SD in the criminal one (treason counting as criminal). But the RSHA never abandoned hope and knew only too well that an excellent way of achieving their ambitions would be to prove that treason was rife in the *Abwehr*. Consequently the members of the two organisations led a cat-and-dog existence in which contact was frequent and trust small. Each side busily collected dossiers about the deeds or misdeeds of the other. One of the reasons why Canaris was picked for the job of heading the *Abwehr* was that Heydrich, before being sacked from the navy for trouble over a girl, had been his subordinate and might therefore treat him with some respect. They lived close to one another in the suburbs of Berlin where Heydrich used to play in string quartets with Frau Canaris.

People who have worked in big organisations in wartime will be familiar with situations in which one unit comes to regard victory over a rival in a neighbouring field as more important than victory over the common enemy. But, in the case of the two German intelligence organisations, this rivalry was spiced by the knowledge that at least some of the side which lost would have to pay for their failure with their lives.

14 Work in the *Abwehr*

September–December 1939

T H E work on which Helmuth now embarked involved a major issue of principle. The Hague Conventions of 1899 and 1907 about the laws of war had been drawn up in days when wars were still thought of as things fought by rival armies, with civilian life remaining relatively unaffected. Once the object of war was extended beyond the defeat of the enemy army in the field to the destruction of its supplies and therefore to the continued capacity for resistance of its industrial machine and population, many of the rules became inadequate and a host of new situations arose for which no agreed rules existed. Air warfare, with its inability to distinguish between combatants and non-combatants, added a further complication. In this situation, and more particularly in Germany in 1939, the lawyers faced two alternatives.

The Nazi leaders, who had neither respect for nor understanding of law, expected it to be used as a tool to further their purposes and looked to their legal advisers to find pretexts justifying whatever they wished to do. This on the whole was the course followed by the Legal Division of the OKW under Dr Wagner, whom Helmuth christened the Poison Dwarf/*Giftzwerg*.* If suitable pretexts could not be found, the law must be flouted. The alternative course, however, was to apply existing rules in such a way as to discourage extensions in the scope of hostilities. The new methods of warfare were bound to expose innocent civilians to greater risks and more undeserved suffering than before. But by appealing to the intention which underlay the rules, the total amount of suffering caused by the war might be kept in bounds. The *Abwehr* lawyers who, with the encouragement of Canaris, exerted their influence in the second direction, thereby making things easier for many people who never knew of their existence, had two main lines of argument. On the one hand the idea of abiding by regulations was deeply embedded in the army and officers could often be induced to refrain from action by the mere demonstration that it was not legally sanctioned. But many of them could also appreciate that arbitrary cruelty was capable in the long run of making Germany so hated as to provoke retaliation by the enemy, besides complicating the task of military governors. Helmuth and his colleagues spent much time in trying to convince not only officers but also party functionaries that law was not

* Below, p. 283.

simply a tiresome device of humanitarians to hamper the effectiveness of German action but something which had been shown by experience to be in the long-term German interest.

Unfortunately the *Abwehr* were handicapped in their efforts by the agreement barring them from the political field, for it was there that most Nazi excesses occurred. Great ingenuity was used to get round this limitation; on one occasion, for example, views of German doctors unfavourable to Nazi policy were reported as having appeared in the foreign press so that they could be brought to notice as 'military intelligence'. Unfortunately also one of the worst violations of the traditional rules began to be perpetrated before Helmuth even joined the *Abwehr*. The SS and SD followed the army into Poland, having been entrusted by Hitler and Göring with the task of eliminating the Polish upper classes, Catholic leaders and Jews. Complaining that the military courts were being too slow and too lenient in dealing with guerrillas, they took things into their own hands and proceeded to exterminate large numbers of people who were not guerrillas and who by the laws of war ought to have been protected. As knowledge of this spread among senior officers, there was considerable indignation. But nobody was anxious, particularly in the euphoria of victory, to face the head-on collision with the party which would have followed from an attempt to insist that what happened in the conquered territories should be decided by the people who had done the conquering. The question soon, however, arose as to what was to happen next time.

On 10 October, when the success of the Polish campaign had done much to offset the shock caused by the British and French declaration of war, Hitler summoned his service chiefs to him and ordered preparations to be made for opening a campaign against the west. The generals, who were told to start an offensive in November, were doubtful of their capacity to defeat the combined French and British armies, and convinced that, of all the times to start a campaign, November was the worst. They, and in particular Halder as Chief of Staff, began once again to think of removing the Führer by force. The idea was sedulously fostered by Oster and Groscurth, by Beck in his retirement and by Goerdeler. One of the things which the conspirators wanted to do before acting was to secure from the enemy a promise that they would not take advantage of internal confusion in Germany and would be prepared to make peace on reasonable terms with a new German government. During the winter, negotiations to this end were pursued through a number of channels in Switzerland and Scandinavia but notably through the Vatican where Pope Pius XII took an active part. The British and French governments were disposed to co-operate provided they could be sure that the offers were seriously meant and that action was really going to be taken against Hitler.[1]

Developments at sea took a different direction. On the one hand the navy was the only service currently engaged in actually fighting the enemy. On the other hand it found itself hampered in several ways. To begin with, it did not have enough submarines. To go on with, the actual commander of the fleet Admiral Boehm and his Chief of Staff Captain Weichold thought it too dangerous to make offensive use of their light vessels near the English coast. Finally the government, in an attempt to learn the lessons of the 1914–18 war, had laid down the most rigorous instructions against submarine or air attacks on ships belonging to or likely to be carrying neutrals.* Although the Germans modified these when the British proved to be less squeamish (e.g. by extending the list of goods to be considered as contraband), they still allowed England to import all her vital requirements, and left English exports completely unaffected. In mid-October Raeder, as naval Commander-in-Chief, decided to get tough. He replaced Boehm and Weichold with more adventurous officers and submitted a 38-page document to Hitler recommending that a statement by Chamberlain on 26 September should be used as a pretext for declaring a 'siege of Britain'.[2]

> The main target of our naval strategy is the merchant ship, and not only those belonging to the enemy but any merchant ship which puts to sea in the service of the enemy's economy either by importing or by exporting.... Military success can be most confidently expected if we attack British sea communications with the greatest ruthlessness; the final aim of such attacks is to cut off all imports into and exports from Britain. We should try to consider the interest of neutrals, as far as this is possible without detriment to our military requirements. It is desirable to base all military measures taken on existing international law; however, measures which we consider necessary from a military point of view ... will have to be carried out even if they are not covered by existing international law. In principle, therefore, any means of warfare which is effective in breaking enemy resistance should be based on some legal conception even if that entails the creation of a new code of naval warfare.

> Once it has been decided to conduct economic warfare in its most ruthless form ... this decision is to be adhered to in all circumstances. Every protest by neutral powers must be turned down. The more ruthlessly economic warfare is waged, the earlier will it show results and the sooner will the war come to an end.

The paper recommended that all neutrals should be asked to keep armed enemy merchantmen out of their harbours, to keep their nationals

---

* The attack on the *Athenia* on 3 September was due to a U-boat commander disregarding orders.

off enemy ships and to keep their own ships far from enemy coasts. The way would then be clear to sink any enemy merchantmen without warning anywhere and to sink neutrals after warning (if necessary from a distance). The bombing of enemy ports, hitherto left unattacked, was also recommended.

Raeder admitted that Germany could not have enough U-boats or aircraft to make a 'siege' effective until 1941, and that the measures proposed might be unwelcome to neutrals, particularly the United States. It could therefore be argued against him that the measures he was proposing would involve a loss of neutral good-will out of all proportion to the advantages which Germany could for the time being gain. Restraint in sinking and observance of the conventions of international law would by contrast amount to a 'moral conquest' of the neutrals.

This was the debate which raged for the rest of the year and provides the background to Helmuth's letters, though the destruction of the *Abwehr* files makes it impossible to be sure of the exact references in many cases.[3] The main forum in which it was fought was a new body set up in the OKW on 23 October to co-ordinate questions of trade and economic warfare (*Handelskrieg und Wirtschaftliche Kampfmassnahmen*, hence HWK). Raeder, to emphasise its importance, put a senior officer, Vice-Admiral Karlgeorg Schuster, in charge of it, a place being found for Weichold as his Chief of Staff; the other members were senior representatives of the services, of the AA and of the economic departments. In the long run the HWK failed to fulfil the hopes placed in it and Schuster is said to have come to the conclusion that it was a stillborn child.[4] It lasted, however, throughout the war.

For nearly a month Helmuth complained of not having enough to do. Then, as he began to find his feet in the office, he wrote that 'the work gets more interesting every day'.

14 October 1939

The last twenty-four hours have not been without interest in that I have had two sharp battles in the division, one over questions of sea warfare, the other over the duty to keep our superiors, and particularly the leaders of the three services, informed about unfavourable as well as favourable developments. At the first discussion [which may have concerned the German reaction to a British Admiralty radio message of 1 October, ordering all British merchantmen to ram any U-boat which came their way. On 17 October U-boats were in consequence authorised to attack without warning any enemy merchantman recognised as such] the sailors were incredibly dour and unperceptive. The second was sensational because I was told that we must guard against a loss of nerve and therefore be selective in what we pass on. Can you believe it? How thankful I am that my purely technical work in all these fields involves me in no responsibility!

18 October

I am to give a talk to the people concerned in the responsible ministries about the seizure of enemy property. That basically suits me, since it enables one to stave off a lot of nonsense [*manchen Unfug verhüten*].

25 October

Everything goes on much as before. More and more people see the misfortune which is impending and, in proportion as the general atmosphere gets worse, my own spirits rise.

29 October

The time is out of joint and there is no prospect of things improving. My head can see no reason why anything should get better for many years. And unfortunately I can see plenty of reasons why things should get materially worse.... At the moment, it looks as if a little respite had been secured. If only it would last till the spring. Everything is easier to stand in summer than in winter.

On 17 November Hitler decided that enemy passenger ships might be torpedoed without warning if it could be established that they were armed, and that all tankers, including neutrals, could be torpedoed if met in the zones proclaimed by the Americans as dangerous in connection with their neutrality legislation.[5] On 24 November, neutrals were warned that their security could no longer be guaranteed in the North Sea unless they kept to specially indicated channels. These measures were considerably less drastic than those for which Raeder had originally asked and the discussions which led to the modification are probably reflected in some of the following letters.

30 October

The quiet day which I was expecting turned out a stormy one. At 10 this morning the draft of a new law landed on my desk for immediate comment; it ran completely counter to my views. I had to challenge it root and branch, which I have done successfully to the point of getting another meeting of all the relevant ministries called tomorrow at which I for my sins must play the leading role.

10 November

Another long day is far from over. My new remit has in fact brought me to grips with one of the basic questions about the whole conduct of the war and perhaps put me in a position where I can in minor respects set limits to the misery. The underlying principle is, however, so big that the details involved are on a scale I never dreamt of and affect hundreds and thousands of individuals. I got the job this morning and have been at it ever since. Now it is 7 and I am on the point of starting a draft which is going to take most of the night. Then I shall have to fight for my point of view with each unit in turn and see no prospect of being finished before the middle of next week.

11 November

I have been sleeping badly lately because I have got too worked up about my jobs. Having to fight for men's lives is certainly pleasing but terribly unsettling. Tomorrow I have got to hold forth for practically the whole day in front of the chiefs* and that will spark off the really big battle.

12 November

This morning I went to the OKW at 9. Now it is 5 and I have just got back. But, wherever there was a chance of success, I have secured it. It will be the same every day this week. I opened the discussion with a talk lasting almost two hours, which was largely concerned with questions of strategy – a subject on which I don't feel exactly at home. But it went well and the people in my division, who were my initial target, are convinced. That is an important step because from now on I shall be putting forward not just my own view but that of my division. The next stage is to convince the [legal and economic] divisions of the OKW and then with luck my view will become that of the OKW as a whole.

13 November

This morning I have just given another lecture. Now it is 12 and there is a short midday pause. At 3 the fight starts again. I am dying to see how much I can put across. The worst thing that could have happened now seems unlikely to materialise, though that would be almost too good to be true. If so we shall at least have gained some time and secured a chance of being spared the worst.

16 November

I have been holding forth for three hours. I was thoroughly exhausted but seem to have put my case across. I am at any rate slowly getting into a position to torpedo one of the more deplorable measures. But a lot more work will still be needed.

At the beginning of October Halder told Groscurth that for some

---

* Bürkner and the chiefs of the other three *Abwehr* divisions who held a daily 'Situation conference' with Canaris and Oster.

time he had been taking a pistol with him whenever he was summoned to 'Emil' – as they called Hitler behind his back – but could never get around to using it. Brauchitsch, the Commander-in-Chief, was then needled by Halder and others into trying to tell Hitler on 5 November that an attack was unthinkable, but such was the tirade which this evoked that he collapsed into ignominious silence. It was bad weather, not rebellious generals, which led to 12 November being abandoned as the starting date. Before the new date arrived, two other things happened. On 8 November a disaffected carpenter, working as it would now seem completely on his own, came near to killing Hitler by planting a bomb in the Munich beer-hall where the Party gathered annually to celebrate the ignominious failure of their revolt in 1923; only the fact that Hitler had cut his speech unexpectedly short and gone off ahead of schedule to catch his train saved his life.[6] Next day two British agents, who had for some weeks been tricked into negotiating with disguised SD men in the belief that they were encouraging an army revolt, were kidnapped across the Dutch frontier at Venlo.[7] German propaganda then adroitly put responsibility for the Munich explosion at the door of the British Secret Service and two chains of activity which had in fact been entirely unconnected were linked together. The net effect was to make everyone more cautious. The date of the attack was again postponed, and more than once. Before it was finally put off until the New Year, Hitler on 22 November gave Brauchitsch and other military leaders such a series of harangues about his own ruthless determination and their defeatism that any remaining inclination which they may have had to action ebbed steadily away.

17 November

I slept miserably because for the time being I am too worked up about the possibility of heading off the catastrophe which seems to be impending. In the past few days this possibility has grown a bit and perhaps can be exploited. But it has driven all other ideas out of my head. I have got a few steps closer to my goal today. I can't, however, act myself but am limited to putting arguments to other people which induce them to act, with the result that each involves an indescribable effort.

20 November

I have to speak to a paper on Thursday (23).... The audience consists basically of the senior representatives of the ministries, along with several admirals and ambassadors. In other words, an exalted lot. It will be very comic.

25 November

Yesterday from dawn till well after dusk I spent fighting in a minority of 1 to 25 against a piece of wartime legislation. It was a beastly strain, especially as the rest of them quoted against me an order already issued by the Führer. [Presumably an early version of Instruction/*Weisung* No 9 laying down the guiding principles for the conduct of the war against England, which was finally issued on 29 November.] As a result the decision went against me. This morning I made representations to my chief [Bürkner] who gave me full support. On the strength of this I reopened the battle and by 2 p.m. had managed to shake a few people's views and get them to take the question up again with their ministers. As soon as that has been done, there is likely to be a fresh discussion either tonight or early tomorrow. Meanwhile I have been mobilising the lawyers in the other offices. None of them would ever have had the guts to revolt on their own, but they plucked up the necessary courage when they saw that I had my chief behind me so that we were backed by a senior officer. The position now is that I've succeeded in shaking people's convictions and hope as a result I can still prevail against the five and twenty.

27 November

Today I won my case. But it is like fighting a hydra. No sooner have I cut off one of the monster's heads than ten new ones grow. In any case I felt so rotten after the victory that I retired home and made myself a cup of tea.

28 November

After the hectic events of the last few days on which a final decision is to be taken today – the discussion with the Führer begins in an hour – I find dealing with normal affairs again rather an anticlimax.

The directive on economic warfare against England to which Hitler finally put his signature on 29 November was in much more general terms than those originally proposed by Raeder and connected this aspect of the war much more closely with the proposed land operations. The difference between the two documents is the measure of the success – or failure – achieved in the interval by Helmuth and his colleagues. England was described as the 'animator of the fighting spirit of the enemy' making her defeat essential to final victory. She was to be attacked with economic weapons which were to be employed in close conjunction with military ones. If the army were to succeed in defeating the Anglo-French armies in the field, and secure a sector of the coast opposite England, the task of the navy and air force to carry the war to English industry would become paramount.[8]

December had not gone far before Helmuth was engaged in a further battle, again with Bürkner's support. His principal opponent was the chief AA expert on economic matters, Ambassador Karl Ritter.* The nature of Ritter's activities can be guessed from a telegram which he sent to seventeen diplomatic missions on 6 December explaining that 150 neutral ships had by that date been detained and the number was increasing daily. As the legal justification for such detention was shaky, the AA was trying to avoid legal aspects in its diplomatic discussions of the subject, and was averse to any kind of systematic method of control, since that might easily make the release of the ships inevitable. The German objective was, by dint of procrastination and chicanery, to induce the various neutral exporters to agree not to supply goods to enemy states or to other neutrals.[9] Involved in this was an argument as to what was to happen when a neutral state allowed some of its ships to be chartered by the British. The AA proposed to regard all other ships of that state as eligible for seizure in reprisal. *Ausland/Abwehr* for the OKW argued that this was contrary to international law.[10]

9 December
Yesterday evening I won through third parties a victory over Ritter, who had to retreat in a pretty important matter in face of a concentrated attack from all sides. He just overplayed his hand.

10 December
Yesterday afternoon I had a message from Schuster to say that he had come round to my point of view in the matter on which I was putting up so much resistance. He was going to put it on the agenda again for the 11th when he wanted me to state my case once more. . . . This transfers the main burden of the battle from my shoulders to the Admiral's. He carries more weight but is more vulnerable because he has something to lose.

11 December
We had a meeting from 12.30 to 3.30 out of which I am glad to say that I emerged victorious. Ritter retreated with the remark that flexibility was just as important in economic warfare as in military. So I hope this chapter is now closed. We have gone straight on to open a new one in which I should be able to operate more successfully.

12 December
I am well but feeling lazy and indisposed to do anything before

* Head of Economic Department of AA 1934–7; Ambassador to Brazil 1937–8; Ambassador for special assignments and liaison officer with OKW 1939–45; Member of NSDAP; condemned to four years' imprisonment at Nuremberg 1949.

Christmas ... At that point my telephone rang and I was called to a meeting which is now at 6.30 only just over.... Ritter's second proposal has come to grief. But it meant the end of my peace and quiet and tomorrow I have another meeting at 10.30.

13 December

See what nice letters [from his grandparents] arrived today. Carl [Deichmann, who was spending much of his time in Holland] forwarded them from Cologne.... I've had a good day all round because my hopes for an early end to the war have been materially fostered. I am ready to bet that we will be celebrating Christmas 1940 in a post-war chaos.

17 December

I am now beginning to reap the first fruits of the seed which I planted in September and October. When I look back over the last few months, I feel I have never staved off so much evil or achieved so much good. It amazes me. And what is pleasant about it is that nobody will ever know about or notice it so that nobody will want to take counter-measures....

Today [a Sunday] is completely quiet. I shall work here in the office till 12 or possibly 2 or 3. Then I shall go home, have a meal, work, read, have a cup of tea, telephone to you, have supper and go to bed. The only human voice I shall hear during the entire day will be yours on the telephone. This is the kind of day I really treasure. One is left in peace for 36 hours on end and can't be disturbed. Curiously enough I can only enjoy such days if the weather is fine. If it is wet, they irritate me.

19 December

At the moment I am used as a sort of Reference Bureau on every conceivable aspect of English law.

20 December

Yesterday I suddenly got in a panic that something which I had managed to get held up – by omission rather than commission – would be settled while my back was turned. I thought I detected signs of my absence being deliberately exploited for that purpose. So I immediately set about drafting a minute on it to tie down at any rate my own division to my standpoint.

[This has been understood as referring to Raeder's proposals of mid-October, p. 101 above. But not only had the discussion on these been to a large extent decided by Hitler's Directive of 29 November; it is attaching altogether too much importance to Helmuth to suppose that he could hold up proposals made by the Naval C-in-C to the Führer for two and a half months by doing nothing about them! The reference may be to some item in those proposals which had not yet been dealt with.]

15 Waiting for the Attack
January–April 1940

A T Christmas Helmuth was in Kreisau but came back to Berlin on 5 January. With the New Year he began what was to be the most important of all his wartime friendships, for on 10 January he wrote:

> At midday I lunched with Peter Yorck, the brother of Davy [the wife of Hans Adolf von Moltke] – or rather, at his house. He lives out at the Botanic Garden in a house that is small but very well appointed. I believe we found ourselves very much in agreement and will see a lot of each other.

The backgrounds of the two were so similar that their failure to establish close relations earlier is surprising. Both bore names famous in Prussian military history, for in 1812 Field-Marshal Yorck von Wartenburg had started off the campaign, which led to the battle of Leipzig and the overthrow of Napoleon, by disregarding his king's commitments to the French and signing the Convention of Tauroggen with the Tsar. Both had family estates in Silesia. Klein-Oels had a bigger Schloss, a better soil and more land (7,500 acres) than Kreisau but Peter was only a second son and lived in a smaller house at Kauern. Born in 1904 he was Helmuth's senior by three years and had a more distinguished academic record. The family had a considerable reputation as progressive intellectuals and patrons of the arts, but had also ingrained in them the Prussian Lutheran belief that position and privilege carry with them an obligation to serve the community.

Peter Yorck had studied law at Bonn and taken his doctorate at Breslau.[1] He then became a civil servant, although at one stage he went on leave and worked in the Labour Service while this was still voluntary. In 1934 he had obtained the post of counsellor in the Breslau headquarters of the provincial government of Lower Silesia. The *Oberpräsident* at the time was Josef Wagner who, though a Party member and indeed *Gauleiter*, was a practising Catholic and distinctly moderate in his political views – or rather in the methods which he was prepared to use in advancing those views.* In October 1936, as part of the Four-Year Plan to make Germany self-sufficient in time of war,

---

* Wagner, Josef (b. 1899), *Gauleiter* of Silesia 1934–9. Price Commissioner 1936–41. Had a thrombosis (partly due to alcohol) 1942. Executed April 1945.

Wagner was made Reich Commissioner for Prices (a post previously held by Goerdeler). He brought Yorck to Berlin and gave him responsibility for organising a system of price-control offices throughout the country. Peter continued to work in the Price Control Office as long as Wagner held the job, although in August 1939 he was called up as a reserve lieutenant and served in the Polish campaign (in which one of his brothers was killed). As Wagner paid more attention to ability than to politics in his choice of staff, the office quickly became a stronghold of anti-Nazis, with Peter prominent among them, although, as their functions did not give them the same opportunities for action as were possessed by the *Abwehr*, it never acquired the same significance as an operational centre.

Peter was a considerate person who spoke slowly and preferred asking questions to giving answers. Although open-minded and distinctly progressive in his views, he was less ready than Helmuth to accept the confiscation of private property or the merging of Germany into Europe. His revulsion against National Socialism was shared by a number of friends with a similar background, such as Count Fritz Dietloff von der Schulenburg, Count Ulrich Wilhelm Schwerin von Schwanenfeld, Albrecht von Kessel and Count Conrad Uexküll. The Stauffenbergs were his cousins. The Gestapo were in due course to pin on this circle the label of 'Group of Counts'/*Grafengruppe*. For some months, Peter Yorck had been holding discussions with these friends much as Helmuth had been doing with his, and in due course he came to be the main link between the two. Helmuth should not, however, be regarded as a member of the counts group; most of them regarded him as lacking in loyalty both to his class and to his country and inclined to belittle him as a mere theorist. He for his part thought that they failed to realise the scale of the changes which would be brought about in Germany, and indeed throughout Europe, by the war.

Helmuth's next letter shows him engaged in the thankless task of trying to explain the English to the Germans.

17 January

I have been made very cross recently at the way people are tending to underestimate the English. As I think this underestimate might well prejudice the chances of peace, I want to counter it. What is more I am responsible for this attitude because I called attention to one or two English articles describing difficulties over there and circulated extracts.[2] The conclusion which I drew was that the English with their usual hard-headedness had spotted where the present economic trends could lead and that we must expect remedies to be adopted soon. Other people took the articles as signs of weakness on the ground that the English would never admit to weaknesses unless these had already got very serious. These people are quite blind. The silliest part of all is that the naval operations staff, who haven't had any success for a long time, are now telling themselves that these weaknesses are due to their efforts, which is a highly dangerous illusion.

Two days later he suggested in the HWK that, instead of remaining content with the purely negative aim of stopping the enemy's imports, they should try to exploit Germany's geographical position so as to make it a European clearing house and thereby deprive Britain of much of her trade with Eastern Europe.* This would not merely help the neutral countries and thereby win good-will for Germany but would also constitute a step towards a European economic community which he already regarded as an essential part of any post-war settlement. On 19 January he submitted a paper expanding this idea and suggesting that a committee be set up to pursue it.

> Such a system needs to be planned well in advance. Consequently we should not content ourselves with establishing that our transport facilities are for the time being stretched to capacity. What we really need to be asking is, what long-term measures must be taken in the field of transport if we are to make the most of our geographical position.[3]

He proposed the creation of a central agency to lay down transport policy in which the OKW would be represented as a vitally interested party. The policy, and the issue of the necessary documentation, would be carried out by German consulates abroad so as to enable trade to flow unimpeded through Germany from one country to another.

Meanwhile the question of an attack in the west continued to be the subject of argument. On 10 January two German air force officers, flying down to deliver the operational plans, lost their way in a fog and landed on the wrong side of the Belgian frontier. The consequences of this blunder were not as serious as might have been expected, for the enemy could not help suspecting it to be a deliberate exercise in strategic deception, while the alternative plans drawn up instead were in fact the ones which in May decided the campaign in Germany's favour. But the very need to work out something different, combined with a hard winter, meant a delay of several weeks. Helmuth's division was in the centre of things for, on the day after the mishap, Bürkner, though properly speaking not involved, spent two and a half hours with Hitler[4] and was lucky to get away unscathed.

---

* The reader is reminded that this is evidence not of anti-British feeling on Helmuth's part but of the expedients to which he was driven in order to get his superiors to pay attention to his proposals. See also below, p. 132.

23 January

The misfortune has now finally vanished. 'Finally' means for a considerable time, perhaps months. It is an enormous relief. Moreover and just to get us used to the continual switching from one extreme to the other, a very small silver streak has appeared on the horizon in the last three days. Very small but the first since September. I can't allow myself to hope but I am in the fortunate position of being able to help in a minor way to develop it.

[This probably refers to an attempt at bringing Army commanders in the west to the point of rejecting Hitler's orders. Their uneasiness about the operation which they were expected to embark on had been increased by the stories seeping through from Poland and elsewhere about excesses.]

25 January

Yesterday I spent the whole day working on a single subject in the OKW. That is the kind of thing I most enjoy. I had the precedents from the last war looked up and made a thorough job of it. At 5 I took it to the chief expecting him to take a quick look at it and give it his blessing. In any case I expected him to ring up the head of naval operations and make sure that nothing irrevocable would be done till we had had our say. And lo and behold, we intervened at the psychological moment! They were just on the point of putting their feet in it. So we let fly and succeeded in getting the brakes applied. That is always gratifying.

[Probably refers to some proposed measures of sea warfare disadvantageous to the neutrals.]

28 January

I am distinctly optimistic. There is no doubt that six intensely strenuous and exciting months lie ahead. But the prospects of everything turning out all right are better today than they ever have been since the war began. It looks as though the days when you were here last marked a turning point and that too on account of the events [the errant officers] about which I told you.

[Probably refers to various steps which were in train to bring pressure to bear on Brauchitsch. If so, the hope was ill-founded because ever since his encounters with Hitler in November, he was too intimidated to run any risks.]

Yesterday I had a long talk with Schuster at the Kieps'.* He was

* Kiep, Dr Otto (b. 1886, in Scotland). Consul-General in New York 1931–4 (in which capacity he attended a lunch in honour of Einstein). 1936–8, German representative on Non-Intervention Committee for Spanish Civil War. 1939–44, Liaison Officer between AA and OKW.

very nice to me. I gave him some advice. That was a thing which I had long had in mind but felt some hesitation about. It was advice about the way he ought to do his work. He was obviously pleased with it so I imagine I had encouraged an idea which he had had already. He told me always to put such suggestions forward to him and to go and see him whenever I had one. What could be more friendly?

29 January

Schuster asked me today if I would like to join him. I long to know if anything will come of this. A lot will depend on a meeting tomorrow in which my plan [of 19 January] is to be discussed. If they decide to go into it seriously, I will certainly be moved across and Schmitz will take over my work.

9 February

At 11 I had to go to a meeting with Schuster at which some pretty serious matters were ventilated [in connection with the Plan already mentioned]. At 2.30 there was another meeting at a high military level with me as the only participant who wasn't a general – which was pretty amusing. After that I had to brief Bürkner so that it was 5 before I was finished. I decided to go home and have some tea, wishing that you had still been there to share it. Now Fräulein Breslauer [his secretary] is due for some work and then I will devote the rest of the day to the tax return.

13 February

I started work with Schuster today and now I spend half the time here and half with Schmitz. The new job looks like providing considerable possibilities.... In any case I am now far more likely to be in on everything decisive than hitherto. For we are a staff of only five here, not counting Schuster, so will work much more closely together than in the big foreign division.

14 February

It is midnight and I have just got home.... At the moment I have four offices simultaneously and four secretaries!* ... It was a frantic day. But things will settle down slowly and get less strenuous. What makes it bad at the moment is the need not to fail Schuster when he wants me. After one or two months I shall know the tempo of work there, they will know my methods and then it won't be so important for me to be continually on hand.

15 February

It is remarkable to be all of a sudden in an office where one gets access to operational plans automatically and as a matter of course,

* The HWK, the *Abwehr*, the Institute and his private law office.

whereas previously one had difficulty in seeing them and then only bit by bit.

This improved access to military secrets was, however, a mixed blessing. Thanks to it he got early information about the plans for invading Denmark and Norway. He also seems to have learnt of the growing impatience of Brauchitsch and Halder with the *Widerstand*, illustrated by the removal of Groscurth from his post as liaison between army headquarters and *Abwehr* on 15 February.

> *18 February*
> I continue to be very disturbed. Last month's hopes have vanished and a lot of unsatisfactory things have developed instead. At the same time the stupidity at some of the top military levels cries aloud and is difficult to believe.

On 14 February a British reconnaissance plane spotted a German ship, the *Altmark*, sailing southward in Norwegian territorial waters. The *Altmark* had acted as a supply ship to the pocket battleship *Graf Spee* before that warship was cornered in the River Plate in the previous December. The British knew that the *Altmark* had aboard a number of British seamen, captured from the ships sunk by the *Graf Spee*, who were being taken to Germany as prisoners-of-war. The Norwegian authorities had failed to detect these and allowed the *Altmark* to go forward. On the night of 16–17 February the British destroyer *Cossack* entered Norwegian waters, attacked the *Altmark* and rescued the men. As can be imagined, this case involved a great deal of work for the international lawyers on both sides.

> *20 February*
> Today was another full day which is far from over yet. The *Altmark* took up a lot of our time but all questions of naval strategy in the spring and early summer involve a lot of work. So for the moment I am really up against it, as is Schmitz. I ate in the mess today which was foul. I only had some soup because everything else struck me as beneath contempt – at any rate in present conditions. In the afternoon we had a meeting, and when that ended soon after six I was famished and got myself some tea which I am still sipping. Einsiedel is due for supper afterwards. Tomorrow I have a fantastic programme: first of all, getting ready for a big meeting on Thursday afternoon, i.e. drawing up the agenda, drafting Schuster's speech and discussing both these opera with Weichold and Schuster. Secondly, a report for the foreign and economic branches of my division on the present position of trade warfare and on the practical objectives of such warfare; thirdly a talk to Schuster's staff as to how the *Altmark* case affects and is affected by international law. Each of these

deserves a day to itself and heaven only knows how I can cram them all and the current business on top into twenty-four hours.

21 February

I have got off surprisingly lightly. It is now half past five and I am already sitting at home having had tea.... Deuel comes about 8. My drafts for tomorrow's meeting were virtually accepted so that I didn't have to revise them, and my report on the situation over trade warfare has been put back till 2 o'clock tomorrow and my report on the *Altmark* reflected the conditions in which it was prepared.

22 February

I really have nothing to tell you. For nothing really has happened. One is waiting for the spring and the troubles it will bring. The chances of avoiding it grow steadily fewer and less likely. I have got to the point at which I can scarcely think of anything else. That is far from pleasant.

5 March

I believe less than ever in the attack on the west. But how can one break free from this immobility?

The outlook here is as grim as can be. The prospects for a change of direction which seemed to exist at the beginning of the year have now dwindled again. It is remarkable that I am still convinced, against all the evidence, that it won't go on for long. If I ask myself frankly why, I can't reply and yet I have a feeling that it is not just wishful thinking.

6 March

The meeting yesterday went splendidly and like clockwork. Whereas everyone had expected it would last between two and two-and-a-half hours, we were through in seventy minutes. I am very pleased that this first job of mine should have gone off so well, especially as the subject was, until recently, a terrible bone of contention.

7 March

There has been a big row today and I wonder whether they won't finally decide to throw me out. I was outvoted again in the big committee, deserted this time by Bürkner, over a question which in my opinion will have a quite decisive influence on Germany's position in the post-war world. As important as the Polish question* but in a different field.

* This may refer to either (a) the position of the SS in relation to the *Wehrmacht* in Poland, above, p. 100 or (b) the belligerent status of those Poles who, having escaped from their country, had joined the Polish forces being organised in France. The Nazis wished to treat them as *francs-tireurs* and shoot any who were captured.

After the meeting was over, I went to Weichold and said I had been left in a minority of I to X. But I had remained unconvinced and would like to exercise the right of every official to have my dissenting opinion recorded in the minutes. A big row. I was an officer and as such had no right but must simply obey. I said I was sorry but in this case a question of responsibility to history was involved and for me that had priority over the duty to obey orders. The matter was referred to the Admiral [Schuster] and after listening for five minutes he said he agreed with me. He obviously had felt like that all along but had been hesitating and my intransigence had given him courage. In the meeting he obviously couldn't say anything because it was his business to ascertain and record the views of other people and not put forward his own standpoint.

Result: the Admiral will certainly put the office's point of view forward officially but will have his own personal dissent recorded in the minutes and speak to these minutes in front of the Führer. That naturally removes the need for my disagreement to be put on record and I escape from the firing line. But whether the Admiral will survive this (figuratively speaking) I don't know.

8 March

Today I celebrated a great triumph. Yesterday's battle was joined again with all the top military brass mobilised. In the end Schuster succeeded in getting Keitel on my side and Keitel in turn succeeded in getting the Führer on to my side and at 6.30 there arrived the Führer's order containing my conclusions and my arguments.* It is a scandal for such a thing to be possible without the whole government coming to bits because in the long run it just won't do for one minister to sabotage the collective decision of all the others. But a terrible tragedy has been averted and in spite of everything I get satisfaction in thinking that many non-German wives have your husband to thank for the continued existence of their husbands. For this decision is in the last resort simply and solely that of your husband against all other ministries and against my own superiors! Isn't that pleasing? By the way, only five people know this – Schuster, Weichold, Bürkner, Tafel and Schmitz. So keep it to yourself.

---

* Extensive research has failed to identify this order. The most suggestive clues are that (a) on 28 February the HWK instituted an inter-departmental inquiry into the effects of an extension of the war into Norwegian and Swedish territorial waters as a result either of British or of German action (Doc W.I: MI 14/707 in Imperial War Museum Documents Centre). (b) Jodl recorded in his War Diary that on 7 March Hitler signed an order (*Weisung*) for the Norwegian operation which was not thereafter to be changed. But on 8 March he wanted special instructions (*Anordnungen*) about it to be cast in a different way (I.M.T., xxviii, p. 411).

E

12 March

Since Saturday I have been once again engaged in heavy fighting against a certain strategic plan. [Probably the attack on Scandinavia since this affected the HWK more directly than the attack on the west.] I gave them everything I've got, unfortunately without success. Tomorrow I will allow myself a break because I simply can't do anything more.... I am so tired I have pains in the head and there's no sense in that. Today I have thought out a new plan of campaign for taking up the matter again. But for that I must make certain people, including Bürkner, Schuster and Weichold, read an old essay by Schmitz. Thereby I shall gain a breathing-space and nothing more will happen till next week.

13 March

I talked to the Admiral [Schuster] for a long time today about the relationship between international law and strategy. He continues to listen in a very friendly way although I can't disguise the fact that I regard certain military measures as mistaken.

17 March

Today is a long peaceful day. That at any rate is what I am hoping for because it is still early. I got up slowly, washed a little, enjoyed a leisurely breakfast and listened to [Bach's] suite in B minor which I have become very fond of. Then I read the Bible again for a bit, an activity in which I take more pleasure than ever before. Previously I regarded it as so many stories, at any rate the Old Testament, but today it is all real. It holds my attention differently from before. Previously I used to be irritated over the space taken up by passages which didn't matter and the brevity of the passages which did. Today I realise that things which matter can either be said in a single sentence or not at all. Consequently if anyone tries to expand a passage which matters, it is a sure sign that he can't put it into words at all.

Freya was in Berlin for several weeks at the end of March, making letters unnecessary. The German invasion of Denmark and Norway began on 9 April.

13 April

Today sees the start of the process by which Denmark is to be gradually made like Poland. [This was not strictly speaking true. The Danish Government, after surrendering, remained in existence and its functions were not taken over by Germans until 1943.] I have done everything I could to prevent it, but the people who could have stopped it had sold the pass before I ever came to hear about it.

14 April

I went into the office this morning to find out how things were going. In the course of doing so I got into a discussion with Bürkner about the strategic aspects of the present operation. That took up an hour, more to his profit than mine.

I began by complaining that we are always told merely how an operation is to be conducted and never why it is to be conducted which is the really interesting thing, so that we are reduced to discovering the latter little-by-little. I have noticed this time after time. It seems to be a German characteristic to avoid answering the 'Why' of important questions and to push the 'How' to the front instead and to delight in answering that as well as possible. But this means continually disregarding the question whether the thing one is doing ought to be done at all. Germans seem to have a genius for tactics but to be hopeless at strategy.

When this defect is translated into military terms it means that these people get so obsessed over operations and victories that they lose sight of the goal, that the object of a war is in fact to win it. Instead of judging each problem by the test of whether its solution brings the winning of the war closer, they judge how the problem can best be solved. I have had the experience of seeming to wake someone out of a dream when I naïvely asked whether he thought that his suggestion was likely to help in winning the war. Schuster and Weichold are the only people whom I haven't so far detected making this mistake.

The northern operation is a case in point. I have by this time asked a whole row of people why we have occupied Norway. And not one has been able to give me a satisfactory answer. It was not just that their answer didn't satisfy me but that by the end of the conversations I always noticed that it didn't satisfy them either – or rather no longer satisfied them. The position is that for the moment I know a better answer than anyone else, but the possibility of this answer hasn't yet struck anybody because it involves certain preparations which haven't been made.

It was the discussion of this problem which took up my time with Bürkner. Then Canaris came in and we started from the beginning again. But in military matters Canaris' thinking is really very primitive.

[This is the first mention in Helmuth's letters of an actual meeting with Canaris although the head of a Department would hardly have embarked on a discussion of this kind with a subordinate whom he did not know. Canaris' secretary said that Helmuth did have a number of dealings with the Admiral, who trusted him – more than Helmuth, for the time being at any rate, seems to have trusted the Admiral! Halder reported that Canaris more than once praised Helmuth in his hearing.]

16 April

It is days since I read a newspaper. And today I was talking to a man whose judgment I highly respect but who gets his information from the papers. He had a picture of events which was the diametrical opposite of my own and I found his comments highly embarrassing.... What on earth can the papers be saying?

I am completely obsessed by recent events and even more by the expectation of further events. It seems to me that things are going to go much faster than I ever imagined and that a process is going to be compressed into the next half-year which in the normal way would take years, perhaps decades. I can't shake off the idea that I must go on thinking and planning in order to keep one jump ahead of events.

18 April

Last night I had a disturbing dream. I was sent on duty to Holland and had a free week-end. Whereupon I decided to go to London with an American passport belonging to a friend who otherwise did not figure in the dream. I got to London early on Saturday morning and went from Liverpool Street station to 5 Duke of York Street where I surprised Michael at his morning toilet. He had to go to his office and I went into the Temple and sat down in John Foster's room where I made various telephone calls and where a wide variety of friends and acquaintances came to see me. Lionel Curtis was unfortunately not in London. For some military reason or other I couldn't go to Oxford so he said he would come up. So we walked through London on a Sunday through the Parks which were already looking very springlike. C had grown rather fatter but was well and spry. For some unexplained reason I missed the evening train which would have got me back to the Hague in time for work on Monday. And with that an otherwise nice dream came to an unpleasant end. I found myself confronted with the need to choose between two alternatives – either to be shot in England as a spy or in Germany as a traitor.

[5 Duke of York Street was the address of the flat belonging to Lionel Curtis in which Helmuth had stayed in August–September 1938. M.B. started to rent it in February 1940. Soon afterwards he sent a letter to Helmuth through an address in Holland (probably that of his brother-in-law Carl) in which he told him this among other personal and family news.]

The army, in the light of what had happened in Poland, had demanded that all Germans in Norway, including the police, should come under its orders. Hitler began by making difficulties, then agreed and then on 19 April appointed Terboven *Reich* Commissioner, adding a higher SS and police leader to his staff a few days later.

22 April

Today was another terrible day because we are now starting to behave in Norway as we did in Poland. It is terrible. The SS have been sent in and you will soon see in the papers the organisational changes which have been decided on. And the soldiers agree to it all. I am terribly depressed.

On 25/26 April Helmuth went to Hamburg to attend a session of the Prize Court. He was dissatisfied with its judgments, one of which he declared to be 'completely and unquestionably wrong'. Perhaps the most interesting point about the journey was that he made it in company with Berthold von Stauffenberg, the elder brother of Claus and cousin of Peter Yorck, whom he had heard of at the Hague five years earlier.* Berthold was now working in the naval headquarters as adviser on questions of maritime international law, and was therefore a close colleague of Helmuth. Their general attitude to affairs must have been very similar and Berthold too used his position to relieve the sufferings of men who would never hear of him by name. But he was a gentle and lonely character, lacking somewhat in drive, whose real heart was in the world of the arts. Like his brothers he was a Catholic and a disciple of the poet Stefan George,† who had made him his heir. Helmuth, who found the poetry of his friend Erich Kästner‡ more to his taste than that of George, was not the person to appreciate this background and, though he and Berthold liked and respected one another, they never became close friends.

* Above, p. 66.
† George, Stefan (1868–1933), symbolist poet who sought to develop among the youth of Germany a new nobility of spiritual beauty and to transform life through art. Withdrew to Switzerland to escape Nazi patronage.
‡ Kästner, Erich (b. 1899), satirical poet, novelist and children's author. Books forbidden in Third *Reich*.

16 The Crisis of Confidence
May–June 1940

HELMUTH spent the first three weeks of May at Kreisau, taking his first real holiday since the war began. Consequently he was out of the office when the western campaign began on 10 May, and by the time he got back ten days later the Dutch had capitulated, the vital break-through in the Ardennes had taken place and the German armour was racing to the Channel.

These events and their sequels produced a major mental crisis, as is evident not merely from the letters written at the time but even more from others written during the succeeding eight months, when he blamed himself bitterly for having been so upset by day-to-day devel-opments. On 19 May he wrote (from Breslau) that 'the main object of my work has disappeared'. On 21 May he described himself, in a fine mixture of metaphors, as 'threshing straw in a siding'.

> Everything that I could have been doing has been overtaken by events.... For the moment I prefer to do nothing because I see nothing useful to do. Everything is in flux and in a few days, weeks, months all one's basic assumptions will be turned upside down.

> *25 May*
> I have done practically no work at all again today ... I have never before known myself be made physically ill by merely having to look on at an external situation.... At times I am unable to eat, at times I feel about to be sick, at times I suffer from collywobbles. [He did in fact go to see a doctor.]

He was not the only person in Western Europe who felt in those days that the foundations of their world were collapsing. For the German *Widerstand* as a whole, however, the outlook must have been almost more disillusioning than it was in the countries which were being over-run. For Helmuth in particular the situation was even worse in that he, unlike a number of his more nationally minded friends, had never seen any good whatever in Hitler. And while he had never believed that the Third *Reich* would be as transitory a phenomenon as the cabinets of the Weimar Republic, only in his most pessimistic moments had he thought of it as likely to outlast his own life. Yet he and the rest of them had

had to watch their sources of hope disappear one after another. Communists, Socialists, Protestants, Catholics had all been trampled into impotence. The leaders of the armed forces had lacked the nerve to act even when they believed Hitler to be leading Germany to ruin, and now his glittering victories seemed to be proving their hesitations justified. Hitler had long been scornful of the pessimists in the army high command and in his triumph showed his scorn by disregarding them. 'Nothing, or virtually nothing, is happening in the office,' wrote Helmuth on 29 May. 'Nobody listens to us any more and we merely discover every now and then what is going on.' During the last two years, as it grew clear that an internal revolution was almost out of the question, the great hope had been that the other nations of the world would act to restore civilised government in Germany. But they had proved as divided and susceptible to Hitler's exploitation as his internal opponents had done. Now they had been shown to lack even the necessary military strength (though historians will for long argue as to whether they lacked the strength because they lacked the will, or whether their lack of will was due to awareness of inadequate strength).

All this evidence therefore seemed to suggest that the Third *Reich* would last, if not quite for the thousand years about which it boasted, at any rate for the indefinite future. Action to counter it or reduce its cruelty must have seemed both impracticable and pointless. Those who were not prepared to fall into line behind the leader had to face exclusion from meaningful activity, from the earning of a livelihood, even from life itself. Moreover this development was bound to raise in many people's minds questions about the morality of the universe and the whole purpose of existence. If evil could thus get enthroned in high places, was there any valid reason for being good?

Several things combined to make Helmuth's cup particularly bitter. One was the failure to come to supper of a friend working for the Confessing Church;* efforts to discover the reason led to the news that the man had committed suicide.† Another was the revival of interest in the plan which he had proposed in January for exploiting Germany's geographical position to develop trade between European countries.

24 May

We can now dictate where I wanted to plan.... It was heart-rending to watch the scheme which I intended to promote co-operation after the war now being misused to bleed the conquered. The

---

* The organisation set up in 1934 by those Protestant pastors such as Bishop Wurm and Pastor Niemöller who were not prepared to accept the measures proposed by the men put by Hitler at the head of the Protestant Church.
† This was not actually true. He had simulated suicide and escaped to Holland, only to be caught there later and sent to Buchenwald concentration camp where he died.

arguments to which nobody would listen when I used them four months ago are now quoted to me on all sides as the height of wisdom, and the Führer's very letter to the King of Sweden has a whole paragraph devoted to this subject with a sentence taken out of one of my papers. Thus the project is being corrupted by the power which now stands behind it. If the war were to end, it could never be used again because it would be compromised. It is as though one had designed a house for a lot of guests and carted the building materials to the site. But, at the very moment when the guests arrive to inspect the house, the workmen use the materials to throw at them. It drives one desperate.

A third source of frustration was the brilliant summer weather. This would anyhow have made Helmuth want to get out of the city to Kreisau, but now when things were going wrong he longed more than ever to escape to the peace of his home and the relative good order of his estate. This attitude was to remain with him almost to the end. Through the remaining years his letters are full of references to Kreisau, speculation as to what was going on there, instructions and suggestions as to what needed to be done. In June Freya acquired some bees, whose well-being immediately became a major concern of Helmuth's so that the reader who wants to learn from the letters about the progress of affairs in Berlin finds himself continually diverted into apiculture! But, as will appear later, the bees have a vital part to play in the story. And those who have had to work for long hours at a desk will know the relief and stimulus which can be provided by being able to turn the mind to something completely different and more congenial, with the ultimate prospect of being able, by ending the work in hand, to devote one's full time to one's distraction at some distant date. For some people it is birds; for some, music; for others, the classics; for many, including Helmuth, it is a home or garden in a loved countryside. In his case where the strain included a permanent element of physical risk, the need for relief must have been all the greater.

Yet, although he told Freya that he thought of Kreisau as a haven of refuge, particularly for her, he realised the danger of allowing himself to escape from reality.

25 May

I turn everyone whom I see into a distraction with the result that I never get finished. Kreisau and everything about it, lovely and lovable as it is, is equally a distraction and I have got to get the better of this affair.

By the beginning of June he was struggling through towards a balance. Freya had refused to listen to news bulletins and been accused by her mother of sticking her head in the sand. She asked Helmuth for his view.

1 June

Instead of averting our eyes from the thing we find repellent, we have a duty to analyse it and synthesise it into a wider picture, thereby enabling ourselves to make sure of it. Anyone who does look the other way, because he lacks either the capacity to recognise it for what it is, or the strength of mind to rise above it, certainly is sticking his head in the sand. What is unimportant is whether one gets to know about individual details, or discusses them or learns about them, on Thursday rather than Friday. On the contrary the effort to know about them makes one attach much too much importance to them and thereby overlook the really important task which is to sublimate these facts and get them into perspective. If one chases after the details one no longer has the strength to rise above them. The ability to do so is undeniably greater in a peaceful atmosphere than in a tense one and anyone who is able to disseminate this peaceful atmosphere is helping others and encouraging them in the right direction. Peace is not the same thing as *complacency*. Anyone who for the sake of peace and quiet calls black white and evil good certainly doesn't deserve peace and really is sticking his head in the sand. But someone who never for an instant forgets what good and evil are, no matter how complete the triumph of the evil may seem to be, has taken the first step towards overcoming the evil. That is why a peaceful atmosphere is enormously important and must not be put at risk.

It is odd that I should be writing to you like this at the very moment when I can't do anything right myself. But perhaps that is precisely why I see the need so clearly. I hope I shall have recovered my balance by [the time you come on] the 8th. But you must stand up for the methods by which you have kept the Berghaus so peaceful and make no compromise in this field.

I have just picked up a book on the History of Philosophy[1] which contains the following dedication:

> *To my wife*
> *Grow strong, my comrade, that you may stand*
> *Unshaken when I fall; that I may know*
> *The shattered fragments of my song will come*
> *At last to finer melody in you:*
> *That I may tell my heart that you begin*
> *Where passing I leave off, and fathom more.*

In his fight for sublimation, Helmuth availed himself of two therapeutic tools. In the first place he started to read widely. The first book he mentions is a life of his distant relative Charles XII* – presumably Voltaire's – but later we find him at Spinoza, Kant, Freiherr vom Stein and Tolstoy. Those who are not philosophers may be relieved to know that even his powerful mind found Kant hard going.

George Kennan has described seeing him immersed in the study of *The Federalist*, which F. S. Oliver had taught Lionel Curtis to venerate.†

> The picture of this scion of a famous Prussian military family, himself employed by the German general staff in the midst of a great world war, hiding himself away and turning, in all humility, to the works of some of the Founding Fathers of our own democracy for ideas as to how Germany might be led out of its existing corruption and bewilderment has never left me.[2]

He had frequent recourse to Curtis's *Civitas Dei*. All this was not accidental. It was part of an attempt to think matters of political and economic organisation through to first principles with a view to answering the question 'If we were ever to have a clean slate, what kind of a society would we start establishing in Germany?' These questions may have been under discussion already[3] but Helmuth now turned to them with a new intensity. And if one of his reasons, perhaps only in part recognised, was to keep his balance by diverting his mind, by trying to see Nazism in perspective, it was out of this process that there arose the activity which was to preoccupy him for the next four years and ultimately cause his death.

Nor should the process be regarded merely as a means of therapy. It was a profession of faith, an affirmation – or rather, a re-affirmation – of the belief that, although National Socialism might reveal the depths of which human nature is capable, it yet ran so counter to the other higher elements in human nature that it *could* not last indefinitely, that there was bound to come a time when rebuilding would be both possible and necessary. Those who reflect on European history would do well to remember that at the darkest hour, when the occupied countries were still stunned by the blow which had hit them, there were men in Germany prepared to make a profession of this kind.

On 16 June (six days before the French Armistice) he wrote a letter to Horst von Einsiedel whom he had known ever since the Waldenburg days and whom he had been meeting fairly regularly during the winter.‡ On 17 June he wrote a parallel letter to Peter Yorck. The opening paragraphs of both give a clear idea of their purpose.

* Above, p. 1.
† Above, p. 68.
‡ When Einsiedel came to England in the autumn of 1937, Helmuth gave him introductions to several friends, including M.B.

Dear Einsiedel.

We failed to reach clarity on a number of subjects because we thought that events would come to our aid [probably in the sense that Hitler would be removed by force] and allow us to try out in practice points which we had failed to think out rightly or perhaps were incapable of thinking out rightly.* Today the situation has altered. Events are not going to come to our aid and we shall only be able to master them after we have reached clarity about them and got the better of them inwardly. We are still as far away from the turning point as Voltaire was from the French Revolution when he adopted the practice of ending his letters with the words: *écrasez l'infame*. What a long way it must have seemed to him then and what a short way it seems to us today, the distance separating mental conviction from practical execution. We must console ourselves with this reflection and start to think afresh.

I have a lot of questions about the organisation or planning of the economy which I would much like to put to you, for answer at your convenience. First of all I think there is a danger of a planned economy assuming a position in human affairs which has all the disadvantages of an idolised state and yet will be appraised solely from the standpoint of its material advantages. How can such a danger be avoided?

[He then went on to lay down four fundamental principles with regard to economic affairs on which he invited Einsiedel's criticism. The text of these will be found on pp. 290–1 of Dr van Roon's book.]

Dear Yorck,

We must today reckon with having to live through a triumph of evil and, whereas we had steeled ourselves to face any amount of pain and misery, must now prepare to do something which is far worse, namely keep our heads above water amid a flood of public good-fortune, self-satisfaction and prosperity. This makes it more important than ever to be clear in our minds about the basic principles of a positive doctrine of politics. I want to use this letter as a contribution to that process of clarification – in my head rather than yours! – and to link it with a conversation which I had with you and Schulenburg not quite a fortnight ago.

You will perhaps recollect the wager. Schulenburg was ready to bet that within ten years a state would have come into existence of which we could fully approve. I was ready to maintain the opposite of this proposition. We went on to the question of defining such a

* This is clear evidence that discussions had been going on during previous months.

state and I proposed as a criterion that of justice,* so that Schulenburg would have won his bet if within ten years we had as just a state
as the imperfections of human nature allow.

That left us with the problem of defining justice and we agreed
that justice consisted in the ability of the individual to expand and
develop himself within the framework of the state as a whole.

The next stage in this discussion and the one with which I want to
link up was reached when you said you wanted to impose a heavy
mortgage [i.e. limitation] on this ability of the individual, and I
replied that I thought enough allowance had been made for your
reservations, at any rate as far as our wager was concerned, by including the words 'within the framework of the state as a whole'.

[What Yorck seems to have been saying, in English terms, was that,
once the individual was thought of as possessing a right to so much
freedom, the state was in danger of anarchy. Helmuth was arguing that
the individual's right carried with it the duty to serve the community
and that this was an adequate safeguard against anarchy.]

At that point we broke off the discussion. I would like to start
from here and discuss with you the nature and range of this 'mortgage', for therein lies one of the most important and fundamental
questions of political reconstruction and we ought not to leave the
matter as we did in our conversation.

[He then went on to lay down three fundamental principles about
political theory on which he sought Yorck's comments. The text of
them will be found on pp. 291–3 of Dr van Roon's book.]

The scale and purpose of the present book would be upset if any
attempt were made to trace in detail the steps by which the thought of
Helmuth and his friends developed from this first rather amateur
formulation to the much more elaborate, though still incomplete shape
which it had assumed three years later. In any case the full texts of
these, as of all the more important surviving documents, are available in
Dr van Roon's book. All that therefore will be attempted here is to
record the chronology in outline and then to give at an appropriate
point† an outline of the position which was finally reached.

Peter Yorck replied on 7 July, questioning whether it was right to
describe the German victory without reserve as 'the triumph of evil'.
'Even if – as I hope – we are today living through the sensational end of

---

* 'Justice' is an inadequate translation of the German word used, *Gerechtig-
keit*, because the German *Recht* means both 'right conduct' (as opposed to
evil) and Law, so that Rightness means both 'Morality' and 'Legality'. It is
the *Dikaiosune* of Plato's *Republic*.
† Below, Chapter 24, pp. 237–57.

an epoch, we must not overlook the seeds which will enable new life to spring up out of the ruins.' Helmuth's answer of 12 July opened as follows:

I want to begin by answering your first point about the current situation.

Throughout my adult life I have worked with people of other nations and have in particular tried quite systematically since 1935 to help the 'new forces' in England to get their way in face of the dominance of the last generation but one (the last having practically vanished in the World War). I did this because I believed that only if this new generation came to power in Great Britain could war be prevented. I remain therefore of the opinion that this contact with these men must be re-established as soon as possible.

This holds good for all collaboration in intellectual fields. But it does not in my view apply to political reality.

[He then goes on to develop the difference,[4] adding that the people who had caused the old order to collapse were incapable of creating a new one.]

He sent further letters to Yorck and Einsiedel on 15 July. Yorck then sent him a paper by an unnamed author on 'The Image of the Western State' which he returned on 21 July with an explanation as to why he found it unconvincing. They met on 20 July and 23 August and between 16 and 19 August the Yorcks, Einsiedel and Waetjen paid a week-end visit to Kreisau at which the various questions received a good airing (though it would be quite wrong to regard the occasion as a formal conference).[5] He wrote again to Yorck on 1 September and later in that month spent some days with Freya at Kauern on a visit which again was primarily social. Meanwhile Dr Otto von der Gablentz had written to Helmuth on 9 August, in answer to a letter which has not survived (or possibly a conversation), about the basis for public morality. A reply of 31 August produced another letter of 7 September.[6]

All through these exchanges, the initiative was coming from Helmuth himself – as he said, it was his own head that he was trying to clear! – and it was he who on 20 October completed the drafting of an eight-page document 'On the Foundations of Political Theory' which reaps the harvest of this first period.[7] He discussed it with Einsiedel and Gablentz on 9 November and with Yorck next day, after which he wrote further letters to Yorck and Gablentz on 16 November, seeking to remove such differences as remained between them.*

In addition Dr Fritz Christiansen-Weniger† has put it on record that

---

* But see p. 159 below.
† Christiansen-Weniger had recently returned from Turkey.

he attended a discussion on agriculture during this summer and Baron Hans Christoph von Stauffenberg has also recorded[8] that he was asked by Helmuth about this time to write a paper on the relations of the United Kingdom to the Commonwealth but after reflection replied that he did not feel competent to do so. Adam von Trott, who had only got back from America (via Siberia) in March, had then fallen ill and thereafter married, came to see Helmuth on 27 May and 11 September but these calls seem to have been merely for a general exchange of views. Hans Peters was also present on 27 May and Adolf Reichwein came on 28 June and 20 August. Fritzi Schulenburg, who made the original wager, was away with his regiment from 7 June so that he inevitably dropped out of the picture.

* Stauffenberg was now working in the *Auslandsabteilung* of the *Abwehr*.

17 Keeping a Head above Water
July–December 1940

H E L M U T H continued to work with varying intensity in the *Abwehr* and HWK. But his letters no longer give the impression that he felt this to be a sphere in which something important could be achieved. Hitler could, and would, do what he wanted and, as long as the German armies went on being successful, there was little prospect of getting the war fought or conquered territories governed in a different way. As Helmuth put it on 30 June, he was 'living without expectations, doing more watching than acting'. The most that could be hoped for was to prevent or reverse individual acts of cruelty and injustice – *in Detail Unglück zu verhüten.*

At the end of May Schuster was appointed naval Commander-in-Chief in France and was succeeded by Admiral Groos, who was said to be 'a very nice educated man, primarily a historian'.* Soon afterwards Weichold was sent to take charge of the naval liaison staff in Italy and was not replaced. By 21 August Helmuth was writing that

> I had a long conversation today with Groos over the basic principles of naval strategy. I am pretty critical of our Naval leadership and absolutely furious with the AA, which keeps on indulging in exaggerated ideas of what the navy and air force can achieve at sea. Their swans always turn out geese. I am at loggerheads with them again and unfortunately have Groos on my side. The 'unfortunate' bit of it is that G has completely swallowed my proposals and is no longer regarded by the AA as an arbiter but as a party to the case.

[On 17 August neutrals had been warned of a major extension into the Atlantic of the area in which their shipping would be at risk. The dispute with the AA may have concerned the implementation of this.]

The general impression which emerges, however, is that from now on the HWK lost steadily in importance.

---

* b. 1882. Wrote in 1929 *'Seekriegslehren im Lichte des Weltkrieges'*, D.Phil. hon. caus. Bonn. 1932–8, Chief of *Marinekommandoamt*. In 1940 wrote a book on *'Die Grenzen der britischen Seemacht'*. Head HWK June 1940–4. From February 1941 Chairman of Military Committee of Three-Power (Axis) Pact.

With the *Abwehr* things were different. At the end of June Helmuth and Schmitz had to argue fiercely in a meeting of the Academy for German Law over a memorandum of Himmler's about the treatment of the Poles in the occupied territories.

27 June

Some of the views advanced were really unbelievable.... It was simply awful. Alas Schmitz and I could cut no ice but at least we didn't let the case go by default.

Five days later they

put up a great fight against the Slave Trade, i.e. the trade in people whom we propose to hand over to others in order to get reciprocal favours from them.

About this time there was a proposal to send him to Wiesbaden to join in the French Armistice negotiations and the preparations for the Peace Treaty which was never to be concluded. It did not come to anything because he insisted on being the only lawyer representing the armed forces and this condition the authorities were not prepared to accept. In any case he had no desire to leave Berlin where he had got involved in a number of minor jobs (not to mention the 'mind-clearing' operation) and from which Kreisau was more accessible than it would have been from Wiesbaden. His tactics all along had therefore been to get the right conditions for the post and then turn it over to Schmitz.

In the background, however, was a more fundamental plan.[1] Reference has already been made to the inadequacy of traditional international law under conditions of total warfare and to the dilemma in which this placed German international lawyers.* On 20 June 1940 Helmuth and Schmitz drafted for General Keitel a memorandum which began:

The moment when peace is being re-established provides an opportunity to obtain the recognition of all States for our interpretation of the fundamental principles of the laws of war. The validity of this interpretation has been borne out by the present war and the proposed step, which would have to take into account the changes brought about by the peace, would lead to them being accepted as generally binding. This could be brought about by a joint declaration of all belligerent states and important neutrals about the principles of law in the fields of sea warfare, air warfare, land warfare, economic warfare and neutrality.

The memorandum went on to argue that, by taking the proposed initiative, Germany would secure the sympathy of all neutrals not

* Above, p. 99.

already friendly. This would be a logical extension of the effort, which Germany had been making ever since the outbreak of war, to undermine the British viewpoint about the rights of a belligerent in command of the seas. The OKW was therefore invited to entrust to an expert committee the drawing up of a programme of work, on the basis of which final proposals would be formulated by the Gladisch Committee for the Laws of War, which was affiliated to the OKW and contained representatives of the three services, the AA and the Ministry of Justice.

Keitel, by now a field-marshal, had already approved the idea of Helmuth and Schmitz being given a free hand to work on questions of international law in preparation for a Peace Conference. He now agreed to a committee being set up to include Helmuth, Schmitz and Berthold von Stauffenberg with as chairman Admiral Gladisch, a friend of Canaris who had been C-in-C of the Navy until 1933 and was one of the trustees of the Institute for Foreign Public Law and International Law. The operation was to be kept as quiet as possible so as not to arouse hostility in high places. At a meeting in Gladisch's room on 30 August the starting point assumed for the work was described as follows:

> Germany heads a group of European States to which England does not belong. The strength of England's position lies in a transatlantic alliance with the U.S.A. Germany controls colonies in Africa and possesses naval bases in the Atlantic as well as an adequate navy and mercantile marine (navy in the proportion *second to one* [sic]). Germany's enemies are assumed to be, firstly the transatlantic alliance, secondly Russia and thirdly Japan. This situation makes it appropriate to start with the laws of sea warfare.

The committee held its first formal meeting on 7 September at which Gladisch spoke on lines already described. Helmuth was in Kreisau when the second meeting took place on 30 September but contributed a paper about the importance of formulating laws for economic warfare. He created some consternation, even among people who were generally sympathetic, by the rigour with which he pointed out the logical implications of proposing principles of warfare simply because they happened to suit Germany. His proposals were sidetracked, and instead the committee decided to draw up lists of the most important problems in the fields of land, sea and air war and neutrality.

When the list relating to the sea was discussed on 8 October, Helmuth pressed for the abolition of the right of seizure and of contraband, while in relation to land war he stressed how important it would be to settle by, or soon after, the end of the war the question of the use and training of coloured troops. He personally supported the English point of view which was that, as the states outside Africa were to become self-governing, they must be allowed to train armed forces but that, as there was no intention of extending self-government to Africa, such training in that continent constituted an unmitigated danger.

When the committee turned to discuss the rights of an occupying power, its minutes contain a fascinating passage:

> Count Moltke said that the rules of land warfare were based on the idea of private property. This was out of date.
>
> The chairman asked whether that statement was universally valid.
>
> Count Moltke thought that it could be applied to all European states. This would be even more the case after the present war, and that would be true of America as well. The basic organisation of the occupied territory must be maintained. Large factories should not be dismantled. Trade secrets should not be extracted. When seen in the context of the total duration of a war, the factories making specific goods in Belgium and France, which were in process of being dismantled, fulfilled a purpose in the economy of those countries which was of benefit to the occupying power. If they ceased to function, the result was unemployment and discontent. To counteract this the employees were brought to work in Germany. The result of this was that a man who had been in Belgium a skilled machinist for a particular job did something quite different when he got to Germany, was separated from his family and as a result dissatisfied. By contrast we should have done much better from an economic point of view if we had left the factories where they were. To have done so might have involved a short-term disadvantage but we should undoubtedly have gained in the long run.*
>
> The Chairman did not think that this topic was relevant to the laws of war.[2]

At the next meeting Helmuth got his way about the separate treatment of economic warfare. But perhaps the most important point which he and Schmitz made was that the section of international law most affected by technical developments was that concerning neutrality. Helmuth at one point asked whether it was consistent with the principles of neutrality for a belligerent to exert pressure on a neutral to adapt its own economy to suit the belligerent's way of waging economic war. As belligerents did not want to increase the number of their enemies, they must be interested in enabling as many states as possible to preserve neutrality, and this they could best do by respecting it themselves.

---

* Three years later similar views were to be expressed by no less a person than Speer as Minister of Armaments and Munitions: see A. Speer, *Inside the Third Reich*, pp. 309–11.

Such a conclusion was hardly the sort of thing which one would expect to emanate from Nazi Germany – and this is perhaps the chief interest of the whole operation, for with the prolongation of the war and the dwindling prospects of Germany being able to impose her will on anybody, it gradually ran into the sand. In this connection a remark made by Helmuth to Hans Peters is illuminating:

> An interdepartmental group of officials and officers has been formed with the full approval of the OKW ostensibly to formulate the wishes of the armed forces in the event of final victory: in reality one is trying to discuss, under a cloak of legality, what should be done when the National-Socialist régime ends.[3]

It was a technique which was to be used more than once in the *Widerstand*, notably by Oster and then Claus von Stauffenberg in working out, ostensibly as a plan for action in the event of a rising by the SS or foreign workers, the details of the *coup d'état* against Hitler (Operation Valkyrie). The Committee submitted a preliminary report on 3 December and on 19 February 1941 was authorised by Canaris to pursue its discussions.

In August the office routine and the tension of waiting for the attack on Britain was interrupted by a six-day trip to Belgium and France which Helmuth made in company with his friend Otto Kiep, with Kiep's superior Dr Ernst Woermann, the head of the Political Department of the AA and with a Major Count von Schlieffen who was also working in the *Abteilung Ausland*.* Before the excursion began, Helmuth told Freya it was going to be 'a kind of joy-ride/*Festfahrt*'. He presumably owed his presence on it to his acquaintance with Kiep who may have chosen to include some of his own friends in an outing which he was ordered to arrange for his chief. Schlieffen's presence almost suggests that the scions of the two most famous Chiefs of the General Staff were being taken to see what the current generation had achieved (or more accurately what had been achieved by a civilian Führer in spite of them!). There is not space to quote Helmuth's fourteen-page record of the trip in full, especially as much of it is merely concerned with describing things seen, but some passages are of wider interest.[4]

---

* Woermann, Dr Ernst (b. 1888), was Chief of International Law Dept of AA 1932–5; Chief of European Section of Political Dept 1936; Counsellor in London 1936–8; Head of Political Division 1938–43. He was then sent to Nanking as ambassador. The latter move (according to Hassell, *Vom anderen Deutschland* p. 312) was due to Ribbentrop's animosity against career diplomats but Hassell also expresses a poor opinion of W.'s capacities. He was condemned to seven years' imprisonment at Nuremberg 1949.

Major von Schlieffen was probably Count Karl Wilhelm von Schlieffen (b. 1888), killed in action 1945. If so, he belonged to a different branch of the family from the Chief of Staff.

The party left Berlin by car at six o'clock on the morning of 7 August and travelled via Cologne and through the Eifel to Spa and Liège.

8 August

The picture was that of a peaceful landscape into which somebody had at intervals blindly pushed his fist without rhyme or reason. A better way of describing it might be to say that at every seven leagues a boot had come down.

After inspecting the forts at Liège they went on to Brussels.

Totalitarian war seems to be very like totalitarian politics. The material resources are left intact and the human beings destroyed. One notices that everywhere. If it were the other way round, the human beings, whose capacity for thought largely depends upon what they can perceive, would realise what they were up against and how to protect themselves. But as things are, the damage which they suffer internally is not reflected at all in their surroundings or in the concrete factual world. The process thus exceeds their capacity to understand it and they do not know how to fight it or how to rebuild.

The other thing which made the journey from Liège to Brussels extraordinarily interesting was the farming methods. I have never seen fields to match them and doubt into the bargain whether such fields could exist in Germany. For fields of that kind are only possible where there is a high-quality labour-force and our present policies are never going to achieve that.

At Brussels they were put up in the best hotel and much impressed by the outward appearance of the city, which Helmuth had not visited before.

To our eyes the shops give the impression of being full to bursting with luxuries. But, if one looks more closely, one notices that the back shelves are completely empty and that the lavishness is superficial. It is like a hive without many bees; only the front combs are filled with honey, the majority are empty. The way our people are buying things up is shameless. Not merely the officers but the rank and file as well act on the principle of devil-take-the-hindmost and that in a land which is facing a scarcity of food and other supplies hitherto unknown in Western Europe. There are two forms of German purchasing which are particularly objectionable. One consists of tours by Rhineland housewives run by the 'Strength through Joy' organisation (and heaven only knows how the tickets are distributed!), the other buying by officers with bags and briefcases. This in particular has caused bad feeling and has been stopped. But there is not much left....

We had a fantastic dinner [with the Commanding Officer, General von Falkenhausen*] in a restaurant in a park: caviare, ham in burgundy, duck, crêpes. The drink was obviously out of this world; vodka, a claret 'Enfant Jésus', champagne and armagnac. I didn't touch any of it but the others seemed blissfully happy. Afterwards at about 11.30 we went back to Falkenhausen's hotel, where whisky and beer were laid on. Woermann was thoroughly tight and most of the rest, including Kiep, distinctly jolly so that the only people really sober were Falkenhausen and myself and for most of the time between 11.30 and 1.30 we entertained one another. I welcomed this because at dinner I was inevitably too far away to talk to him.

The conversation at dinner was mediocre.... I was anyhow irritated by being offered such a lavish meal in a country on the verge of starvation, and this bothered me because I didn't want to be rude and yet didn't want to seem to be giving the proceedings my blessing. But I got over this in view of other people's behaviour, with the result that the two hours with Falkenhausen when alcohol had rendered the others *hors de combat* were very pleasant. He is an outstanding and courageous man and we talked freely about Belgium's economic situation, the German plundering and its economic and political consequences. In the end he told me how far he was prepared to play along and the points beyond which he wouldn't go.... The man is concerned with human beings, not with any *gloire* or *grandeur*. He is obviously seriously worried that we are behaving again as we did before and cannot restrain ourselves. One remark of his which sticks in my mind was 'when colleagues of mine come through, I tell them, "Your job is to destroy as quickly and as completely as possible and you get honoured and decorated for doing it. My job is to repair as quickly and completely as possible but by comparison with your activities, that is a very slow process which brings no public recognition." '

[On getting back to Berlin, Helmuth told Wally Deuel of the attempts he had made to convince Falkenhausen that he was accountable both morally and under international law for the Party's treatment of Belgium and the Belgians. The general was horrified at the thought that anyone would blame him for what the SS and other party elements were doing. He was only a simple soldier fighting for his country and was in no way responsible for the behaviour of the party.][5]

* Falkenhausen, General Alexander von (b. 1878), 1934–9, Military Adviser to Chiang Kai-shek. 1939, GOC Wehrkreis IV (Dresden). 1940–4, Military Commander, Belgium. Dismissed just prior to 20 July 1944 and subsequently to that date arrested. Taken from Flossenbürg towards Italian frontier April 1945. Imprisoned after capitulation and condemned by a Belgian court to six years' hard labour 1951 but released in consideration of time already spent in prison. Died 1966.

Next day they went on to the Flemish coast, Dunkirk and Calais where they looked at the preparations for invasion. Thence to Paris.

13 August

The troops are strictly controlled in Paris, which is fortunate. You never see a girl in a military vehicle and anyone who tries anything of the kind is severely punished.... The German civilians and party representatives, however, make a less pretty impression. One sees high functionaries in large cars driving through the streets and shopping with their wives. The most repulsive are the people from Berlin and other parts of the *Reich* who come for a day to Paris and lay in everything. If one is a German, one simply can't go into a shop.

The numerous demobilised French soldiers to be seen in the streets don't make too depressing an impact and on the whole one has the feeling that even before the fighting began the French powers of resistance were small. The main overall impression which I have brought back is that French morale was simply non-existent. The planes failed to take off before the Germans attacked, the troops ran away with their officers in the lead, the troops in fortresses and tanks laid down their arms at the first suspicion of an attack.... The verdict [of a Yugoslav friend] was: 'I shall go back to Yugoslavia as soon as I can get a pass. One can't live in a land whose menfolk have lost the courage and will to work and whose womenfolk no longer know what honour is. This country can only recover under a bolshevist régime after equality of misery has prepared the ground for it.'

There was a good deal of talk about the prospects of invading England.

14 August

The most significant thing to report from these conversations is that clearly no soldier with any knowledge of the situation believes in the success of the current operations, so that all reckon with a long war. But haven't the soldiers in a position to know always been wrong up to now and mayn't we against all our expectations yet see a moral collapse in England? I don't believe it. Falkenhausen summed up his views as follows: 'If I hadn't experienced so many military miracles in the last few years, I would say that this operation is hopeless.'*

On the way home they inspected the Maginot Line.

This whole system is impressive to look at because the careful and methodical planning is so obvious and because when one looks at all

---

* Helmuth's criticisms of the exaggerated expectations of the AA (above, p. 131) were made just a week after he wrote this passage.

these arrangements one is bound to say that this line is impregnable, if it was really defended. At the same time the expense, the waste of money and of space, with thousands of square miles of fertile land taken out of cultivation, is depressing. This whole area is just given over to growing thistles and other weeds and the wind which sweeps over it bears away whole cart-loads of ripe thistle-seeds to infect fields a hundred miles or so away in Germany which may well never know where the thistles come from. In short, such a defensive system is unnatural and morbid. If Europe can't exist without such things, then we deserve what we get. In spite of the marvellous planning, the whole thing is an unhealthy and infectious phenomenon which ought never to be repeated.

Soon after getting back to Berlin, Helmuth found himself fighting 'like a lion' for the life of a French officer whom Göring wished to see executed. Only on the following day, when the question was on the point of being submitted to the Führer, did it emerge that no such officer existed. 'That was really extraordinarily funny and a typical muddle.'

24 August

Churchill's last speech was outstanding and one gets the impression that the English have now perhaps surmounted their crisis of morale. The speech is more modest and more self-confident. It emphasises that all must do their best and ends with the following sentence: *and if we exert ourselves to the limit of our capacity, and after we have done all that is in our power, we can only pray that God may consider us worthy to give victory to our cause.*[6] The tone has changed. The Almighty is no longer being invoked as a champion on one's own side but is being left to judge whether the English deserve to win.

Militarily it is too early for anyone to form an opinion. There are still a few weeks between us and the big decision and an enormous amount will depend on it. The most important thing politically is the rapid preparations of the U.S.A. to reach full union with the Empire. I have the impression that this union, no matter what you like to call it, will really be achieved by the end of the year in which case the second great decision of this year will have been taken.

25 August

I have been skimming through Goethe's educational theories.[7] Do you remember? Children are to be brought up to reverence three things: what is above us, what is beneath us and what is equal to us? What a splendid way of putting it! National Socialism has reminded us of the need to reverence what is beneath us – material objects, blood, ancestry, our bodies. To that extent it is right and we should not forget the lesson. But it has destroyed the reverence for what is above us, namely God – or however you like to describe him – and has tried to put him beneath us by exalting things temporal which fall into the category of what is beneath us. National Socialism has also destroyed reverence for what is equal to us, in that it has tried to put some things of this kind beneath us. By contrast the degenerate form of Liberalism preaches reverence for what is equal to us, to the neglect of both other kinds of reverence. But it is precisely in keeping a balance that wisdom lies and only a liberally minded countryman can really attain this wisdom because everyone else has so little to do with the living things beneath us that they can hardly acquire reverence for them.

The more I think about it the more sure I am that 'Freedom' and 'Natural Order' are the two poles between which the art of government must move. And these two poles are not susceptible of further resolution or definition. All attempts to elaborate them are futile because we really reach them by intuition, not by reason. That is why all discussions about them are so sterile. A man can only be free within the confines of the natural order and an order is only natural when it leaves men free. If this state of affairs is achieved, we won't be able to describe it but will see it and feel it. How it is to be achieved nobody can say – that is what we must explore. It is a process of *trial and error*.

Last night I played the charming Mozart which you got for me. It is enchanting and so very catching. Whenever I play the gramophone, I think of Caspar; he must get used to listening to it as early as possible. I missed it completely in my childhood. We always made our own music so that we only heard strumming, never anything complete and properly played.

8 September

I have been reading the whole morning: Voltaire, *The Times* and Junger's *The Worker** which Yorck thrust into my hand, and which seems to me romantic Humbug.

---

* Jünger, Ernst (b. 1895), published between 1920 and 1949 a series of novels which caught the mood of the German public and became best-sellers. *The Worker* appeared in the autumn preceding Hitler's assumption of power. It exalted the warrior-worker, whose function it was to put the achievements of technology at the service of the national community in the fight against the bourgeois state with its obsolete ideals of freedom, reason, peace and tolerance. Jünger helped to set the stage for the Third *Reich* though he drew aside when confronted with its realisation. His work tended to evoke passionate enthusiasm or antagonism but seldom, as with Helmuth, cold disdain.

10 September

My meal with Brandenburg* was well worth while. A good man. But I am continually astonished to find how far all these men have lost their sense of direction. It is just like blind-man's buff. They go round in a circle with bandages over their eyes and can't any longer tell right from left, forwards from backwards.

11 September

Trott turned up yesterday with Bielenberg† less to exchange news, as I had expected, than to be told what attitude to adopt. They too have lost their sense of direction and allow themselves to be influenced by external events and expect these events to provide solutions which they don't think they can discover on their own.

10 October

Deuel was here last night. His successor has arrived and he leaves from Lisbon on 12 December. It is a great relief to him. Kirk is off tomorrow. [Alexander Kirk had been Chargé d'affaires at the American Embassy ever since the *Kristallnacht* had led to the Ambassador's withdrawal and Helmuth had met him regularly. According to George Kennan[8] it was largely from Helmuth that Kirk had derived his conviction that the war would end badly for Germany.] The departure of both of them will make a very big gap for me. The position in the U.S.A. seems unchanged: it is hardly a question of 'whether' any longer, much more one of 'when'. . . .

What a clearance this war is going to make! It offers a really big chance of breaking through to a really stable epoch. I feel it so close that I have little patience left and I find it terrible to have to wear a mask all the time. But I must wait and join in the comic dance. And thereby this solution is threatened by dreadful dangers which could lead to everything being destroyed. I think I see these dangers, I see them growing and yet there is nothing I can do except wait and look on in the crisis which these dangers will precipitate.

I have a lot to do which in the next few weeks will turn into a very great deal. Basically I have only one objective – to obtain a staff of soldiers who see the problems of a peace treaty clearly and with whom one can work. It is not a question of senior officers but of people at my own level who can sit in the outer rooms and do the real work.

For the rest my thoughts are primarily in Kreisau – the shrubbery,

---

* Brandenburg, Ernst Bruno (1883–1952), till 1933 head of Air Transport Division in Transport Ministry, then of Road Construction and Railway Division. Appeared as a witness for Pastor Niemöller. Prematurely retired 1940.
† Peter Bielenberg's relations with the *Widerstand* are described in Christabel Bielenberg, *The Past is Myself* (1968).

the stones for the wall, the walnut trees, the cherry trees to be planted on the slope, the root-crop harvest, the food for the bees.

6 November

The U.S. Presidential election is over. I had certainly expected that Roosevelt would be re-elected but I know nothing about the U.S.A. and so I didn't allow myself to trust my own judgment. . . . If R. uses his opportunity, he could go down to history as one of the greatest men of all time, as the man who succeeded in reversing the Wars of Independence, in carrying through the fusion of the Empire with the U.S.A. and thus re-establishing the uncontested and incontestable supremacy which is the precondition for a lasting peace. It is a really great day and I feel I ought to indulge in a large-scale celebration. It doesn't matter how long and how difficult and how steep the road may be provided it goes in the right direction. There are still many difficulties to be overcome, but not merely has today seen a reef circumnavigated but – and this is much more important – America's recovery of her freedom of action has created a situation in which further reefs can be circumnavigated.

The remainder of the letter can be read as an example of the well-bred man turning up his nose at the common people. But closer consideration may suggest a doubt as to whether this interpretation is adequate. Helmuth was not so much criticising the human beings as the system which had turned them into types. It is an echo of the Rosenstock theory* that the natural harmony of society had been shattered by the speed with which industrialisation had occurred. Moreover Helmuth saw in the creation of these rootless apathetic masses a necessary pre-condition for the rise of National Socialism.

I spent the time from 11.30 to 1 on Monday evening in the hall of Breslau station and, as the waiting-room was full, sat on the luggage-counter of the cloak-room in a corner. During these ninety minutes I watched the people coming through; 90 per cent soldiers, older men who looked tired and jaded and were laden with packages of all kinds, young lads, airmen especially, who were obviously proud and well satisfied with their present life, older career soldiers; the majority were, however, typical forces of occupation. Along with the soldiers went the girls who attached themselves to or belonged to them, trivial camp-followers. The remaining people were travelling officials – perhaps 5 per cent – who felt important, were badly dressed and left little impression. Among them a few Poles who were coming to work in Germany. They looked thoroughly wretched and worse off than the Poles on our estate and they were so dirty that I

* Above, p. 29.

should have hated to have any of them sit down next to me.

But all these passers-by were types, not human beings. They were material to be slaughtered or set to work, machines which had a definite function in a process. I literally didn't see another human being except for my very nice porter. The current into which all these people had been dragged had torn them from their human moorings. In Africa one calls this 'detribalisation' and associates it with the idea that the natives are thereby rendered incapable both of ruling and of being ruled. The same thing is happening with us.

10 November

Molotov's impending visit is announced in today's paper. That is the result of a personal letter from the Führer to little Joseph [Stalin]. All the same it is of considerable interest whether we succeed in keeping the Russians as sweet as they have been. In any case relations with them have deteriorated in the last few weeks.

28 November

Deuel and I felt thoroughly mournful yesterday over our last evening together. It really hurts me that he won't be coming any more for I am fond of him and have always found talking to him a great help. Of all the people whom I meet like this and talk to at length, he is the only one who doesn't, so to speak, look to me to strengthen his faith. Even Yorck, who is in some ways the most self-sufficient, wants that. The result is that all the others, for all their friendships, take more out of me than Deuel. As a parting present I gave him the two records of Mozart overtures and the Paumgartner* Mozart.

[Deuel subsequently said that at this meeting Helmuth gave him three messages for friends outside Germany (*a*) he himself still thought as he had done before war broke out, and so did others, (*b*) he was pessimistic as to the prospects of effective opposition inside Germany, (*c*) Hitler was doing everything he could to compromise *all* Germans, so that there would be nobody with whom the Allies could or would make peace. Deuel also stressed that at no point had Helmuth ever told him anything which even a Nazi could consider a military secret.]

2 December

Another entire day has run without a stop and I am correspondingly exhausted. However a case [has been disposed of]† which looked very dangerous because our Hermann [Göring] had committed himself deeply over it. I intrigued for all I was worth and

---

* Paumgartner, Bernhard (1887–1971), Austrian conductor and musical scholar. Removed by Nazis from Directorship of Mozarteum in Salzburg 1938–45.

† Verb omitted in original.

pushed the *Reichsmarshall* into a retreat which still looked like a victory. Of course it is all stupid but excellent practice in manœuvring.

On 11 December Helmuth lunched with Peter Yorck and Hermann Abs,* a banker who had known Peter since 1929 and who was in the next thirteen months to join in seven more discussions about plans for financial and economic affairs after the war.

On 12 December Helmuth went to tea with General von Rabenau,† who represented the army in the Field-Marshal's trust and was in consequence involved in the plans for celebrating the fiftieth anniversary of the Field-Marshal's death in the following April. There he met the Austrian General Glaise‡ and a yonng Chinese Dr Chi who had been private secretary to Chiang Kai-shek and as such had had dealings with the latter's two German military advisers General von Seeckt (famous as the architect of the post-Versailles 'apolitical' army) and General von Falkenhausen (the commander in Belgium). In due course the conversation turned to the war. To appreciate the full flavour of what ensued, the reader must remember that the two generals concerned were the highest official authorities for Germany and Austria respectively on matters of military history.

And lo and behold! [Dr Chi] was the first person beside Deuel to share my basic ideas about strategy, though to be sure I don't know how far he had had them before. But when I noticed that I was carrying him with me, I was so delighted that I couldn't resist giving a sort of lecture about strategy in world wars.

His agreement grew with each word I spoke and while at the outset the two generals ventured on a few interjections, after about ten minutes the conversation was confined to Chi and myself and we had simply squeezed out the career soldiers. That went on for over an hour, during which neither of the generals dared to put a foot forward; they just sat there and listened and from time to time said 'really?' while we two sang the great hymn of maritime supremacy as

* Abs, Hermann (b. 1901), head of Foreign Department of Deutsche Bank, member of board 1945, later chairman. Now chairman of supervisory board of Bank and of many other companies.
† Rabenau, General Friedrich von (b. 1884), till 1943 Head of Heeresarchiv Potsdam, Friend of Goerdeler. Arrested after 20 July. Executed at Flossenbürg April 1945.
‡ Glaise von Horstenau, General Edward (b. 1882), Austrian plenipotentiary at Brest-Litovsk 1917–18. Director of Kriegsarchiv in Vienna 1925–34. Wrote life of Count Beck, Austrian Chief of Staff: Minister in Schuschnigg's cabinet 1936; Vice-Chancellor 1938. GOC Agram 1942–4. Committed suicide in U.S. internment 1946.

the only decisive force in the world. I was a bit embarrassed afterwards and wrote Rabenau a letter of apology....

My dear, there may be only one real task facing us – to get the better of our own chaos. If we can succeed in doing that, then there will be a period of peace, of secure peace ahead of us which will outlast the longest span of our lives. I assure you I don't underestimate the difficulties but here is a war which really will decide the burning questions, which won't be followed by a fresh war about the same questions. Today I have the same feeling as I had in 1930 when I saw a way out of chaos for Kreisau. Naturally everything can go wrong but that is rather different from being in a hopeless position.

18 Interlude

January–22 June 1941

A F T E R spending Christmas at Kreisau, Helmuth returned to Berlin in January. On 1 February he again went to the Yorcks and there met Albrecht Haushofer, son of Professor and General Karl Haushofer whose 'geopolitics' had influenced a number of Germans, including Hitler, and who at one time had had a pupil called Rudolf Hess. The younger Haushofer, born in 1903, was a teacher in the same field who was also employed intermittently in the Information Division of the AA. Having acquired considerable familiarity with Britain, he had tried through Hess to warn the German leaders of the danger of provoking British hostility. With the knowledge of Hess (and probably Hitler as well) he tried in September 1940 to open negotiations for a compromise peace through the Duke of Hamilton, whom he had first met in 1936. The Duke did not reply and in April 1941 Haushofer, this time encouraged by friends of Goerdeler, started similar soundings through Carl Burckhardt, the Swiss who had once been high commissioner in Danzig. These had not had time to get anywhere when Hess, on 10 May, without Haushofer's knowledge, made his flight to Scotland. Haushofer was arrested and, though soon released, remained suspect.[1] His main contact among Helmuth's friends was with Schulenburg; Helmuth in February found more in common with him than he had done previously, and met him again on 19 April and 10 December. He also noted that he himself and Peter Yorck had got on very well together, 'although I am a good deal more to the left than he is'.

At this point, however, Helmuth proceeded to take some seven weeks' holiday, or more accurately sick leave. During his nervous crisis of the previous summer he had applied for such leave; it was now granted and he decided that a change of scene would help the process of recovery.

25 January 1941

I myself am exclusively to blame for my 'illness'. I am completely and utterly dissatisfied with the way I conducted my life in 1940. I made cardinal mistakes which I hope I shall never repeat. I lost my equanimity in the most scandalous way and was not exactly graceful in my manner of recovering it. I shall always look back on 1940 as a thoroughly black period; I was frankly not up to it and shall be thankful if a holiday costing RM1000 puts me back where I was in

April 1940 and enables me to atone for the sins of May to October....

Perhaps you haven't realised that I owe it to you that I have put the six bad months behind me; in case you don't realise it, I can now say so in so many words.

Now he and Freya went to the Dolomites. Thence they travelled through Rome (where he saw Weichold) to Taormina, and there spent thirty-six hours with Helmuth's youngest brother Carl Berndt who was serving in the ranks of the air force. Any differences which may have threatened by Carl Berndt's youthful enthusiasm for Nazism* had long ago been removed by Helmuth's kindness and care, and this particular visit must have been a consolation in the following December when news arrived that Carl Berndt had been shot down over North Africa.

Helmuth did not get back to Berlin till just before Easter when on Good Friday he and Freya went to the St Matthew Passion together. At first the break did not seem to have brought the desired result.

28 March

As far as I am concerned, nothing has happened since my visit to France last August. That surprises me but it is a fact. I am looking for fresh slants, changed ideas, improved plans. But all my thoughts start not from the present but from a point which still lies in the future.... I thought that after the five weeks I would see everything differently, and have new inspiration. But I have come back with the same eyes as I took away....

I have only one desire – to come to Kreisau, to concern myself with the farm and the garden, to dig and sow and plant and prune, and wait until events have caught up with my picture of their future course. But that is the attitude of Kaiser Barbarossa who waits until the ravens take wing.

At the beginning of the war, Helmuth had been graded by the doctors as 'fit for working in an office but unfit for active service'. His letters have a fair number of references to headaches, insomnia, colds (particularly sore throats) and influenza. But, in fact, his health soon began to improve, as a Nazi downfall turned from an article of faith to a practical possibility and as in consequence the prospect opened before him of doing constructive work for the common good. He had always been prepared to drive himself hard when need arose, but his letters during his remaining years of freedom testify to an increasingly exacting programme. Yet the growing belief that he might after all be some use in the world enabled him to stand up to it and in October 1943 the doctors (whose standards were admittedly dropping as the need for

* Above, p. 61.

cannon-fodder rose) passed him as fit for active service. When asked how he was, he used often to answer, 'Well enough/*gut genug*.'

On 24 April he was able to gratify his longing for a visit to Kreisau, but in company with General Rabenau, three other generals, his cousin Hans Adolf, the Yorcks and various other members of the family, to celebrate the fiftieth anniversary of the Field-Marshal's death. This occasion had been foreseen some time in advance and there had been a good deal of discussion in the Berghaus as to what form it should take. The mausoleum and its surroundings had been renovated for the occasion and Helmuth's practical mind made him anxious for a present of two tons of horse-manure from the nearest cavalry-barracks to benefit the newly planted shrubs! He accepted, however, the need for something rather more formal – but laid down that no flags must be flown and the occasion remained a family and military one without the Party intruding. Nor can it have been altogether an accident that, as already mentioned, he put the date on a new document which set out his views on the European social situation, the goals to be aimed at after the war, the probable position at the end of the war and a list of the questions which needed answering – in short, a résumé of his past work and an agenda for the future.[2] Two days before the German attack on Russia, he produced a further version, shortened from eleven pages to three.

In the office, after his return from Italy, he discovered – or thought he had discovered – that Admiral Groos, anxious to get rid of the British Ambassador to Switzerland, Sir David Kelly, and unable to find any easier way of achieving this, had given instructions for the *Abwehr* to ask the Gestapo to murder him. Helmuth went to Bürkner and got him to put an absolute veto on the request, which he described as a totally improper one for any organisation connected with the Services to put to the Gestapo.[3]

27 April

I do nothing but read. I find it very interesting, for it extends my knowledge of the thinking of our friends on the other [i.e. the English] side. It is astonishing how hard it is in wartime to avoid intellectual isolation even when one is in such a relatively favoured position as I am. The cutting-off of news, due partly to our own censorship but partly to the blockade and to the drop in traffic with the outer world, has devastating consequences and it will be a hard job to bring oneself up-to-date again with world developments once this war is over.

[Perhaps it was the fear of this isolation which led him on 11 May to write a letter to Freya, concerned only with trivialities, in English and on 22 May to go to see an English newsreel showing bomb damage in London.]

1. HELMUTH IN 1931

Although Helmuth brought Fräulein Schneefuss to Kreisau to make
a picture of him as a present for his parents, he declared that he was
too busy to sit inactive while she drew, so that this charcoal sketch
had to be made while he was working at his desk.

2. THE
SCHLOSS

3. THE
BERGHAUS

Helmuth had
this picture
with him in
Ravensbrück.

4. HELMUTH'S PARENTS

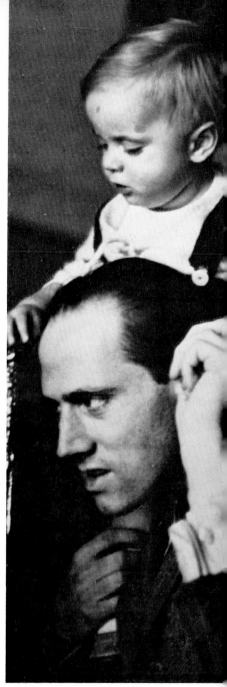

5.[a] DOROTHY AND FREYA

b] HELMUTH AND CASPAR, 1938

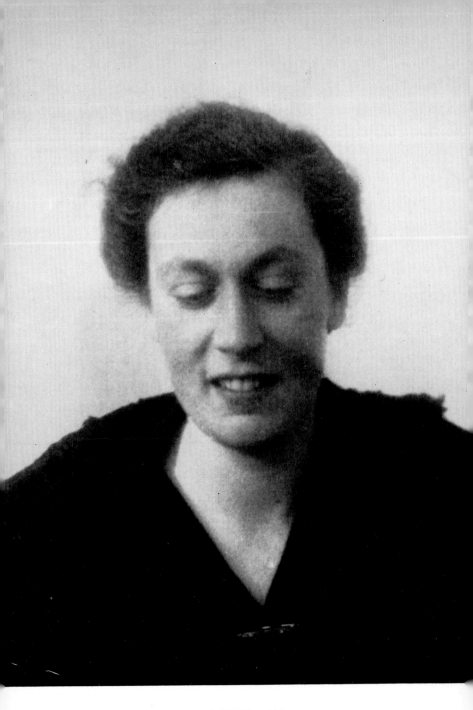

6. FREYA, 1946

7. HELMUTH AT HIS TRIAL
Freisler on the left.

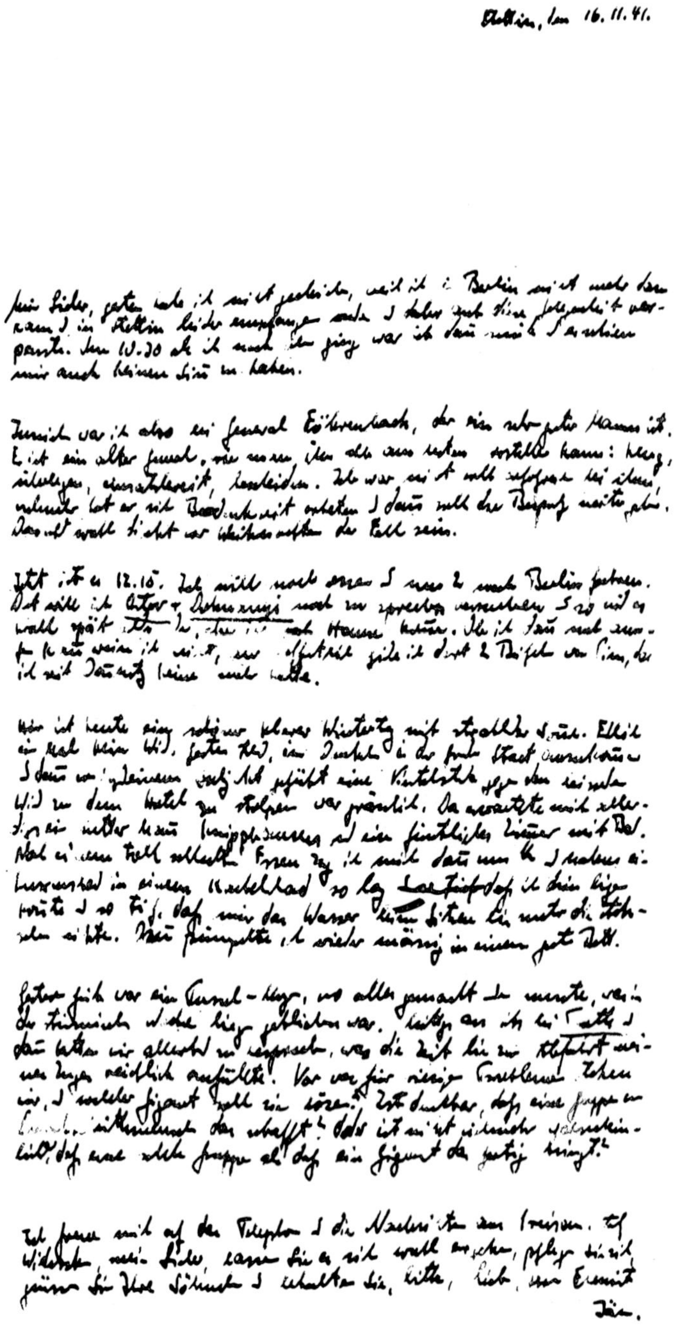
Stettin, den 16.11.41.

8. LETTER OF 16 *November* 1941
Actual size.

29 April

A serious row has suddenly blown up over a matter of principle involving Schmitz who is in Belgrade [Germany had invaded Yugoslavia on 6 April]. I must see how I can best defend him. Fortunately I have worked my way into the foreground and am consequently likely to have to explain things to Canaris myself tomorrow or the day after. That will be very interesting because a question of basic principle is involved on which Canaris can hardly avoid taking a decision. I shall present it in as fundamental a way as I can and see what happens. I shall be alone with Canaris so that he will have no pretext for ducking the issue, unless I give him one.... My text is: what is right benefits the nation, what is internationally right benefits the conduct of the war.*

30 April

My interview with Canaris lasted an hour and was thoroughly satisfactory. I left no doubt about my attitude and he thoroughly agreed with me. Nothing has yet been decided but I hope that things will go all right. In any case I was pleased to know where Canaris stands.

9 May

I had lunch with Peters yesterday. He was as nice as ever. The most interesting thing is that quite obviously his surroundings in the Air Ministry are entirely different from the ones I am accustomed to here. There belief in the Party and hurrah-patriotism openly prevail to an extent I have never met anywhere else. It goes so far that the Führer's remarks in his last speech about the arms needed for 1942 have been interpreted as a mere ruse to deceive the English whereas in reality everything will be over this year.

13 May

I am always thinking about Kreisau, wondering how it is looking and planning all the things one might do. But a black cloud hangs over everything in the shape of the impending political decision which is as imprecise as it is unexplained. [A reference to the attack on Russia.]⁴

14 May

My talks with Trott and Haeften† were very satisfying. In our previous [unrecorded] discussion I had less success in convincing

---

* The point recurs here that *Recht* in German means both 'morality' and 'law'.
† Haeften, Hans Berndt von (b. 1905), the son of the soldier who, in the First World War as liaison officer between the AA and High Command, had sought to mediate between Ludendorff and such moderate civilians as Prince Max of Baden. His father-in-law was Julius Curtius who had been one of Strese-

F

them and bringing them over to my line. But yesterday evening I was
on my day, I penetrated Haeften's hard shell easily and Trott then
joined the hunt. Winning such people for the 'big solution'* involves
a great effort because they are too familiar with routine affairs. But if
one once succeeds, then one has gained a companion who can be
depended on – I mean Haeften.

21 May

There is nothing I like to think about so much as your bees [*die
Bienchen, mein liebstes Meditationsobjekt*] !

25 May

This afternoon I am going to a meeting with Gramsch,† in which
he and I will be the protagonists. As it is about a big basic question
of economic planning, this naturally pleases me a great deal. There is
nothing to beat a good opposite number; if I can have one, I am
prepared to put up with poor colleagues although it is still pleasanter
to be on one's own as today.

---

mann's closest colleagues under the Weimar republic. His uncle was Brauchitsch, the commander-in-chief of the army. He had joined the Foreign Service
in 1933 and while posted to Vienna had blotted his copybook irretrievably in
the eyes of the Party by insisting on unmasking one of its foundation members
as a swindler. He had come back to Berlin at the end of 1940 as Deputy Chief
of the Cultural Affairs Division, and was working closely with Adam von Trott
who brought him into touch with Peter Yorck and Helmuth.

* Officers training for the German General Staff were taught to distinguish
between 'big', i.e. large-scale, solutions to strategic problems and 'small',
i.e. short-term, ones.

† A Ministerialdirektor in the Office of the Commissioner (Göring) for the
Four-Year Plan.

19 Fresh Impetus

22 June–December 1941

THE RUSSIAN WAR

T H E Russian campaign had been under way for nine days before Helmuth's letters contain any comment on its progress. His initial attitude may seem out of keeping with his obvious hopes in 1938–40 that Hitler would be defeated by the British and French. One might therefore have thought that he would want Hitler to be defeated by the Russians, whereas he clearly came close to wanting and expecting the Germans to win. The explanation is that he regarded Nazism and Communism as much of a muchness; in 1938 he had complained to his grandfather that *'the whole outlook and atmosphere'* in Germany was *'definitely Bolshevist'*. His social views may have been well to the left of Peter Yorck's, but the object of the changes which he wished to introduce was to increase the freedom and responsibility of the individual, whereas he considered that Communism as well as Nazism decreased them. This, taken with his habitual inclination to pessimism, makes it easier to understand why he showed so much concern at the bad news which came from the Russian front.

1 July 1941

I am not very impressed by the military news. In Russia we have not yet reached the main defensive line anywhere and even so there has already been very heavy fighting with very big losses. All the same I imagine that things will go all right but there is certainly no question of its being a military walk-over supported by internal disturbances.

3 July

I'm still uneasy about the Russian war. A big new attack starts today, however, and will perhaps have more decisive results than the first battle. But the fighting spirit and the tactical leadership of the Russians are far better than we expected and I am coming to realise that all our information about Russia has clearly been quite wrong. That at any rate applies to me.

4 July

Today's war report says explicitly that the Russians have held out against waves of dive bombers. Up till now only the English have been capable of that. And the fact that more than half the forces engaged at Bialystock fought to the death and that only the rest surrendered is eloquent testimony to the Russian army's quality.

8 July

A man who came from the Führer's headquarters yesterday said his impression was that people there were satisfied with the progress: they were expecting to make a breakthrough in a few days' time and would then roll up the whole line from behind. I can't judge whether this diagnosis is correct but it is certainly possible. All the same, fighting has been going on for several days on a completely stationary front and that doesn't look to me like a breakthrough but much more like an orderly Russian retreat.

13 July

We are now engaged in breaking through towards Moscow. In my opinion such a move makes no sense. There seems to be some doubt as to whether our armour is in a condition to exploit the move successfully. But what everybody agrees about is that, if it comes off, all our tanks will then have to go in for repair. And what is going to happen then leaves me guessing, for the prize of this war is not Moscow but the Ukraine and the Caucasus and to get them we shall have to throw in everything we've got.* Moscow by comparison is a mere *sideshow* and a liability because in terms of food it is an industrial area so that our troops cannot support themselves there for long. In short this move gives me the impression that people at headquarters have lost their nerve. If that is the case, so much the worse for us.

16 July

Optimistic ideas about the war in the east are being put round. I hope they are right. The General Staff's version is that the Russians have no more reserves within call, so that once the present battle is over the way will thereafter be free. That would at any rate be something. But where to? Moscow? One can't see the end of this adventure and I bitterly regret having given it my private support. I was misled by prejudice into believing that the Russians would collapse internally and we could then set up a régime there which would not constitute a threat to us. But there is no sign of that happening. Russian soldiers go on fighting far behind the front and so do peasants and workers – it is just like China. We have stirred up something terrible and it will cost us heavy sacrifices including the lives of good people.

* But see 26 September, below, p. 154.

21 July

The war in the east goes slowly ahead. Various changes have now been made and the hope is that some particularly obstinate pockets of resistance can be mopped up. But I get more and more sceptical about the military outcome. Moscow is now going to be bombed [by air], which seems to me a sign of weakness since what point is there in it if we are going to get there soon? Today I have the impression that Kiev, Moscow and Leningrad are not going to fall next week. [Kiev was not occupied till 19 September, Moscow and Leningrad never.]

22 July

I detect no change in the military situation in the east. According to the latest appreciations (i.e. reports which are not altogether reliable) the Russians are retreating systematically in the Ukraine taking the harvested grain eastwards with them. If they manage to do that, we shall find ourselves pushing into a vacuum and what will happen then, heaven knows! One thing at any rate seems to me certain – between now and 1 April next year more men will come to a miserable end in the area between Portugal and the Urals than ever before in the world's history. And this seed will come up. Who sows the wind, reaps the whirlwind, but if this is the wind what will the whirlwind be like?

25 August

Churchill has made a really great speech. [Broadcast of 24 August on Atlantic Charter meeting.] Another of those speeches which will go down to history as a classic. It is less the factual content than the form and the impression of mastery which give this effect. One feels as one reads it that, while we are still in the valley of history, he is speaking over our heads to the statesmen of the classical past.

26 August

The news from the east is again terrible. We clearly have suffered very very heavy losses. But that would be endurable if hecatombs of corpses didn't already weigh on our shoulders. One keeps on hearing reports that only 20 per cent of prisoners and Jews survive the journeys they are sent on, that there is starvation in the prisoner-of-war camps, that typhus and all the other deficiency diseases have broken out, that our own people are collapsing from exhaustion. What is going to happen when the whole nation realises that this war is lost and, what is more, lost in quite a different sense to the last one? With an amount of bloodshed which cannot be made good in our lifetime and indeed never forgotten, with an economy which is completely ruined? Will men arise who will be capable of distilling from this punishment the penitence and remorse which will gradually bring new creative forces into existence? Or will everything collapse in chaos? In 12 months we shall know the answer to most of these questions.

[This is the first time since the German victories in 1940 that he talks as though the loss of the war was a foregone conclusion.]

6 September

The war situation looks to me worse than even *I* expected it to be by now. And if the situation goes on developing to our disadvantage, then when it comes to negotiating our hand will have lost the cards it so badly needs. . . . We must face the fact that prospects are black and that the anxiety and suffering ahead of us surpass the limits of our imagination.

24 September

Nothing fresh to report. The U.S. Neutrality Act will be repealed during the next few days and then the way will be clear for sending American ships to England and to Murmansk. The soldiers here are brimming over with confidence. It seems to me this time to be forced rather than genuine because each wants to feel good just once more before the revenging nemesis overtakes him. But once again it is impressive to see how these people in their preoccupation with a single battle lose sight of the ultimate objective, namely the winning of the war.

26 September

Hopes are still high in the south and there is talk of reaching the Caucasus by November. That seems to me militarily very optimistic but also militarily very pointless unless one has previously eliminated the threat from Timoshenko's army on the north flank. The longer the flank gets, the more dangerous is Timoshenko. But even if one reaches the objective and can prevent the danger, I don't see how it's going to affect the result except to make the line of retreat longer and the retreat more difficult and expensive.*

One result of the war which affected Helmuth personally was that in September the sympathetic Lt.-Col Tafel, his nominal superior as head of Branch VI, was called to the front and replaced by an ex-policeman called Werner Oxé. The latter seems to have arrived without any firm anti-Nazi feelings but gave his subordinates a free hand and created no difficulties for them.

28 September

The days rush past. It seems so fast to me because I can see the

* But see comment on 13 July, above, p. 152.

disaster which lies ahead and each day which passes without any check being put on this misery and murder is as good as lost. What's more, each day costs 6,000 Germans and 15,000 Russians, each minute 4 and 10. That is a horrible price which now has to be paid for inaction and procrastination. Thanks to the resistance of Kiev the Russians have got their second wind. A new line has been established. Admittedly they have few tanks left and fewer guns but we have appreciably fewer tanks and guns and the others have just as many aircraft as before. Nobody knows where they got them from but there it is. And the Russian announcements reveal complete confidence. 'We have lost many men and a great deal of equipment, but the Germans forget that when we are fighting in our own country our army is only our first line of defence and that in these circumstances every Russian is a fighter.' These are great words, very great words, and if the determination of the Russians needed strengthening our treatment of them will have done it.

On 8 October Hitler ordered his press chief Otto Dietrich to announce to the world that the eastern campaign was for all practical purposes over and that the Russian armies were beaten. Goebbels, who in spite of being Dietrich's superior had no control over him, was furious at this violation of the principles of prudence in propaganda but it was afterwards excused on the ground that it had been necessary to prevent the German generals from losing their nerve and retreating.

9 October

The news from the east is excellent. Contrary to everyone's expectation Timoshenko's army seems to be the weakest of the three. For the first time the resistance is not described as very serious or concentrated and one can't avoid the impression that in this case we could succeed in bringing about a complete collapse on the Russian front before winter. Objectively this would not make much difference but it would give a colossal moral boost at home, perhaps also abroad, i.e. among the neutrals and in occupied countries. But we must wait and see.

17 October

The weather at the front is very bad. . . . I cannot escape the impression that once again we have only been successful in the limited sense which I imagined.

[After this Helmuth spent about ten days at Kreisau.]

18 November

I get a bad impression of the war. The current joke about the campaign is 'extended for another month in view of outstanding success'. A bitter saying! I don't think we shall make much real progress before the New Year.... The millions of wretched troops who now freeze out there, get wet, perish! Comparison with the 14–18 World War isn't possible because then there were fewer men, who could consequently be better provided for, and there were still houses in which they could shelter.... What sort of an army shall we have by next March – no appreciable leave, no adequate supplies, no accommodation, no suitable clothing, no military victory?

PLANS FOR POST-WAR

After the last quoted letter, comment on the eastern front virtually ends. At the time of Pearl Harbor Helmuth was away on a visit to Vienna and the entry of the United States into the war went unrecorded. But the five and a half months between 22 June and 7 December had produced a complete change in the world scene, even though the effects of that change took almost another year (until November 1942) to become obvious. By the end of 1941 it was clear – even to Hitler – that the German attempt to knock out Russia with another lightning campaign had failed and that if the Germans were to win at all it could only be by a long struggle, straining the national resources in a way which had not occurred before. Moreover, if it came to a long-term trial of strength the resources available to Germany, Italy and Japan in terms of men, industrial capacity and raw materials were smaller than those of the other side (especially as the latter controlled the sea). Well-informed Germans therefore found it increasingly hard to avoid the conclusion that their country had lost the war and that the only thing to do was to try to save as much as possible from the wreck by concluding a compromise peace. As Hitler was clearly unprepared to compromise with anyone and as the other side were equally clearly unprepared to compromise with Hitler (assuming that they were willing to compromise at all), the removal of Hitler and his immediate associates came increasingly to be seen as necessary for the national good. A fresh impetus was thus given to the planning of Hitler's elimination and of the régime which should succeed him.

The method of eliminating Hitler was initially thought of as being a *coup d'état/Staatsstreich* in which one or more commanding officers would refuse to obey the Führer's orders and take over as much of the government machine as they could compel or persuade to obey them. If the coup was to succeed, Hitler's person would have to be seized at a fairly early stage and in the process of seizure he might well get killed. But his assassination in cold blood was not thought of as the essential starting-point of the coup. What made it become such later was the unwillingness of senior commanders to start the revolt. Those at the front who had most reason to regard Hitler's leadership as disastrous were afraid that defiance of him might involve capitulation to the enemy – for internal war is notoriously hard to combine with external. Those at home lacked the nerve, feared civil war or (if they were outside Berlin) doubted whether a coup started by them could succeed. Those more junior officers who felt action to be imperative realised that they for their part could not succeed without senior backing. But they also realised that that backing would be more easily forthcoming once a crisis had been precipitated by assassination. Thus an *Attentat* gradually (but only gradually) came to be seen as the inescapable preliminary to the *Staatsstreich*.

Helmuth had for long been convinced that a coup must be left to the generals. Early in the war, he said to Hans Christoph Stauffenberg 'We're not conspirators, we're not capable of being, we've not learnt how to do it, we shouldn't try to make a start now, it would go wrong, we would make an amateur job of it.'[1] But he was not much more convinced about the ability – or readiness – of the generals to make a revolt. He was, however, keenly alive to the daily cost of Hitler in human suffering – a matter which as will be seen impressed itself acutely on him this autumn – and for that reason was prepared more than once to contemplate a coup by the generals, even to join in attempts at instigating one.

His remarks to Stauffenberg ended, however, with the words: 'What we ought to devote some thought to is what is going to happen if someone takes it into his head to throw Hitler over or what is going to happen if he has an aeroplane accident. An event like that mustn't find us unprepared.' Long ago Eugen Rosenstock had emphasised that the problem which would matter, and give real scope for individual initiative, was not the elimination of Hitler, since that was likely to happen anyhow in one way or another, but the question of what would happen afterwards. To this problem Helmuth now devoted an increasing amount of his attention, gathering together a collection of men who were not so much like-minded and congenial as representative of the elements whose help would be needed in the rebuilding. He believed that, for such a group of men to have a chance of exerting influence by acting together at the crucial moment, they must previously have learnt to trust one another and to have taken steps to clarify by discussion the nature of their aims. The decision was taken to work out systematic statements of view on all the major political issues.

The form of post-Hitler Germany had, of course, been exercising his mind for a long time and must have been the subject of many informal conversations with friends like Carl Dietrich von Trotha, Horst von Einsiedel and Eduard Waetjen. This circle had gradually been enlarged by people like Gablentz, Reichwein, Furtwängler and Yorck. What is noticeable is that a number of people who later played a prominent part, like Mierendorff, Haubach, Trott (and indeed Yorck), had crossed Helmuth's path at an earlier stage of his life without his establishing any particularly close connection with them. There are signs that, even before the Russian campaign began, he was trying to sound out possible recruits and widen the number of people with whom he was in touch. After 22 June the process went steadily ahead and took on a more purposeful character. In particular, contacts were strengthened with the churches (hitherto principally represented by Gablentz who was in touch with the Geneva office of the World Council of Churches) and the workers (whose views had previously been principally voiced by Reichwein).[2]

It seems to have been at this time that Helmuth asked Hans Christoph Stauffenberg, 'You have a cousin [Claus] in the Führer's headquarters. Can any use be made of him?' Hans Christoph replied that he had not seen Claus for some time but would make inquiries, which he did through Berthold (itself a commentary on Helmuth's relations with the latter). A few weeks later Claus' answer came back by the same route. His view was that the war had first to be won. 'During the war one must not try anything of that kind, above all not during a war against Bolshevism. Afterwards, however, when we arrive back home, we will get rid of the brown plague.'[3] On 1 September 1941 Helmuth wrote, 'A new Stauffenberg is coming to lunch tomorrow, sent by Guttenberg* who himself is on leave.' But there is no evidence that Claus Stauffenberg was absent at this time from his post at headquarters in East Prussia; the member of the family referred to is more likely to have been Berthold's twin brother Alexander.[4]

On 4 July Carlo Mierendorff is mentioned for the first time. Born in 1897, he had served through the First War, latterly as an officer. He then became a student in Darmstadt and Heidelberg, shifting his interests from literature and the arts to politics as he grew increasingly concerned with the state of the world around him. Known to his friends as 'Mr Loud Mouth'/*Herr Vielgeschrey* because of his habit of expressing a decided opinion about everything, he went into the Social Democratic Party in the hope of adapting it to a society in which it was no longer a self-sufficient outcast but a source of innovating thought. He was made to work his passage through the party machine and had just become a member of the *Reichstag* by 1933. Although he was in Switzerland when Hitler took power and had made himself much unloved by the Nazis, he refused to desert his working-class companions and came back to Germany, only to be put into a concentration camp where he remained for five long years. On release he found work in a firm

* For Guttenberg, see below, p. 162.

handling synthetic petrol but was forbidden to meet old political friends
and had to be extremely careful not to arouse suspicion. Einsiedel put
him in touch with Helmuth to whom he was welcome not only as a
practical, intelligent, amusing and courageous person but also because
his links with the workers helped to fill a gap of which the group was
very conscious.[5]

After this the letters illustrate what was happening:

11 July. Lunch with Gramsch and an assistant of his called Kadgien.

The conversation was for me a considerable surprise for there
came to light a far greater amount of agreement than I had expected
both in the diagnosis and in the picture of what should happen *post
festum*.... They were just as surprised to discover that I had been
occupied in the same activity for a long time.

Supper with Furtwängler who, in view of first-hand acquaintance with
India before the war, had just gone to work with Adam von Trott in the
Indian section of the AA's Information Department, where they were
trying to use Chandra Bose as the spearhead of a movement for Indian
independence.[6]

We argued again about India. But I have the impression that he
has come a little closer to me. At any rate, he no longer wants complete independence for India, but rather dominion status. That is a
small concession.

[Helmuth had no doubt argued that, in the interests of World Order,
the British Commonwealth needed to be left in existence, though as a
group of self-governing states.]

12 July. Supper with Yorck and Einsiedel.

The other two spent most of the evening arguing and I sat by as
critic and arbitrator, since I understood much less about the subject
[clearly an economic one].

15 July. Lunch with Gablentz and Yorck.

The occasion lasted from 1.30 to 4.30.... G was in good form.
During the winter we had reached deadlock* and apart from the fact
that I have learnt a certain amount since then, he too had obviously
been upset by it, had concerned himself with the question on which
we differed and had for his part come to fresh conclusions and was
visibly pleased that I took up the matter again.

Supper with Yorck and Gablentz.

Yorck and I know one another a bit too well by now so that the

* Above, p. 129.

third is apt to become a target instead of a partner.... All the same Gablentz had the great advantage over us that he knows something about the actual position of the Protestant Church and theology.

21 August. Lunch with Trott.

He is going on leave tomorrow. I gave him some homework [the drafting of a paper on foreign policy].

5 September. Tea with Bishop Count Konrad von Preysing, the Catholic Bishop of Berlin. This was an important new contact, not only because of the Bishop's eminence but as a step towards bringing an additional sector of German life into the talks. Count Preysing, a Bavarian aristocrat who had been a lawyer and a diplomat before taking orders, had been appointed in 1935 at the age of fifty-five to the see established by the Vatican in 1919 in the predominantly Protestant capital of Prussia. He was the firmest opponent of the Nazis among the Catholic hierarchy: more letters were addressed to him by the Pope between 1934 and 1944 than to any other German bishop. Helmuth's introduction to him was due to Hans Peters who was a Catholic, and to a lawyer friend who held a position in the diocese. The Bishop lived near the Unter den Linden in an eighteenth-century palace in which, as the office of the General Staff, the Field-Marshal had worked as a young man.

The afternoon was very satisfying. I thought he was satisfied too. The 2½ hours passed quickly and we covered or touched on a wide field of human relations. In any case he told me on the spot to come again which I will do at regular intervals of about 3 weeks....* I asked him about [Bishop] von Galen [of Münster, who had just caused three of his sermons against the Nazi introduction of euthanasia to be read in all the churches of his diocese]. He assured me that he is a perfectly average fellow-citizen of limited intellectual powers who until recently had not seen where things were leading and had been inclined to compromise. That makes it all the more impressive that the Holy Ghost should have enlightened and inspired him! How much more significant a sign like this is than it would have been in the case of an outstandingly clever man.†

* At one point Helmuth was anxious to bring a 'social democratic politician' (probably Mierendorff) to meet the Bishop but Preysing refused, judging that he could learn all he needed from Helmuth and that each new acquaintance increased the risk. W. Adolph, *Kardinal Preysing und zwei Diktaturen* (1971), p. 181.

† Preysing himself preached a sermon condemning euthanasia on 2 November 1941. Dr van Husen went to see Bishop von Galen several times on behalf of Helmuth. The remarks quoted about Galen are not altogether fair since in March 1933 he, along with Preysing, had led the opposition among the German bishops to the Centre Party voting for Hitler's Enabling Bill.

On 10 September Helmuth had lunch with Hans von Dohnanyi*
and Justus Delbrück,† afterwards going with them to a display of
show-jumping and dressage at a cavalry barracks outside Berlin.

13 September. Lunch with Yorck.

Unquestionably I get on better and faster and more profitably with
him at present than with anyone else. What's more, we are so completely similar, I mean think on similar lines. Although I know
Einsiedel nearly as well, for some reason or other I have the edge on
him and that troubles me. Yorck is really the only one from whom I
seek advice. With all the rest it is really a matter of using the process
of seeking advice to conceal an inquiry as to how far they are prepared
to go along and what they want to do. That then always leaves the
responsibility with me, or at any rate the burden of the responsibility.

17 September. Steltzer. Theodor Steltzer had first been brought into
touch with Helmuth in the autumn of 1940 by von der Gablentz.[7]
'When I [Steltzer] first met him, he was sunk in melancholy which
later abated as our discussions led to concrete plans. I had the feeling
that he regarded the position as hopeless and did not believe our efforts
could be successful.'[8] A handsome, talented but slightly aloof man of
fifty-six, Steltzer was a native of Schleswig-Holstein and the son of a
judge. Until the end of the 1914–18 war, he had divided his time
between the university, where he was influenced by the 'academic
socialists'/*Kathedersozialisten*, and the army where he worked as a
close assistant to General Groener in organising transport and munition
supplies. He then became the *Landrat* of Rendsburg in Schleswig but
was pensioned off in 1933 and for a time imprisoned on a trumped-up
charge. He was much involved in the ecumenical work of the Protestant
Church, with contacts in Switzerland and Scandinavia. In 1939 he got
recalled to the army as a reserve officer and in 1940 was posted to
Norway as transport officer to the GOC. Here he established close
relations with the Norwegian Resistance and in particular with Bishop
Berggrav.

23 September. Supper with Einsiedel and Poelchau. Poelchau was the
son of a protestant Minister and a minister himself. He was a pupil and
friend of the progressive theologian Paul Tillich who advocated the
need for a 'religious socialism' and soon after 1933 emigrated to
America. Poelchau himself was appointed in 1933 chaplain to the

* Above, p. 96. Helmuth first mentions having met him in August 1940.
† Delbrück, Justus (1902–44), son of Hans Delbrück, Professor of History in
Berlin and editor of *Preussische Jahrbücher* 1883–1919. An industrial lawyer,
joined *Abwehr* on outbreak of war. Friend of Dohnanyi since childhood, sister
married to Klaus Bonhoeffer.

prison of Tegel in the north-west suburbs of Berlin, the first such post to be created.

I like P very much; young, bright and enterprising. It is a mystery to me how a man can retain his ability to put across a spiritual message, keep his nerves and be good-humoured into the bargain when he is perpetually having to attend executions. What he had to say about the outlook of the workers was thought-provoking and for me novel: he clearly has a really close connection with them.

25 September. Lunch with Gladisch, Yorck and Steltzer.*

The talk was good and brutally frank which in Gladisch's case surprised me a little.

26 September. Lunch with Dohnanyi and Guttenberg. Carl Ludwig Baron von und zu Guttenberg (1902–45) was another official in Division Z of the *Abwehr*. He came of a conservative Bavarian Catholic family and edited from 1934 to 1943 a periodical with corresponding views called 'White Leaves'/*Weisse Blätter*.[9] He had known Helmuth since at least 1938 when he had introduced him to Hans Christoph von Stauffenberg.

The meal was very nice. Both D and G were brisk and lively. D especially talking more than I have ever known him to do. In practical terms our conversation was satisfactory, particularly because D has at last handed in his contribution [about the legality of the Armed Forces' Oath of Loyalty to Hitler and the legal justification for *Widerstand*] so that it can now be put into circulation.

28 September. Supper with Yorck and General Beck. This meeting is an important landmark because ever since his opposition to Hitler culminated in his resignation as Chief of the army General Staff in August 1938† Beck had been widely looked up to as the leader of the *Widerstand* and the potential head of state in succession to Hitler. Helmuth and Peter Yorck already had a number of contacts with people close to Beck but an ex-Chief of the General Staff would in any case have been disposed to accept an invitation from two people with their names. The meeting thus indicated that Helmuth and his friends were beginning to link up with other *Widerstand* groups.

It was a successful evening and one can only hope that it will contribute to the forging of the iron.

8 October.

Poelchau described how five of his protégés would be told at 7

* For Gladisch, see p. 133.
† Above, p. 82.

o'clock in the evening that they were going to be executed at 5 the next morning. He would sit with them from 7 until 5, though yesterday someone else had replaced him. I got him to describe this night; it was dreadful and yet somehow or other inspiring. But he said that no men were ever so thoroughly prepared for death as these and he said that in his eight years of duty there was nobody – with the exception of hysterical women – who had not gone peacefully to the scaffold. What an achievement such a night represents! It is dreadful and frightful but it raises questions which don't otherwise present themselves so uncompromisingly, openly and absolutely. He never offers Communion but 50 per cent of those entrusted to him ask for it spontaneously.

10 October. At a conference of the Academy for German Law Helmuth met Carlo Schmid, a law teacher from Tübingen who was working in the German Military Government at Lille. He had already shown signs of being helpful and his contribution on this occasion so much pleased Helmuth that he was asked to lunch on the spot and, after a two-hour conversation, began to act as a channel between Helmuth's friends and the French resistance.* (Carlo Schmid is half French.)

12–13 October. Helmuth went with Peter and Marion Yorck, Adam von Trott and his wife and a couple called Wussow† on a week-end visit to an estate at Gross-Behnitz, some thirty miles west of Berlin, owned by Ernst Borsig, a younger brother of Arnold.‡ The visit, which was to be repeated three times in the course of the next eighteen months,[10] was only superficially social; the host was very interested in problems of agriculture and the intention was to discuss what should be done in this field after the war. On the first evening 'the discussion was opened by Wussow and Borsig but after ten minutes developed into a duel between Trott and me about the justification for thinking out how the state should be set up'. This was a criticism which a number of people made against Helmuth's method of proceeding, arguing that it was a waste of time to plan for an unforeseeable situation. Any plans which were made were bound to be rendered more or less inapplicable by the course of events preceding the Nazi downfall. Helmuth on this occasion argued that 'the justification' was to be found in 'the individual's heart' and didn't need any prompting from outside. He presumably meant that any conscientious individual should feel the Third *Reich* to be evil and want to find something better with which to replace it. He was 'in good form' and was backed by Yorck so that he seemed to get the

* After the war Schmid (b. 1894) became active as a Social Democrat, ending up as Minister for Federal Affairs in the 'Great Coalition' 1966–9.

† Wussow, Botho von (1901–71), landowner, at one period in diplomatic service.

‡ Above, p. 87.

better of the discussion. But he could have well added a further argument to strengthen his case. For the value of planning lay as much in the process as in the content. The mere act of engaging in it was a training exercise for those who would need to co-operate later. Admittedly the plans would have to be adapted to events and could not be regarded as final or sacrosanct. But at least their formulation would make the participants more aware of what the problems were and establish the general direction in which the answers were to be sought.

During a long walk next day Helmuth had a discussion with Borsig about agriculture.

> He advocated very liberal theories – 'improvement of farming by competition', 'free play for market forces', etc., whereas I in contrast argued that one must at the outset picture to oneself what sort of life people are to live in the country, how many people and of what kinds need to live on the land, and that one must then go on to employ means calculated to achieve these results without bothering how acceptable one finds these means in theory, because it is a question of remedying an unhealthy situation. But he was wildly obstinate and I wasn't in my best form so that we spent our time at cross-purposes.

14 October, evening.

> Guttenberg came with the head of the Jesuit-province of Munich, which includes Württemberg, Baden and the Allgäu. As far as I could make out, he is immediately responsible to the Vicar-General of the Order in Rome. A farmer's son with an outstanding brain, fluent, well educated, with a mind of his own. I liked him very much. We also talked about concrete questions of pastoral work, of education and of collaboration with the Protestants; he seemed reasonable, objective and ready to make considerable concessions.

Father Rösch's own account of this meeting, given twenty years later, was that, when in Berlin to negotiate some matter with the OKH, he heard over loudspeakers in the street a speech in which Hitler announced that Russia was defeated. This caused him considerable anxiety because he knew that the end of the war would be a signal for renewed Nazi attacks on the churches – particularly the Jesuits. Just at that moment he met Baron Guttenberg whom he knew in Bavaria. As any real conversation was clearly impossible in the street, Guttenberg told Rösch to follow him without giving any sign that they knew each other. 'When I stop at a garden door and light a cigarette, go through the next garden door, up to and round a big garage and up some stairs behind it. There is a flat above. Ring there, my name is the code word. I will come by a different route.' In the subsequent conversation, Rösch asked Helmuth if he had heard Hitler's speech. Helmuth replied that such things didn't interest him because he was in touch with the outside world and knew the truth. When Rösch told him what the speech contained Helmuth was indignant at the lies and omissions, and told Rösch what he himself knew from official reports about Russian reserves. 'Remember, Father Provincial, if we are still alive; in the early summer of 1945 the Russians will be in Berlin unless someone succeeds in taking the leadership out of Hitler's hands.' This last operation had to be the business of the generals. Then the Russians would have to be halted. In this way a tolerable peace could be achieved and Europe saved. They then went on to discuss Germany's internal situation and the position of the churches.* Helmuth said about this, 'We must fight and do everything we can to save what can be saved, for the others are frightened again. If they encounter opposition, they stop and wait.' In discussing the Protestant Church, he said, 'I will tell you one thing, speaking as a Protestant Christian – Christianity in Germany can only be saved by the Catholic bishops and the Pope.' That was why it was essential in his view for the churches to work together. Helmuth then asked Rösch if he was ready to join in this common work.

15 October. Dohnanyi and Oster. This and another meeting on 16 November are the only mentions of Oster in Helmuth's letters and he gives no details. But these two facts, the frequent mention of Dohnanyi at this time, the meeting with Beck and various other details in the next two months† suggest strongly that Helmuth was involved in plans for a *Staatsstreich*, sparked off by the mounting disagreement between Hitler and Brauchitsch about what to do during the winter on the Eastern front.

13 November. Preysing. On this occasion he and Helmuth first talked about a paper which Peters had written on Church questions, and which neither found altogether satisfactory. Secondly they discussed the case of St Clemens church which had been sequestrated by the Gestapo: Preysing's letter of protest to the Minister of the Interior had gone unanswered and Helmuth urged him to press his case. This he did by writing a further letter to the Gestapo. When that also failed to extract a reply, he sent a Pastoral Letter expounding the facts to all Catholics in

* There are three reasons for thinking that Fr Rösch's memory may have faded a little in giving this account. One is that Helmuth's version in no way suggests that the Jesuit's arrival was accidental. The second is that Hitler's speech was delivered on 2 October. It may have been a recording which was being played on 14 October, but in that case one would have expected Rösch to be familiar with it. Thirdly, it is incredible that Helmuth could have predicted three and a half years in advance the exact date of the end of the war, especially as his remarks elsewhere suggest that he expected catastrophe to arrive a good deal faster.

† There is evidence (van Roon, p. 170) that in the winter of 1941–2 Leuschner made preparations for calling a general strike, to coincide with a military revolt.

the diocese. This led Goebbels to complain that 'a couple of [Nazi] know-alls had acted very injudiciously'.[11]

The third subject of conversation was the Jews, against whom a fresh wave of persecution had broken out.* Preysing had confirmed some who were going to be taken away the same evening to the Litzmann-stadt camp whose inmates only received a quarter of normal rations. Preysing described the Gestapo interrogation of the Provost of his Cathedral, Bernhard Lichtenberg, who had been prosecuted in 1928 for praying for the Jews; he was arrested in 1942 and died a year later on the way to Dachau concentration camp.[12]

In these weeks the discussions had made so much progress that on 27 November Helmuth could tell Freya how he had been discussing with Peter Yorck the allocation of responsibility for the week-end meeting which they were already planning to hold at Kreisau in February (though in practice it was postponed till Whitsun). But his activities at this time were not solely theoretical. On 16 November he not only met Oster but went to Stettin to see a General Föhrenbach.† 'The best kind of old general, clever, judicious, enterprising, modest ... rather how I picture the Field-Marshal.' He gave no details of the proposal which he put to the General but it seems to have been nothing less than a sug-gestion that he should raise the standard of revolt against Hitler: General Halder, talking after the war about the lack of anyone suitable to lead a *Staatsstreich*, said, Föhrenbach was too old and too little known.'[13] Whatever it was, Helmuth was not wholly successful. The General asked for time to think the proposition over.

'The matter is very good. I know no better way but I am not good enough for it.' That is very good. So might Daddy [Sir James] have spoken and the Field-Marshal.

He promised to discuss the matter again on 18 December in Berlin with Helmuth and Beck. On the evening of his return to Berlin, Helmuth had supper with Dohnanyi to prepare for a meeting with Beck on 22 November and another with Halder who was still the army's Chief of Staff. 'I hope we shall now manage to take two or three big steps forward before Christmas.'

Helmuth is said to have travelled to Munich in November[14] and he certainly went to Vienna early in December, ostensibly to buy a new

---

* Below, p. 171.
† Föhrenbach, Max (1872–1942), retired in 1931 with rank of general. Rejoined in 1940 with the same rank and was made deputy-commander of II Corps. *Wehrkreis* II Stettin. In 1941, when the corps went off under its commander to Russia, Föhrenbach, in accordance with regular practice, became Commander of the *Wehrkreis* at home which provided its base. Retired April 1942, died in the same year.

suit! The inference is tempting that he was looking for a substitute or a reinforcement for Föhrenbach. In 1943 he certainly thought that defiance of Germany could start in the south-east and may well have done so two years earlier. The Brauchitsch crisis duly came to a head, only to prove as damp a squib as its predecessors. On 17 December the Field-Marshal, who had had several heart attacks, renewed his proffered resignation. Two days later Hitler accepted it and announced that he would be taking over the job himself. On 8 February 1942 Helmuth was to write to Freya:

> Instead of telling me 'it is too early', as they were all doing before Christmas, the view now obtains that 'it is too late'. It is sad to see how correct Peter and I were in our diagnosis that 18 December was the right day.

Whatever may have been going on behind the scenes, the outcome of the episode, and the person of Brauchitsch's successor, made it harder than ever to expect an initiative from the top of the army.*

In this context and at some date between 11 December (Helmuth's last letter before Christmas) and 18, a meeting occurred about which we only know through an entry which Ulrich von Hassell made in his diary on 21 December after getting to his Bavarian home. Hassell (1881–1944), a distinguished former diplomat and son-in-law of Admiral Tirpitz, had been recalled in 1937 from his last post as ambassador to Italy and thereafter became closely associated with Beck and Goerdeler. His diary entry reads:

> I have felt all along that we had too little contact with the younger generation. This wish has now been satisfied, but has brought fresh and serious difficulties in its train. First of all I had a long talk with Trott, in which he fought passionately to avoid any trace of 'Reaction', 'Herrenklub', 'Militarism' whether at home or abroad. Consequently, although he is himself a Monarchist, no Monarchy now under any circumstances. Otherwise the public will be apathetic and foreign countries mistrustful. 'Converts' – by which he means Social Democrats who had turned Christian (among whom he mentions a former M.P. by name [almost certainly Mierendorff]) – would under such circumstances have nothing to do with us and wait for the next model. He made up for his negative attitude by putting forward

---

* On 17 November General Udet of the air force, an 'air ace' of the First World War, committed suicide. He was declared to have been killed in an accident and given a state funeral. In fact, he had grown desperate about Germany's prospects and was caught making plans against Hitler. The news gave Carl Zuckmayer, who knew Udet, the inspiration to write his play *The Devil's General* which he later dedicated to Helmuth, Carlo Mierendorff and Theo Haubach.

the positive idea of making Niemöller Chancellor, as being on the one hand the man best known outside Germany as an exponent of anti-Hitlerism, and on the other as symbolising a change which would be popular and evoke a response among Anglo-Saxons.

Afterwards I met the clever cultured Yorck, a genuine scion of his intellectual but sometimes rather theoretical family, who propounded similar ideas. Finally I went a few days ago at Yorck's invitation a second time to his house where I found Moltke, Trott and Guttenberg and was worked on by all four (at Trott's instigation) with great passion. On the day I left Berlin Schulenburg sang the same tune. Of the five younger men he has the best judgment and political sense but on the other hand was the one most opposed to the Crown Prince [whom Goerdeler was proposing to make the new Head of State].

There was one other person whom Helmuth met in 1941 who must be mentioned here, although his connection with the planning of postwar Germany was rather different. When Alexander Kirk left the American Embassy in October 1940 he turned over his contact with Helmuth, as the most delicate and valuable one which he possessed, to his First Secretary George Kennan. Both parties recorded their impressions. Helmuth mentions a visit by Kennan to the Derfflingerstrasse on 13 September:

> Very nice. More fruitful than the evenings with Deuel. He has accepted my proposal to do something definite, will leave the service at Christmas, go home and devote himself to this task.* He is a good and nice man and I hope that he will really prove a positive influence for us. It always surprises me when people say that, to interest men in something, one must emphasise and demonstrate their personal interest in it. I can't do so because I don't think like that myself and my experience is exactly the opposite. What most men want to be convinced of is precisely the fact that they haven't any personal interest in the matter – that is what they long for. '*You know my personal affairs are all in a muddle just now and I did not know how to get out of it. But this work will put me right again and I hope by that way to be able to repay my debt of gratitude to Europe for the most important fifteen years of my existence.*' So speaks Kennan. I have no idea what he means by the first sentence, I know nothing about his private life. But what I find over and over again is gratitude when one says to somebody: do this, it will be useful and bring you

---

* Mr Kennan was unable in 1962 to remember what the task might have been but supposed it was to persuade the Allied governments to establish contact with Helmuth and his friends. When Kennan finally reached the United States in May 1942, he decided not to tell the administration what he knew about Helmuth as he did not trust their discretion.

nothing, at the most hard work, anxiety and danger. God knows I have no grounds for putting a low estimate on the people I go around with.

The last of four meetings mentioned by Helmuth took place at Kennan's house five days before Pearl Harbor. Kennan, after referring to visits to the Derfflingerstrasse in the black-out, goes on to say that later, when the Russian campaign was on, Helmuth became for some reason bolder.

He cheerfully came to lunch, one time, with my wife and myself. He once filled me with astonishment and consternation by walking into the American Embassy in broad daylight and asking to see me. I received him immediately, took him out on to the balcony of the office, where traffic noises were likely to drown out the effectiveness of microphones, and asked him how he had dared to do this. 'Oh,' he replied, 'the Gestapo would never believe that anyone coming this openly could be coming for anything other than a legitimate purpose.'

I consider him, in fact, to have been the greatest person, morally, and the largest and most enlightened in his concepts, that I met on either side of the battle lines in the Second World War. Even at that time – in 1940 and 1941 – he had looked beyond the whole sordid arrogance and the apparent triumphs of the Hitler régime; he had seen through to the ultimate catastrophe and had put himself to the anguish of accepting it and accommodating himself to it inwardly, preparing himself – as he would eventually have liked to help prepare his people – for the necessity of starting all over again, albeit in defeat and humiliation, to erect a new national edifice on a new and better moral foundation.

The image of this lonely, struggling man, one of the few genuine Protestant-Christian martyrs of our time, has remained for me over the intervening years as a pillar of moral conscience and an unfailing source of political and intellectual inspiration.[15]

THE RELIEF OF PRESENT EVILS

Even before the Russian campaign began, the *Abwehr* had been at odds with the national leadership over the way in which the conquered territories were to be treated. On 13 May Keitel had signed an order calling for immediate execution without trial of any Russian found obstructing German activities; German troops were to be immune from punishment for anything done to Russians unless these acts impeded German success. An annex – the notorious 'Commissar Order' – laid down that political commissars and other captured persons suspected of believing

in Communism were to be done away with as soon as they were identified. A supplementary order reinforcing these instructions, and providing for commissars to be handed over to the SS, was signed on 8
September by General Hermann Reinecke, the head of the General
Office of the Defence forces/*Allgemeines Wehrmachtamt* (AWA) in
the OKW.[16] Reinecke, the chief exponent of the 'hard line' among the
OKW heads of departments, provided Hitler's '*Lakeitel*' with a lackey
of his own; no love was lost between him and Canaris, who was technically his superior and tried to avoid personal dealings with him.* One
of the difficulties in opposing this policy was that the Soviet Union had
never fully adhered to the 1907 Hague Convention or to the 1929
Geneva Red Cross Convention about Prisoners-of-War.

Helmuth and his colleague Jaenicke drew up for Bürkner and Canaris a memorandum which the latter signed on 15 September.[17] It
shines out among the evidence of Nazi ruthlessness as a good deed in a
naughty world. For it began by claiming the existence ever since the
eighteenth century of general agreement that no punishment or revenge
should be imposed on prisoners-of-war, whose handling should be
designed to exclude them from any further part in hostilities. 'This
principle has developed in company with the view valid in all armies
that it goes against military ideas to kill or injure people who cannot
defend themselves.' The document went on to show how the orders
already issued contravened this principle and argued in seven further
paragraphs that the application of these orders would damage the reputation of the German army and complicate its tasks. An annex contained instructions issued by the USSR Council of People's Commissars which (if they were observed) would make the handling of
German prisoners conform closely with international regulations and so
remove one of the chief excuses for German policy. These arguments
were, however, brushed aside by Keitel who wrote on the memorandum,
'These doubts correspond to military ideas about wars of chivalry. Our
job is to suppress a view of life. For that reason I sanction the measures
proposed and give them my support.' His action did not go unnoticed
when he was tried at Nuremberg.

Helmuth also circulated evidence to disprove the story that the
Russians were taking no Germans prisoner. When the Nazi authorities
held up the letters which came through from prisoners in Russia, so as

* When Hitler finally decided, in late 1943, to override military objections and
appoint political commissars in the German army, and Party and generals were
as a result at loggerheads as to which of them should have charge, the job was
given to Reinecke as a person who was both a soldier and a convinced Nazi. On
the evening of 20 July 1944 he was put by Hitler in command of all troops in
Berlin and thereafter sat with Freisler on the Court which condemned to death
the surviving officers (including Peter Yorck) who had joined in the attempt.
In 1949 he was sentenced at Nuremberg to life imprisonment.

to buttress up this story, members of the *Abwehr* got hold of some, put them in small batches into post-boxes all over Berlin and thus conveyed them undetected to their intended recipients. Finally on 14 November Helmuth was able to write:

> As regards prisoners, my main opponent General Reinecke has finally found himself compelled to propose that the Red Cross should look after the treatment of German soldiers in captivity. The consequence must be that we allow the R.C. in on our side too and therewith change our methods.

When in January the AWA, in conjunction with Himmler, proposed announcing that five hundred Jews would be transported eastwards for every German soldier killed in Russian captivity, so as to make Jews in enemy countries press for humane handling of German prisoners, *Abteilung Ausland* found it easy to show that the proposal was as full of practical difficulties as it was devoid of legal authority. The treatment of Russian prisoners does seem to have shown some slight improvement, partly because fear of what would happen to them in captivity increased the desperation of their resistance, partly because the German war machine came to need more of them as labour. As Helmuth wrote on 6 November:

> Headquarters have issued instructions which make one doubt the sanity of the people who sit there. When taken with everything else, it is downright comic. All of a sudden large numbers of the Russian prisoners are now to be given places in the economy and a parenthesis says that 'the need to provide them with adequate nourishment goes without saying'. They behave as though they knew nothing of the previous orders.

16 September

> The generally unsatisfactory position with its reactions in the occupied countries has led to a wave of measures of intimidation intended to keep these countries down. One has finally to realise that the death penalty no longer works. But instead of drawing from that the conclusion that you have got to get the people you are ruling on your side instead of against you, the conclusion has been drawn that something more frightening than death has got to be found. The Führer has personally thought out two measures in this direction which certainly are noteworthy [shooting of hostages and mass executions]. They will all recoil upon us and rightly too! It is all evidence of weakness and incohesion which can do us no good.

21 October

> The day has been so full of horrible news that I can't write col-

lectedly although I came back at 5 and have had tea. What cuts me
to the quick at the moment is the inadequacy of the soldiers' reaction.
Falkenhausen [GOC Belgium] and Stülpnagel [GOC France] have
returned to their posts instead of resigning after the latest incidents,
dreadful new orders are going out and nobody seems to find them
remarkable. How can one bear one's share of guilt?

In one part of Serbia two villages have been reduced to ashes,
1,700 men and 240 women of the inhabitants have been executed.
That is the punishment for an attack on three German soldiers. In
Greece 240 men were shot in one village. The village was burnt
down, the women and children left on the spot to mourn their husbands and fathers and homes. In France extensive shootings are
going on as I write. In this way more than a thousand men are being
murdered for a certainty every day and thousands more Germans are
being habituated to murder. And all that is child's play compared to
what is happening in Poland and Russia. How can I bear this and sit
just the same in my warm room and drink tea? Don't I make myself
into an accomplice by doing so? What shall I say when someone asks
me, 'And what did you do during this time?'

They have been collecting the Berlin Jews since Saturday. They
are taken away at 9.15 in the evening and shut for the night into a
synagogue. Then they go off with what they can carry in their hands
to Litzmannstadt and Smolensk. The authorities want to spare us the
sight of how they are left to perish in hunger and cold so arrange this
in Litzmannstadt and Smolensk. A friend of Kiep's saw a Jew collapse in the street: when she wanted to help him, a policeman intervened, prevented her and kicked the body as it lay on the ground so
that it rolled into the gutter. Then he turned to the lady with a last
vestige of shame and said, 'Those are our orders.'

How can one know things like this and yet walk about a free man?
What right has one to do so? Isn't it inevitable that, if one does, one
will one day find oneself in that position and be rolled into the gutter? This is all summer lightning, for the storm has yet to come. If
only I could be rid of the awful feeling that I have let myself be
corrupted, that I no longer react keenly enough to such things, that
they torment me without producing spontaneous reactions! I have
misrepresented myself, because in such matters I over-react. I think
about possible reactions instead of acting.

In November a letter from a friend produced a further outburst of
indignation:

What distinguishes his attitude is fear of having to take responsibility for a group which is too big to be visualised. The whole
question of physical courage which seems to be involved is only

camouflage. Of course it is more convenient to feel oneself responsible for only a few people and at the same time to be prevented by
blinkers – or rather by lack of will – from seeing the kind of evil that
is brought about by the way such responsibility is discharged, not
seeing that one is protecting murder and robbery. In reality these
people rather than the criminals are the crux of the evil. There are
criminals everywhere and always have been but it is the inescapable
duty of all right-thinking people to keep crime within bounds and
whoever evades this duty is more guilty than the criminal himself.

He returned to the same theme two days later.

I am so bitter, not to say furious, with men of this type, because I
have more difficulties with these smooth characters than with anyone
else. They are the kind of people who have got us the reputation in
the world of not being fit to govern ourselves, let alone other people.
These men lack vision, they fail to see that every action has its
consequences, that everything is connected, that a murder in Warsaw
has repercussions in Calcutta and Sydney, at the North Pole and in
Kurdistan, not political repercussions but moral ones. As for the self-
sacrifice involved in war, I only believe in it up to a point. It is a
kind of self-satisfaction, of a cloak, which will be disposed of later
on. One doesn't fight for something but against something; hate is
the dominant passion of war, not love. What war breeds is cowardice,
cant and mass psychosis. To give you an example, yesterday I was at
a meeting in the Foreign Office about the Jewish persecutions. It was
the first time that I had been involved with this question officially.
Single-handed against twenty-four other people I attacked an ordin-
ance and for the time being held it up after it already had the
approval of all ministers and of the chief of the OKW. And then I
came back and the responsible official in the OKW asked me, 'Why
have you done that? You can't change anything about it now; naturally all these measures lead to catastrophe.' I am not insensitive to
the charm and qualities of people like that but their actions are determined by expediency and have no moral basis. Like chameleons they
make a good impression in a healthy society, a bad one in a depraved
society. In reality they are neither one thing nor the other. They are
stuffed shirts. True, there have to be stuffed shirts. But what is intolerable is when a stuffed shirt, who has sat by and let the depravity
spread, acts as though he had a moral justification for doing so. Yes,
I know I am being extremely severe. But it is necessary if one isn't to
slide into hypocrisy without noticing it.

9 November

Today I spent the morning with some Jewish people who needed to have their affairs put in order before being deported. Some 10,000 more have been ordered to hold themselves in readiness during the last three days. It was gratifying to see how well these people kept up their spirits and I can only wish that we shall behave as well when our time comes.

11 November

A difficult day. In the fight against the latest Jewish order,* I have at any rate achieved getting the three most important generals in the OKW to write to the fourth [Reinecke] to say he must withdraw forthwith the approval which he gave on behalf of the Chief of the OKW. The next stage is therefore to see whether he does this. The real battle will then begin. Wouldn't this be a wonderful issue on which to be thrown out of this outfit? [i.e. sacked from the *Abwehr*]

12 November

In the fight for Jews and Russians, or alternatively to stop the spread of savagery in the military mind, I have made such surprising progress that I am pushing at a succession of open doors.

13 November

The last few days were extremely difficult not so much because there was anything substantial to be achieved as because I had to exert myself to get all the decent people in line. Also I slept very little for two nights because I woke up at three and thought about Jews and Russians. To return to our correspondents. My patience with these people is completely at an end and yet I mustn't show it; sometimes I can hardly manage that.

The man I saw yesterday had completely broken down. But do you suppose he feels any obligation to do anything to get out of the mess which he has helped to create? Far from it! When I merely said that we should have to be prepared to write off a lot in good time, he said with obvious indignation, 'We can never write *that* off.' [This probably applies to the surrender of German territory.] And in twelve months [after an armistice] he would again be giving his blessing to a *Freikorps*† to operate against enemy armies of occupation which were trying to maintain order. And if I were to remind him that I had prophesied to him, before the war and during its opening months, precisely the situation which he now sees, and that he answered me, 'Then try to create a more optimistic outlook among your acquaintances', he would still regard my diagnosis then as something that no patriotic man ought to think, let alone utter. I say no

---

* Probably an order about the handling of Jews who came into German hands in Russia.
† Above, p. 21.

more, I've written these people off, want nothing more from them and will merely take care not to turn them more against me than is necessary. But you anyhow will understand that there is no patience left in me for these people and no patience for their excuses. To them applies the motto that they think they can save themselves

> If together we cling
> Singing God Save the King
> And throw men overboard to the sharks.

Well, what has happened? My memory of the last two days is none too good. Russian prisoners, evacuated Jews, Russian prisoners, shot hostages, gradual spreading into Germany of measures 'tested' in the occupied territories, evacuated Jews again, Russian prisoners, a nerve clinic where SS men are cared for who have broken down while executing women and children. That is what the world has been for these two days. Yesterday I said good-bye to a Jewish lawyer, once well known, who had the Iron Cross, the Hohenzollern family Order, the Golden Badge of the wounded, and who is going to commit suicide with his wife today because he is due to be taken away this evening. He has a nice daughter of about nineteen who wants to live and is determined to face what lies ahead of her. I have given her my 'permanent' address in case we and she survive the deluge and our address still makes sense. Very probably this will not happen.

Meanwhile I've actually succeeded in putting a few obstructive spokes in the wheel of the Jewish persecution. My self-assumed representation of the rights of the *Wehrmacht* has been backed by Canaris and Thomas.* I dictated the letters for each of them to sign and both were obviously pleased, just as in general a surprising number of people are willing to make a stand as soon as anyone else does. But there has always got to be somebody to go on first; nobody will do it alone. And apart altogether from the unpleasantness and strain of going ahead, how seldom do I get a chance to do it! But when one does, the success is pleasing. Thus it was nice to see how an old colonel suddenly got red in the face with pleasure that for once someone had done something.

14 November
I have made a certain amount of progress this week. In the Jewish affair I have achieved for the moment a veto by the OKW.

17 November
I have spent the whole day with the Jews again and actually got all divisions of the OKW behind me on the question. Tonight a colonel

* Thomas, General Georg (1890–1946), head of the Economic Defence and Munitions Division of the OKW and an anti-Nazi.

is going to Keitel and will propose to him tomorrow that an objection should be entered against the intended order. So in two or three days I should know whether I have really won a victory on the limited issue. [In the end he did not, as Keitel rejected Helmuth's views.] Hunger, illness and anxiety spread all the while under our rule. No one can ever guess the consequences which that will have, or how quickly they will develop. Only one thing is sure. The Horsemen of the Apocalypse are beginners compared to what is ahead of us: *Certus an, incertus quando.* Every day brings new insights into the depths to which men can sink.

18 November

What is more, the situation at home is appreciably worse than I had imagined. The Jewish persecutions and the church affair have produced a great deal of unrest. The promises of military victory, of leave or discharge for soldiers won't and can't be fulfilled. Hunger is creeping closer to everybody, there is nothing left to buy, and there is nobody to help do the necessary jobs.

11 December

—'s letter is such complete nonsense that I wonder how an inherently intelligent man can get into such a state of mental confusion. It just shows what a 'yes-man' he is! He takes the world as it comes and then paints for himself a picture of the world which fits in with the way it treats him. He overestimates material and might, he treats war as more important than any other political factor, he despises the individual and he ignores the basic foundation of all European culture, namely that each human being is an independent creation of the Divine Mind. Instead he takes refuge in the Old Testament and in Asiatic notions. Well, the next few years are going to change his notions a bit.

The various experiences through which he was passing were all combining to deepen Helmuth's faith. One of the things which pleased him so much about Carlo Schmid was that within ten minutes of starting to talk they had got on to the subject of religion. 'This always happens with people who really share my views – though he is more of a mystic than I am.' And it is a most striking thing that all the most determined members of the *Widerstand* either were or gradually became convinced Christians. The only exceptions to this – and ones which prove the rule – were the Communists. It would seem as though a mere attitude of humanist benevolence is not enough to see one through a time of such trouble; those who start with it either compromise with the evil or feel the need to find an anchoring point beyond the visible world. The furnace of horror and danger through which they were passing gave fresh reality to any conventional beliefs which they may have inherited and convinced them that, if the rest of the world was to be saved from going in the direction to which Nazism and Communism pointed, it must find again a faith for individuals to live by.

Helmuth asked Adolf Reichwein for advice about religious education for children. His own concern about the bringing up of children was all the more keen because on 23 September Freya and he had had another son Konrad.* Helmuth wrote M.B.'s name into the Gräditz church register as one of the boy's godparents. After his October visit he wrote, with reference to his remark of 30 September about few islets escaping the oncoming misery:

> As always it was lovely being with you. I only hope it will be possible to preserve the islet so that one can keep at least one foot in peace. Oh! I found it so very very delightful and was enjoying it again in my mind on the journey back.

Once in October Helmuth described how, after waking at 4 a.m. he had spent his time thinking about Kreisau, his family and the war, an activity which, instead of distressing him, had led him pleasantly into a fresh day.

> It gave me the opportunity to become conscious of a change which has taken place in me during the war and which I can only ascribe to a deeper awareness of Christian principles. I don't think I am any less pessimistic than I used to be, I don't think I am less sensitive to human suffering now that it has assumed crude material forms, I consider even today that the murderer is more to be pitied than the victim, but all the same I can take it more lightly; it inhibits me less than in the past. The realisation that what I do is without purpose doesn't hinder me from doing it because I am much more firmly convinced than I was in the past that the only things which have any purpose at all are those which are done in the realisation of the purposelessness of all action. I sometimes argue with myself reproaching myself for having constructed this theory for my own convenience. Perhaps I have, but all the same I can't give it up.

* In 1965 Konrad was married, by Harald Poelchau, to Hans Berndt von Haeften's daughter Ulrike.

20 Steps Forward

January–Whitsun 1942

'J A , Serpuchoff.'

One of Helmuth's first letters in the New Year starts with these words. He had appropriated the name of a town* sixty miles south of Moscow for the mythical Russian manager who was going to take over the Kreisau estate after Germany's defeat and live in the Berghaus.† In the course of the next two years the family came to know this man so well that he was almost a friend; when Freya failed to put out the best jam or marmalade, she was jocularly accused of 'keeping it for Serpuchoff'.

The prophecy that the Russians would reach Berlin had been made to Rösch in October, while George Kennan reports Helmuth as having said that 'my own homeland of Silesia will go to the Czechs or the Poles'. According to Steltzer he said that he would feel no compunction if Silesia were to be joined with Poland or Czechoslovakia, with Prague or Warsaw as its capital.[1] In judging this marked lack of national feeling, one must remember not only that Helmuth considered Hitler to have provoked the loss of Germany's eastern territories by attacking Russia unsuccessfully but also that he was convinced of the need for Europe to work together as a continental unit if its self-destruction and decline was to be arrested.

But Helmuth was under no illusions about the probable attitude of Serpuchoff and his friends; in the letter referred to, he says that he has been talking to Mierendorff whose information led him to suppose that for Freya to await the Russian arrival in the Berghaus (as she was in fact to do) would be tantamount to suicide and serve no useful purpose. He therefore went on to discuss friends in Austria, etc., where she might arrange to take refuge.

The only Russians who came to Kreisau at this stage arrived in a different capacity, being prisoners-of-war brought to work on the estate. Helmuth arranged for the scanty food which they received in their camp to be supplemented by a midday meal and for those who died to

* There were two places in which he might have come across the name. It was mentioned as the scene of a German repulse in the Russian communiqué for 8.xii.41. It occurs in Chapter III Book XIII of *War and Peace* which he read that autumn. Indeed it seems to have been the farthest point reached by both the French and the German invaders! There is no knowing how far he realised this.

† The Polish manager is in fact said to be doing so today!

be buried in the cemetery with a cross to identify the grave. He once told Bishop Preysing in fury how one of them who had broken ranks to seize a raw beet in hunger had been shot out of hand by the guard. When the incident was reported to the camp commandant, his only question was, 'How many shots were needed?'[2]

Soon afterwards Helmuth had another remarkable – though less accurate – vision of the future which he recorded in a letter of 23 March. He had been at the funeral of one of the Kreisau smallholders. He went on to look at the family mausoleum and over a stretch of a hundred yards on the way back seems to have fallen into a reverie.

> I was a very old man and had outlived you all. . . .
> I had achieved everything that I wanted. The world looked as I had wanted it to do but it had cost an enormous effort and you had not lived to see the success. That was the bitterest part. I could no longer tell you that all the sacrifices and renunciations and struggles had borne fruit. I thought about these sacrifices and worries and wondered whether the success had been worth them. And then I thought, although it pained me to do so: even if it had meant that I had to torture myself, that you hadn't had what you were entitled to have, that I had no family or friends left because I had neglected the former and outlived the latter, even if it meant too that I didn't even have a happy old age but had to live here alone with a housekeeper, I still had to act as I did and would do so again.
> And then I found myself at Reetz' cottage and was sixty years younger. Remarkable, wasn't it?

Freya, when this letter was written, was away with the children for a month in Switzerland. But this meant that letters to her had to cross a frontier, which may explain the fact that none contain any news of interest between 8 February and 15 April. The freedom with which Helmuth usually wrote to her may seem surprising. But his letters would have been difficult to identify at the Berlin end, while at the Kreisau end not only were the people in the post-office on good terms with the Moltkes but they were simple country folk who would have understood little of what Helmuth was talking about. If the interception had been made in Schweidnitz or elsewhere en route, the delay would have been noticed. Helmuth's incoming post was more susceptible to control but Freya's letters to him contained little or nothing that was incriminating. There was one further safeguard. His minute compressed handwriting was hard enough to read at the best of times – he usually made things easier for his friends by using a typewriter – and only a little extra effort and a few abbreviations or codewords were needed to make it indecipherable except to an initiate or a skilled cryptographer.

Helmuth's valued colleague Schmitz was killed in January in a skiing accident and was replaced in June by the transfer from the Institute of Dr Wilhelm Wengler who soon became no less valued and who since the war has become a distinguished authority on international law. Another name which begins to figure about this time, with a first mention on 15 December 1941, is that of Wilhelm Leuschner, always referred to as 'the Uncle'. He was a man of fifty-four and a former trade union leader who had been Social Democratic Minister of the Interior in Hesse from 1928 to 1933 and as a result spent some years in a concentration camp. He provided Goerdeler's chief link with the working classes and was now brought to Helmuth by Mierendorff as an important man to consult about social and trade union questions.

Helmuth's letters at this time show a gradual improvement in his spirits:

6 January 1942

[Hitler's veto on withdrawals will mean] that the Russians certainly won't make any territorial gains but our eastern army will just be ground to powder where it stands. And the soldiers still fail to realise this. They aren't generals but technicians, military technicians and the whole thing is a gigantic crime.

[To do the generals justice, a number did give orders to retreat from hopeless positions, only to be relieved of their commands, dismissed from the ranks and even condemned to death.]

9 January

[After dwelling on the satisfactory state of his relations with Gablentz, Mierendorff, Preysing and Haeften.] So there is a lot to be pleased with on the human side, only the problem is to see how this can be turned to practical advantage.

10 January

[At a smart dinner at a steel magnate's.] It was instructive to see how many people still haven't had their eyes opened to the real causes and still attribute the mistakes to people other than themselves. 'The English are to blame for everything.' 'The last thing we wanted was this or that.' Uexküll and I joined forces in making clear to these people how at the end of the day they will deserve just what they get.

The next letter was written nine days before Heydrich convened a meeting in the Berlin suburb of Wannsee at which he explained to fifteen representatives of the SS and various ministries the Nazi Government's intention to exterminate all the eleven million Jews within its reach.

11 January

I can't stop myself wondering how the present state of affairs, and the developments likely in the next four weeks, are going to be broken to the German people and how they will react. Unless a miracle occurs, even the Cassandra-like utterances which I have been venting since the beginning of the war will pale into insignificance beside the reality. When that happens, will anyone be in a position to master the chaos? Will each individual realise his guilt? Will East Germany or Prussia then be missionised and converted to Christianity. Or will everything vanish into a maelstrom of heathen materialism? Whatever happens, the battle that began at Christmastime means a bigger turning-point for better or worse than the cannonade of Valmy.* Perhaps it is the final end of the Holy Roman Empire, perhaps the resurrection.

23 January

I hope you can get [during the visit to Switzerland] a rosy gleam through the dark clouds. You must keep up your spirits, allowing for the worst to happen but set to encounter something less serious. If we can keep our nerves and our strength, we shall pull through.

24 January

Don't be *downcast*, there's no point at all in that. We shall have to be prepared to take much worse news yet without losing our capacity for action. Churchill ended one of his speeches by saying ... '*Great Britain is still the sole master of its destiny.*' That is a very good phrase.[3]

27 January

Yes it is good that you are regaining courage. Courage is vital. One must make up one's mind that nothing is going to make one knuckle under or stray from the right path. Whether one then has the strength to hold to the resolve and the capacity to recognise which path is right is not solely within one's own control. But the will is what matters.

The second meeting at Gross Behnitz occurred from 13 to 16 March. This time the Trotts and Wussows were absent and were replaced by Friedrich Zitzewitz-Muttrin (a Pomeranian landowner who was a friend of the Borsigs), Frau von zur Mühlen (the widow of Dr Ohle), Father Hans Galli (an agricultural expert sent by Rösch) and Fritz Christiansen-Weniger. When Helmuth invited the latter to attend this or some other meeting and explained the nature of the activity which

* By which in 1792 the French armies repulsed the attempt of the European Powers to suppress the Revolution. Goethe, who was present, said on the previous night, 'Here and now a new epoch in world history is beginning.'

G

was afoot, Christiansen-Weniger, although agreeing to join in, said he considered the work more dangerous than service at the front. He got the reply, 'We must be clear about that. If I am hanged, I shan't be the first Moltke to whom that happened and I hope I shan't be the last.'

In the middle of April, from the 10th to the 18th, Helmuth was sent at short notice to Scandinavia on behalf of the *Abwehr*. In the previous February, Quisling, on being made Prime Minister of Norway, had quarrelled with the church over the control of youth and forbidden the Provost of Trondheim Cathedral to hold services. This had led first the Norwegian bishops and then, on 5 April, the pastors to lay down their offices. Quisling's reply was to arrest Berggrav, the Bishop of Oslo and prime mover in the resistance, on Easter Sunday. He was subsequently put in prison. Helmuth and Steltzer had already discussed this contingency in the light of the fact that the German GOC was forbidden to report back on such matters as the behaviour of the SS. They had agreed that, if it arose, Steltzer should immediately cable a code-word to Berlin. On receipt of this message, Canaris and Oster decided to send two members of their staff to Oslo to investigate the position and make representations. They were on the one hand to point out to the civilian authorities that, if the whole Norwegian population was provoked into unrest, a number of German troops would be tied down in the country when badly needed elsewhere: on the other, they were to encourage the Norwegians against giving way.

The two people picked for this mission were Helmuth and Dietrich Bonhoeffer, who was at the time working for the *Abwehr* under his brother-in-law Dohnanyi. Helmuth was regarded as the senior of the two – he got a distinctly better hotel room in Oslo than Bonhoeffer! They travelled there by the Sassnitz–Trälleborg ferry and Malmö. On the way Helmuth had – or rather avoided – an encounter with some of the people who provided a main source of support for Hitler:

The ship was comfortable but our travelling companions simply excruciating and frightful. I would have preferred to speak nothing but English so as to distinguish myself from this bunch of robbers and clots. Apart from a few people who were tolerable and the stewards and a few German foremen, who travelled third-class, there was nothing on the ship but the scum of the German middle-class. Employees of firms who work in Oslo and whose only activity consisted in talking about how to profiteer and in seeing how much they could eat, drink, smoke and buy while on board. They immediately formed queues in front of the tobacco counter. Fortunately the meals were very modest, which moved the clots to blasphemy. I didn't go to lunch (at four o'clock) at all because the idea of sitting in a room with such people for an hour was too much for me; it would have embarrassed me in front of the stewards. So I ate later and virtually alone – only the captain and first officer and perhaps five other people with me....

In Oslo they were looked after by Steltzer, who boasted of having all the faculties of a university represented on his staff, and divided their time between him, Falkenhorst* the German GOC (who had once stayed at Kreisau, loved the sound of his own voice and told tedious stories), his Chief of Staff, the local *Abwehr* representative and various Norwegians.[4] The main (clandestine) meeting with the latter took place in the flat of a sympathetic German industrialist who, however, did not join in the talk. Besides encouraging the Norwegians to stand firm, Helmuth took the opportunity to tell them something of the work which he had organised in Germany and discussed the idea of asking the King and Crown Prince of Norway (who were in London) to plead with the Allies for contact to be established with the *Widerstand*. Such a move was thought in the end to be premature. Helmuth unfortunately had a bad feverish cold throughout the visit, which is perhaps why he reminded his hosts of Saint Sebastian.[5]

The security authorities had been planning to bring Berggrav before a 'People's Court' on the very morning after Helmuth and Bonhoeffer arrived, but this was postponed and on the third and last day of their stay in Oslo a telegram arrived from Bormann in Berlin instructing the Reich Commissioner to transfer Berggrav from prison to house-arrest at his home in the suburbs.† The guards placed there over the Bishop soon told him that they were on his side, and would be glad to lend him a policeman's uniform any time he wanted to go into the city, at the same time putting a dummy in his bed so that they could answer inquiries by saying he was asleep! On one occasion Steltzer was disconcerted by the entrance of a bearded policeman into one of his meetings with the Resistance until the intruder asked, 'Don't you recognise me?' and rejoined the episcopate by taking off cap, glasses and beard. When asked how he had got there, he replied, 'By the suburban railway.'

Helmuth and Bonhoeffer then travelled back via Stockholm and Copenhagen. Prior to April 1940 Norwegian firms had placed contracts for ships with Swedish builders; the boats were nearly ready but the Swedes were contesting the German demand for them to be handed

---

* Falkenhorst, General Nikolaus von (b. 1885), GOC German troops invading Norway 1940. GOC Norway till 1944. Condemned to death by British–Norwegian Court 1946; sentence commuted to long imprisonment. Released 1953.
† This telegram was probably instigated by Himmler who had met Berggrav in 1941. It was certainly not the outcome of representations which the two emissaries caused to be sent from Oslo since the letters make it pretty clear that Helmuth did not agree the terms of his report to Canaris with Falkenhorst until the 15th, the day the telegram arrived.

over to the occupying power. Helmuth's call on the German embassy in
Stockholm on this matter was, however, only a cover for the main
purpose of his visit which was to despatch letters to friends in enemy
countries through Maria Strindberg.* Two of these, which in fact
reached London in June through the Special Operations Executive,
survive.

The first, addressed to Lionel Curtis, read:

*I will try to get this letter through to you, giving you a picture of
the state of affairs on our side.*

*Things are worse and better than anybody outside Germany can
believe them to be. They are worse, because the tyranny, the terror,
the loss of values of all kinds, is greater than I could have believed a
short time ago. The numbers of Germans killed by legal process in
November was 25 a day through judgments of the civil courts and at
least 75 a day by judgments of the courts martial, numbers running
into hundreds are killed daily in concentration camps and by simple
shooting without any pretence of a trial. The constant danger in which
we live is formidable. At the same time the greater part of the population has been uprooted and has been conscribed to forced labour
of some kind and has been spread all over the continent untying all
bonds of nature and surrounding and thereby loosening the beast in
man, which is reigning. The few really good people who try to stem
the tide are isolated as far as they have to work in these unnatural
surroundings, because they cannot trust their comrades, and they are
in danger from the hatred of the oppressed people even when they
succeed in saving some from the worst. Thousands of Germans who
will survive will be dead mentally, will be useless for normal work.*

*But things are also better than you can believe, and that in many
ways. The most important is the spiritual awakening, which is starting up, coupled as it is with the preparedness to be killed, if need be.
The backbone of this movement is to be found in both the christian
confessions, protestant as well as catholic. The catholic churches are
crowded every Sunday, the protestant churches not yet, but the
movement is discernible. We are trying to build on this foundation,
and I hope that in a few months more tangible proof of this will be
apparent outside. Many hundreds of our people will have to die before this will be strong enough, but today they are prepared to do so.
This is true also of the young generation. I know of two cases where
a whole class of schoolboys, the one in a protestant part of the
country, the other in a catholic part, decided to follow the calling of
priests, something which would have been quite impossible 6 months
ago. But today it is beginning to dawn on a not too numerous but*

* Née Lazar, above, p. 58.

active part of the population not that they have been misled, not that they are in for a hard time, not that they might lose the war, but that what is done is sinful, and that they are personally responsible for every savage act that has been done, not of course in a mortal way, but as Christians. Perhaps you will remember that, in discussions before the war, I maintained that belief in God was not essential for coming to the results you arrive at. Today I know I was wrong completely wrong. You know that I have fought the Nazis from the first day, but the amount of risk and readiness for sacrifice which is asked from us now, and that which may be asked from us tomorrow require more than right ethical principles, especially as we know that the success of our fight will probably mean a total collapse as a national unit. But we are ready to face this.

The second great asset which we are slowly but steadily acquiring is this; the great dangers which confront us as soon as we get rid of the NS force us to visualise Europe after the war. We can only expect to get our people to overthrow this reign of terror and horror if we are able to show a picture beyond the terrifying and hopeless immediate future. A picture which will make it worthwhile for the disillusioned people to strive for, to work for, to start again and to believe in. For us Europe after the war is less a problem of frontiers and soldiers, of top-heavy organisations or grand plans, but Europe after the war is a question of how the picture of man can be reestablished in the breasts of our fellow-citizens. This is a question of religion and education, of ties to work and family, of the proper relation of responsibility and rights. I must say, that under the incredible pressure under which we have to labour we have made progress, which will be visible one day. Can you imagine what it means to work as a group when you cannot use the telephone, when you are unable to post letters, when you cannot tell the names of your closest friends to your other friends for fear that one of them might be caught and might divulge the names under pressure?

We are, after considerable difficulties, in communication with the christian groups in the various occupied territories with the exception of France, where, as far as we can find out, there is no really effective opposition on a fundamental basis, but only the basis of casual activity. These people are simply splendid and are a great accession of strength to us giving trust to many others. Of course their position is easier than ours: moral and national duties are congruous even to the simple-minded, while with us there is an apparent clash of duties.

Happily I have been able to follow the activities of my English friends, and I hope they all keep their spirits up. The hardest bit of the way is still to come, but nothing is worse than to slack on the way. Please do not forget, that we trust that you will stand it through

*without flinching as we are prepared to do our bit, and don't forget
that for us a very bitter end is in sight when you have seen matters
through. We hope that you will realise that we are ready to help you
win war and peace.*

Yours ever,
James

The second, to M.B., was only sixteen lines long and consisted mostly
of family news, notably of Konrad's birth and of M.B.'s nomination
as his godfather. But it did contain the sentences:

> *I expect to be able to come to Stockholm again in autumn. Might
> it be possible for you to come? If so, please communicate to Fru
> Strindberg, Stockholm, Essingbrogatan. I suppose that I could
> arrange any date in September or October and I trust a meeting
> might be useful.*

M.B. was at that time working for the Political Warfare Executive
and, on getting the letter at the beginning of June, asked his chiefs for
leave to fly to Stockholm (which was only possible in an RAF Mosquito) and take up the invitation. They had no objection but were not
qualified to give authority. In July it seemed that the necessary permission would be forthcoming, but shortly before he was due to leave
M.B. was told that the scheme had been turned down. All he could do
was to send a letter which was never delivered, because Helmuth refused to meet anyone belonging to the enemy whom he did not already
know. A friend in a key post afterwards said to M.B., 'I thought the
question of your trip would go high but I was a bit surprised when it
reached the Prime Minister!' M.B. subsequently heard through Lionel
Curtis that Churchill had mixed up Helmuth with his cousin Hans
Adolf von Moltke, then German Ambassador in Madrid, but neither
this nor the story that Hans Adolf had also been putting out peace
feelers can be substantiated. (The Foreign Office certainly knew the
difference between the two Moltkes.)*

On his way from Copenhagen to Berlin, Helmuth visited the estate
of Hans Schlange-Schöningen near Stettin. Dr Schlange-Schöningen
had been Commissioner for Eastern Aid/*Osthilfe*† under Brüning and
was later to be head of the German Food Administration in the British
Zone and the first German Ambassador in London after the war. His
children had become close friends of Henry Brooke, who had stayed
with them in 1938 and visited Kreisau with one of the sons on his way
back to England. Helmuth was anxious to see the extremely efficient
estate and obtained some plants for the Kreisau garden. But in the

---

* Hans Adolf died (of appendicitis) in March 1943.
† Above, pp. 61–2.

course of inspecting the estate he discussed politics and asked whether his host would be prepared to join in the planning for post-war. Schlange-Schöningen gave a tentative consent and a retired senior civil servant, Karl Passarge, who was a close friend and present at the conversation, later met Helmuth and Peter Yorck in Berlin but without any practical result. A mutually convenient date could not be found for a second visit by Helmuth to Schöningen in September.

On getting back to Berlin, Helmuth presented his report to Canaris: it was then submitted to Keitel who wrote on it 'one of his well-known NS Party phrases'.[6] There is no evidence that Dietrich Bonhoeffer and Helmuth ever met again. This may seem strange. Here were two implacable opponents of Hitler who were both convinced Christians, both more than ordinarily intelligent. Helmuth would certainly have endorsed Bonhoeffer's view that it was the duty of a German who was a Christian to pray for the defeat of his country. He was also at this time particularly interested in the proper relation between church and state. One might have expected them to become fast friends. But in fact there were a number of reasons why this should not have happened. They certainly differed on the question of whether it was wise and consistent with Christian principles to work for the assassination of Hitler. Paradoxically, it was the pastor who was convinced of the need and justification, the layman who had objections. Helmuth is not likely to have felt much at home in Bonhoeffer's abstract theological discussions nor would he have taken kindly to the horse-play with which, by some accounts, the cleric offset the intensity of his devotions. Helmuth already had links of his own with the Protestant churches who satisfied him but were in some cases antagonistic to Bonhoeffer. Finally Bonhoeffer was by this time a marked man, employed in the *Abwehr* because he had been forbidden to preach or teach, and his attendance at discussions might have attracted unwelcome attention to them. In any case he had arranged to be in Switzerland at Whitsun.

This was the date, from 22 to 25 May, on which the first of the Kreisau meetings took place, making the present an appropriate place to say a word about the so-called 'Kreisau Circle'/*Kreisauer Kreis*. The first thing to realise is that this label was never coined or used by the people concerned but by Neuhaus, the SD official who, after 20 July 1944, was put in charge of this field of investigation. In their inquiries the SD turned up a vast amount of evidence which they found it hard to sort into any kind of system (for the very good reason that what had been going on was not at all systematic). As an aid to clarification, they began to give names to groups of people who seemed to belong together, just as they had given the code-word 'Red Band'/*Rote Kapelle* to the Soviet spy ring with its headquarters in the Air Ministry which was uncovered in August 1942. Among the labels used were the

*Grafengruppe,** the *Kreisauer Kreis*, the *Solf Kreis*, the *Thadden Kreis*† and the Trade Union Clique/ *Gewerkschaftsklüngel*.

The 'Circle' was not in any sense formal: it had no definite member-ship. Helmuth and Peter had begun by turning to their friends for advice. Those friends brought in other friends, particularly where they felt that the person concerned had experience or contacts which could usefully supplement their own. In the circumstances, this was a natural way of proceeding but the resemblance to the methods of Lionel Curtis and the Round Table,‡ even to the week-end meetings at a house in the country, is too obvious to be just coincidental. But one result is that the question 'Who belonged to the Kreisau Circle?' is not one which admits of a precise answer. A possible line of reply is to list the people who went to one or other of the three occasions[7] when, in order to devote a continuous period of time to the study of a particular subject without attracting attention, the Moltkes invited friends to spend the week-end with them at Kreisau. But this is inadequate because there were several people who were too prominent or too suspect to be able to come to Kreisau. Moreover week-end gatherings were held at the Yorck estates of Kauern and Klein Oels and at Gross-Behnitz as well as at Kreisau. And patently the Kreisau gatherings were only an extension of the meetings which, as has been seen, were going on incessantly in Berlin. A second approach is therefore to list all the people whom Helmuth mentioned in his letters to Freya as having joined in such meetings. But that too is inadequate because his letters were far from exhaustive and a number of meetings took place without him being present. Many people had work outside Berlin which prevented them from attending, at any rate frequently. Yet, if these reservations are kept in mind, the two lists do throw some light on the question as to who the main participants were (see pp. 193–4).

Among these people Helmuth could fairly be described as 'the mov-ing spirit'. He started the whole process off, he assigned particular jobs to particular people, he chased laggards and he arranged for the gradual assembling of the various pieces into a whole. After the week-ends he drew up, in consultation with Yorck, a summary of conclusions which was then agreed with those of the participants who were within reach. As has been and will be seen, he argued vigorously for his own views about the overall approach and certain of the details but there were other areas in which he frankly admitted ignorance and was content to be guided by others. At no stage could he impose his views. Indeed, it was essential to the whole approach that views were not to be imposed by anyone but were to be evolved in the process of discussion. His position can best be compared to that of foreman in a gang of labourers

* Above, p. 111   † Below, pp. 296–8.
‡ Above, p. 68.

who, while having overall direction, does basically the same work as the rest.

The meetings at Kreisau were genuine 'week-ends', partly but not wholly to divert attention from their main purpose. The time was not devoted exclusively to 'conference sessions' – people went for walks and talked at leisure. The guests overflowed from the Berghaus into the Schloss and the accumulation of provisions to feed them had taken considerable forward planning. Throughout the war Helmuth insisted on rationing and similar regulations being strictly observed. 'If we are going to defy the government over big things,' he would say, 'we must be careful to keep its rules over little ones.' Peter Yorck's wife Marion was present as well as his sister Irene; there were on this first occasion five children in the house. The meeting was devoted to discussing partly the proper relationship between church and state, partly education. Steltzer led the discussion on church and state; Rösch explained the Catholic position; Peters the law as laid down by the 1933 Concordat between Germany and the Vatican; Reichwein spoke on schools; Helmuth on university reform. This choice of subject may seem surprising; if Englishmen and Americans were to sit down to work out a new form for the state, it is unlikely that this is where they would begin. But the choice of subject was more than a convenience of programming. To begin with, it was politically the most innocent of their various themes; if they proved to have overestimated the chances of keeping their talks quiet, the trouble into which this topic might get them would be relatively small. Moreover, Germany had been split ever since the Reformation to a greater extent than any other state in Europe by the Catholic–Protestant antagonism and even after 1870 this had proved a weakness. For one thing, the political spectrum was complicated by the existence of a specific party, the Centre, dedicated to advancing the political interests of the Catholic Church. To go on with there was the deep division already mentioned* between the Protestant Church and the Social Democrats. The Church of England has been described as 'the Tory Party at prayer' but the association in Germany between the various Protestant Churches (for each state in the Reich had had its own) and the German Nationalist People's Party, the group furthest to the right in Parliament, was even closer.† Harald Poelchau had deplored the tendency of Protestant theologians to lay emphasis not on the world of industry and of the class struggle but on *volk* and race. The typical attitude of many German Protestants even in face of the Third *Reich* was that the task of religion was to concern itself with saving individual souls and not to consider how society should be organised. Significantly the Protestants whom Helmuth invited to work

* Above, p. 30 *et seq.*
† Cf. Bethge, *Bonhoeffer*, p. 91.

with him were people who disagreed strongly with this point of view. If the deep divisions in Germany which had done so much to weaken its political effectiveness were to be overcome on a liberal basis, then the Protestant Church must be induced to concern itself with social reform and not hold people at arms' length simply because they were Socialists. The Catholic Church had shown greater vision in this respect, but Catholicism's character as a religion of authority had to be reconciled with a free society (a process which was assisted by the experience of life under a non-religious authoritarianism).

But there was more to it than this. Germany had not merely to be given a sense of community on a voluntary rather than an imposed basis but the havoc which National Socialism had brought to German moral values had also to be repaired. Helmuth and most of those associated with him believed that this could only be done on a religious foundation. Their experience in resisting evil had suggested to them that benevolence was not enough. The difficulty, of course, is that one cannot get faith in a divine purpose for the world accepted just by showing it to be a social necessity. But such an objection is not going to stop people who believe that that faith has been vindicated in practice. They therefore wanted to bring religion back to the heart of German life, but as a unifying and no longer as a divisive factor. And since the Churches are so much concerned with education and since German education had always contained such a strong authoritarian element, the whole question of church schools and educational reform was naturally brought in too.

The informal character of Helmuth's group needs to be remembered in considering two documents which were transmitted to the British at this time. The first was a 'Memorandum for the English Government' which was given by Adam von Trott to Dr Visser't Hooft* in Geneva at the end of April 1942 and brought by him through Vichy France to London. There are slightly conflicting accounts of how it was prepared but the probability is that its contents were exhaustingly discussed by Trott, Haeften and Eugen Gerstenmaier in Berlin during the winter of 1941/2; Trott carried the upshot in his head to Geneva and there wrote it down, possibly showing the result[8] to Kessel and Dr Hans Schönfeld. The second document was handed by Schönfeld to George Bell, Bishop of Chichester, in Stockholm on 1 June. This[9] was certainly drafted by Schönfeld on his own responsibility but in the light of a memorandum

* Dr Willem Visser't Hooft was General Secretary of the Provisional Committee of what was to become, in 1948, the World Council of Churches. Dr Hans Schönfeld, a Lutheran pastor, was its research director. The Geneva headquarters of this organisation performed for the Protestant Churches during the war somewhat the same function of intermediary as did the Vatican in a bigger way for the Catholics. Dr Bell was chairman of the Universal Christian Council for Life and Work, the forerunner of the World Council of Churches.

by Trott and others which had been made available to him on his journey through Germany. Dietrich Bonhoeffer had heard of Bell's impending visit and also went, on a travel authority supplied by Canaris and Oster, to Sweden to meet him. Whether Bonhoeffer knew of Schönfeld's journey is uncertain: there was a past history of conflict between him and the German Church Office for External Affairs (in which Gerstenmaier was assistant to Bishop Heckel) and he may have thought that Schönfeld's close links with the Office might prejudice what he said to Bell about conditions in Germany.[10]

There has been a good deal of discussion as to how far these two memoranda should be regarded as 'Kreisau documents'. They clearly had not been discussed at Kreisau, for the first was handed over before, and the second only a week after, the first Kreisau meeting. If the question is rephrased to ask 'how far they represented the views of Helmuth and his friends', the answer is that the people responsible for preparing them were, or (in the case of Gerstenmaier) were about to become, Helmuth's close collaborators. He had in the previous August asked Adam von Trott to draft a document on foreign policy and saw Adam about once a month throughout the winter, though apparently not between 7 April and 17 June. It would be highly surprising if he had known nothing about what Adam planned to do in Geneva, while in Sweden his written good wishes were sent to Lionel Curtis through Schönfeld and Bell.[11] On 30 June he reported hearing from Adam (who had been on another trip to Geneva) 'the first English and American reactions to our efforts' which were 'not too bad'.

On the other hand Helmuth does not mention Gerstenmaier's name in a letter until 3 June and never mentions Schönfeld at all nor gives any indication of knowing him (though in fact he did). When expecting Adam von Trott on 17 June, Helmuth comments that he was eager to see whether his visitor would make up his mind to join fully in the work (*ob er nun den Absprung finden wird*). The truth would seem to be that the two documents represent the views of the people who were going to exercise a major influence on the subsequent thinking of the group on foreign affairs but, at the time when they were drafted, that thinking had not got to the stage of being at all precisely formulated.[12] Helmuth knew of the general line which was being taken[13] and there is no evidence of his having disagreed with it. But this was not an operation which stemmed from an initiative of his.

Nowhere in his letter to Lionel Curtis did he give any sign of asking for negotiations (though this may have lain behind his invitation to M.B. to meet him in the autumn). The implication in the Curtis letter is that the war would go on to the end. His invention of Serpuchoff and his other remarks quoted at the outset of this chapter hardly suggest that he expected the Russians to stop before they reached Germany.

Such attitudes are not altogether in line with the approach of the documents transmitted through Dr Visser't Hooft and the Bishop, which argue in favour of a peace to be negotiated (after the overthrow of Hitler) between the new German régime and the Anglo-Americans. The aspects of those documents which raised doubts in London were the failure to deal with the future of the German armed forces and the disregard of the obligation which Britain had undertaken in July 1941 *not* to make peace separately from Russia. The obvious policy for any country which finds itself up against a superior coalition is to try to split its enemies. This is precisely what the Nazis themselves were to do later on, and by anticipating them the authors of these two documents drew on themselves the suspicion that they were being used as naïve catspaws, by the army leaders if not by the Nazis. Few of the *Widerstand* leaders could bring themselves to believe that the British and Americans (which really means Churchill and still more Roosevelt, for these matters were decided at the very highest level) judged the dangers involved in leaving Germany to dominate Central Europe to be greater than those involved in allowing Russia to reach the Elbe. The *Widerstand* attempts at negotiation were condemned to futility by the failure to realise that the things which they did not like about Anglo-American policy were due to something more fundamental than a failure to think of the arguments which Goerdeler, Trott and others propounded to them. There is no evidence that in these matters Helmuth sympathised more with the Anglo-Americans than with his colleagues but his habitual pessimism is likely to have made him sceptical about the prospects of their endeavours.*

* A full discussion of the rights and wrongs of Allied policy towards a negotiated peace with Germany would take up more space than can be afforded in this book but readers are invited to consult *International Affairs*, Vol. 46, No. 4 October 1970, pp. 719–36, Michael Balfour, 'Another Look at Unconditional Surrender'.

PARTICIPANTS IN DISCUSSIONS

As mentioned in letters,[a] and supplemented by other knowledge.
To be taken in the light of reservations mentioned in the text.

	Kreisau Meetings[b] Nos	Meetings in Berlin and elsewhere 1940	1941	1942	1943–4	Total
Yorck	1, 2, 3	18	45	39	39	141
Einsiedel	2, 3 (?)	15	15	16	16	62
Trott	3	6	12	15	29	62
Mierendorff	nil	nil	6 (4 July)[c]	26	16	48
Waetjen	nil	12	11	8	11	42
Reichwein	1, 3	5 (28 June)	10	13	10	38
Gerstenmaier	2, 3	nil	nil	15 (3 June)	18	33
Guttenberg	nil	nil	16 (10 May)	11	5	32
Steltzer	1, 2	nil	5 (17 Sept)	16	10	31
Haeften	nil	nil	11	9	10	30
König[d]	nil	nil	nil	11	13	24
Peters	1, 2	3	8	6	4	21
Preysing	nil	nil	4 (4 Sept)	7	10	21
Gablentz	nil	5	6	6	1	18
Trotha	nil	2	4	6	5	17
Husen	3	nil	nil	2 (15 June)	15	17
Furtwängler	nil	14	1	nil	nil	15
Haubach	2	nil	nil	nil	14	14
Göschen	nil	nil	nil	5	8	13
Schulenburg	nil	2	1	7	3	13
Dohnanyi	nil	2	8	2	1	13
Gramsch	nil	nil	2	8	nil	10
Kessel[e]	nil	5	4	1	nil	10
Rösch	1	nil	2 (13 Oct)	4	4	10
Delp	2, 3	nil	nil	7 (31 July)	2	9
Poelchau	1	nil	2	4	3	9
Abs	nil	1 (11 Dec)	6	1	nil	8
Rantzau[f]	nil	3	3	1	nil	7
Leuschner	nil	nil	1 (15 Dec)	4	1	6
Delbrück	nil	nil	1	1	4	6
Borsig	nil	nil	1	4	1	6
Leber	nil	nil	nil	nil	5 (8 Aug)	5

4 mentions: Christiansen-Weniger, Haushofer, Lukaschek, Maass, B. Stauffenberg, Wurm
3 mentions: Beck, Bielenberg, Krüger[g], C. Schmid
2 mentions: Blessing, E. Harnack,[h] Lehndorff, Oster, C. Uexküll
1 mention: Bonhoeffer, Luckner,[i] Popitz, Schlange-Schöningen, Schmölders, Schneider[j]

Notes

[a] The figures are based on *all* Helmuth's letters, not just those transcribed.
[b] The number given in column 1 (as distinct from those in the other columns) is that of the meeting or meetings attended, *not* a total. Attendance at the meeting in August 1940 has been reckoned in the 1940 column.
[c] Where a day of the month is given, it is that of the first mention.

[d] In the case of König, it is possible to check meeting dates from his own diary and there is an almost complete discrepancy. This is yet another reason for handling these figures with caution.

[e] Kessel, Albrecht von (b. 1902), counsellor in AA, went to German Consulate in Geneva 1942, to Embassy to Vatican 1943 as deputy to Weizsaecker, whose secretary and confidant he had been in 1938.

[f] Rantzau, Josias Clemens von (1903–50), counsellor in AA, died in Russian captivity.

[g] Krüger, Hans, a Socialist, formerly *Staatssekretär* in Ministry of Agriculture.

[h] Harnack, Ernst von (1888–1945), son of Adolf Harnack the theologian; civil servant 1911–32, dismissed as Social Democrat; went into commerce, worked with Beck, Goerdeler and Leber; arrested Sept 1944; executed March 1945.

[i] Luckner, Heinrich Count (1891–1971), painter.

[j] Schneider, Reinhold (1903–58), writer and poet.

Biographical details about other persons are given where they occur in the text and can be traced through the index.

People known to have been primarily office contacts have been omitted. Helmuth described the meeting with Luckner and Schneider as 'more a social commitment than a serious discussion'.

21 The Turning Point
Whitsun–Christmas 1942

THE first job after the Kreisau week-end was to transmit to other people who had not been there the conclusions which had been reached and summarised in a thousand-word note of 'results'.[1] Helmuth took on himself the task of doing this with the church leaders and left the socialist and trade union side to Reichwein. Neither found it easy going. Helmuth had two difficult and lengthy sessions with Preysing, of which the second was a 'regular stand-up fight'/*ein richtiger Grosskampf*. Fortunately he himself was 'in good form' and a lot of the difficulties were surmounted. Later he brought in Rösch and the latter's secretary König to help him, who also found the Bishop 'a hard nut' but not beyond cracking. The main bone of contention seems to have been the proposal that after the war all German schools (or at any rate all primary schools) should become Christian but interdenominational. The main initiative for this idea is said to have come from the Protestants, who doubted whether they would be able to find enough genuine democrats among their teachers to man their schools,[2] but it was undoubtedly welcomed by other members of the group as an important step towards bridging the gap between Catholics and Protestants; some Catholics, however, were inevitably nervous that it would reduce their influence over their children.* Another progressive idea likely to horrify those who did not understand what lay behind it was the proposal for *'Una Sancta'*, a German (and indeed a world-wide) Christian Community to which all Christians would belong regardless of their confession and which would ensure that the Christian standpoint got a full hearing in political and social discussions.

While not unsympathetic to these ideas, Preysing was not prepared to take the lead in pressing them on his fellow-bishops. Rösch approached Cardinal Faulhaber of Munich whose attitude was much the same. Archbishop Gröber of Freiburg was next cast for this awkward rôle and Helmuth travelled there on 13 July: the Archbishop, who in spite of having once belonged to the SS[3] was being closely shadowed by the Gestapo, took refuge in technical difficulties and, although Helmuth thought he had found a way out, nothing substantial came of it.

* On the whole denominational schools were re-established in West Germany after the war; they are now in process of being replaced by interdenominational Christian ones.

All the same such hold-ups are events of some importance and give one an opportunity which might never arise if things went well of making one's own views and methods clear. In such cases what is always decisive is simply one's own ability to master the difficulties. Unfortunately we have still some way to go and the tension will last for some time yet.

At the end of July an approach was made to Bishop Dietz of Fulda but this too had no real success.

Things went rather more easily with the Protestants where the main person to be persuaded was Bishop Wurm of Württemberg.* It was in the process of making an approach to him that Helmuth first came into real contact with Eugen Gerstenmaier, an almost exact contemporary who himself hailed from Württemberg and who, in addition to his work in the Church Office for External Affairs, had held since the beginning of the war a post in the Information Department of the AA.⁴ Thanks to preliminary work by Gerstenmaier, Gablentz and others, and to careful preparation by Helmuth himself, his meeting with Wurm on 24 June was so successful that after it he had a distinct sense of anti-climax. There was probably another meeting with Wurm on 19 July.

On the other side, Mierendorff's reaction was not to contest but rather to enrich the ideas which had been ventilated at Kreisau. At first things seemed to be going well with Leuschner too but before long trouble developed. This was due not so much to any particular passage in the Kreisau note as to the whole approach which was being developed. The aim of Helmuth and his friends was to build society from the bottom upwards and overcome the individual's sense of isolation in an alien world by creating a strong sense of community at the local level. They therefore regarded with mistrust all central organisations which might make claims on the individual's loyalty and thereby impede his willingness to work together with his immediate neighbour. Leuschner had been brought up in the tradition of German trade unionism and thought that the ability of the Nazis to gain power had been largely due to the failure of the workers to stand together. He hoped to prevent a repetition of this in post-war Germany by strengthening the unions and reducing their numbers (some people even wanted to keep the unitary German Labour Front which the Nazis had established). The emphasis on the locality, and even on the individual factory, made him nervous lest it should result in a weakening of loyalty to the centre. Moreover,

* Wurm, Theophilus (1868–1953), Church President of Württemberg 1929. Took title of bishop 1933. Dismissed for opposing Hitler over church policy 1934 but reinstated on account of public protest. Co-operated with Kerrl, Minister for Church Affairs 1936. Protested against euthanasia 1940 and treatment of Christian Jews 1943. Chosen as chairman of reconstituted Evangelical Church of Germany 1945. Retired 1949.

the concept of an endemic struggle between the classes had for long been fundamental to German socialist thought (even if sometimes belied in German socialist practice). It was not easy for even a moderate socialist like Leuschner to think of doing away with the class struggle (except by the victory of the proletariat). But this was precisely what the Kreisau group was aiming at since, among the factors which had ham-strung German democracy, they attached more importance to the divisions between the classes than to the divisions inside the working class. What is more, Helmuth actually talked of doing away with trade unions, on the ground that his other changes would give the workers so much say in society as to make them unnecessary. To convince a trade union leader that this was not visionary was bound to take some doing.*

After a 'terribly strenuous' discussion on 7 July, Leuschner was induced to admit 'Yes, if the attitude adopted by these factors is really as you suggest, then a completely new situation has arisen and in it we can reach other results.' Another discussion a week later brought more progress and after it Leuschner nominated a former socialist youth leader called Hermann Maass to represent him in further talks. Maass, who was employed by Leuschner in the metal firm which he had set up both as livelihood and cover, was working to create through Germany a network of clandestine cells to bring the growing numbers of anti-Nazi workers into touch, so as to be ready for action in the event of a coup. Maass first came to a meeting on 30 July and to another two days later. He proved to lack both humour and a sense of proportion, which led to long discourses.

> The rest of us slept through long stretches of the lecture, Peter and I shamelessly while Friedrich's† extinct cigar kept dropping out of his mouth, at which he woke up, looked at me, smiled, put it back in his mouth and went to sleep again. But these ninety minutes made us realise that here there was a man talking who really had something to say about the position of the workers and the ninety minutes included high points where we all listened with fascination while several pearls were concealed among the banalities.

Maass had the advantage of not being violently anti-clerical which was important because this was the point at which Helmuth was trying to bring the representatives of the workers together with those of the churches. With this in view he had, through Rösch, brought into the circle in August a young Jesuit sociologist called Alfred Delp. The fact that these encounters took place without a breakdown meant that a major object of the whole operation seemed on the way to being accomplished. For the Catholic Church and German Social Democrats to be

* Below, pp. 248–50.
† Cover name generally used for Mierendorff.

brought to agree on a social programme was a considerable achievement.

But the effort had taken a lot out of Helmuth and he found his inability to get to Kreisau bitter. The three days which he did spend there at the end of June stood in retrospect 'like precious green islands in a torrent.... What would the river be without the islands? But would the islands be quite so beautiful if there were no river?'

Fortunately the *Abwehr* made no great claims on his time, or if it did he was too busy to record much about it. Dr van Roon has recorded interventions made on behalf of Portugal and Spain during September.[5] Helmuth came across a report in *The Times* that a South African brigadier had been dismissed the service for assaulting German prisoners and another that the British government had refused a Soviet proposal to try Hess as a war criminal; these he used as evidence to prevent the Germans from mishandling prisoners whom they themselves had taken. He also protested with some success against the fettering of prisoners taken during the raid on Dieppe in August 1942, though the retaliatory action of the British on German prisoners undoubtedly did more to make the Nazis give the practice up. This only illustrated one of Helmuth's basic arguments about the reasons for observing international law.[6]

In October the committee which Helmuth had started in 1940 to revise the laws of war held one of its periodic meetings which Helmuth used to attack German policy in Russia. 'From the standpoint of economic warfare, the occupation of areas of Russia is an obvious failure which has led to economic resources being wasted and inescapable claims being made on the stocks of investment goods in order to keep the economy in any sort of working order.' After a long discussion about the relative advantages of autarky and internationalism, the committee produced a report saying that autarky was virtually impossible. This appeared to run counter to a report produced by the managing director of the Hamburg–Amerika line, Dr W. Hoffmann, and the last recorded action of the committee was a meeting with him in June 1943 at which it emerged that the two views had been based on different premises.[7]

Towards the end of August Helmuth and Mierendorff went on a trip to Bamberg and the Neckar valley where they met Bishops Dietz and Wurm.[8] On 16 September he again visited Scandinavia for a week. He arrived in Oslo on the same plane as a general of the Waffen SS which led to his having to join, in civilian clothes, in inspecting a guard of honour. His instinctive revulsion against such an act was, however, mitigated by the fact that it was pouring with rain and he alone had an umbrella! He and Steltzer had four meetings, usually late at night,*

* This was the occasion on which grouse was served. Above, p. 1.

with the Norwegian Resistance and this time Bishop Berggrav was able to evade his house-arrest for a talk lasting between three and four hours. Helmuth encouraged them in their opposition and made plans for co-operation. He showed them the notes of the Kreisau talks, which caused 'a first-class sensation'. Indeed, what he was able to tell them of the post-war plans as a whole, particularly with regard to European co-operation, helped in Norway, as later in other occupied countries, to prevent the Resistance from adopting a bitter attitude to all Germans without exception.

Helmuth also found a warm welcome from General von Falkenhorst, whom he decided to be 'a proper old blockhead but with fewer faults than his colleagues habitually attribute to him'. He was invited to sit at the general's table which automatically put his presence in Norway beyond challenge and opened a number of doors. He principally set his cap at the new Chief of Staff, General Bamler.*

> As cool as a cucumber and not altogether pleasant but very intelligent – at any rate the most intelligent of the bunch. I want to establish a situation here which will make my periodic appearance be regarded as something quite natural which needs no further justification.

Towards the end of the visit they went out for two hours together and Helmuth, having noticed that the whole group felt rather on the edge of things, succeeded in providing enough Berlin gossip for Bamler to urge him to make a habit of such visits. 'So I hope that I have induced the most dangerous man among the high-ups to think well of me.' Two Swedish generals and the German military attaché from Stockholm were in Oslo and had to be amused, an exercise in which Helmuth joined because of the opportunities thereby afforded of talking to officers whose help he needed. The only disconcerting moment came when they were taken for tea to a villa with a wonderful view. Helmuth, knowing the owner to be in a concentration camp, could not avoid

---

* Bamler, Rudolf (b. 1896), in *Abwehr* (counter-espionage and then head of military-political information in *Ausland/Abwehr*) 1927–39. Boasted of having been first officer in army to turn National Socialist. Also drank too much. Removed by Canaris as being too close to Heydrich and sent to command an artillery regiment. Chief of Staff XLVII Corps, Sept. 1939–41. Chief of Staff, Danzig, 1941–2. Chief of Staff, Norway, 1942–4. Sent to Russia as GOC 12th Infantry Division 1.vi.44. Captured 27.vi.44. Signed appeal to *Wehrmacht* to surrender 22.vii.44, acted for Soviet authorities as a spy on recalcitrant German prisoners, attended a Russian anti-Fascist school, returned to Russian Zone of Germany as Director of Police school at Glöwen, studied further in Soviet Union 1950, became head of school for technical officers, Erfurt, 1952, became adviser in East German Ministry of State Security 1959, still serving there 1965.

feeling like a thief who had broken into a stranger's house and began to think of Serpuchoff.

From Oslo he went on to Stockholm which he admired greatly. 'One recovers here the feeling that man is in the world to beautify it and that nature can by his hand be enlivened and enabled to realise its full potentialities.' 'I would go so far as to claim that anyone who has not seen this city has no conception of what a big modern city has to offer.' He is almost bound to have met Adam von Trott who got there three days before he did. But there was nobody to meet him from London.

The second week-end gathering at Kreisau took place from 16 to 18 October. The subjects this time were the organisation of the state and of the economy. Steltzer and Helmuth led on the constitutional problem and in particular the degree of decentralisation involved in a federation, while the other guests were the Yorcks, Einsiedel, Gerstenmaier, Delp, Maass and Haubach (a new participant, representing his friend Mierendorff).* On Sunday they all went to church, though not together. There was less time available than there had been in the summer and, in spite of the considerable preparations which Helmuth had organised, the subjects proved so controversial that the two notes of conclusions, each about the same length as the single one at the first gathering, were only completed after an all-night session,[9] and even then the paper on 'The Economy' was not thoroughly considered.

All through these weeks there was a continual series of discussions going on in Berlin. Helmuth was particularly pleased with the contribution made by Gerstenmaier.

8 September 1942

He is a man over whom one must take pains and who does not automatically fall into the category which is convenient but that is why his help is worth while and, if I can succeed in integrating him with us completely, it will be an appreciable step forward. ... I availed myself of the opportunity of a talk with him to get myself filled in on various questions of theology and church history such as

---

* Haubach, Theo (1896–1945), has been described as follows: 'He was of slender build, almost gaunt, dark-haired, with a narrow face shaped by divergent tensions, and a manner that concealed the soft and gentle side of his personality behind a deliberately stressed vigour. Intellectual distinction was united in his features, his language and his bearing with soldierly discipline, a readiness to serve and to command – a rare combination. Even in the periods of his political activity he had none of the commonplace shallowness of the ordinary activist. He used no propaganda clichés in his speeches and writings. Even at the beginning of his political activity he despised all trite formulations, all vague unexamined phraseology. Like Carlo [Mierendorff], his original interests had been literary and artistic. But for him poetry and music were not means for personal release or emotional intensification, but objects of sober, searching investigation.' Carl Zuckmayer, *A Part of Myself*, p. 198.

the significance for the present day of the Council of Trent and the Confession of Augsburg, the position of Karl Barth, etc.

3 November
It is really gratifying what an accession we have had in Gerstenmaier.

13 November
The crystal-clear character of Gerstenmaier's intellectual apparatus is of appreciable benefit to any conversation.

Gerstenmaier as a result quickly took over the function of the group's main liaison man with the Protestant church, a function previously performed by Gablentz, who thereafter fell out of the picture.

Trott from now on played an increasing part in the discussions, but the co-operation was not always smooth.

5 November
Trott was very obstinate but was softened with Gerstenmaier's help in a three-hour discussion. He is astoundingly intelligent but handicapped as a result. It keeps on being funny. Besides he has for some quite inexplicable reason an inferiority complex towards me which always results in his adopting very aggressive attitudes and expressions.

Fritzi von der Schulenburg also showed up again. He had left the army and during the winter of 1942/3 was working in the Ministry of Food.

10 September
I have never had such a stimulating and uncontroversial talk with him. We had a *tour d'horizon* and discussed the reasons for my steps and on the whole he was not only satisfied but also convinced of the necessity for certain things which had previously displeased him. We passed on to Russia where he completely shared my view, indeed went still further and, for example, volunteered the opinion that 'the relationship between officers and men in the Red Army is quite simply a model and defies imitation'. In all other matters too we agreed on the conclusions even if our diagnoses were in some respects different. He, for example, attributed much to the good quality of the Russian man whereas I held it to be a result of education.

11 November
It takes a long time to get Fritzi completely in line with us but he is well on the way to being so and I much hope that now we shall soon succeed. He had a whole heap of *constructive criticism* to offer to the Kreisau texts but it was concerned with details, was sometimes

based on misunderstandings and dealt in part with things which we too had never liked, such as the National Technical Offices/*Reichsfachämter*.

25 November

The slight distance at which Fritzi always kept from us has visibly diminished and is well on the way to disappearing entirely.

Schulenburg, however, according to his wife,[10] on several occasions remarked, 'I am of course stupid, Moltke is clever', and it may well be, as Dr Gerstenmaier has suggested,[11] that this was said ironically and implied an element of criticism, because his intellectual attainments were considerable. Though he saw a good deal of the group in the next four months, the gap never was completely closed. He was one of those who tended to criticise the planning on the ground that it was too far removed from reality, but this does not seem to have stopped him from producing a document of his own in the autumn of 1943.[12]

When Helmuth saw Preysing again in September after a two-month break, he found the Bishop so concerned with the sorrows of the time as to be once again seriously ill. In October he plucked up his courage and wrote a letter calling on the Bishop to take a firm line. 'Comic that I now find it a matter of course to do something which a few months ago would have appalled me.' The letter arrived at an opportune moment for the West German bishops had just commissioned Preysing to re-draft a pastoral letter originally drawn up for them by Bishop von Galen. On 28 October Helmuth, who found the Bishop of Berlin 'in sparkling form', was shown a copy of the new draft and had every hope that it would prove a 'masterpiece'. In fact it proved too much of one for his colleagues and he was forced to tone it down; when Helmuth saw a revised version on 17 November he told Freya that it was 'good but not very good and not very compelling. It is aimed at those who can hear, not at the deaf.' It was in fact the Pastoral Letter on Right/Law (*das Recht*) which was read throughout West German dioceses on 13 December and attracted widespread attention at home and abroad; while admittedly couched in somewhat abstract terms (because anything more would have provoked a crisis), it amounted in practice to a condemnation of Nazi conduct.[13]

With Leuschner and his friends things seemed at first to be going well. Maass came to one meeting to report reactions but only for as long as was necessary for that purpose – in other words, ninety minutes! But later Leuschner and Delp got at cross purposes and the whole work was held up until shortly before Christmas Helmuth managed to establish a precarious truce.

Nazi misdeeds were going on all the while. Fourteen Norwegians were shot in Berlin at the beginning of October. In the same month

Helmuth had lunch with a man recently returned from Poland who gave him details about the SS gas chambers. 'Previously I had not believed it but he assured me it was true; 6,000 people are "processed" daily in these chambers.' On one occasion Helmuth told Preysing that he had met a drunk nurse on a tram who said to him, 'I expect you are cross with me for being like this.' He replied, 'Not cross but sorry.' She then explained that she worked in a hospital for SS men and all the time heard patients saying, 'No, I can't do it any longer! I won't do it any longer!'[14]

Soon afterwards there was trouble in the office about prisoners-of-war. A decision had, as so often, been taken without the *Abwehr* being consulted.

12 October

Now it has to be changed and our advice is asked. I am glad that this should be so but it has meant a stormy day.

23 October

All in all I would have plenty to do without any work in the office but they unfortunately want some help from me. There are some idiotic orders on the stocks once again and I must make sure that my revered bosses stay firm and don't let themselves be overridden so that at any rate no responsibility falls on us.

3 November

Yesterday evening I had a decisive talk with Bürkner. He was reluctant to sign something to which I attached great importance and argued with me about the justification for an absolutely murderous order of the Führer's. Whereupon I said to him, 'Look here, Admiral, the difference between us is that I am incapable of arguing about such things. So long as orders exist for me which no order of the Führer's can annul and which have to be acted on even in the face of an order from the Führer, I can't allow such things to pass, because the difference between good and evil, right and wrong is fixed for me *a priori*. That's got nothing to do with the expediency of the arguments' – whereupon he signed without hesitation. I was interested to see once again how such people can be got on to the right side if only one takes up a resolute attitude.

On the whole, mention of the war dropped completely out of the letters written at this time. There is, for instance, no reference to Stalingrad. But when events reached what Churchill has described as 'The Hinge of Fate', Helmuth did not fail to realise it, even if his English sympathies led him to expect too much. During the three days after the news arrived of El Alamein and the Anglo-American landings in Morocco and Algeria, he expanded on their significance.

7 November

I find it really difficult to concentrate on other things since I keep noticing that my thoughts are there even while I am reading here. An enormous amount will be decided in these days and Britain's prestige as a World Power will be influenced more decisively and for a much longer time by the daring and success of these operations [Alamein] than by any previous ones. It is striking how all of a sudden an enormous number of things depend upon one decision. Those are the rare moments in which a single man can suddenly really count in history. Everything which went before and comes after depends on masses, on anonymous forces and faceless men. And then suddenly one has the feeling that all these forces hold their breath, that the vast orchestra which has been playing till now stops for one or two bars, in order to let the soloist give the key for the next movement. The pause only lasts for a heart-beat but the one note which sounds out all by itself gives the direction to the entire orchestra. And this note is what one waits for. One has the possible melody in mind, one can imagine a number of variations but one does not know for certain what it is going to be. And so this one heart-beat lasts for an eternity. While I sit here the decision on which everything hangs has long been taken but I listen eagerly to catch the note. Up to now there has only been one such moment previously in this war: after Dunkirk.

8 November

The Mediterranean will be an English lake in four weeks' time, unless something quite surprising happens, and nobody else will have any say there. The fleet which left Gibraltar on Friday evening consisted of 4 capital ships, 4 aircraft carriers, 45 cruisers, 50 destroyers and 390,000 tons of transport vessels. That must have been at least 4 divisions. This is Oom Jannie's [Smuts] decisive hour, for this plan is assuredly his.

10 November

I can't remember ever before feeling so well and fit for work in November. I can't deny that the sense of approaching crisis and danger stimulates me enormously. ... I am also convinced that the majority of Germans fail to see what has happened in the Mediterranean during the last few days. The battle of El Alamein is probably the battle which has brought the formal decision of the war. But the least that can happen is that we are now certainly confined to the defensive and that there can be no more talk of the offensive. I wonder if contemporaries failed equally to understand the battle of Trafalgar?

This analysis, however, suggested that the war would end sooner than was to be the case; even among the Allies, Churchill's statement on 10 November that this was only 'the end of the beginning' came as a damper on hope (as it was doubtless intended to do). The over-optimism, however, made it seem all the more important to get the planning completed and Helmuth continued to drive his team forward. One main field still to be covered was that of foreign affairs, particularly Germany's relationship to the rest of Europe. There was also the question of detailed arrangements for the days immediately after a coup or collapse; it was probably to these that the 'list of appointments' referred which at one stage he talked of getting settled before Christmas. The trouble with Leuschner, however, held things up and 1943 was on the whole to be a year of disappointment.

22 Argument and Frustration
January–April 1943

T H E first event of importance in 1943 was the fullest meeting ever to take place between the Kreisau Circle and the older group centring round Beck and Goerdeler. The initiative for this came on the one side from Popitz* and on the other from Gerstenmaier. Schulenburg acted as a convinced intermediary. Gerstenmaier secured the support of Adam von Trott, while Helmuth, who was antagonistic and only gave way in deference to his friends, described Peter Yorck as 'much less negative' than himself.[1] The meeting was held in Yorck's Hortensienstrasse house on the evening of 8 January, with Beck, Goerdeler, Hassell, Popitz and Jessen† on the one side, Helmuth, Peter, Adam von Trott, Gerstenmaier and Schulenburg on the other. Two accounts have survived, the first being Hassell's:

> Extremely interesting but fundamentally unsatisfying was a big discussion between the 'juniors' and 'seniors' at Yorck's. The juniors, who in contrast to the seniors presented a united front, were led by the very witty Moltke who thinks along Anglo-Saxon and pacifist lines. I was again very favourably impressed by Gerstenmaier with whom Popitz and I had a talk beforehand. Beck presided, extremely weakly and keeping too much back. Goerdeler provoked but tried unsuccessfully to conceal a sharp collision between himself and the juniors, chiefly in the social field. Goerdeler is really a kind of reactionary. The 'unity' of the 'juniors' does not incidentally really include Fritzi Schulenburg who is much more of a realist in political matters. I am happy to think that the 'juniors' have enough confidence to discuss their doubts with me.[2]

Helmuth, who had cast himself in the role of 'Leader of the Opposition', wrote as follows:

> My evening was remarkable because we didn't really come into conflict at all till 11 but every attempt to get on to fundamentals was diverted by the other side into issues on which agreement was easy.

* Popitz, Professor Johannes (b. 1884), joined Prussian Civil Service. Prussian Finance Minister 1933–44. Received golden Party badge 1937.
† Jessen, Dr Jens Peter (b. 1895), political adviser to Nazi Party 1931–3. Professor of Political Theory in University of Berlin, employed on staff of quartermaster-general.

But a chance finally presented itself and on the theme too about which we had the all-night session at Kreisau [representation of workers].* After a little skirmishing on our part, they gave vent to a really idiotic statement; flabby and totally lacking in imagination, etc. Thereupon I seized the opportunity and declared there was no point left in answering it at 11.35 because that would be the beginning of the real discussion. We would therefore answer some other time. I also shot in an arrow which I had had in my quiver for some time about a 'Kerensky solution'.† It quite obviously went well home and with it the affair ended – dramatically and, I'm glad to say, not flabbily.[3]

Goerdeler and Beck set out their ideas about post-Nazi Germany in a long essay called 'The Goal' written in the latter part of 1941. Indeed, Goerdeler was tireless in producing and distributing documents and plans, though he preferred to do so on his own instead of evolving a mutually agreed plan by discussion with other people. He talked far too freely, which was a reason why many people gave him a wide berth, but he was not good at listening. Helmuth referred to the Beck–Goerdeler group as 'Their Excellencies' because they had held relatively high office. They came from a fairly narrow group of soldiers and civil servants who had been young men in the years before 1914 (to which they looked back with some nostalgia) and who mostly belonged between 1919 and 1933 to the German Nationalist Party; Helmuth, by contrast, had deliberately brought into his discussions representatives of the two groups, the workers and the churches, which he considered (rightly, as it proved) to have much to offer to a new Germany. It is true that in some respects the gap between the Goerdeler plans and the Kreisau ones does not look large. Both attached great importance to re-establishing the role of law and public morality on a Christian basis. Both emphasised local self-government and wanted to build from the bottom upwards. Both contemplated the dissolution of Prussia and the re-organisation of Germany into between fifteen and twenty-five units roughly equal in population. Neither made any mention of the party system. Both looked for European economic collaboration.

But along with these similarities went wide differences. In the economic field Goerdeler proposed a sweeping return to individualism and the freedom of the market, whereas to Kreisau the economy and the

---

* Above, p. 200.
† Kerensky, Alexander (1881–1970), was leader of the Provisional Russian government after the March Revolution of 1917 but was superseded by Lenin and the Bolsheviks in the October Revolution. Helmuth's remark was therefore intended to imply that any group which aimed at seizing power after the Nazis must be prepared to pursue a radical policy unless they wanted to find themselves quickly superseded.

activities of individuals in it must be made to serve the community as a whole and the interests of the ordinary citizen. This would involve the regulation of the economy by the state in accordance with a centrally devised plan and the socialisation of basic industries (including, as far as Helmuth was concerned, land). In the course of time and in the face of criticism, Goerdeler was prepared to allow the unions a place in the political structure (which induced Leuschner to throw in his lot with this group rather than Kreisau). But the attitude towards labour was still paternalistic, whereas Helmuth sought to make the workers one of the state's main pillars of responsibility. As regards political forms Goerdeler seriously proposed re-establishing the monarchy, although initially in the shape of a regent. In foreign affairs he assigned to Germany a much more dominant role than Kreisau would contemplate, and failed to realise the full extent of the difficulty which faced her in recovering the good-will of the oppressed countries. In spite of the proclamation of the demand for unconditional surrender on 24 January he felt confident throughout about the possibility of winning the British and Americans to an anti-Communist crusade. Even as late as the autumn of 1943, he imagined that after the war Germany would be able to keep her 1914 frontiers in the east (i.e. including large parts of 1919–39 Poland), Austria, the Sudetenland and the German-speaking parts of of Alsace. Kreisau at no stage made any precise proposals about frontiers.*

Helmuth's aim was to make a complete break with the past in order to re-establish Germany on new foundations. He wanted to make a deliberate bid for the support of those elements which had hitherto been denied their due place in society and classed the workers along with the Jews and the Poles as people for whom compensation must be obtained in view of their maltreatment by the Nazis. In foreign affairs, he wanted to establish Europe as a political entity and was quite prepared to see Germany dissolved into a number of states inside a European Federation if that would help his main end (though in this few even of his companions could follow him). He believed that Goerdeler, though no doubt sincere in wanting to make a new start, was too set in his ideas to realise what a really new start involved. This belief underlay Helmuth's doubts about the utility of discussions with the other group and his anxiety, when the discussion occurred, to centre it on fundamental principles rather than on superficial issues. Goerdeler both repaid and justified this mistrust by talking about the others as 'parlour Bolsheviks'!

Hassell, on hearing of Helmuth's arrest a year later, repeated the

---

* The 1942 documents mentioned on p. 190 proposed the creation of a free Polish and a free Czech state, in one case with the reservation that they should be based on ethnographical frontiers.

criticism that he lacked political realism. Though such realism was hardly a quality in which Goerdeler was outstanding, there was perhaps a little in this charge; Helmuth underestimated the extent to which politics is the 'art of the possible' and the frequent need for compromise. He was inclined instead to believe that, if only a man would stick to his convictions and argue with cogency for what he believed, he would get his way. But it must be remembered that Helmuth and most of those around him were still in their thirties, without any experience of responsibility in high office. They were also continually engaged in fighting a régime about whose evil character there could be (at any rate for all who shared their principles) no dispute. This must have made it easier to believe that the right course would usually be obvious and to forget that political decisions often involve choosing between alternative goods.

But there is something more to be said. It would probably have been easy, by concentrating on the superficial issues, to achieve a working agreement between the two groups, and Helmuth might seem to deserve blame for obstructing unity at a time when the prime need was for as many people as possible to join in overthrowing the Nazis. But, if one believed, as he did, that through one means or another such an overthrow was inevitable, then what became important was what followed. Here Helmuth's aim was firstly to break with those elements in Germany's past which had made it possible for Hitler to gain power, however much they might by now be opposed to him. It was also to avoid half-measures, for fear that they would not last but only open the door to Communism, something as objectionable in his view as Nazism; here his phrase about a 'Kerensky solution' is crucial.[4] German circumstances meant that the *Widerstand* drew its active membership from an élite which possessed financial independence and the protection of institutions like the General Staff. But there were many respects in which these people did not represent the masses who might be expected, on the overthrow of Hitler, to recover their ability to organise and with it their political influence. This prospect made it important to design the immediate post-Hitler régime on lines which would be attractive to those masses and not merely to the élite. But the exact way in which Hitler would be overthrown, and therefore the precise problems which would confront the post-Hitler régime defied prediction. Therefore only by sticking to principle and avoiding detail was there a chance of getting a decision about the character of that régime which was both clear and susceptible of application in practice.

These questions are difficult to judge even in the light of thirty years hindsight. Small wonder then that they led to considerable controversy among Helmuth's friends. But they were also divided by the more immediate question of the justification for making an attempt on Hit-

ler's life. A number of Helmuth's remarks about this question have
survived and render his position reasonably clear. He felt as keenly as
anyone the need to get rid of the Third *Reich* at an early moment,
although he found the reason more in the suffering which was being
inflicted on humanity and less in the damage which was being done to
Germany. He was therefore prepared to approve a *Staatsstreich* by the
army and to help in bringing one about. But he had a low opinion of the
ability of generals as conspirators – he once remarked that 'when
generals conspire, they almost always score a near miss'[5] – and therefore not much hope of achieving anything by these means. The increasing realisation that he was probably right led a number of his friends –
and others in the *Widerstand* – to support the idea of assassination as
the essential step to force the generals into action. Helmuth's high
standards of Christian ethics – rather than any lingering influence of
Christian Science, as has been suggested – made him firmly opposed to
this. As has been seen, he differed from Bonhoeffer here. He said to
Hans Christoph Stauffenberg, 'Why are we opposed to the Third *Reich*
and to National Socialism? Surely because it is a criminal system/
System des Unrechts and one ought not to begin something new with a
new crime. Murder is always a crime.'[6] He told Father Rösch that 'we
have no right to complain about the innumerable murders in the concentration camps if we are prepared to commit murder ourselves'.[7] If
the generals were a vain hope, however, the question arises of how then
Hitler should have been got rid of. Helmuth would probably have
answered this by saying that it must in that case be left to the Allies.
Hitler must even be left in power to face the consequences of his
crimes,[8] a course which would also have the advantage of showing
unmistakably to the German people what the consequences of those
crimes were, a demonstration of which the effects would be impaired if
the lesson could again be evaded by a claim that Germany's defeat was
due only to internal treachery. Helmuth did not overlook the danger of
creating another 'stab-in-the-back' legend – and it must be remembered
that up to the end of 1944 a number of Germans believed Hitler's
allusions to a 'secret weapon' with which he would ultimately win the
war.[9] The solution of 'leaving it to the Allies' was, of course, easier to
adopt in the spring of 1943 when the time which they would take over
finishing the job was apt to be underestimated. Later in the year, Helmuth's faith in this solution seems to have weakened again.* Goerdeler,
though equally opposed to assassination, was always naïvely confident
about getting the generals to act.

The worries attending these debates and the fact that Freya had been
ill led Helmuth to slip away to Kreisau for the week-end of 17 January,
a thing he was seldom able to do:

* Below, pp. 246, 376.

I long so much to be in Kreisau alone with my family.

It was particularly pleasant to be in Kreisau on our own for once and without visitors. .... It's never happened before. I only hope you will keep well. Think how important that can be. Up to now I have never included in my calculations the possibility of our having to leave something necessary undone because you did not feel up to it. Not only am I deeply grateful to you for that but I very much hope it can stay like that, for it is precisely in the period which lies ahead of us that this freedom of manœuvre can be very necessary. Take care of yourself!

Thanks to the Trust having finally sold Wernersdorf to Hans Adolf, Kreisau was now at last completely free of debt. One day as Helmuth and Freya were walking from the station to the Berghaus he told her that this had finally been achieved; when she remarked, 'Now it will go either to the Nazis or to the Russians', his only comment was, 'Better free of debt.'

Back in Berlin, argument continued:

21 January 1943

I would so much like to be at home with you, and get no joy from being here. I am too completely convinced that there is nothing else to do for me to believe in all the activity of the others. But waiting is always more difficult than acting and trying to get people to do so is a thankless task.

22 January

Haeften, Peter and Gerstenmaier were here for lunch. Nothing fresh came out but the three are much more positive in their assessment of the chances than I am and this gives rise in practice to considerable differences. I am going to suggest to them that it would be better for me to sit out this dance.

24 January

[After a four-hour discussion with Peter Yorck, Trott and Gerstenmaier]

I am glad that by giving in at the New Year and the resulting attempt at a compromise with Their Excellencies, I have won over to my side Peter, who was then much less negative than me. Today he and I took a pretty uniform line. I am afraid, however, that we shan't yet be able to get our way but will have to allow the impossibility of the other course to be tested out further.

The discussions of the last few months have taken a lot out of me. I feel myself pumped so dry in this respect. The explanation is that from the start I represented a line of my own for which I had in consequence to be continually arguing and that as a result I felt a responsibility not to endanger the coherence and capacity for action of our squad. So I had difficulty in keeping to the right line and didn't always succeed.

26 January

I got a letter from Steltzer today which completely supports me in my relatively intransigent line.

4 March

Even König and Delp, who thanks to their discipline must really have learnt to wait, can't do so, and if an action is followed by the inevitable set-back they become restive and do not see that the down will in due course be followed by another up. Adam, who was excessively confident when I last saw him, is now excessively worried again. All these changes of mood seem to me so uneconomical; it must take a lot out of one to join in them.

On 10 January Helmuth had been in Munich to see Rösch, König, Delp and the lawyer Josef Müller, who was the main channel of communication between the *Abwehr* and the Vatican, and was another of the people introduced to him by Guttenberg. He also saw the former Bavarian ambassador to Berlin, Franz Sperr (who was the leading spirit of another *Widerstand* group), another lawyer Franz Reisert[10] (a disillusioned member of the Nazi Party) and Prince Fugger von Glött. (According to Fugger, Steltzer and Mierendorff were there as well.) In seeking to enlist their co-operation, Helmuth laid emphasis on his view that the future German state would have to have a federal character and indeed be merged in a federal Europe, so that Bavaria would have considerable autonomy (though at other times he alarmed them by suggesting that Franconia should be split off). It must have been on this occasion that he went to the Michaelskirche to hear Cardinal Faulhaber preach. Afterwards Rösch brought him together with Faulhaber and they discussed the position of the church in a future state but they did not get very far because Faulhaber was unwilling to depart from the idea of a concordat or treaty between the Vatican and the German government defining the rights of the Catholic Church.[11] At some stage also Helmuth had contact with Franz Rehrl, who had been until 1938 the governor/*Landeshauptmann* of Salzburg.

In the following month Munich was the scene of a significant demonstration of opposition, when the two students Hans and Sophie Scholl started openly distributing leaflets signed in the name of 'The White Rose' which they had been sending out for some months anonymously and through the post. The text condemned National Socialism in terms of moral indignation and called on the population to rise against it. No such rising occurred. The college porter gave their names to the police and on 22 February they were executed.* Sophie, who appeared in court with a leg broken, said to the President of the People's Court, Roland Freisler, 'You know as well as we do that the war is lost. Why are you too cowardly to admit it?' It was a classic example of the powerlessness of the righteous individual under a modern tyranny. But the fact of their having given their lives for a principle did become known and they were honoured if they were not imitated.

Helmuth was particularly impressed by the episode. Long ago he had told Dorothy Thompson that the students were 'the worst class'; here was a sign that things might be changing.† He asked Ernst von Borsig, who had studied in Munich, to go there and try to find out if there was anything still going on.[12] He and Peter Yorck called Günther Schmölders‡ to Berlin in the hope (which proved vain) that something similar might be on foot in Cologne. He collected information and the text of the leaflet which he took with him when he went to Scandinavia on 16 March. He gave the story not only to the Norwegian underground press but also to Ivar Andersen, the Editor of *Svenska Dagbladet*;[13] it may not have been a coincidence that the first stories giving the world the details of the Scholls' action appeared in two Swedish papers (and not, as might have been expected, in the Swiss press, closer to Munich) in the third week of April. Helmuth is further said to have arranged for a copy to be sent to England.

On his visit to Oslo Helmuth had another long talk with Berggrav, who was much impressed by his personality. He asked the Bishop whether it would be right for a Christian to kill Hitler. He explained that he personally had always been opposed to such a deed not so much because he regarded it as ruled out by Christian principles as because he doubted whether a régime inaugurated in such a way could prosper. A further more practical difficulty was that the planning of an assassination must be confined to a small circle so as to prevent the whole network from being compromised if things went wrong, whereas the planning of a new government must necessarily involve a number of people. He himself saw his chief function in the latter field but if the killing of Hitler could not be done without him, he was ready to play his part. Berggrav, who later described it as the most difficult matter on

* An intermediary had tried to bring about a meeting between Fr Delp and Professor Huber, who stood behind the Scholls and was executed later, but failed to do so in time. If such a meeting had occurred, Delp was likely to have advised The White Rose to hold their hand until there was a better chance of acting with effect. Van Roon, p. 163.

† Above, p. 30.

‡ Schmölders, Professor Günther, economist, friend of Yorck's, joined in several discussions, especially at Klein-Oels, and prepared memoranda. He mediated between the would-be planners and those more faithful to private enterprise.

H

which he had ever been asked for advice, said that in certain circumstances the murder of a tyrant could be justified but that in his opinion it was already too late to kill Hitler. Those who were contemplating such a deed ought to command not only the means to assassinate him but also, and still more important, be able to form a new government which could secure peace. The war, however, had reached a stage at which, in Berggrav's opinion, no new German government could any longer do this.[14]

In Stockholm Helmuth made another attempt to sort out the question of the Norwegian ships* which had got into a thorough muddle, largely because too many departments were involved on the German side without the responsibility for deciding action being firmly assigned to any of them. He arranged for this responsibility to rest in future with the Stockholm Embassy, as the only body capable of taking decisions in the light of all the available and up-to-date information.[15]

He wrote to Freya on Thursday 18 March that he had to go to Stockholm on the Saturday evening because a man whom he needed to see was leaving early on the Monday. Steltzer had to go to Berlin and could not get to Stockholm until Wednesday evening. 'By that time I shall have fought the main battle there. It is a little unfortunate but perhaps has the advantage that we shall get a new impetus on Thursday.'[16] He spent a night at Sigtuna with Dr Harry Johansson, the director of the Nordic Ecumenical Institute there. Dr Johansson had been involved in the Bell–Schönfeld–Bonhoeffer meeting at the Institute in the previous year and had thereafter formed a group of Swedes (including Ivar Andersen) to act as a link between the *Widerstand* and the Allies in the event of the latter being willing to negotiate. Helmuth may have met Johansson the previous autumn (when Adam von Trott certainly did) and Johansson's group may have been the scene of the 'main battle'. Johansson has recorded finding Helmuth wrestling one morning with the question of whether he should try to fly to England with the news about the Scholls so as to convince influential quarters there of 'another Germany'.[17] Perhaps it was as an alternative to this that he wrote and left with Johansson for transmission to Lionel Curtis a letter which depicts with remarkable vividness what life in Nazi Germany was like. For this reason and for the way it illustrates Helmuth's analytical and descriptive powers at their full development, it deserves to be quoted in full.

* Above, p. 183.

Lionel Curtis, Esqu., *Stockholm, March 25th. 1943*
Hales Croft, or All Souls' College,
Kidlington Oxford.
Oxon

Dear Mr Curtis,
    This letter has a chance of getting into your hands without passing any censor. And I want to take this singular opportunity of giving you an analysis of conditions in my country, and to make some proposals as to how matters could be speeded up.

1

    I have to write a preface to what I have to say. From my experience I distrust judgment and discretion in matters of internal political developments of everybody connected with missions abroad. For one thing we get highly confidential stuff from practically every British and much worse still every American legation or embassy. Probably your people repay us the compliment in tapping the stuff inside our legations; but in the first case such information has killed more than one man whom we can ill spare. I have the impression that diplomats are so used to live in their very limited circles prying on each other and lauding each other that they are naïve as soon as it comes to the facts of life. Indeed one sometimes has the feeling that diplomats lead such a secluded life, that they simply cannot imagine what life really is like on our continent. There are grand words to describe the conditions of life on the Continent; but for lack of imagination what that looks like in reality these words do not really convey anything to the person using them much less to the one hearing them.
    There is a further caution in the same line, that is the prevalence of the secret service view as opposed to the political point of view. From the point of view of the secret service everything I do and with me many men and women is simply destructive of the third realm, thereby destructive of the chief enemy and therefore laudable. But from the point of view of politics the same rule applies in dictatorships or tyrannies as in democracies: you can only get rid of one government if you can offer another government, and that means, that the mere process of destroying the third realm can only get under way if you at least are able to propound an alternative. This view is not in sight of the man with the secret service point of view, and this lack can have very grave consequences not only for the post-war-period but also for the chances of destroying the third realm with assistance from inside.
    By the way this argument has been propounded to me by more than one man from the underground organisations in the various occupied countries.

2

People outside Germany do not realize the following handicaps under which we labour and which distinguish the position in Germany from that of any other of the occupied countries: lack of unity, lack of men, lack of communications.

Lack of unity: *in all countries under Hitler but Germany and France the people are practically united. If it be in Norway or Poland, in Greece, Jugoslavia or Holland the vast majority of the people are in one mind. In Germany, and to a lesser extent in France this is different. There are a great many people who have profited from the third realm and who know that their time will be up with the third realm's end. This category does not only comprise some few hundred people, no it runs into hundreds of thousands and in order to swell their number and to create new posts of profit everything is corrupted. – Further there are those who supported the Nazis as a counterbalance against foreign pressure and who cannot now easily find their way out of the tangle; even where they believe the Nazis to be in the wrong they say that this wrong is counterbalanced by a wrong done to us before. – Thirdly there are those who – supported by Göebbels' propaganda and by British propaganda – say: if we lose this war we will be eaten up alive by our enemies and therefore we have to stand this through with Hitler and have to put him right, i.e. get rid of him thereafter: it is impossible to change horses in midstream. – You may disagree with those reasons just as strongly as I do, but you must take them into account as politically effective to make for disunity. Therefore while, practically speaking you can trust every Dutchman, Norwegian etc. as to his intentions, you have to probe deep into every German before you find out whether or not you can make use of him; the fact that he is an anti-nazi is not enough.*

Lack of men: *In our country we have, practically speaking no young men left, men of the age-groups which make revolutions, or are at least its spearhead. You have got young or at least fairly young workers in your home factories, you have your young men training in your own country. All this is different with us, all our young men, even those in training, are far beyond our frontiers. Instead we have got more than 8 million foreign and potentially hostile workers in the country, and their numbers are going to be swelled to 10 millions and not a man younger than the age-group of 1899 in the country. The exceptions to this rule are but for the secret police of the SS negligeable. And those who still are there and are active are terribly overworked and have no strength to spare. The women, if they are not engaged on war-work of one kind or another are fully occupied – physically but especially mentally – in keeping their houses in order. The worse the economic strain gets the less likely a revolution be-*

comes, *because people are so occupied in simply living. Food-distri-*
bution is fairly allright, though it takes also a lot of time; but if you
endeavour to buy anything else you will have an exhausting experi-
ence. If you need an envelope, want your shoes repaired, your dress
mended, your coat cleaned, if you are so audacious as to ask for nails
or a toothbrush, for glue or a cooking-pot, a piece of pottery or glass,
if you try to park your child anywhere or need a doctor you will find
the fulfilling of anyone of these desiderata a full-time job. You have
to wait and to run, to stand and to bid, to press and to plead and in
the end you will probably only get what you want if you have some-
thing to offer in return, be it services or goods. And all this additional
work falls on the women. While the men forget in their job of soldier-
ing completely what work is like, the women are thoroughly over-
worked. And that means not only that they are occupied physically
with these jobs, they are of course, but the worst is that their head is
full of thoughts about stratagems to get what you need be it a tooth-
brush or a doctor. When a woman goes to sleep her last thought
probably is: "I must not forget that they said they might get some
envelopes at three, and the doctor's office said, he might be back by
6.30; but what do I do with my child while waiting for the doctor: it
may be 9 before I come back." There is no time even to think of the
war.

Lack of communication: *That is the worst. Can you imagine what*
it is like if you

a. *cannot use the telephone,*
b. *cannot use the post,*
c. *cannot send a messenger, because you probably have no one to*
   send, and if you have you cannot give him a written message as
   the police sometimes search people in trains, trams, etc. for docu-
   ments;
d. *cannot even speak with those with whom you are completely*
   d'accord, because the secret police has methods of questioning
   where they first break the will but leave the intelligence awake
   thereby inducing the victim to speak out all he knows; therefore
   you must limit information to those who absolutely need it.
e. *cannot even rely on rumour or a whispering-campaign to spread*
   information as there is so effective a ban on communications of all
   kind that a whispering-campaign started in Munich may never
   reach Augsburg.

There is only one reliable way of communicating news, and that is
the London wireless, as that is listened in to by many people who
belong to the opposition proper and by many disaffected party-
members.

3

*Some of this devilish machinery has been invented by the Nazis,
but some of it has been produced by war itself. But this machinery is
used to great effect by the ruling class. Their first aim is to keep the
army out of touch with the political trends in the country. They
succeed in this to a great extent. None but men on leave and those
manning anti-aircraft guns are in the country. When on leave they do
not want to be bothered and their relatives do not want to bother
them. When out of the country, the information they get by post is
very scanty as their womenfolk dare not write to them for fear of
repressive measures which are and have been taken. Besides the
soldiers lead a fairly secluded life. Where they are they usually
appear in great strength and have only the enemy to cope with. Most
officers especially lead a life far above their status in civilian life.
The normal soldier does not know more about conditions in Germany
than you, probably a great deal less. And besides the soldiers are
continuously led into positions where there is no choice but to fight.
Their mind is occupied with the enemy as fully as the housewife's is
occupied with her requirements. "The German general and soldier
must never feel secure otherwise he wants to rest; he must always
know that there are enemies in front and at his back, and that there is
only one thing to be done and that is to fight." This remark Hitler
addressed to field-marshall Manstein who proposed to fortify some
line way behind the front line.*

*But even in Germany people do not know what is happening. I
believe that at least 9tenths of the population do not know that we
have killed hundreds of thousands of jews. They go on believing,
that they just have been segregated and lead an existence pretty
much as the one they lead only farther to the east where they came
from. Perhaps with a little more squalour but with out airraids. If you
told these people what has really happened they will answer: you are
just a victim of British propaganda; remember what ridiculous things
they said about our behaviour in Belgium in 1914/18.*

*Another fact: German people are very anxious about their men or
boys who have been reported missing in Russia. The Russians have
allowed our men to write home, which was a very wise thing for the
Russians to do. Well these letters are, on their arrival in Germany
locked up or destroyed but not allowed to reach the relatives. About
1000 of these cards had passed the censor through some technical
error. The recipients who then tried to answer in the normal way
through the ordinary channels were there upon arrested, questioned
and kept in confinement until they had realised what it would mean
to them if they ever talked about the fact that they had received news
from their men. Things like that go on in Germany for months and*

perhaps years and this is a bit of information for which Germans are eagerly waiting; you cannot explain it away, as you could with the example given about the jews, with the argument that the Germans are impolitic and do not want to hear, that they have put jews to death. No, even these facts about the communications from Germans in Russia are neither known nor, where you tell them, believed. And where the facts become known as with officials dealing with the cards or their relatives, their is a widespread belief, that the cards are faked and that the Führer in his magnanimity does want to prevent the raising of hopes by the beastly Russians which are unfounded and must give way to still deeper dispair once the facts become known.

A third fact: We now have 19 guillotines working at considerable speed without most people even knowing this fact, and practically nobody knows how many are beheaded per day. In my estimation there are about 50 daily, not counting those who die in concentration camps. – Nobody knows the exact number of concentration camps or of their inhabitants. We have got a concentration camp only a few miles from our farm, and my district-commissioner told me, that he only learnt of the fact that there was a concentration-camp in his district when he was asked for orders to stop an epidemic of typhoid from spreading to a neighbouring village; by that time the camp had existed for months. Calculations on the number of KZ-inhabitants vary between 150.000 and 350.000. Nobody knows how many die per day. By chance I have ascertained that in one single month 160 persons died in the concentration-camp of Dachau. We further know fairly reliable, that there are 16 concentration-camps with their cremation apparatus. We have been informed that in Upper-Silesia a big KZ is being built which is expected to be able to accommodate 40 to 50.000 men, of whom 3 to 4000 are to be killed per month. But all this information comes to me, even to me, who is looking out for facts of this nature, in a rather vague and indistinct and inexact form. We only know for certain, that scores, probably many hundreds of Germans are killed daily by the various methods, and that these people die not a glorious death as those in the occupied countries do, knowing that their people consider them heroes, but an ignominious death knowing that they are classed among robbers and murderers.

4

What is happening to the opposition, the men "of whom one hears so much and notices so little" as a headline in a paper lately said.

Well, first of all it looses men, at a considerable rate. The quick-working guillotines can devour a considerable number of men. This is a serious matter; not alone because of the loss of life; that has to be faced, as we will not be able to get out of the quandary into which we have been led without considerable sacrifices in men. The worst is that this death is ignominious. Nobody really takes much notice of the fact, the relatives hush it up, not because there is anything to hide, but because they would suffer the same fate at the hands of the Gestapo if they dared telling people what has happened. In the other countries suppressed by Hitler's tyranny even the ordinary criminal is a chance of being classified as a martyr. With us it is different: even the martyr is certain to be classed as an ordinary criminal. That makes death useless and therefore is a very effective deterrent. Secondly the opposition has thrown sand into the machine. It will probably never be known to what extent this has helped your people. But the extent to which that has been done is very considerable especially in the higher bureaucracy. There is seldom a week when I do not notice something that must have been done in order to prevent a command from being executed or at least from becoming fully effective.

Thirdly the opposition is saving individual lives. We cannot prevent the ferocious orders from being given, but we can save individuals. And this is done in all walks of life. People who have been officially executed still live, others have been given sufficient warning to escape in time. This is especially so in occupied countries: their is no denying the mass-murders, but once the balance is drawn, people will perhaps realise, that many thousands of lives have been saved by the intervention of some German, sometimes a Private and sometimes a general, sometimes a workman and sometimes an high-ranking official.

Fourthly the opposition has made many mistakes. The main error of judgment has been the reliance placed on an act by the generals. This hope was forlorn from the outset, but most people could never be brought to realise this fact in time. The same reasons which made it impossible for the french generals to get rid of Napoleon prevent this happening in Germany. To expound the reasons would be too long a process. The main sociological reason is that we need a revolution not a coup d'état, and no revolution of the kind we need will give generals the same scope and position as the Nazis have given them, and give them today.

Fifthly the opposition has done two things which, I believe, will count in the long run: the mobilisation of the churches and the clearing of the road to a completely decentralised Germany. The churches have done great work these times. Some of the sermons of the more prominent Bishops catholic as well as protestant have become known abroad, especially two sermons of the Bishop of Berlin Count Prey-

sing, of May 16th (?) 1942* and December 20th. 1942. But the most important part of the churches' work has been the continuous process by which the whole clergy practically without exception have upheld the great principles in spite of all the intense propaganda and the pressure exerted against them. I do not know of a single parson who in a church demolished by British bombs held a sermon with an antibritish strain. And the churches are full Sunday after Sunday. The state dare not touch the churches at present, and in order to get over this difficulty the churches have been requisitioned in many places for storing furniture saved from bombed houses; thereby the state hopes to make church-work slowly impossible.

The breaking down of the idea of a highly centralised German state has made considerable progress. While two years ago the idea of a completely decentralised Germany was considered an utopia it is today nearly a commonplace. This will ease the transitory period between war and peace, and may, perhaps, make a meeting of the minds possible.

<h3 style="text-align:center">5</h3>

Two general observations can be added: one on war-criminals and one on the threat of communism. The punishment of political criminals once the third realm has come to an end will this time be very popular with the German people. You must realise that we have a concentration-camp-population of some 250,000, certainly once again that number of men have lost their lives through the nazis' hands, and probably another 250,000 have once been in a camp but have been released and fight or work somewhere. These 750,000 men and/or their relatives have only one big desire: to kill the person whom they consider responsible for their special case. And this by the quickest procedure possible, if attainable with their own hands. And those who are killing people in occupied countries are to a great extent the same people who have killed or imprisoned Germans, unless they are drawn from other countries, especially from Latvia. – By the way most of the most brutal SD-men, murderers etc. have been drawn either from Austria or from the Sudetenland, the minority are toughs from the smaller Germany, and probably a quite minute minority only from Prussia. – Therefore it is a need of the internal German politics to bring these men to justice, perhaps even to death without justice, and the only way in which this could be prevented would be by making these toughs national heroes suffering for Germany instead of being punished by Germans.

---

* No sermon of this date is known. Probably Helmuth had in mind that of 28 June 1942 on the Christian conception of law. For the sermon (Pastoral Letter) of 20 December, see above, p. 202 (where on the basis of Dr Schwerdtfeger's biography of Preysing, p. 104, the date is given as 13 December).

The "danger of communism" is in our position very real. But as things are this danger arises mainly in the group of intellectuals and not among the workmen. The reason is that those workers who would go communist are already nazis. And those who are nazi are ready to go communist any day. If one does not take care, one will find all those brutal SA and SS men posing as persecuted communists, who now have to avenge themselves on their opponents. But those workers who are not nazi now, and that is the majority of the older and highly skilled workers, are completely fed up with all kinds of totalitarianism. These are the workers on which we must build not on those who can escape with a simple change of colour without change of heart. You see the fight against nazism is not confined to one class or another: it goes on inside the classes and there are adherents to each creed at all levels of the society at the top as well as at the bottom. If there is anything you can say about classes it is this: broadly speaking the middle classes are nazi or at least most highly afflicted by one form of totalitarianism or another, and the lower ranks of the Prussian nobility as far as it still possesses land is least afflicted, is in fact practically immune from any kind of totalitarianism. The nobility of the higher ranks from dukes upwards and the nobility of the South and West of Germany is much more afflicted by this disease and the urbanised nobility is really part of the middle-classes. These middle-classes tend, where they are anti-nazi to be philo-bolshewist, philo russian etc. They feel uncertain of themselves and hope for the great new strength that shall come from the East.

6

Now my plea in these circumstances is for a stable connection between the German opposition and Great Britain and a connection not based on secret service relations, not used mainly to extract information but a political connection. I do not want this in order to discuss possible peace-terms, possibilities of a post-war world. I want this connection in order to assist our war against Hitler, our internal war. I enclose a note I made about a certain event which has occupied us lately. If we had had a stable connection with Great Britain we could have discussed common strategy in exploiting these facts. As we have not got this connection we have to grope about in the dark hoping that the information which comes to your people will not be used in such a way as to discredit and perhaps andanger us. – Occasions like this will recurr, and other occasions will make contact useful. But I hope that this one example will show you what I mean without further details or examples.

7

Now how can this be done technically? We would have to have a man in Stockholm who knows Central Europe and who, working under the general guidance of the ambassador would have special functions to keep in touch with the various underground movements in Europe, especially in Germany and would have to deal with them on a basis of political discussion and cooperation. We would supply him with addresses here which would contact him with the oppositions in various countries under Hitler. Preferably it should be a man whom I know or about whom I know something, because time is precious and with a stranger it will take some time to get intimate and real personal contact is required.

But there are two main points one about his position and one about his powers. Although subject to the general guidance of the ambassador he should be free from all entanglements of secret service work. As far as I can make out the channels of all secret services of the various nations are the same, and most agents will work for at least two parties. Therefore whatever you put into the secret service of one country will in due course be known to the secret service of all other countries. As a result the secret services of all countries are secret to everybody but its opponent. There may be an all-important time-lag before one bit of information available to one secret service percolates to the other, but in the end it will get there and there is not much to be thankful for, if the guillotine is simply postponed for 3 months.

As to the powers I have to offer the following remark: the man must be able in certain circumstances to provide one of us with everything necessary to get to Britain and back in a short time, so that if necessary common plans can be discussed viva voce.

Well, these are the proposals and I hope you will be kind enough to give them a thought. Perhaps they will be brought to you by one of our Swedish friends, if not, they will contain the address of one of our friends, with whom you could put a man you sent here in contact. You will realise that you must please not mention my name in this connection unless it is to a man placed so highly as to be able to decide himself without handing the information with the name on to some superior. The name must most certainly never appear in writing anywhere.

As far as I am concerned I would, of course, prefer to have Michael here in Stockholm be it as principal or as an adviser to the principal.

I do not feel able to add personal notes to this letter. I have written separate letters to Michael and Julian and have given them

all the news. They know that they shall show their letters to you, and
perhaps you will be good enough to show them from this letter what
you think worth while showing.
I send my love to you both, Yours ever

This letter put Johansson in something of a dilemma because he
thought it too dangerous to send on as it was; he may also have been
afraid of compromising Sweden's neutrality. Accordingly the full text
remained in his archives until it was published in 1970.[18] But in the
following July he received a visit from Tracy Strong the American
General Secretary of the YMCA. He asked Strong to memorise the
letter as best he could and repeat it to Bishop Bell on his way home.
This was done. In England Strong wrote out a précis of the letter
running to about a sixth of its original length and including no precise
indication of its source. Bell sent this to Curtis with a covering letter[19]
explaining how the document had come into his hands and particularly
emphasising the request that 'a thoroughly trusted Britisher' should be
posted to Stockholm with whom the *Widerstand* could establish contact. Exactly what Curtis did with the letter is not known but he is
almost certain to have passed it to the Foreign Office and MI5. Bell had
also sent a copy of the document to Sir Robert Bruce Lockhart, the
Director-General of the Political Warfare Executive in which M.B. was
working. Sir Robert, however, never showed or mentioned the letter
to him or to the head of the PWE German Section, though a copy of the
document, without any indication of source and without any of the
references to establishing a channel of communication, may have been
circulated in the department (where in its truncated form it would have
attracted little attention). No action is likely to have been taken on the
request for someone to be sent to Stockholm because earlier in the year
the British authorities in that city had tried in vain to get M.B. sent
there to meet Helmuth of whose forthcoming visit they were aware.
Their request was refused on the authority of a general directive from
the Prime Minister that any approaches from Germans were to be
disregarded.[20]

On getting back to Berlin, Helmuth is likely to have heard of two
disappointments which the *Widerstand* had suffered but which went
some way to confirm his own views. Since the beginning of the year and
the final surrender at Stalingrad Oster, working in close conjunction
with Major-General von Tresckow on the eastern front, had renewed
his efforts to get Hitler assassinated. This led, after several disappointments, to a bomb being smuggled on to Hitler's aircraft by Lieutenant
Fabian von Schlabrendorff on 13 March and to another being concealed
about his person by Colonel Gersdorff on 21 March so that he could
blow up both himself and Hitler while he was in process of showing the

Führer an exhibition of captured weapons. The first attempt failed because the altitude impaired the bomb (captured from the British) which failed to go off, the second because Hitler went through the exhibition without stopping to be shown anything. Nothing could have demonstrated more clearly the measure of the problem of how to get at Hitler. The Kreisau group had not had any detailed knowledge of what was going on, for that had to be confined in common prudence to a small circle. But the mere awareness that some sort of action was to be expected soon had produced a state of tension, followed, after the failure, by depression.

Only a fortnight later, the *Widerstand*, already hampered by Beck falling seriously ill, received a further blow. In May 1942 Heydrich, who in addition to being head of the RSHA was acting as 'Protector' of Bohemia and Moravia, was assassinated outside Prague by Czech parachutists from England, with terrible consequences for the Czech people. His security post was left unfilled until January 1943 when SS General Ernst Kaltenbrunner, hitherto Chief of Police in Vienna, was appointed to it. His arrival added force to the efforts at undermining the *Abwehr* which were already being pursued by Walter Schellenberg, the former head of the Counter-Intelligence Branch of the Gestapo who had been promoted in 1941 to become head of the Foreign Countries' Intelligence Branch (Amt VI) of the SD. If only some treasonable charges could be made to stick against members of the *Abwehr*, its independent existence might be brought to an end. Particular interest was therefore paid to any of its members who got into police hands.

One such was a businessman called Schmidhuber who had worked for the *Abwehr* in Munich (where he was honorary Portuguese consul) and was arrested in Italy in November 1942 for currency offences. He was handed over to the Gestapo for questioning and his interrogation was entrusted to a Dr Manfred Roeder who had just distinguished himself by breaking up the *Rote Kapelle* spy ring, as a result of which forty-six people were condemned to death.[21] Under cross-examination, Schmidhuber managed to cast suspicion on various members of the *Abwehr*, principally Dohnanyi, Bonhoeffer and Joseph Müller. Initially their offence was that they had rescued Jews by sending them out of the country as *Abwehr* agents and getting their money to them as payment for their services. But a good deal more began to come out and 5 April saw the arrival of Roeder in Canaris' office with a warrant for Dohnanyi's arrest. According to the latter's wife, Helmuth had warned him of his danger[22] but this does not seem to have led him to remove all incriminating material from his desk. Oster, as his superior officer, had to be present while the room was searched and, misinterpreting a signal from Dohnanyi, was caught by a Gestapo officer trying to conceal a document. The net result was that Dohnanyi was taken to prison and soon after his wife, Dietrich Bonhoeffer, Joseph Müller and Frau Müller were all arrested. What was perhaps worse was that Oster was ordered to quit the office and remain at home on indefinite leave. Though the SD did not realise it, they had removed the linch-pin of the team which was trying to remove Hitler. Moreover the whole *Abwehr* had been brought under even greater suspicion than ever.

Canaris seems to have sensed that the odds were against his maintaining his position for much longer. The approach of defeat was paradoxically increasing the influence of the more radical elements among the Nazis. Not only did their smaller chances of escaping lightly from a collapse make them more reckless but they could argue that drastic measures alone still offered a chance of avoiding such a collapse. Himmler, it is true, seems to have been playing a completely double game, leaving at liberty people whom he knew to have contacts with the Allies and making overtures himself to the *Widerstand* in August 1943 through Popitz and a lawyer called Carl Langbehn. But an Allied message (said to be neither British nor American) from Switzerland reporting these overtures was deciphered by the Gestapo so that the *Reichsführer SS*, to save his own skin, had to pretend he had been behaving as an *agent provocateur*, order the arrest of Langbehn (but not of Popitz) and exploit his new position as Minister of the Interior to the full against anyone reported for defeatism or subversion. During the summer Canaris began to change the form of his foreign organisation to make it less vulnerable to a take-over but, in contrast to his earlier practice, did not venture on any substantial attempt to rescue his captured subordinates.

Dohnanyi's arrest had made Helmuth wonder how much longer it would be possible for him to go on working in Berlin. About this time, he asked his friend Wilhelm Adam, the *Landrat* of Schweidnitz, whether a job could be found for him in the provincial administrative office in Breslau. But this did not prevent him from criticising Canaris for inaction, probably because he did not know nearly as much as we do about the latter's difficulties. On 5 May he wrote to Freya:

> I had a talk with Bürkner this morning about the little sailor's bouts of weakness. I said to him that things could not go on like this. B was sympathetic and has given me permission to discuss the matter with the little sailor tête-à-tête. That will take place at the beginning of next week. I long now to know what will come of it –

but tantalisingly the next letter to be preserved comes from a fortnight later and gives no hint of the outcome. Dr Gisevius, who was at this time acting as liaison officer between *Abwehr* headquarters and Switzerland, has, however, provided a picture which to some extent fills the gap:

I can still today see [Moltke's] tall thin figure standing in front of me – it must have been shortly after the blow to our office. Our conversation revolved round the question whether one ought to put pressure on Canaris, whose position was so obviously threatened, and get him to use the last vestige of his influence in persuading the military chiefs to move against the rule of terror. Moltke's view was that the Admiral should restrict himself to firm action on a strictly legal basis on behalf of his arrested friends. Moltke stood motionless, with a thin file pressed to his chest like a parson's Bible, his gaze directed into the distance as if he were a revivalist preacher. This added fascination to the restrained force with which he spoke; sharp as the words were, he did not once raise his voice and his arguments remained balanced, matter-of-fact, one might almost say completely unruffled and imperturbable – he might have been pleading as a barrister in an English court.

Our talk went on for hours. For I must admit that, after all that has happened in recent years, I understand him less than ever. But when I consider what can be said twenty years later in Germany itself not against the unsuccessful action on 20 July but against the moral and political reasons behind an attempt at insurrection, I must hasten to add I could not today argue against the dead Moltke with the same conviction which I deployed against the living one.[23]

23 Hard at Work
April–August 1943

DURING the remaining ten months of liberty left to Helmuth, his activities fall broadly into two groups. In the first place he was occupied in completing the drafts of the post-war plans to which he may be said to have put his final touches in September, and in working for the *Abwehr* in Berlin. Secondly he made two visits to Western Europe, two to Turkey, one to Poland, one to Austria, a further one to Scandinavia and several to South Germany. The two groups overlap in time and purpose, for the earlier journeys were made before September and all were in one way or another connected with his various activities in Berlin. But they can be followed more easily if they are treated separately.

The net result of all these activities was, however, to put him under considerable strain. It was not always quite as bad as on 6–7 August but his calendar on those days ran as follows:

> Kiep had lunch here on the 6th. Steltzer came at 2.30, Peter at 3, Adam and Haeften at 3.30, then I had to go to the office, then to my private office, then at 8 back to the main office, where I had arranged with Fräulein Thiel to go through and divide up the papers, as I simply had no time for this during the day. That took so long that I didn't get into bed until 2, and at 6 had to get up again because there were a lot of urgent matters which had to be disposed of early. They took me till 11, when [Berthold] Stauffenberg arrived. When he went, Adam came and when Adam went, Hans [his brother-in-law] who stayed till 1. I then had various things to settle and found Peter already waiting for me when I got home. He and Steltzer had lunch with me, Husen joined us at 2.30 and by the time we were through, it was ten past five and I had to go off hastily on my bicycle to Konrad [Preysing] who expected me at 5. When I came in again at 7.30 Friedrich [Mierendorff] was sitting there, who stayed till 12.

Yet the only person still surviving from that list of visitors declares that he found Helmuth relaxed and in good shape!

Writing to M.B. on 25 March,* he had said:

> *My two younger assistants have been taken away for front-line duty and those which I have collected to replace them are wounded*
> * See note, p. 376.

*officers who have had several years of front-service and have thereby
completely forgotten how to work. So it is easier for me to do the
work myself than to trust it to them. It is most unhappy, but the two
boys will shape allright, as they have the right spirit and the right
will. Only it will need a great deal of patience on my part.*

The arrest of Dohnanyi seems to have given him a premonition that
his own time might be limited:

12 April

Haven't you rather too much to do? You sounded a little like it on
the telephone. Spare yourself. The time for unlimited effort hasn't
arrived yet and you must look after yourself till it does. You above
all people, because you must always allow for the possibility that later
on I shan't be there any more, whether physically or geographically.
Please don't forget that.

19 April

The farm concerns me enormously – the sheep and the cows, the
fodder and the new cropping programme, the building, the water-
trough in Wierischau, the new machines, etc. There is such a fearful
lot to do, to think over, to plan that I grudge every day I can't be at
home.

In May after another short week-end with Freya at Kreisau he men-
tions reading in the train back to Berlin not merely reports of House of
Commons debates (Hansard) but also the plans of J. M. Keynes and
Harry Dexter White for an International Monetary Fund and Bank.*

27 June (a Sunday)

The day was spent in cooking, eating, reading *The Times*, playing
Patience a little. It was not productive because I wasn't at peace with
myself. I had the feeling once more that I only had a really short
time still ahead of me and that I must leave such an enormous lot
unfinished. These are days in which I find it really difficult to keep
control of myself.

15 July

I am full of pleasant thoughts about Kreisau and only sorry that
you aren't there. I don't like that at all. I feel so very much more
secure when I know that you are on the spot at home.

17 July

There's nothing more to report. The hour-glass is slowly running

* Readers of Sir Roy Harrod's biography of Keynes (p. 544) will recall
another occasion when those documents were read in a train. Helmuth would
have appreciated the suggestion that the American one was written in
Cherokee.

out and the people who haven't looked at it for years are shocked to find how little sand is left. Time and again I find it hard to understand how people can be under illusions about that.

Simultaneously with Dohnanyi's arrest, Helmuth found himself in the thick of a controversy about the use of former Dutch, Belgian and French conscripts on forced labour in Germany.[1] In 1940 the Germans, thinking the war virtually over, had released their prisoners-of-war and let them go home. Nobody had bothered to define their exact legal status. Now the voracious appetite of the eastern front for manpower and munitions had caused a labour shortage in Germany which the authorities proposed to fill by calling on the men to report again for duty, with penalties if they did not come. Helmuth's branch as usual heard of this at a late stage. He had to work till midnight with Wengler and a secretary and then start again at 8. By 11.30 he had got Bürkner's signature to a teleprinter message to all commanding officers in the west, which seems to have taken the line that the prisoners' release had restored their civilian status. Some who had later helped the enemy had been punished under the occupation regulations, which would have been improper if they still had the status of prisoners. If on the other hand they had only been released on parole, without any alteration of status, the Red Cross convention on prisoners forbade their being set to work on armaments. And, if they did come to Germany as prisoners, they were entitled to be under the control of the army rather than the SS.

9 April

Whether it will be any use I don't know but in the first place I have satisfied my conscience and secondly it may act as a brake. In any case it has been noticed in the Führer's headquarters because they have been at me today for explanations.

A week later he reported having been suddenly called to the AA against whom he had succeeded in mobilising all relevant sections of the OKW.

They were in confusion and I came at the right moment. I injected a little stiffening and worked out a ploy with Schlitter* so that I hope to have saved the situation again. And no matter what happens I have enabled hundreds of thousands of men to go on living their normal lives for ten days longer. That always gives one satisfaction.

* Schlitter, Oskar, junior official in AA, known to Helmuth since at least 1940. After the war, Counsellor in London and Ambassador in Athens. Died 1970.

Delay was in fact all he did achieve for on 29 April General Christiansen,* the GOC in Holland, announced the recall of former P.O.W.s for work in Germany, thereby provoking a general strike. It was experiences like these which led Helmuth to say once to Wengler, 'Anyone who wants to see his proposals translated into reality had better not come to work with us.'[2]

Another subject of controversy at this time concerned the taking of hostages. An occupying power which encountered resistance was entitled by international law to take hostages, provided that they were not treated as convicts. The Nazis, who had been taking hostages since 1940, tried to prevent resistance by punishing and even shooting some of them when it occurred. In practice this policy had the opposite effect to that intended, as Helmuth had forecast. He was in constant touch with the authorities in Belgium on the matter but had more difficulty in getting information from those in Holland and France. This was the chief (ostensible) reason behind the journeys to those countries described in Chapter 25. It may well have been this issue on which he reported a clash with the soldiers on 17 June.

> I went yesterday to a meeting which gave me much pleasure. For I was called on to advise the murderous group of generals and officers in the OKW† who hang on the Führer's every word and I put them one and all to flight by wild attacks. They called my attention to the fact that what I wanted conflicted with a directive of the Führer, whereupon I answered, 'But gentlemen, you can't creep to shelter behind a directive of the Führer's. We would be failing flagrantly in our duty to the Führer if, sitting round our peaceful table, we were too cowardly to say to him that he was wrongly advised when he issued this directive and if, as a result of our cowardice, our troops away on service were to lose their lives.' That was roughly the line with which I jumped on these filthy toadies and, although one or two got indignant, they all turned tail in the end.

Argument also continued about the treatment to be given to nationals of countries like Poland, France and Yugoslavia whose official governments had surrendered to Germany if such men later joined 'free' forces fighting with the Allies and were captured. A similar problem arose over Allied personnel fighting with Resistance forces. The Nazis wished to treat all such persons as guerrillas and shoot them on capture. Helmuth's branch on the other hand sought in each case to find valid

---

* For Christiansen, see below, p. 259.
† This may refer either to the Command Staff of the Wehrmacht/*Wehrmachtführungsstab* under Generals Jodl and Warlimont, which handled actual military operations (except on the eastern front, handled by the OKH) or to the AWA under Reinecke.

grounds in international law for giving them protection. The Free French were claimed initially to be fighting as part of the British army and after November 1942 under a *de facto* government of their own in North Africa (though in fact the Committee of National Liberation in Algiers was *not* recognised by Britain or the United States as a provisional government). As regards Yugoslavia, the argument was advanced that combatant status did not depend on the country to which the persons concerned claimed to belong but on whether a belligerent (e.g. Britain) included the area in its strategic operation. One British officer, Captain Christie Lawrence, was later to describe how after capture in Yugoslavia he had been brought to Berlin to be shot but was rescued by Helmuth who succeeded in getting him handed over to the army authorities as a prisoner-of-war and in the process of transfer took him to his flat and gave him an 'English breakfast'. The inadequacy of international law in such matters may have meant that some of the arguments used in the cause of humanity were flimsy but that only makes more admirable the resource with which they were deployed.

By the end of July British air raids, in particular the three fire-raids on Hamburg and the prospect that Berlin's turn would come next, were forcing the German government to drastic action.

2 August

I have come back into a mad house. The difference in atmosphere since last Friday is enormously funny. Everything is in total dissolution and in another fortnight we shall have no machinery of government left. Early yesterday Dr Goebbels favoured his subordinates with the attached fly-sheet which discloses sheer panic. Not a word of confidence, of thinking big, no call for people to keep their heads, not a hint as to why these sacrifices must be made, no indication that the authorities have orders to protect the population and look after those who have suffered. Nothing but anxiety and panic. But this fly-sheet is nothing compared to the state of affairs in the Ministries. Work is at a standstill. Everyone is packing. Our female staff were sent home today to pack their own things. I have with great difficulty got action for us put off for a fortnight. Everything has got to happen immediately and everyone has got to go immediately.

3 August

We are suddenly the centre of interest because everyone is anxious to safeguard our files which are going to be indispensible for their justification [i.e. as showing to the victors that the *Abwehr* had opposed Nazi crimes]. It is madly comic. Everyone is at me to evacuate my files, and myself as well, as quickly as possible. I am having the greatest difficulty in withstanding such demonstrations of affection. If I didn't, I would be off to Zossen [army headquarters twenty miles south of Berlin] this very week. ... Conditions at the stations are insane. The police have to use their truncheons to separate those who have to stay from those who are allowed to go. The panic is simply indescribable and is increased by people being told there is bound to be a raid the very next night, in order to hurry them up.

10 August

Everyone here is getting out in panic. It is terrible. Nothing ever gets done, the people you want are not there and when they are aren't interested in business, only in their own salvation. ... I enclose a new will. I now think that the right thing is for Caspar to get Kreisau and know it and prepare himself for it.

Most of Helmuth's division, including Bürkner, retired to Zossen, while part of the Institute went to the Harz. Helmuth himself refused to budge, primarily because of the difficulty he would thereafter have found over keeping in touch with his friends. (It was the same motive which led his eminently practical mind to seize his telephone whenever an alarm sounded and take it with him to the shelter, for instruments were scarce yet without them communication became extremely hard!) He was left alone with Oxé and a staff of two. This in some ways made it easier for him to follow his own line with such other officers as remained in the city, but created problems when he had to consult his colleagues and superiors, especially when communications had been disrupted by bombing. Domestically he took to sleeping at Peter Yorck's Hortensienstrasse house and only used his own flat in the daytime. The Allies, in damaging their enemies, inevitably made things difficult for their friends.

All the same consultations continued actively. In April and May Helmuth recorded meetings with Peter Yorck (who had had to leave the Price Control Office and was working in the Economic Division of the OKW), Preysing, Lukaschek, König, Adam von Trott, Görschen (a German businessman with Dutch nationality, resident in the Hague and former employer of Carl Deichmann, who since the previous autumn was being built up as liaison man between the *Widerstand* and the Dutch Resistance), Gerstenmaier (who had been in Rome),* Mierendorff, Reichwein, Einsiedel, Delbrück, Poelchau, Peters and Waetjen (who was by now attached to the German Consulate-General in Zürich and acting as liaison with the Americans under Allan Dulles† in place of Gisevius who had incurred suspicion along with Oster and dared not

---

* He reported 'a completely negative attitude of the Vatican towards Russia'. This surprised Helmuth who had expected the opposite.

† Dulles' assistant, Gero Gävernitz, was the son of the Professor Schulze-Gävernitz who had lunched at Kreisau on 18 September 1927. Above, p. 32.

leave Switzerland). There was also another meeting with Bishop Wurm on 6 May while he was in Berlin for a meeting of Protestant leaders to protest against anti-Jewish measures. But there was still trouble over the future form and function of trade unions.

13 April

Unfortunately Maass has had a bad relapse now that he is no longer under continual observation. [Mierendorff] was in a fury with him and Reichwein gave a marvellous description of his interview with Mierendorff, who sat the whole time with his back turned to Maass under the pretext that he wanted to warm his feet in the sun. It must have been a lovely sight. All the same it is a very unfortunate break-down and [Leuschner] and his comrades will have to exert themselves to make up for it.

14 April

I had a detailed discussion with Adam and Eugen [Gerstenmaier] about problems of foreign policy and to my great joy the differences in the previous talks have been completely overcome. This was partly because we started from a different angle but secondly because the English discussion and the Russo-Polish conflict [following the German revelations of the Katyn massacres] have helped a lot. So to my surprise we proved to see eye-to-eye. In particular they accepted for all practical purposes my thesis about the island.*

The third and last week-end gathering at Kreisau took place at Whitsun from 12 to 14 June. The guests this time were Peter, Marion and Irene Yorck, Delp, Gerstenmaier, Reichwein, Trott, Haubach, Husen† and (probably) Einsiedel. There were three main subjects of discussion. First came post-war foreign policy (including economic relations) on which Adam von Trott took the lead.‡ The second was the action to be taken by the German community to punish those of its

* Dr Gerstenmaier can no longer remember exactly what this refers to.

† Husen, Dr Paulus van, had been dismissed in 1934 from the Upper Silesian Mixed Commission (above, p. 21) for having used the League of Nations Minority Statutes to protect Jews from persecution. He then secured a succession of appointments in Prussian Courts. In 1940, although forty-nine, he took the place of a colleague who should have been called up and was posted to the *Wehrmachtführungsstab* (above, p. 23).

‡ The informal character of the Kreisau arrangements is illustrated by the fact that on this Whit Monday Mierendorff (who kept away from the meeting on security grounds but had Haubach present to speak for him) drafted along with others (unnamed) in Berlin a proclamation containing a programme of Socialist Action (Text, see van Roon, p. 378). A copy was preserved by Helmuth along with the other Kreisau documents. The proclamation (among other demands in line with Kreisau thinking) calls for co-operation with all nations 'and particularly in Europe with Great Britain and Soviet Russia' while the 'Action Committee' is said to include Communists.

members who had been guilty of crimes against the law. This was something on which many members of the *Widerstand* felt keenly that action must be taken by the Germans instead of being left to the Allies. The latter, however, remembered the German failure to do anything effective against considerably less serious offences after 1918 and had as early as January 1942 announced their intention of bringing 'war criminals' to justice themselves. The discussion at Kreisau sought for a compromise between these two views. It was based on a paper drafted by Husen and redrafted in the following month by Helmuth himself. The third subject was the document of instructions to the Land Commissioners/*Landesverwesern* who, it was intended, would take over in each part of Germany after a collapse.* Here the initial draft was Helmuth's. The selection of these *Landesverwesern* was part of the list of appointments which Helmuth mentioned towards the end of 1942.† The names of about half a dozen are known and more were probably approached but it seems likely that soon afterwards the process of selection and nomination was taken over by Claus von Stauffenberg and the military as part of their plans for a *Staatsstreich*; according to these plans, each Commander of a military district was to have a political adviser. Most of the persons named for this work seem, however, to have been nominated by the Beck–Goerdeler group.

Once the third Kreisau meeting was over, all the major subjects had been covered and papers embodying the conclusions prepared. There were, however, still a number of other people whose adhesion was thought to be desirable, while experience was to show that participation and agreement at Kreisau gave no immunity against a change of mind later. Thus in the latter part of 1943 Husen and Lukaschek, to Steltzer's great indignation, went back on the agreement that schools should be Christian but undenominational and arranged that each church should keep its own schools. Consequently discussion continued in Berlin. On the one hand was the desire to have a cut-and-dried scheme ready to be applied if the Nazi downfall came suddenly; on the other the desire to adapt proposals in the light of further argument and of changes in the world picture.

Between Whitsun and the end of August the names which crop up in the letters are nearly all familiar: the one newcomer is Karl Blessing‡

---

* For details, see below, pp. 252–5. *Land* is the German term for the administrative unit between the national and local levels. It has more autonomy than is conveyed by 'province', less than is conveyed by the American 'state'.

† Above, p. 205.

‡ Blessing, Karl (1900–71), assistant to Dr Schacht in Reichsbank 1926–30; in Bank of International Settlements 1930–4; with Schacht in Economics Ministry 1934–7; Director of Reichsbank 1937–8; in German subsidiary of Unilever 1938–41, chairman 1949–58; president of Bundesbank 1958–70.

who came with Waetjen on 24 August for 'a good and altogether fruitful talk'.

The main problem remained that of trade union organisation, where Carlo Mierendorff was a tower of strength:

8 August

The evening with [M] was very satisfactory precisely because of the great difficulty of the subject. In fact he and I are fundamentally in agreement, which makes everything else by comparison simple. I think we have now found a way of going, admittedly not back to where we were but forward to a positive solution.

10 August

We [H, Husen, Steltzer, Trott] assembled at 8 at Peter's [Yorck] where [Mierendorff] and Haubach joined us. M was in absolutely splendid form – clear, resolute, clever, tactful and witty. The result of the night session, which lasted till 5 o'clock, was that the gap which the Uncle [Leuschner] created has been filled, in that M will see to it that the comrades come over to us with him and leave the Uncle isolated. An enormous step forward has been achieved in both a practical and a theoretical direction.

This then was the background against which Helmuth drafted a 2,500-word document entitled 'Fundamental Principles for the New Order'/*Grundsätze für die Neuordnung* and two subsidiary 'Instructions for the Land Commissioners'/*Weisungen an die Landesverwesern* of 1,000 and 250 words respectively.* He originally dated these documents 9 August but in fact went on making minor amendments till 10 September. They are the last of the surviving documents dealing with the picture as a whole in which he had a hand and this makes the present an appropriate place to say something about the plans resulting from all the activity which has been chronicled.[3]

* For texts, see van Roon, pp. 347–57. The three documents went closely together, since the 'Fundamental Principles' were designed to give the Land Commissioners guidance as to general policy. They therefore repeated and summarised many of the conclusions reached in earlier documents but did not supersede them.

24 Plans

M O S T Germans who tried during the war to think about what should be done after it was over faced a dilemma. For them to agree on repudiating National Socialism was as easy as it was later to be for the Western Allies and the Russians. Equally the majority of them repudiated Communism, in which indeed they saw similarities to the Third *Reich*. But they also agreed that Western democratic forms, as tried in Germany between 1919 and 1933, had not worked either. While some certainly found satisfaction in this conclusion, to others it was a matter of regret that the preconditions of tradition and social integration which had enabled democracy to succeed in the West were lacking in Germany. In 1941, when Helmuth started systematic discussions, parliamentary democracy had vanished from the mainland of Europe (except for Switzerland and Sweden) and the assumption was easily made that its day was done. He and his friends were therefore in search of some other political and social forms which might bring to their country – and to Europe – peace, plenty, justice and individual freedom. Instead of examining whether there were any other Western institutions or methods which might prove more effective than the ones used by the Weimar Republic, they nearly all turned to the well-established idea that there was a distinct German, Central European tradition to be followed which was neither Eastern nor Western and that sticking to the indigenous would yield better results than importing the exotic. Some of them, including Helmuth, may have thought of this merely as the best way of creating the preconditions in which democracy in the Western sense could function effectively; others looked to it as a lasting solution.

The foundation of the 'German Way' was the supremacy of a law which laid down explicitly for each individual citizen not only his rights and liberties but also the limits of those rights and the duties which went inseparably with them. It was the Nazis' refusal to abide by the rule of law which had done more perhaps than anything else to drive the German upper classes into opposition. It involved a code of law more systematic than the Anglo-Saxon combination of common and statute law. Secondly there was the ideal of a community to which each citizen belonged and in which each citizen had duties as well as rights, so that position and privilege carried responsibility. Hegelians like Adam von Trott might be inclined virtually to identify this community with the state, others (including Helmuth) condemned the idolisation of the state. The idea was not unlike Lionel Curtis' principle of 'the infinite duty of each to all'. Thirdly there was the view, always associated with the reforms which Baron vom Stein had introduced but left uncompleted in Prussia in 1812–15, that liberty and self-government started at the bottom, in the towns and communes/*Gemeinde* which were not merely free in Germany to decide on anything not explicitly assigned by law to higher bodies but had in many cases habitually acted as the executive agents of these bodies.

Certain corollaries of this approach deserve notice. Firstly there was an underlying assumption that, if things were working properly, all citizens ought to be agreed. It is probably true that liberal democracy will only work well where the great majority of its citizens are agreed in giving its maintenance priority over all other more divisive sectional objectives. But rightly or wrongly the German expectation was for something rather more, probably because for so many centuries Germany had suffered from ideological and geographical divisions. The pluralistic idea of a society which deliberately organises itself so as to bring divisions to light in the hope of reconciling them was something which shocked most Germans. Even Helmuth who, influenced by Eugen Rosenstock's teaching and British example, saw the importance of discussion, expected it to lead to agreement on a voluntary basis. But many other Germans saw little wrong with the idea of agreement being imposed by the established authorities who after all had a duty to act in the general interest. Characteristic of this was the important position assigned to the administrative official such as the *Landrat or Bürgermeister* who was certainly to be advised by popularly elected representatives but was not their servant to be given orders. As many decisions as possible ought to be taken on an administrative technical basis rather than on a political one, by calculating facts rather than by weighing values.

The system had not worked satisfactorily either in the Second *Reich* (1871–1918) or in the Third, although in some respects the latter was a hypertrophied travesty of it. The question therefore was what was wrong. Some members of the *Widerstand* saw the mistake in bad leadership. Put the right people at the top and all would be well (though they were less precise about the way to find the right people and get them to the top. As an American is reputed to have said, 'We all want to vote for the best man but he's never a candidate'). The answer which Helmuth and the more radical members of the *Widerstand*, including the trade unionists, favoured was that a real community had never been achieved. Besides the split between Catholics and Protestants, the workers had been regarded as outcasts.* Moreover, the tendency of the large-scale industrial state to treat the individual as a type, a mere cog in the machine, deprived them of the sense of participation in the processes governing their own lives. As Helmuth wrote, 'The responsibility of the individual is in process of disappearing. All small communities, in which individuals still bear responsibility, are in process of disappearing. The functions of such small autonomous communities are all gradually being taken over by the state.'† The result was that, as President Nixon put it in his State of the Union message on 18 January 1971, people became increasingly frustrated 'as everything has grown bigger and more complex, as the forces that shape our lives seem to have grown more distant and impersonal'. The remedy was to bring all classes into the community, to enable them to participate effectively and to give them a motive for doing so other than self-interest and other than the national appeal which the Nazis had exploited till it was discredited. 'We must reawaken in the individual the awareness of owing a personal allegiance to values which are not of this world. Nothing else will make possible the restoration of his freedom. In this way the individual will recover an awareness of responsibility which will enable a feeling of true community to blossom.'‡

GENERAL PRINCIPLES

This approach explains the opening sentence of the 'Fundamental Principles':

> The Government of the German *Reich*§ sees in Christianity the foundation for the moral and religious renewing of our people, for the surmounting of hate and lies, for the rebuilding of the European Community of peoples.
>
> The point of departure lies in the recognition by men of the divine order of things on which human existence is founded both inwardly and outwardly. Only when it proves possible to make this order the test of relations between men and peoples can the disintegration of our time be overcome and a genuine state of peace be created.
>
> The internal reordering of the *Reich* is the basis for the establishment of a just and lasting peace.
>
> The power complex which is collapsing had become irresponsible

---

* Above, pp. 29–30.
† Document of 24.iv.41, above, p. 148.
‡ Ibid., p. 148.
§ *Reich* is best left untranslated. The nearest English equivalent to it is 'realm' but it does not necessarily imply a monarch.

and was based exclusively on the supremacy of technology. The main task now facing mankind in Europe is to get this divine order recognised. The solution lies in the resolute and vigorous realisation of Christian values. The *Reich* government is therefore resolved to realise by every means in its power the following essential demands:

1.   Law which has been trampled under foot must be re-established and made supreme throughout human affairs. If interpreted by conscientious, independent and fearless judges, it provides the foundation on which alone a peaceful world can in future be built.

2.   Freedom of belief and of conscience will be guaranteed. Existing laws and ordinances which conflict with these principles will be immediately repealed.

3.   An end will be put to totalitarian interference with the individual conscience. The inviolable dignity of human life will be recognised as the foundation on which we will seek to build a peaceful and just order. Everybody will bear a full measure of responsibility in whatever spheres of social, political and international life their work may fall. The right to work and to own property will be officially assured without regard to race, nationality or religious belief.

4.   The family is the basic unit of a peaceful life in common. Both education and the external necessities of life, i.e. food, clothing, housing, a garden and health, will be officially assured to it.

5.   Work must be so organised that it encourages and does not stunt the taking of responsibility. This can be secured not merely by the character of working conditions and opportunities for further education but also by assuring to everyone in a concern a genuine share of responsibilty for its conduct and by this means for the whole framework of the economy to which his work contributes.... Those in control of the economy must see to it that these basic requirements are met.

6.   Each individual's personal political responsibility requires that he should make his voice heard in the self-government which is to be resuscitated in the small face-to-face communities. It is these which will secure to every individual the right of having a say in the State and in the national community, through representatives of his own choice, and which will in this way transmit to him an active conviction that he* has a share of responsibility for political development in general.

* The German text throughout uses masculine forms rather than ones which would cover both sexes. Possibly it is this which has given Professor Mommsen the idea (*The German Resistance to Hitler*, p. 116) that 'Kreisau regarded women as ineligible'. This was certainly not the case.

7. The special responsibility and loyalty which every individual owes to his national origin, his language and the spiritual and historical heritage of his nation must be respected and protected. They must not, however, be exploited to produce concentration of political power or to humiliate, persecute or oppress alien nationalities. The free and peaceful development of national cultures is no longer compatible with the maintenance of absolute sovereignty by individual states. Peace demands the creation of an order which embraces the individual states. Provided that the free consent of all participating nations is guaranteed, those on whose shoulders responsibility for this order rests must have the right to call on every individual to obey and respect them and if necessary to put life and property at the service of the highest political authority of the Community of Nations.

To appreciate these paragraphs, the reader must remember that they were written as a confession of faith which might cost the lives of the men who made it, since it summed up the issues dividing them irrevocably from the tyranny which controlled their country.

POLITICAL STRUCTURE

The document then goes on to discuss the way in which the *Reich* is to be built up. It opens by saying that 'the *Reich* remains the supreme political authority of the German people'. This phrase represented something of a defeat for Helmuth. Three considerations had led him to toy with a different idea: the desire to decentralise, the conviction that Europe must be united and the knowledge that after the war Germany must reckon with the hostility of all her neighbours. He thought that all three might be met if Germany and France, instead of entering a United States of Europe as single entities, joined as several states, each comparable in size to Belgium or Denmark. But though his colleagues were all prepared to swallow the loss of national sovereignty to a federation (as stated in Point 7 above), the idea of Germany ceasing altogether to exist as a separate unit was too much for them. All that remained of Helmuth's proposal was a requirement that the *Reich* should be built up in such a way as to make its incorporation into a European Federation possible. Otherwise its constitution was to stem from the full co-operation and responsibility of the nation; to involve the three natural units of family, commune and land; and to follow the principle that each level should be self-governing in the way already described. The whole was to 'combine freedom and personal responsibility with the needs of order and leadership'.

This phrase – and indeed the document as a whole – may call to mind the German saying that 'the devil's in the detail'. Sonorous phrases like these are easy to put on paper but harder to realise in practice. The Kreisau addiction to general principles at the expense of concrete proposals is what has earned the group a reputation of being unpractical theorists. But they had two reasons for not going into further detail. One was that in some matters they were not yet agreed among themselves as to what form the detail should take. The second was precisely the argument used against planning at all – that one could not foresee the circumstances in which the plans would be applied. The Kreisau answer in effect was that, if one decided in advance what one's general principles were, one would be able to proceed more quickly to agree on how they should be applied to the situation which had developed, whereas if one had not settled one's general principles, one would either live from hand-to-mouth by improvisations or have to lose valuable time in arguing over principles (as the Frankfurt Parliament had so memorably done in 1848). The man who stuck to general terms was, for the time being, more practical than the man who went into detail.

'The political will of the people is to be formulated in the framework of a face-to-face community.' This generalisation was, however, particularised as implying a system of indirect election by which every citizen of either sex over twenty-one would be entitled to vote in communal elections. The omission of any stipulation as to the votes needed to win election suggests that it would be by simple majority. Heads of families were to get an extra vote for each child below voting age. The same rules were to apply in choosing representatives for the next stage in the hierarchy, the county/*Kreis* councils and the city council of towns large enough to be independent of the counties. In both, constituencies which were too large to be 'face-to-face' were to be subdivided. But election to the next tier of land parliament/*Landtag* would be done indirectly by the county and city councils, and the members of the *Landtag* would then elect persons to represent it in the *Reich* parliament/*Reichstag*. At *Land* and national levels, half the representatives had to be chosen from non-members of the electing body (so as to prevent people from being active at too many levels at the same time). Each *Land* was to have between three and five million inhabitants – rather less than the average in Western Germany today. Members of a *Land* government had to have their 'hereditary home' in the *Land*. The administration of each *Land* was to be supervised by a Land Commissioner/*Landesverweser* who was to be elected for twelve years by the *Landtag* and confirmed by the head of state.

Besides the *Reichstag* there was to be a *Reich* council/*Reichsrat* consisting of the Land Commissioners, along with other councillors chosen by the head of state with the consent of the *Reich* government for eight years. But the council was to have few powers beyond choosing for a twelve-year period of office (after the start when Beck was to fill the post) the head of state, to be called *Reich* administrator or regent/ *Reichsverweser** (the Kreisau group were unanimous in opposing the restoration of the monarchy).

The *Reich* government was to be headed by the chancellor, who was to be nominated by the *Reichsverweser* with the consent of the *Reichstag* (presumably voting by simple majority though this is not specified). But the *Reichsverweser* could dismiss the chancellor whenever he wished, provided he immediately appointed another. The *Reichstag* had, however, the right to demand, by a two-thirds majority, the dismissal of a chancellor provided that at the same time it voted in favour of a specific successor. This provision resembles the 'constructive vote of no confidence' in Article 66 of the Basic Law of the Federal Republic and it is interesting that the Article should have been taken from the Baden–Württemberg constitution and that the person who had suggested its inclusion there was Helmuth's friend Carlo Schmid.[1] The powers of Kreisau's *Reichstag* over its chancellor would certainly have been rather limited and this is the point at which one begins to wonder how far the details had been really thought out.† The wonder is increased when one finds that there is no provision for dissolving the *Reichstag before* its term of office expired and indeed no stipulation as to what the period of office of the *Reichstag* (or any other body) was to be.‡

The truth is that, when the Kreisau plans did advance from the general to the particular, the particulars were regarded as provisional rather than final. The members of the group did not foresee (or, if they foresaw, did not think it necessary to take into account) their imprisonment or execution as the result of an unsuccessful coup. They assumed that when the Nazi overthrow occurred they would move into action as a group, in continual contact with one another, and would be able to modify or elaborate their plans as the situation required so as to apply their basic principles to changing circumstances. This makes it desirable to use caution in drawing deductions as to their views or political intentions from the precise stage of formulation which their plans had

---

* Most Germans would be reminded by this title of Archduke John of Austria who in 1848–9 was appointed to a post carrying it by the Frankfurt Parliament. He too had met his future wife – a Postmaster's daughter – beside the Grundlsee.

† If the *Reichstag* had voted by a two-thirds majority for a successor to a chancellor whom it rejected, would the *Reichsverweser* have then been entitled to dismiss him?

‡ Such omissions are not peculiar to the Kreisau documents. The main Beck–Goerdeler plan (*Das Ziel*) fails to specify how the chancellor is to be appointed.

reached when Helmuth's arrest, and subsequently the failure of the 20 July coup, turned them for ever into mere historical documents.

The other Ministers were to be nominated by the *Reichsverweser* on the proposal of the chancellor. There was no provision that they had to belong to the *Reichstag* but such membership has never been regarded as essential in Germany and the use of the term departmental ministers *Fachminister* suggests that, as again is not unusual, their responsibility was to be confined to their own department instead of being collective as in Britain. Indeed, the impression is that they were to be technicians rather than politicians.

Besides the vital question of the relationship between the legislature and executive, the most striking features about this whole scheme are the idea of indirect election and the apparent exclusion of political parties. Upon this latter, intentions seem to have differed among the *Widerstand* generally. The Weimar experience, with a multiplicity of parties, had soured many people with the whole idea. Parties were thought to be divisive and to keep differences of opinion alive instead of achieving a reconciliation between them. Some people wanted to get rid of parties altogether, some to organise a single party to which all citizens of good-will would belong, some favoured three parties representing the middle class, the workers and the farmers respectively. Whatever views the members of the Kreisau group may have had prior to May 1945, it did not prevent a number of the survivors from working actively to re-establish parties after that date – Steltzer, for example, was one of the co-founders of the Christian Democratic Union in Berlin.

Helmuth, it is true, gave no indication of having been interested in this question. But what he was above all concerned with was bringing back life to the small unit – not merely in the political field. By making the vote in the communal elections the key to participation in the state, he hoped to make people take an interest in local affairs. In this way they could practise self-government in a sphere about which they knew something and choose as their representatives people whose talents and character they were able to judge by personal observation. As the same thing would happen all the way up, this would, it was hoped, solve the problem of getting the best men to be candidates. This was how the élite was to be formed on whom the successful development of the new Germany would depend.

The whole idea is perhaps more interesting today than at the time when it was evolved because it represents an attempt to remedy the exclusion of the individual from any real say in the conduct of the overcentralised bureaucratic state and this is a failing of which liberal democracy is now widely accused.[2] Moreover, it was an integral part of the plan to give the local units as wide powers as possible. One of the few things on which all wartime thinkers about the post-war world, both Anglo-Saxon and German, seemed to agree was the desirability of decentralising as a safeguard against authoritarian government.

Yet the plan is open to several criticisms. Interestingly enough, it flies in the face of one principle which Helmuth should have absorbed from his reading of *The Federalist* and from Lionel Curtis – namely the need for a direct relationship between the central government and the individual citizen. The process of transmitting the will of the individual voters up the long chain from commune to *Reich* might well have proved as frustrating as the supposed inability of the individual to influence government policy by casting a single vote once every four or five years. And, if the lower units had proved lively, the *Reich* government might have found great difficulty in getting them to co-operate in its measures. The problem cannot be evaded by saying that the powers of the centre would have been strictly limited. The reason why so many pressures today tend to increase the powers of the centre is that the alternative is confusion and waste of resources, growing so obvious that common sense demands co-ordination by the centre to eliminate them. The Kreisau group themselves saw the need to give the centre over-riding powers for economic and environmental planning. The participants with administrative experience, such as Schulenburg, intervened to emphasise the need to leave powers with the centre. Local autonomy and consultation of individual interests can only too easily mean delay, indecision, changes of course, overlapping, inconsistency and narrow-mindedness. The problem of overcoming these defects without taking too much freedom and responsibility away from the average man, of reconciling efficiency with liberty, may well be inherent in the human situation and capable only of a relative rather than an absolute solution. Certainly it has got no easier since 1943.*

Secondly the authors of the document seem insensitive to a problem which local election on a non-party basis might have presented for the central government. For that government, if it is to be effective, needs to feel reasonably sure of its ability to translate its intentions into reality. To do so, it needs to know that a majority of members of the legislature can be relied on to vote in a consistent way. The provision of that assurance is the function of the party system. If the members of the central legislature (or indeed of the legislative bodies at any level) consist of wise and honourable men each of whom votes exactly as seems to him best in each individual instance, then either the course of action for which there is a majority will vary from day to day, making the executive's task almost impossible, or the wise and honourable men, recognising the importance of consistency, will organise themselves into some

* Although the Kreisau intention was so clearly to decentralise, the word federation/*Bund* does not occur in the document.

I

kind of a party system. But once such a system develops, and once a party's chance of getting into its hands the power and privileges of central government begin to depend on who gets elected locally, local elections will soon begin to be organised on party lines and the community will begin to choose not the best man but the man advocating the policies which they like best. An alternative, of course, is to release the government, whether communal, *Land* or central, from the need to get the approval of the legislature for its individual actions and some of the Kreisau provisions look very much as though this was the intention.[3] But how in that case can the government be said to be responsible?

Helmuth's reply would probably have been that a government responsible for its individual actions to a majority made up of a coalition of parties was only capable of pursuing a consistent policy if it did as little as possible. There are countries in the world today which illustrate this fact only too painfully. Coalition government tends to be weak government, especially when more than two parties are involved. But what this comes down to is that a country in which the divisive forces are strong and the integrating forces weak is bound to have difficulty in achieving self-government at all. And this brings us back to the ultimate problem with which Helmuth and his friends were wrestling – if Germans were not sufficiently integrated to be capable of self-government on Western democratic lines, what form of government was most likely to increase their integration and at the same time be reasonably effective? Nobody could have foreseen in 1941-3 how far reliance on the Christians (acting politically as a unit) and on the workers would go towards simplifying party politics in the Federal Republic (especially when reinforced by a few constitutional devices and hatred of Communism). Even so, the system is being criticised increasingly for its failure to involve the individual in the control of his affairs.

RELIGION AND EDUCATION

The Fundamental Principles went on to deal with religion and education. Here their primary purpose was to restore to the churches what the Third *Reich* had taken away. Freedom of belief, worship and teaching was therefore to be guaranteed. The Christian contribution was to receive a fitting place in all cultural activities as well as film and radio. But the most significant sentence said that the relationship of the *Reich* with the German Evangelical (i.e. Protestant) Church and with the Roman Catholic Church would be regulated afresh in friendly harmony in the spirit of the Principles. This represented a concession by Helmuth, especially as a further sentence said that the 1933 Concordat between the German government and the Vatican was to remain unaffected. He had been so struck by the results of the Hegelian tendency to idolise the state that, far from regarding it as the source of morality, he had earlier wanted to deny to the state any standing in the field of morality at all. 'The state is amoral because it is abstract.' In this way nobody would be able to excuse himself for committing an immoral act by saying it was enjoined, or not prohibited, by law. He therefore wished – and in this he resembled Goerdeler – to dissociate the German churches from the state with which they had always been closely connected.* This idea was what lay behind Helmuth's suggestion to Cardinal Faulhaber that the Concordat should be given up.† It is interesting to note that the document speaks of the German Evangelical Church as a single unit. This was an aspiration rather than a fact except in so far as unification had been brought about by the Nazis, for Germany had not fully emerged from the post-Reformation situation in which each German state had its own Protestant Church. The dissolution of the existing states and substitution of the new *Länder*, often with different boundaries, were naturally expected to result in a reorganisation of these Churches and so create an opportunity for their unification.

Only eighteen lines were devoted to education in the 'Fundamental Principles' but this is largely because the document was intended to give guidance to the Land Commissioners during the early stages after the Nazi overthrow, whereas educational reform was thought of as something longer in term. A fuller picture of the group's views is to be gained from the text agreed at the first Kreisau meeting in May 1942. Even here, however, the concern is more with the kind of person whom it should be the function of the schools to produce than with the practical details of how this was to be accomplished. The school was required to 'realise the right of a child to an appropriate education'. This phrase may have been intended by some of the participants to imply that, when a child's parents could not afford the education appropriate to it, the state would step in. But nothing is said explicitly about the vital question of finance. The state school was defined as a Christian school with Catholic and Protestant religious education as a compulsory subject; this reflected the willingness of most Catholic members of the group to accept inter-confessional schools, though argument about this was still going on.‡

The existing universities were to be divided into *Reichsuniversitäten* – institutions for the pursuit and propagation of learning at the highest

---

* Every German, for example, is required to declare his religion, and unless he professes atheism the state financial machinery will then collect from him tax at a level agreed with the churches and pay it over to whichever of them he says he belongs to.

† Above, p. 212.

‡ Above, pp. 195, 235. Below, p. 300.

level – and *Hochschulen* or Technical Colleges to provide specialist training for the professions. The task of the first would be to relate the various branches of knowledge to one another, that of the second to specialise. Students would be expected to distinguish themselves at the *Hochschulen* before passing on to the universities, which would award the degree of M.A. as the qualification for senior posts in the public service (replacing the student's traditional choice between the state's own examination and the doctor's degree). Members of the group were, of course, well aware of the disappointing record of the universities in opposing Nazism, of the excessive power wielded by conservative professors and of the almost exclusively middle-class nature of the intake. But they had no agreed remedies to suggest and therefore made no precise proposals. Indeed they were largely concerned to free the universities from the state control established over them by the Third *Reich* and to ensure their autonomy.

INDUSTRY AND ECONOMICS

The economic paragraphs open by saying that everyone in the economy has certain minimal duties to fulfil, including good-faith and honesty on the part of employers, and observance of agreements on the part of the workers. Employers have a duty to provide their employees with the necessities of life while everybody should contribute to effacing the losses brought by the war and to raising living standards.

> The *Reich* government sees the foundation of economic reconstruction in regulated competition in production which takes place within the framework of an economic system directed by the government and officially supervised with regard to its methods.

The leaders in the economy are required to see that this aim is not frustrated by monopolies, cartels or excessively large firms.

> The economy's communal interests in heavy industry call for particularly close supervision by the state of these branches of industry. Key undertakings in the coal industry, in the iron and metal producing industries, in basic chemicals and energy will become public property. . . .
> The *Reich* government will encourage the development of each factory into an economic community of the men engaged in production within it. In such a community – called a Works Union – the participation of the workers in management and results, and in particular in increases in the factory's value, will be arranged between proprietor and the workers' representatives.

These proposals were intrinsic to the outlook of the men who drafted the document, and in effect translated into economic terms the idea of participation by the individual in the local community in which he was active. They foreshadow the idea of co-determination/*Mitbestimmung* which has been introduced into German industry since the war. What is not solved or even faced (although Helmuth showed in 1940 that he saw it)* is the problem of how centralised direction of the economy by the state is to be reconciled with local autonomy.

The problem of the single German trade union on which Leuschner laid such emphasis was solved by treating it as in the first instance a transitional institution designed to bring into existence the system just described. The possibility was envisaged that the union could itself be dissolved once its functions had been taken over by the organisations of economic self-administration and of the state. But this idea was far from being conceived in a spirit of hostility to the workers. On the contrary, the Kreisau group wanted these organisations to embody the interests of the working classes. They were set on developing the part which these elements of the population played in the political and economic tasks of the nation. They thought it possible that, if only this could be adequately done, the workers would not any longer need a union to look after their interests. In other words, they thought that social harmony was a matter of good-will, that employers and workers were not bound to differ and that machinery for expressing these differences would do more to encourage than to eliminate friction.

The remainder of the section concerned itself with the chambers of trade, industry and agriculture, membership of which was to be compulsory (as it usually is on the Continent, where such chambers perform a number of administrative tasks in conjunction with the central or local governments). Both employers and workers were to be represented in the chambers of trade and agriculture.

The only group document to have survived about agriculture is a four-page memorandum† summing up the discussion at Gross Behnitz in March 1942. The subject was one in which the participants faced a dilemma. On the one hand they felt passionately that a healthy society required a flourishing countryside, and they would no doubt have liked to follow their usual principle of building up from small units. But they were well aware of the fiasco which had overtaken Nazi promises to establish an economy of small peasants and they knew too much about agricultural economics to suppose that smallholdings could easily be made viable. They realised that Germany must import considerable quantities of food in payment for her industrial exports and that in a customs union including the Balkans German agriculture might be driven to the wall. They knew that things could not be left to the free

* Above, p. 127.   † Unpublished.

play of market forces and proposed a variety of measures in the hope of evading the need to choose between acquiescing in rural decay and turning farms into food-producing factories.

The country population was to be swollen as much as possible by people who only earned their living indirectly from agriculture (such as shopkeepers, teachers, doctors). Food-processing industries were to be attracted to the countryside as providers of employment, though the aim would be to countrify the towns, not to urbanise the villages. Production was to be raised by as much as a third so as to give farmers (and particularly the peasants) a standard of living comparable to townsfolk. The main means to this end would be mechanisation, though tax incentives, easy investment credits and co-operative action should all be brought into play. But machinery must be used to ease work rather than to save labour and mutual or state assistance must not end in bureaucracy. Big landowners had a vital part to play provided that they did not seek to cut out labour but looked after their workers. Many of the problems involved in making the countryside flourish in an advanced industrial state were diagnosed. If no sovereign remedy was found, part of the explanation is that in 1942 it was still hard to tell what the condition of European agriculture would be when the war ended.

FOREIGN AFFAIRS

In the paper which he completed on the fiftieth anniversary of the Field-Marshal's death* Helmuth had said that the end of the war would bring a readiness for repentance and atonement such as men had not known since the year 999 when the end of the world was expected. Almost in the same breath he said it would afford the biggest opportunity for refashioning the world which mankind had had since the fall of the medieval Church. And there can be no doubt that the possession by the victors of dominant military force and the loss of all such force by the conquered and unsuccessful régimes does create at the end of a war a moment when human institutions and relationships are more 'plastic' than at any normal time.

The way in which Helmuth and his friends proposed to take advantage of this opportunity was set out in two papers on foreign policy agreed at Kreisau at Whitsun. The first and more general of these closely corresponds to the opening section of the 'Fundamental Principles'.† It is the second paper on economic policy which goes into more detail.

It opens by saying that the establishment of economic order in

* Above, p. 148.　　　　　　　† Above, pp. 239–41.

Europe is the precondition for the establishment of a peaceful economic order throughout the world, owing to Europe's share in world trade.

Therefore the countries of Europe must agree on a division of labour which will ensure that all factors of production keep step in their development. This would be the best way of ensuring a quick post-war recovery.

The European economy must be set free from the traditional limitations imposed by national sovereignty. The fundamental principle was to be regulated competition in production carried to completion under the supervision of a European Economic Authority. This Authority was also to ensure that the various economies of Europe developed into an organic and articulated unity. This was to be achieved by control of investment in heavy industry, supervision of cartels, and co-ordination of national policies in the fields of taxation, credit and communications.

There then follows a list of some fourteen questions for further consideration about such things as:

The consequences for the individual states of a European customs and currency union. What measures would be needed to ensure a smooth transition?

Could national tariffs be abolished forthwith and, if not, what function would they perform in the transitional period?

What special interim measures would be needed (e.g. to prevent countries which still held relatively plentiful stocks from being plundered)?

What attitude should Europe adopt towards the Keynes and White plans for an International Monetary Fund and Bank?*

What consequences would regulated competition in production have on the existing European distribution of labour in industry and agriculture?

What undesirable consequences would regulated competition in production be likely to have and what safeguards could be devised against them [e.g. what is known in Brussels today as 'regional policy']?

What products would Europe be likely to import from and export to the rest of the world and in what quantities? What would be the size of Europe's share in world trade? How would the interests of non-European participants in such be affected?

What parallel institutions to an International Bank would be needed in the field of visible trade and capital movements?

How far was the 'other side' agreed on plans for the post-war development of the European and world economies and where did their opinions differ?

Though Helmuth could not have realised it, the last of these ques-

* Above, p. 229.

tions was to prove probably the most important. For the Russians, hoping for a Communist Europe, discouraged all plans for European integration, while American thinking was primarily on a world (United Nations) plane. Helmuth envisaged the British Empire as emerging strengthened from the war and more closely associated with the United States than before. He therefore thought of Britain and the Empire as being linked to his European Economic Community by such political and military ties as would make a conflict impossible, but not as being a member of that Community. The attitude of Churchill and Attlee was much the same while de Gaulle was preoccupied with re-establishing France as a great power. The net result was that in 1945 there was nobody in Europe who had both the will and the power to grasp the 'plastic moment' and establish an economic community at one blow, as Helmuth and very many other Europeans had hoped. He proved altogether too optimistic when he stated (in the paper of April 1941) his conviction that it would be possible for the vanquished to convince the victors of their responsibilities in this matter and that their example would give a powerful stimulus to the realisation of the desired objectives.

FIRST STEPS AND THE PUNISHMENT OF CRIMES

The document 'Preliminary Guidance for the Land Commissioners'/ *Erste Weisung an die Landesverweser* was intended, as its opening lines explain, to deal with the emergency which would arise immediately after a Nazi collapse and not for a period when such Commissioners had been constitutionally elected. As has been seen, both the Kreisau group and the Goerdeler group devoted time and energy to looking for and approaching people who would take the lead in each area as the chief civilian representative of the provisional central government. Helmuth was engaged in this from the end of 1942 onwards. It could be – and to some extent afterwards was – argued that in so doing they crossed the line between legality and illegality. The Nazis may have regarded it as a crime so much as to think that Germany could lose the war, let alone discuss what would happen next, but by 1943 it was becoming obvious that a ban on such activities was like using dynamite to stop a flowing tide. Yet to draw up lists of persons who would actually take over was undeniably a further step towards rebellion, no matter how many people regarded it as a sensible precaution.

The document envisaged that, at the time when it began to apply, communication beween the central government and the *Länder*, if not between one *Land* and another, would have broken down. Every Commissioner was therefore enjoined to act on his own initiative as he thought necessary, without waiting for instructions, particularly in making appointments. His primary duty would be 'to sustain and strengthen the internal cohesion of the German Lands as a cultural entity' (*Kulturnation*). For this reason it would be desirable for them all to be acting along similar lines which it was the business of the document with its annexes to describe. The first of these annexes was in fact the Fundamental Principles, which were drafted primarily to serve this purpose. The second was a map, drawn up in the first instance by Schulenburg with some undefined assistance from Haushofer[4] and disguised as a plan for the organisation of market co-operatives under the Food Ministry; it showed the boundaries of the new *Länder* (though these were not to apply to the post or railways). Each Commissioner was enjoined to establish contact as quickly as possible with his neighbours. Great importance was attached to keeping the economy running, and maintaining supplies and services. Except for measures discriminating against individuals on grounds of nationality, race or religion, existing laws and regulations were to be enforced. People wrongly deprived of liberty were to be set free. If a state of emergency had to be declared, the local military commander would still be bound to take the advice of the Commissioner in political matters.

Top priority was to be given to maintaining intact the fighting powers of the armed forces and preventing enemy incursions into *Reich* territory. But, in case these became irresistible, and in the event of an enemy occupation of Germany, a further extra guidance was attached. According to it, Commissioners were so far as possible to follow the instructions already given and only allow themselves to be deflected by the actual use of force, not by its mere threat. They were to work with the enemy authorities on a strictly practical basis to achieve a compromise between the requirements of the occupiers and the needs of the population. They were to make clear that they had no authority to agree to any change in their own status or in the boundaries of their *Land*. They were to protect the population of their *Land* and everyone acting under their authority from arbitrary encroachments, treacherous dissidence and nationalist excesses.

As soon as possible, they were to set about reconstructing the state on the lines of the Fundamental Principles. Nothing is said about the convening of a constituent assembly or the submission of the principles of the new system for popular approval. It has been argued that this is because the document was only a 'preliminary guidance', very obviously designed to meet a transient emergency. Thereafter the intention was to 'play it by ear'. This, though containing some truth, is not altogether convincing; the clear intention of the group was that the Fundamental Principles were to provide the basis on which the new Germany was to be built.* One would have expected the group to have faced up to the question of how far the consent of the governed was to be sought and what was to be done if, when consulted, the governed or their representatives wanted something different. Anything in the nature of dictation would have been quite out of keeping with the known attitude of most members of the group. Nothing shows the incomplete character of their plans more clearly than the absence of any evidence that it even occurred to them to discuss this fundamental point.

A final annex gave guidance about the punishment of those who had violated the law, in the light of the conclusions reached in the third gathering at Kreisau. The solution adopted was to hand over responsibility for trying crimes committed during the war, not to a tribunal of the victors, as they were demanding, but to the International Court of Justice at the Hague. One advantage seen in this was the contribution which it might make to establishing the authority of international law. Anyone was to be punished as a violator of the law who had acted in a way which indicated a wanton disregard for basic principles of divine or natural law, of the law of nations or of positive law generally current in the community of nations. People who gave orders for such acts to be done or propagated views encouraging them were to be regarded as violators. Complicity in, and assistance or incitement to, such acts were to be judged according to the rules of the criminal code. The fact that somebody was acting under orders was not to be a valid defence unless it was established that the action had been taken under duress.

The original intention had been that these measures should be applied retrospectively. But after argument it was decided that the principle of 'no penalty except as provided by law' must apply, largely because the Nazi refusal to observe this principle had been one of the chief charges brought against them by the champions of the rule of law. On the other hand, the group were confident that most of the Nazi crimes would in fact fall under one or other of the basic principles of law already mentioned.

As regards the number of people to be accused, a passage from Macaulay's *History of England* was quoted as a guide:

> The rule by which a prince ought after a rebellion to be guided in selecting rebels for punishment is perfectly obvious. The ringleaders, the men of rank, fortune and education, whose power and whose artifices have led the multitude into error, are the proper objects of severity. The deluded population, when once the slaughter on the field of battle is over, can scarcely be treated too leniently.[5]

One is tempted to attribute this reference to Helmuth but there were

* If it was just a provisional and temporary document, why did it contain provisions for electing Land Commissioners for twelve years?

several other people who might have been responsible for it. The relevance of the quotation is in any case questionable. Macaulay was talking about rebels against political authority rather than about people who had used the occasion of a rebellion (or war) to commit inhuman acts. The discussion which went on among the Allies about 'war crimes' was confused, and very nearly perverted, by their failure to distinguish between political acts, notably unprovoked resort to force in international affairs ('aggressive war'), and others which war does not make necessary and which are morally objectionable. Until there is an international authority, resort to force in the political relations between states cannot be prevented and therefore cannot be unreservedly condemned. This is bound to lead to acts being committed against individuals which in other circumstances would be regarded as wrong (e.g. killing people in cold blood). To execute prisoners and refugees during a war is something quite different. As has been seen, Helmuth had been striving to use international law in such a way as to limit so far as possible the cruelty inseparable from war and to protect the individual, particularly the 'non-combatant'.* He would therefore have been likely to approve of the proceedings taken against crimes of this kind in recent years in German courts. He would have been less satisfied with the Nuremberg trials.

Besides the guidance given by showing them this document, the Land Commissioners were instructed that all who had been in any way leading Nazis were to be relieved completely of their functions. (As it proved, they did not wait to be turned out but disappeared of their own volition!) The question of who was to be arrested was to be decided partly by the likelihood of their interfering with the measures of the provisional government, partly by the extent of their personal responsiblity for crimes. The facts regarding the latter were so far as possible to be established by due process of law.

CONCLUSION

Such, in broad terms, were the ideas about post-war Germany and Europe which Helmuth and his friends had worked out by the end of 1943. There has been some controversy in recent years as to how far they should be regarded as 'progressive' or 'reactionary'.[6] A certain amount has been made, for example, of Maass's statement to the SD, under interrogation after 20 July, that 'the counts group' and in particular Moltke (who was not a member of the counts group)† followed objectives which were political not merely in relation to the state but also in regard to society, i.e. the restoration and maintenance of the

* Above, p. 99.   † Above, p. 111.

privileges of a limited group of persons to which one could only belong if one had the right social background (*eine bestimmte gesellschaftlich umgrenzte Gruppe von Personen*).[7] This is questionable evidence, not merely because of Maass's rather uneasy relations with the group. The Nazi authorities, unnerved by the number of Germans (and of Germans with well-known names) whom they discovered to have been working against the régime, were anxious to discredit the whole affair as inspired by selfish and reactionary motives and therefore made the most of any evidence which seemed to support this line.

Undeniably the majority both of Helmuth's friends and of members of the *Widerstand* belonged to the upper and upper-middle class. But this was largely because only people who had some financial independence or could obtain some kind of official protection in the armed forces, civil service or Foreign Office could lead in Nazi Germany an existence sufficiently independent to enable them to engage in serious anti-Nazi activities.* Until defeat came, the anti-Nazis among the workers could do little beyond keeping in touch, passing information and distributing the occasional leaflet. The lower middle-classes were nearly all pro-Nazi. The army, except the headquarters staff, were isolated from the civilian population.† The first three men whom Helmuth co-opted to speak for labour, Reichwein, Mierendorff and Haubach, came of middle-class families and had had a university education. This was not true of Leuschner, Maass and Leber, but even they had done little manual labour in their lives. Aims rather than origins must therefore be taken as the criterion.

Obviously the Kreisau group were not social revolutionaries. The desire to get rid of Hitler and his crew by force may have made them rebels but one of their dominating aims, as has been seen, was to give Germany greater social unity. The immediate effect of revolutions, however, is to create bitterness and disunity. Helmuth and his friends certainly did not want either to continue on existing lines or to restore pre-1933 conditions. The changes which they wanted to see were far from consisting simply in the overthrow of Nazism. They thought it vital to halt the spread of religious apathy, and would have wholeheartedly endorsed the statement that 'a society with only itself to believe in will not for long retain belief in itself.'[8] They also thought it vital to halt the process by which power and responsibility were being concentrated at the level of the national state to the detriment of the small community on the one hand and of the international community on the other. There can be no doubt that in these respects they were going against the tide of contemporary tendencies. It is probably a valid

---

* Above, p. 60. See also Mommsen in *The German Resistance to Hitler*, pp. 57–64.

† Above, p. 218.

criticism that they allowed themselves to be swayed too easily by dislike of the society which they found around them and did not stop long enough to consider the forces which were making it what it was – and is.

But anybody who proposes to label their attitudes as 'reactionary' can fairly be asked to define what he means by that term. Its usual sense is to denote people who try to recover for themselves undeserved privileges and benefits which have been taken away from them. To say that in that sense Helmuth was the opposite of a reactionary should by this stage in this book be superfluous. The plans which he took the lead in working out (though they cannot properly be called 'his plans') may not have been entirely well designed to secure his ends, but that is a criticism of technique rather than of intention. He wanted the world to move in a direction different to that which it has taken – so far – but that did not mean he wanted it to go backwards. He had attitudes which are not universally popular, such as believing that life has a purpose, that duties are as important as rights and that freedom is as important as equality. He refused to see society in terms of the class-struggle or to give top priority to material enrichment or technological progress. But unorthodoxy is not the same thing as obscurantism, no matter how the orthodox may choose to talk.

25 Travels

April–December 1943

*I have become a sort of travelling agent. There is practically no
month in which I am not dispatched to one European country or the
other, or better to say I dispatch myself. Join the army and see the
world is too ambitious a slogan for me but join the army and see the
continent is quite a feasible proposition. These travels are mostly
depressing to mind and intellect, but they are also elating to the
spirit. You only meet the worst and the best people under circumstances as they rule the continent nowadays, and if you manage to
keep the worst at an adequate distance the remainder is simply
astonishingly good.*

THIS was how Helmuth was already writing to M.B. from Stockholm
in March 1943 and thereafter the journeys multiplied.* The next, in
late April and early May, was to Vienna whence he travelled via
Warsaw to Pulawy in Poland where Fritz Christiansen-Weniger was
supervising 240 Polish scientists, in a big Polish agricultural institute.
On the way to Warsaw Helmuth stopped in Cracow and had an interview (arranged but not attended by Christiansen-Weniger) with Archbishop Adam Sapieha.† The SS had developed the practice of surrounding villages by night and seizing the male inhabitants as a reprisal
against acts of the Polish Resistance; those who were not shot on the spot
were taken to work in Germany. Helmuth wanted to devise a system for
warning villages in advance and had hoped that Christiansen-Weniger
himself could undertake this. He, however, felt that he was too con-
spicuous and too much under suspicion already for treating Poles as
human beings (a warrant for his arrest was issued in July 1944 but
could not be executed as the SS had fled in face of the Russian
advance). Helmuth therefore decided to see whether anything could be
arranged through the Cardinal. What passed between them or what resulted is not known, except that Helmuth on arrival at Pulawy told
Christiansen-Weniger that he was fully satisfied with the result.[1]

The most encouraging thing about the trip was the excellent work

* He had already been on a trip to Paris and Brussels lasting from 7 to 17
February. It was probably on this trip that he spent two nights with Herr
Hans Heinrich von Portatius, an old friend and Silesian neighbour of his
family who was working in the German military government at Béthune.
† Archbishop of Cracow 1925–51. Cardinal 1946.

which Christiansen-Weniger was doing and the good relations which he had established with the Poles who as a result protected him from their own guerrillas. Helmuth was also surprised by the amount of livestock still left in the Polish fields, by the amount of Warsaw which was still standing and by the fact that the people in the streets did not look worse fed than the Germans. But he heard alarming stories of the dangers run by Germans who travelled by train, while a big column of smoke rose over the Warsaw ghetto, where a hand-to-hand fight in catacombs of cellars was going on between German troops and the last 30,000 remaining Jews. Christiansen-Weniger's chauffeur had driven Russian professors before 1914, then German ones, then Polish, then again German and was waiting calmly to see who would come next.

On 30 May Helmuth went off westwards, primarily in the hope of reaching agreement with the German commanders in Holland, Belgium and France about the shooting of hostages.* The recent crop of executions had increased resistance instead of reducing it, and he thought that the moment might be ripe for getting the practice abandoned as militarily ineffective. His inability to get satisfactory replies by letter (except from Belgium) on the matter induced him to see what a personal visit could achieve. He also planned to use the trip to establish or improve contacts with the Resistance movements.

Helmuth's first call in Holland was at army headquarters outside Hilversum where they promptly equipped him with a bicycle for getting to and from the town. The GOC, General (of the air force) Christiansen, was

> a nice Merchant Marine captain such as we have often met in our travels on English and German boats, though perhaps more intelligent than most of them. He is completely adrift on matters of politics and strategy because he has no idea of the right questions to ask. That doesn't worry him, however, in the least. How such a man can be made GOC I just don't understand.† He told me the story of his appointment and of his first weeks in Holland and completely failed to notice that in doing so he had given a complete explanation of why

---

* Above, p. 231.
† Christiansen, General Friedrich, had been in the German Air Force during the First World War, where he met Göring, and thereafter actually had served in the Merchant Marine, largely on transatlantic liners. In 1933 Göring put him in charge of training schools for airmen and in 1940 got him the Dutch job. He was a bad choice, for he had little military experience and had never served on the General Staff. He was no match for the German High Commissioner, Dr Arthur Seyss-Inquart, who was in charge of the civil administration. From September 1944, when active military operations began again in Holland, Christiansen's Chief of Staff Wühlisch had to take over the operational control of troops. Christiansen was sentenced to twelve years' imprisonment by a Dutch court in 1948.

things are bound to go badly there. They couldn't possibly go well. He described for example how at his first interview with General Winckelmann, the Dutch GOC, Winckelmann said 'I take it for granted, general, that you will observe the rules of international law and the Hague convention.' 'D'you know what I replied? "General, did you ever hear of international law at school? I didn't! International law is something that only exists in the newspapers!"' That put the whole table in a roar. Wühlisch (the Chief of Staff)* noticed that the whole story made me restive and critical and said to me in the car on the way home, 'You will understand that with a commanding officer like that one can't get very far on political or military matters.' All the same, Christiansen is a nice man. It's just that several things got left out in his make-up. He dropped another brick when I was leaving. As he said good-bye, he pressed a parcel into my hand, which I still have. I hated taking it but I just couldn't refuse so it is standing still unpacked beside my case. . . . It is the Göring-touch – one keeps on coming across it.

Christiansen's staff, however, left a good impression. Some of them lacked weight but the hearts of the majority were in the right place. Wühlisch, who had only recently arrived, was anxious to avoid executions of hostages as far as possible. Helmuth left Hilversum thinking that the army would back him against the SD. But when he got to SD headquarters in the Hague he had a pleasant surprise. He was warmly greeted and given a lot of attention. He spent two whole days talking to the SD General Harster,† sitting during the second by the latter's sickbed.

This meant that he had every chance to take an intransigent line but didn't do so at all. On the contrary, he was obviously very interested, and that goes for his colleagues as well. Basically and on fundamental issues we are leagues apart but when it came to practical matters our views and interests coincided to an extent that was very gratifying. Among the things he said were 'I come down heavily, very heavily indeed, on people who are guilty, but shooting

* Wühlisch, Heinz von (b. 1892), Lt.-Gen. April 1942 as COS Holland. Previously COS Luftflotte I Konigsberg. Described as having a Nazi attitude and being energetic. Took his life after the war while in internment.
† Harster, General (b. 1904), doctor of law. In Baden-Württemberg Police. Joined Freikops 1920. Joined Nazi Party 1933. Counsellor RSHA. Lt.-Gen. SS. Commander of security units in Netherlands 1940–3. In Italy and Innsbruck 194A–5. Condemned by Dutch Gvt to twelve years' imprisonment 1947. Released 1953. Counsellor in Bavaria 1956. Senior Counsellor. Retired 1963. Brought to trial in Munich for murder of 82,856 Jews deported during the war from Holland 1967. Condemned to fifteen years' imprisonment 1968 but released prematurely. Harster was responsible to Rauter who was one of Seyss-Inquart's four deputies.

people who are innocent is just bloody silly.' 'Each hostage who gets shot is a confession of personal bankruptcy; it simply means that we have failed to find the real offender, or at any rate to find him fast enough.' 'I can't expect the public to keep quiet and not help the bandits if I start laying hands on the innocent.' 'If you want to get the taking and shooting of hostages completely and categorically forbidden, you can count on my support.'

Harster went on to promise that he would gradually, though in the strictest secrecy, release all the hostages who were still under arrest. But, just to make sure that these professions were genuine, Helmuth arranged to send one of his own assistants, Diwald, to the Hague after Whitsun to work through the files. (Hans Berndt von Haeften's younger brother Werner, who was also working for Helmuth at this time, went on a similar errand to Belgium.)

The third meeting in Holland was with Görschen and a Dutch resistance leader called Van Roijen, a member of the Dutch Foreign Service who was after the war to become Foreign Minister and Netherlands Ambassador in London. He had already met Adam von Trott in December 1942.

> The Dutchman is a good man who definitely understands our problems and although he hates Germany is clever enough to realise that all Germans can't be lumped together and must be allowed to live. Besides, the main animosity is not directed against us but against Mussert [the Dutch Nazi leader]. We talked for ninety minutes and I rather think we can establish completely trustworthy relations with this man. In fact I can be a real help to him and his friends thanks to my good relations with the SD, provided they will hold back from active sabotage.

Helmuth went on to Brussels where his first call was on the GOC, Falkenhausen,* who

> discussed the world situation with me extremely frankly. I led him on to the questions which concern us at the moment and found a gratifying amount of agreement, more actually than I had expected.†
> At 11 Craushaar‡ showed up. He was obviously pleased and sur-

* Above, p. 137.
† In Belgium and France the army authorities had succeeded in 1940 in preventing the establishment of a commissioner-general or other civilian authority independent of them so that the two Commanders-in-Chief, Falkenhausen and Stülpnagel, were at the same time military governors.
‡ Craushaar, Dr Harry, a friend of Helmuth's parents and a civil servant in Saxony, was Falkenhausen's Chief of Staff for Military Government: he was promoted *Brigadeführer* in the SS in November 1943. The Chief of Staff for military matters was Harbou. When told to execute hostages, Falkenhausen shot people already condemned to death on other grounds.

prised by the success of my trip to Holland. I very much hope that this will prove to ease matters considerably for the people in Brussels. To my delight I found that as a result of my last visit* no Belgians had since been punished by deportation. This time I have made another push in one particular direction and Falkenhausen has promised to follow suit. In addition I have arranged with Craushaar that he will release on bail the 300 hostages whom he is still holding. That means that in these few days I have secured liberty for over 1,000 men if everyone does as he has promised.

He spent the evening dining with Falkenhausen in the company of, among others, a Princess Ruspoli† and Erwin Planck.‡ They played cards at which Helmuth won 25 francs. He then caught a train at 7.30 a.m. to Lille, where he was to see Carlo Schmid.

He travelled in company with loud-mouthed Germans whom he found without exception ghastly! Four ack-ack girls discussed whether the Bosporus was in Norway. He spent two hours putting Schmid in the picture and got the impression that the latter had already achieved some success in cultivating relations with the French Resistance.§ They also discussed the hostage question. They ate sumptuously with an actress friend of Schmid's in the 'German House'.

> There was everything on offer. The worst part, however, was the clientèle: profiteers, profiteers and still more profiteers. Partly in mufti, but partly paymasters, NCOs and junior officers, who ate for 20 marks a head with casual girl-friends. All of them people whose motto obviously was 'Enjoy your war, peace will be frightful.'

Afterwards Helmuth went back to Brussels and thence by sleeper to Paris.

In Paris he saw General von Stülpnagel‖ the GOC for France who fourteen months later was to be the only German commander outside the *Reich* who took action on 20 July.

---

* In February 1943. Above, p. 258.

† Born Elisabeth Marquise d'Arsche, a Belgian national. Known as Mary.

‡ Planck, Erwin (b. 1893), son of Max Planck, the physicist. Had been Principal Private Secretary to Brüning and other Chancellors. Left the civil service for industry during the Third *Reich*. A friend of Goerdeler.

$ In 1942 Helmuth had told Lionel Curtis (above, p. 185) that there appeared to be 'no really effective opposition' in France 'on a fundamental basis'. Since that date, he seems to have improved his contacts with the French Resistance but no details are known. In August 1943 he speaks of 'our man in Paris' arriving in Berlin but this could have been an *Abwehr* representative or Lt.-Col. Cesar von Hofacker, a cousin of Yorck's who was on Stülpnagel's staff and much concerned with plans for a *Staatsstreich*.

‖ Stülpnagel, General Karl Heinrich von (1883–1944). His connection with the *Widerstand* went back to 1938 when he had been concerned, as senior quartermaster in the OKH, with the plans for a *Staatsstreich*.

I was very pleased with him. Not of the same calibre as Falken-hausen but all the same a good man.... He is completely sound on the things which interest me so that I can count on his support. He showed me his most confidential report on the subject, which he hadn't even given to Falkenhausen, and this mere fact was pleasant evidence that he trusted me. In any case he has assured me that he won't let any more hostages be shot, no matter what his orders are.

The next call was at the headquarters of the GOC in Western Europe (von Rundstedt) at St Germain. The first staff officer whom Helmuth saw was sympathetic, if rather light-weight, but he was more impressed next day by the Chief of Staff, General Blumentritt,* who, while not up to the level of Falkenhausen or even Stülpnagel, 'was ready to go into my proposals for circumventing the Führer's orders and that was what mattered most to me'. Helmuth had spent the intervening evening with an uncle and aunt of Freya where he had met a nephew† of General Falkenhausen.

I talked with less reserve than usual and said a little too much. But F is in very good standing among non-Nazi Germans and I thought it would do no harm to show those of them here that each has a contribution which he can and must make. As it is, all the people here are pinning their hopes on the generals although they really must know better.

It was as they were going home from this party that, according to Falkenhausen, Helmuth said, in relation to proposals for the forcible removal of Hitler:

Let him live. He and his party must shoulder right to the end the responsibility for the terrible fate which they have brought on the German people. This is the only way to eradicate the ideology of National Socialism.[2]

When next morning Helmuth got out of the car lent him by Stülp-nagel at the Hotel Majestic (which has been an office rather than an hotel for most of the years since 1919) the guard presented arms and forced on him the embarrassment of giving the Nazi salute!

He went back to the west three months later between 9 and 17 September. He found a disappointment awaiting him in Holland where

* Blumentritt, General Günther, was one of the foremost of the younger generation of staff officers and did much of the detailed planning of German victories. His readiness to circumvent the Führer's orders was seldom con-spicuous and least of all in France on 20 July 1944.

† Falkenhausen, Rittmeister Baron Dr Gottfried von, Civil Servant attached to German Embassy in Paris. Arrested 25 July 1944; released 20 February 1945.

Harster had suddenly been sent to Italy, which had surrendered un-conditionally on the day Helmuth left Berlin. Helmuth's 'main ally' (it is hard to say who is meant by this) could not be in Hilversum on the evening which he spent there. But he extracted a promise of support from Harster's successor Erich Naumann, even though he had no confidence that this 'weak insignificant' man would maintain it under pressure. (He didn't!) Helmuth achieved some immediate results which were satisfactory, but said nothing as to how far the process of releasing hostages had gone. He also seems to have pitched into General von Wühlisch in no uncertain terms – presumably for failing to act up to his promises.

In Brussels, which he reached on a Sunday, Falkenhausen welcomed him warmly, took him shooting and put him up in his own house. This had its disadvantages. Besides losing 100 francs at poker, Helmuth had to listen to an excessively voluble professor whose lecturing manner he found intolerable after ten minutes. What was worse, he never really got Falkenhausen to himself until the Monday afternoon. In fact he got the impression that the general had deliberately set out to test his patience for 'after I had shown I could take it, things went swimmingly' (*war plötzlich alles in Butter*). Falkenhausen talked without reserve and showed that he had taken and thought over a few hints which Helmuth had thrown out to him the day before. 'A remarkable man with all the makings of an elder statesman.'* After the war Falkenhausen described how on this occasion Helmuth said to him, 'In spite of all doubts we have no other choice open to us except to eliminate Hitler physically.' When Falkenhausen replied that the war must be ended as quickly as possible, to prevent anything worse from happening, Helmuth agreed but added, 'I believe, however, that the German people must first of all be for once completely broken' (*das deutsche Volk muss einmal erst ganz herunter*). Falkenhausen contested this.[3]

The engine of his train to Paris *did* break down completely, with the pleasing result that he arrived at 10.30 after a good night's rest instead of having to get up at 6.30. He again visited Stülpnagel who gave him a memorandum listing the various actions which the GOC had taken against Nazism. But his chief experience was being caught in a raid by U.S. Flying Fortresses as he was walking along the Seine in the early evening. The anti-aircraft fire forced him to take shelter and he only caught the train by the skin of his teeth and the omission of his supper. They got to Brussels ninety minutes late because a rail had been broken and there the restaurant car could not be put on because a wheel had been sabotaged.

* This appraisal may have sparked off the suggestion, made during the following winter, that Falkenhausen rather than Goerdeler should be made chancellor after a *Staatsstreich*.

Cologne looks indescribable. When you are going by train south-wards, you can look across the city and see not just the towers of the Cathedral but the whole building because there is nothing else left standing between the railway and the Rhine.

At the beginning of August he went to Munich for a week-end, which proved an almost unbroken series of interviews interrupted only by attendance at Mass. He went back again at the end of the same month, in the first train to leave Berlin's Anhalter station after the damage done by a severe air-raid had been repaired. On this occasion he saw Speer and Reisert* as well as Rösch, König and Delp.[4] He then went on to Graz where he saw a Captain Taucher.

The discussion was unsatisfactory as regards the diagnosis though there was plenty of good-will shown. I am continuing it this after-noon, i.e. he can at any moment come up with something. At half-past four I will go back to Salzburg.

On 20 September he went to Sigmaringen, the home of the Hohen-zollerns in south-west Germany, for a meeting with a branch of the Finance Ministry which had been evacuated there.[5] His *Abwehr* col-league, Hans Christoph Stauffenberg, lived in the neighbourhood and, after spending the afternoon in meetings, Helmuth caught a local train which deposited him at 7 at a country station where he was met by Stauffenberg whose house was 1½ hours' walk away. Having gone to bed at 10.30, he got up next morning at 5.15 to reverse the journey in time for a meeting at Sigmaringen at 9. He used the occasion to tell Stauf-fenberg about the Kreisau meetings and invite him to attend if another was held (interesting evidence that the series was not necessarily re-garded as complete). On the way south, he had breakfasted with his lawyer friend Reisert in Augsburg. 'What a nice man he is! Our meal was, however, overshadowed by the news that twelve people, including two whom he had defended, were to be executed at midday.' He met Reisert again on the way back with Rösch and Delp in Munich.

The following week he was off to Steinort in East Prussia whither sections of the AA had moved along with their Minister, Ribbentrop, in order to be near Hitler's headquarters at Rastenburg. They were quartered in a house on a vast estate, including 28,000 acres of water.

The Foreign Minister of the *Reich* lay in bed and made an address to the world. The house was in some disorder because the hot-water system wasn't working and the Minister's bath had to be prepared on cauldrons throughout the house.

---

* Above, p. 212.

The owner of the property, Count von Lehndorff,* had served on the staff of Major-General von Tresckow in the Central Army Group in Russia and one of the objects of Helmuth's trip seems to have been to recruit his services as *Landesverweser* for East Prussia. (He did in fact become liaison officer for Stauffenberg with the army command in that area and was executed as a result.) But there was some other business to be transacted with the AA as cover:

> We have found a way by which the principles I was defending can be maintained without leading in practice to impossible consequences.

But two days later, back in Berlin, the settlement needed further attention.

30 September

A man came from Adam [von Trott] who stayed a pretty long time and was a complete wash-out. Adam thought I was very unfriendly to him which I am sorry about, for he was a good-natured middle-aged man. But he had lemonade in his veins, not blood, and no amount of good-nature can make up for that.

The same evening Helmuth went off to Scandinavia. No wonder he once wrote to Freya, 'I hate this living in a suitcase.' But this time the journey seemed urgent, even if a pretext for it had to be hastily concocted. News had spread in Berlin that at long last the Jews in Denmark were to be deported to the eastern death camps and Helmuth wanted to see whether anything could be done to save them. The Danish situation was, however, a great deal more complicated than he realised. The Danes were still being ruled by an all-party Parliamentary government which had succeeded in limiting German interference and notably in preventing any serious steps being taken against the Jews. But, as German prospects worsened, acts of resistance increased and on 28 August, at Hitler's prompting, the Commander-in-Chief, General von Hannecken, proclaimed a state of emergency. But Hannecken was a brutal and licentious soldier who in 1945 was convicted of embezzlement and relegated to the rank of major.† He and the German minister, Dr Werner Best, were at daggers drawn.

Best, a qualified lawyer and civil servant of thirty-eight, was about as near as the Nazi Party ever came to having in their ranks an egg-head

---

* Lehndorff, First-Lieutenant Heinrich Count von (1909–44), associated with the *Grafengruppe*.

† Hannecvken, General Hermann von (b. 1890); 1939, a Commissioner for four-year plan; October 1942, Army GOC in Denmark; November 1943, GOC all German Forces in Denmark; January 1945, relieved of command and re-employed as major; September 1948, sentenced by Danes to eight years' imprisonment; August 1949, released.

who was not a crank. In 1931 he had, at Carlo Mierendorff's instigation, been prosecuted for high treason on account of a document concocted by him and others at the Boxheim Hotel near Worms; it contained plans for seizing power and making radical social changes on the pretext that the Communists would win an election. Hitler and the other leaders had kept clear enough of the project to be able to disown it; Best was acquitted but lost his job, thereby qualifying for promotion when Hitler came to power. From 1935 to 1940 he headed the personnel and legal branches of the Gestapo but found Himmler uncongenial and Heydrich even more so, besides having incipient doctrinal doubts about the racial policies. Accordingly in June 1940 he went to Paris as head (under Stülpnagel) of the German military government in occupied France. Two years later he resigned, joined the Foreign Service and was posted to Copenhagen.

Best was an ambitious man who found himself slipping, and therefore wanted to distinguish himself in Denmark. The first step towards doing this was to get power out of Hannecken's hands, which he planned to achieve by greatly strengthening the German police forces. He saw no other way of getting his superiors to send him extra forces than to tell them that the moment was propitious for rounding up the Jews. But he knew that such a round-up would precipitate a crisis – indeed the case for having more police hinged on its doing so. But if his career as top German started off in such an atmosphere, it might not bring him the success for which he was looking. He therefore sought the best of both worlds by planning to show, as soon as the extra police had arrived, that their use was out of the question. To get evidence of what an anti-Jewish action would arouse, he leaked hints of it to the Danes and promptly reported their indignation to Berlin. But such finesses proved too clever by half. The police were sent, but not put under Best's command. Final responsibility was transferred from the army to the civilians but Berlin insisted on the round-up going ahead. Owing to the advance notice it proved a signal failure and Best ended by bringing on himself the scorn of his superiors and the hatred of his subjects. For the rest of the war, he was in charge of a Denmark which was uncooperative and increasingly restive.[*6]

Helmuth summed up Hannecken accurately – 'a foolish loudspoken man who is completely out of place and fit only for a barrack-square. Best is far and away better.... He's not a bad man, at any rate he's clever.' He also sensed that the root cause of the trouble was Best's desire to get the better of Hannecken, but naturally the intricacy of Best's manœuvres escaped him.

* After the war, Best was condemned to death by a Danish court. The sentence was commuted to a long term in prison but he was released in 1951.

The sad thing is that the consequences of this incompatibility [between Hannecken and Best] fall on the Danes and in my view we are heading for a thoroughly complex and difficult situation in which clashes with the Danish courts and authorities are inevitable.... Everyone I talked to about shootings [of hostages – the ostensible purpose of the visit] gave me extensive and thoroughly satisfying assurances.... What relieved me most was that Best was completely categorical on this point. The only thing is that I don't know how he sees his position in the long term because unless he gets rid of Hannecken, things will never work.

The only man of sense among the soldiers was the Chief Military Judge, Dr Ernst Kanter, who, when the taking of hostages was first mooted, had said that, while permissible as a means of protecting buildings, it should not be used to secure the good behaviour of the population. When executions were proposed, he protested. To arm himself against the criticism of colleagues, he turned to Dr Karl Sack, the head of the Judicial Division of the OKH and a resolute anti-Nazi, who told him to consult Helmuth. When Helmuth's approaching visit was announced, Kanter was warned that he was already under SD observation and should be kept at arm's length.

But Helmuth did not content himself with warning the German army authorities of the trouble which they might bring on themselves by vigorous action. As soon as he could free himself from official calls, he sought out an old journalist friend from Dr Schwarzwald's circle, Merete Bonnesen – not without difficulty because she had been arrested for three days after the state of emergency had been proclaimed and was still giving her own house a wide berth. She and her brother Kim, whom Helmuth had also known in Vienna, were weighed down by the new feeling of insecurity and found difficulty in believing his assurances that in time one got used to it. Kim was an official in the Ministry of Social Affairs and when he learnt Helmuth's news about the Jews, conveyed it at once to high quarters in the Foreign Office, though in practice the head of that office had heard of it three days previously from Georg Duckwitz, a counsellor on Best's own staff.* When Kim's door-bell rang early next morning, he found on the step a smiling Helmuth who exclaimed, 'Hitler wanted to get six thousand but he's not even got two hundred.' He had risked his life for that result – since the SD are bound to have noticed his journey – and it would have made him indifferent to the fact that that journey had not strictly been necessary.

After another journey on which he found his German fellow-travel-

---

* German Ambassador in Copenhagen 1955–8 and Staatssekretär in the AA since 1967.

lers less than attractive, he reached Oslo on 3 October. It was Harvest Thanksgiving and he thought with regret of Kreisau. He found everybody in Norway impatient. Steltzer was beginning to look for results, the Resistance (with whom he had two meetings) were depressed at the prospect of another winter under occupation and the Germans with some misgivings were planning harsher action against the Norwegians. Quisling's position had deteriorated during the last six months, and the hope of establishing him politically on a permanent basis was being given up. Instead he was to become the leader of a group of 'trusties' who would work for German interests. The Norwegian internal position had lost its stability and prospects for the Resistance were not good.

Owing to what he believed to be a confusion, Helmuth's visa for Stockholm failed to arrive and he was unable to stop in that city on his way home as he had intended. Instead he returned as he had come, by train to Malmö and thence by air, stopping for a night in Copenhagen where he saw Kanter and Kim Bonnesen again. The state of emergency had been ended but the general atmosphere had grown worse.

The only trips which remain to be described are those to Istanbul. The first of these took place between 5 and 10 July, the second between 11 and 16 December. The first produced a long letter to Freya giving a vivid description of the city (though no reference to the years that the Field-Marshal had passed there); the second went unrecorded. Helmuth also sent letters of a personal character to various English and South African friends.* The pretext for both journeys was the fate of a fleet of river steamers on the Danube which had belonged to a French company. One of its directors escaped from France to Britain in 1940 and in 1941, when the Germans invaded the Balkans, ordered the boats through the Bosporus to internment in the neutral waters of the Sea of Marmora. Meanwhile the Germans had installed Frenchmen favourable to themselves in the company's Paris office who instituted a suit to make the Turkish government return the boats. Helmuth took Dr Wengler with him on the first occasion to carry the burden of the negotiations, so that he himself would have time to get on with his main objective which was the establishment of contact with the Allies. This was now a major concern of the *Widerstand*. Adam von Trott had already been in Switzerland in January and in Turkey in June: he was in Switzerland again in September and in Sweden at the end of November, when he talked to two British officials. Canaris is said to have been aware of Helmuth's real purpose and to have arranged the journeys in this knowledge.

There were several reasons which made Istanbul a favourable point.

---

* The news had already reached him that both Sir James and Lady Rose Innes had died in the course of 1942.

It had easier connections with the West than Sweden or Switzerland, which could only be reached from Britain by crossing German-held territory. Helmuth had friends among the German colony: the chief *Abwehr* representative was his lawyer colleague of 1938–9 Paul Leverkühn. A Dr Hans Wilbrandt, who had been living in Turkey since 1934, had been a friend since dealing with Helmuth over Kreisau finances when working for a Frankfurt bank before 1933. Perhaps the biggest attraction was that Helmuth's friend Alexander Kirk* was now U.S. Ambassador in Cairo.

During the July visit Wilbrandt put Helmuth in touch with a Dr Alexander Rüstow, a German religious sociologist who had been living in Turkey since 1934 and had contacts with the American Office of Strategic Services (OSS). The three of them discussed at length a proposal by which a German staff officer would fly to England with full details of German military dispositions in the west, allow himself to be captured in an apparent aircraft accident and concert with the British a plan for landing Anglo-American airborne troops in western Europe and opening the western front to them while fighting continued in the east. Helmuth apparently claimed to have discussed this with at least one German general. He made clear that he was opposed to attempts at assassinating Hitler (though not at removing him by force). But he also attacked 'unconditional surrender' and indicated that in any negotiations he would do his best to get this rescinded. Rüstow, while showing sympathy with this attitude, told him that any such attempt was hopeless in the circumstances then obtaining. He further said that the conditions which the Allies might grant at that moment would be more onerous than those which would probably be forthcoming after a collapse of the régime. The chief objective for the time being should be to secure that Germany should be occupied by the Western Allies alone. He refused to give any further help unless Helmuth accepted this position, which the latter with some reluctance did. He wrote a letter to Dorothy Thompson which was handed over to the Americans but which never reached its destination. He is also said to have tried unsuccessfully to get in touch through a diplomat friend of Trott's with the Patriarch of Constantinople, thus with English Church leaders and ultimately with Churchill himself. But, as nothing more could be done in the time available, he asked Rüstow to try to establish contact with Kirk and to arrange either for him to meet Kirk in Istanbul or for him to be flown secretly to Cairo for a day or two. As soon as either could be arranged, a signal was to be sent to him in Berlin and he would then come again to Istanbul.

Kirk duly received this message through OSS. But, knowing the spy-ridden character of Istanbul, the impossibility of concealing his own

* Above, p. 141.

presence there and Helmuth's own unmistakable physical characteristics, he decided that a meeting between them in that city would be too dangerous for Helmuth and informed the OSS intermediary to that effect.[7] The alternative of flying Helmuth to Cairo was not apparently pursued for the good reason that there was no commercial air service (even if there had been, it would have been too public to use) and it would have been impossible to use a U.S. military plane without giving elaborate explanations to the Turkish government, thus running a risk of leaks. The proposal, in short, was more gallant than practical. OSS, however, were reluctant to let the project drop and gave Helmuth's colleagues to understand that, if he came to Turkey in December, his conditions would be met. Their intention seems to have been for him to meet someone armed with documents which would be adequate evidence of reliability.

In the meantime Rüstow had in September brought Franz von Papen, the German Ambassador, into contact with an American diplomat. Helmuth had called on Papen in July to discuss the question of the steamers. Whereas before the interview he had taken the view that Papen could not really be as inept as he was generally painted, he remarked to Wengler (when Papen was called out of the room during their conversation), 'The man is absolutely deplorable'/*Er ist doch ein jämmerlicher Mann.*[8] Papen was pressed by the American to consider joining the *Widerstand* and promised to get advice on the matter during a forthcoming visit to Berlin. When he got back, he professed to have discussed the possibility with Weizsaecker who advised against it.*

On Helmuth's second arrival in Istanbul, not only was there no sign of Kirk or of a flight to Cairo but something would seem to have gone wrong with the Americans' alternative arrangements; probably they had sought, and failed to obtain, authority from OSS headquarters for entering into negotiations.[9] He therefore wrote the following letter to Kirk:

Istanbul 1943

Dear Mr Kirk,

May I in this way send you my best greetings and wishes and my most sincere compliments. Perhaps it would be best to explain first, why I have stated quite definitely that I would be unable to see anybody before having seen you. You will realize that any discussion on the ways and means to end this war and to begin peace requires an enormous amount of confidence on the part of both participants;

* The probability of this story is somewhat impaired by the fact that Weizsaecker had left the AA in April 1943 to become Ambassador to the Vatican. His memoirs do not indicate that he came back to Germany till the war was over.

*on your side because the credentials I could produce would neces-
sarily be incomplete as they can only receive their value from and
through action; on my side for reasons of security as well as of
policy. From my point of view any partner to such discussions must
be able to visualize what life in my country is like, and he must have
the discretion required to use anything I might say in a manner
which will not be harmful to myself and to fundamental, permanent
interests of peace. Therefore I must be sure of talking to somebody
whose personal loyalty is beyond doubt and whose political judgment is up to the complex and tangled situation prevailing in my
country and in several other countries of continental Europe. Obviously such qualifications demand at least personal acquaintance between those who are responsible for the conduct of the discussion and
personally I do not know of any American in this part of the world
who would fulfil these qualifications but for you. I trust that you will
understand this position and that you will excuse any inconvenience
to which you may have been put in consequence.*

*Any discussion would have to start with an appreciation of the
military and political situation. I am under the impression that, all
exhortations by the President and Mr Churchill to the contrary not-
withstanding, some people expect an early termination of the war in
Europe.*

*I would be interested to get your opinion on this point, which is
fundamental to the possibilities of co-operation: if a speedy end
were in sight co-operation would become much easier technically and
much more difficult politically.*

*On the other hand I might be able to give you an account of the
German political scene. You, who know Central Europe and totalitarian states in general would thereby be enabled to gauge the value
of my credentials, although nobody can be exact on this point before
the event. Such a report would furthermore show you the possibilities
and limits of any military or political assistance we can render to our
common cause. I am afraid that to somebody who has never lived in
a totalitarian country the limits of such assistance are not under-
standable while he will have great difficulties in even recognizing its
chances.*

*The political-post-armistice world would have to be touched as far
at least as it constitutes part of the diagnosis of the present situation.
You will understand that the example of Italy has had the most
damping effect on all thought of internal change and it would have to
be made clear by what means a repetition will be prevented.*

*Once these questions of the diagnosis of the present situation have
been disposed of, the main point of co-operation arises. This must be
followed into its military and its political possibilities. You will*

*realize that some unity of purpose on the political side is a condition
of effective military co-operation. As to the military co-operation, I
am of the opinion that for military as well as political reasons only
such co-operation is feasible as will turn the tables with one stroke.
This will require the patience to wait and wait and wait until effective military power on a very considerable scale can be employed,
such in fact as will undoubtedly prove overwhelming once our
assistance is added.*

*As I see it that would be the ground to be covered and I suppose
that we would agree fairly quickly. The remainder is not a question
of policy but of technique and is therefore beyond my competence.
But we would have to agree on ways and means to contact the technicians on both sides.*

*The place for any discussions can be arranged by you. I can leave
Istanbul next time I come for 48 hours. I am completely in your
hands as to this point, relying on you to see that the arrangements
made will keep the risk down. As to the time; I believe that, if I
hurry up with my work at home, I will be able to come here at the
earliest by the middle of February, at the latest middle of April.*

Please accept my best wishes for Xmas and the New Year.

At first Steinhardt, the U.S. Ambassador to Turkey, refused to
handle this letter and insisted on Helmuth seeing his Military Attaché,
Brigadier-General Tindall. They therefore met in the Istanbul office of
OSS but with the results which Helmuth had feared. Each was mis-
trustful. The American was not unimpressed but tried to extract military information which Helmuth was not prepared to give. The letter to
Kirk was, however, handed over but never reached its intended recipi-
ent.[10] Helmuth is said by Wilbrandt to have been anticipating arrest,
to have been anxious to spend Christmas with his family and to have
left with the words 'Now all is lost.'[11] On 10 January Rüstow received
a letter which purported to come from Kirk but did not in fact do so.[10]
It simply said, 'I would always be glad to see you, but I do not see that
any good purpose would be served by our meeting as it is my personal
conviction that nothing short of unconditional surrender of the German
armed forces will terminate the war in Europe.'

Before this letter arrived, but after Helmuth's departure, Wilbrandt
and Rüstow put down on paper what purported to be a statement of the
views which he had expressed. After a preliminary draft had been made
in German, it was translated into English by another German exile in
Istanbul and the only surviving copy is in English. It ran as follows:

5. *Exposé*
on the readiness of a powerful German group to prepare and assist
Allied military operations against Nazi Germany.

Note: This exposé defines the attitude and plans of an extremely influential group of the German opposition inside Germany on the subject of hastening the victory of the Allies and the abolition of Nazism. It has been prepared on the basis of frequent and searching conversations and discussions with a leading representative of this group about the political future of a free democratic Germany, cleansed radically of Nazism, and about the maximum contribution that can be made immediately by determined German patriots towards making this Germany a secure reality.

The exposé is to reproduce clearly and concisely the views and intentions of this group of responsible democratic Germans within Germany.

Background and standing of the German oppositional group

Apart from the Nazi Party hierarchy and its subordinate organs and functionaries, there are left in Germany two elements vested with political power: the officers corps of the Wehrmacht, and the upper ranks of the Civil Service, which, in their ministerial grades at least, represent a fairly closely knit network of officials interconnected by personal acquaintance, official association, often long-standing friendship.

Within the overlapping spheres of high officialdom and professional army circles, three categories of people can be distinguished:

1. Politically non-descript specialists who are absorbed altogether in their service duties, being either too vague or too cautious to express their views or engage in political activity. They constitute the majority, especially among the professional officers.

2. Confirmed National Socialists.

3. Decided and conscious opponents of Nazism.

The third category is again divided in two wings, of which one favours an 'Eastern', pro-Russian orientation, the other a 'Western', pro-Anglo-Saxon trend. The former is considerably stronger than the latter, particularly in the Wehrmacht; in Luftwaffe circles it rules supreme. The driving force behind the Eastern wing is the strong and traditional conviction of a community of interests between the two mutually complementary powers, Germany and Russia, which led to the historical co-operation between Prussia and the Russian monarchy, and between the Germany Republic and Soviet Russia in the Rapallo period (1924), when the *Reichswehr* and the Red Army concluded a far-reaching understanding regarding military collaboration and reciprocal training facilities. Historical bonds of this character are reinforced by the deep impression wrought by the power and resilience of the Red Army and the competence of its command.

Among the Eastern wing the foundation of the German Officers' League at Moscow has evoked a powerful echo, the more so as the leaders of the League are recognized in the Wehrmacht as officers of outstanding ability and personal integrity (by the standards of their caste). This group has for a long time been in direct communication, including regular wireless contact, with the Soviet Government, until a breach of security on the Russian side led to the arrest and execution of many high-placed officers and civil servants early in 1943.

The Western group of the opposition, though numerically weaker, is represented by many key men in the military and civil service hierarchy, including officers of all ranks, and key members of the OKW. Furthermore, it is in close touch with the Catholic bishops, the Protestant Confessional Church, leading circles of the former labour unions and workmen's organizations, as well as influential men of industry and intellectuals. It is this group which is seeking to establish a practical basis for effectual collaboration with the Anglo-Saxon Allies.

Conditions of collaboration with the Allies

The following are the future material factors and present political arguments which form the logical prerequisites of a successful collaboration between this Western Group of the German democratic opposition, and the Allies.

1. Unequivocal military defeat and occupation of Germany is regarded by the members of the group as a moral and political necessity for the future of the nation.

2. The Group is convinced of the justification of the Allied demand for unconditional surrender, and realizes the untimeliness of any discussion of peace terms before this surrender has been accomplished. Their Anglo-Saxon sympathies result from a conviction of the fundamental unity of aims regarding the future organization of human relations which exists between them and the responsible statesmen on the Allied side, and the realization that in view of the natural convergence of interests between post-Nazi Germany and the other democratic nations there must of necessity result a fruitful collaboration between them. The democratic Germans see in this unity of purpose a far safer guarantee of a status of equality and dignity after the War than any formal assurance by the Allies at the present time could give them, provided any such assurances were forthcoming.

3. An important condition for the success of the plan outlined in the following points is the continuance of an unbroken Eastern front, and simultaneously its approach to within a menacing proximity of the German borders, such as the line from TILSIT to LEMBERG.

Such a situation would justify before the national consciousness radical decisions in the West as the only means of forestalling the overpowering threat from the East.

4. The Group is ready to realize a planned military co-operation with the Allies on the largest possible scale, provided that exploitation of the military information, resources, and authority at the Group's disposal is combined with an all-out military effort by the Allies in such a manner as to make prompt and decisive success on a broad front a practical certainty.

This victory over Hitler, followed by Allied occupation of all Germany in the shortest possible time, would at one stroke so transform the political situation as to set free the real voice of Germany, which would acclaim the action of the Group as a bold act of true patriotism, comparable to the Tauroggen Convention concluded by the Prussian General Yorck with the Russians in 1812.

5. Should, however, the invasion of Western Europe be embarked upon in the same style as the attack upon the Italian mainland, any assistance by the Group would not only fail to settle the issue of the War, but would in addition help to create a new 'stab-in-the-back' legend, as well as compromise before the nation, and render ineffectual for the future the patriots who made the attempt. There is no doubt that half-measures would damage the cause rather than promote it, and the Group is not prepared to lend a hand in any collaboration with limited aims.

6. If it is decided to create the second front in the West by an unsparing all-out effort, and follow it up with overwhelming force to the goal of total occupation of Germany, the Group is ready to support the Allied effort with all its strength and all the important resources at its disposal. To this end it would after proper agreement and preparations be ready to despatch a high officer to a specified Allied territory by plane as their fully empowered, informed, and equipped plenipotentiary charged with co-ordinating the plans of collaboration with the Allied High Command.

7. The readiness of a sufficient number of intact units of the Wehrmacht to follow up the orders given under the Group's operational plan, and co-operate with the Allies, could only be counted upon with a sufficient degree of certainty if the above conditions are fulfilled. Otherwise there would be a grave danger that the orders and operations agreed upon by the commanders and staffs belonging to the Group would at the decisive moment fail to materialize for lack of support, or be executed only with great friction.

8. The Group would see to it that simultaneously with the Allied landing a provisional anti-Nazi government would be formed which would take over all non-military tasks resulting from the collabora-

tion with the Allies and the political upheaval that would accompany it. The composition of this provisional Government would be determined in advance.

9. The Group, which comprises personages belonging to the most diverse liberal and democratic parties and schools of thought, regards the possibility of a bolshevization of Germany through the rise of national communism as the deadliest imminent danger to Germany and the European family of nations. It is determined to counter this threat by all possible means, and to prevent, in particular, the conclusion of the War through the victory of the Red Army, followed by a Russian occupation of Germany before the arrival of the Anglo-Saxon armies. On the other hand no cleft must be allowed to develop between the future democratic Government and the masses of German labour. A non-communist democratic home policy will only be possible in conjunction with a whole-hearted policy of collaboration with Russia, designed to eliminate all hostility or friction with that power. In this way it should be sought not to antagonize the strong pro-Russian circles in Germany but to rally them in a common constructive effort and win them over. Finally, what must be avoided at all costs is the development of a situation which would lay a democratic Government open to the reproach of placing foreign interests above national concerns, and unify against this Government the forces of nationalism, communism and Russophily.

10. The envisaged democratic Government, in order to steal the thunder of left radicalism, should operate at home with a very strong left wing, and lean heavily on the social democrats and organized labour, even, if necessary, seek the co-operation of personally unimpeachable independent communists.

11. The initial HQ of the democratic counter-Government would under the postulated circumstances best be Southern Germany, perhaps Austria. It would be advisable not to subject the civilian population of this territorial basis to indiscriminate air attack, since experience teaches that bombed-out populations are so exhausted and absorbed by the effort of providing for their bare survival and subsistence that they are out of play as far as revolutionary action is concerned.

This document was forwarded by OSS in Istanbul through their theatre headquarters in Algiers to the U.S., where it is said to have been submitted to President Roosevelt. According to Rüstow, the President asked Felix Frankfurter to advise him about it and Frankfurter, who had already reported adversely on Trott,[12] took the view that it was a decoy by people who were not sincere in the attitudes expressed.

K

What is not clear is the relationship between this document and another document in the form of a letter, written on the paper of the German Embassy in Ankara and signed Leverkühn, which was soon afterwards brought to the U.S. by General Donovan, the head of OSS. This was shown in New York to Professor Karl Brandt of Stanford University, who in an interview with Adam von Trott in 1939 had decided that he was wrong-headed but honest.[13] Brandt took the view that the 1944 document was genuine but in spite of this, and of General Donovan's support for the idea of negotiating with the *Widerstand*, Roosevelt firmly refused to treat with 'these East German Junkers'.*[14]

Since Helmuth never appears to have seen the Wilbrandt–Rüstow document, it cannot be treated without qualification as a statement of his views. There is an arrogance about it which is uncharacteristic – but then it was written after his departure and he might well have expressed himself more trenchantly in conversation than he would on paper. The idea of surrendering to the Western Powers and fighting with their armies against the East does not seem to have been discussed at Kreisau but the last Kreisau meeting occurred before the Anglo-Americans had set foot even in Sicily, whereas by December 1943 the prospect of a cross-channel invasion had become much more real, and Helmuth and his friends must have discussed how best to react to it. The evidence that he propounded some plan of this kind in Istanbul is circumstantial.

What is more surprising to the present-day reader is the strength which the document attributes to the group inside Germany said to favour overtures to the Russians, since relatively little evidence to support this estimate has come to light. The failure to establish contact with the West had made those who came to Kreisau at Whitsun 1943 sympathetic to the idea of trying to sound out Russian reactions, preferably through Madame Kollontai, the Ambassador in Sweden. In the following month German Communist emigrés in Russia had, with Russian help, persuaded twenty-one German prisoners-of-war to join with them in announcing a 'National Committee for Free Germany' which was followed in August by the more conservative 'League of German Officers'. The accounts of reactions to these developments among German troops and inside Germany are divergent.[15] The Russians on the whole seem to have been disappointed and to have lost

---

* According to yet another story Canaris and Papen made a similar approach to the U.S. Naval Attaché in Turkey but were told to direct all proposals for a surrender in the west to General Eisenhower (Papen, *Memoirs*, pp. 499–523). Assuming that these various stories refer to different approaches and not to different accounts of the same approach, there need be no wonder that the Americans were confused and suspicious, especially when one remembers that reports of similar approaches were arriving frequently from Switzerland, Sweden and Spain.

interest in the movement after it had served one of its purposes by frightening Roosevelt and Churchill into accepting at Tehran Stalin's demands about Russia's western frontier. But the manœuvre seems to have aroused among some Germans, who took it at its face value, a hope that the Russians might be prepared to make peace on terms more lenient than 'unconditional surrender' and this in turn clearly alarmed some members of the non-Communist *Widerstand*. There is little doubt that an effort was made on behalf of the Kreisau group to make contact with Madame Kollontai but the complete absence of any evidence about its results strongly suggests that it was unsuccessful.[16]

But the emphasis in the Istanbul document on an Eastern orientation fits in with the efforts which the *Widerstand* were making at this time, as in Trott's talks in Stockholm and a memorandum prepared by Goerdeler for transmission to the British, probably through the Swedish banker Jakob Wallenberg, to frighten the Anglo-Saxons about the danger of Communism establishing itself in Central Europe. Although this was a fear which the *Widerstand* genuinely felt, nothing was better calculated, in the atmosphere prevailing in London and Washington in the winter of 1943/4, to get their overtures rebuffed. Wisely or unwisely the British, and still more the Americans, had made up their minds to fight through to victory in conjunction with the Russians. Any attempts by Germans to play upon Western mistrust of Communism were regarded as nationalistically inspired moves to save Germany from having her physical and military power completely broken. After great difficulty Roosevelt and Churchill succeeded at the Tehran Conference in overcoming Stalin's suspicions that the West was aiming at a separate peace (which might have prompted him to make such a peace first himself) and they were strongly averse to anything which might upset this hard-won confidence. At the very time of Helmuth's second visit to Istanbul, the European Advisory Commission was sitting down in London to work out plans for a joint occupation of Germany with zonal boundaries as established in 1945; this prospect robbed the dangers portrayed in Paragraph 9 of the Wilbrandt–Rüstow memorandum of a good deal of their terrors.

But there were further reasons why the document was foredoomed to futility. There is, for example, a certain inconsistency between its first and third paragraphs, probably due to Rüstow's insistence that 'unconditional surrender' must be accepted, with the result that plans which assumed its abandonment had to be hastily – and therefore incompletely – revised. How could it be said that the Germans had suffered an indisputable military defeat (the point on which the West was determined not to repeat the mistake of 1918) if they had gone on resisting successfully in the east and had only stopped fighting in the west of their own accord? Again the first sentence of Paragraph 2, renouncing any attempt to make conditions, is incompatible with Paragraphs 4 to 7 which in effect contain such conditions.

The military proposals would have been very difficult to carry out. They would not have been feasible at the time when they were made because the Allies did not then have in Britain the troops and transport equipment necessary to give them the overwhelming superiority which was called for. Even by the following summer there would have been a hen-and-egg quality to the whole arrangement. German co-operation was only to be forthcoming if the Allies could move and win quickly, but the chances of them being able to do so depended on the Germans co-operating, i.e. ceasing to resist. It was not after all by design that the Allied campaign in Italy had moved so slowly.

But finally there was a deeper difficulty. Roosevelt and Churchill had decided that they were fighting not just National Socialism but German militarism and indeed nationalism. The existence of honourable and liberally minded Germans would not on the whole have been denied in policy-influencing circles on the Allied side. But there was serious doubt as to how many of them there were, a doubt which is reinforced when one considers how many in the *Widerstand* had started out as national-ist conservatives. Experience since 1919 had suggested strongly that it was not enough to see that Germany established a democratic constitu-tion and then hope for the best. The problem was how to create a situation in which Germans would be prepared to feel loyalty to such a constitution and operate it in a genuinely democratic spirit. The solution adopted was to show what excessive nationalism led to by bringing about complete and undeniable defeat, followed by complete disarma-ment. To achieve such a clear-cut military decision, the co-operation of the Russians right up to the end was necessary. And (unless Polish interests were thrown to the winds) the frontier terms on which the Russians were insisting were not such as the *Widerstand* could possibly accept, since by doing so they would make it permanently out of the question for them to convince their fellow-countrymen that they under-stood Germany's interests better than Hitler and were therefore acting patriotically in removing him. Most members of the *Widerstand* went on hoping to restore Bismarck's 1871 frontiers to Germany for as long as the course of the war made this seem at all possible. Few of them were prepared to acquiesce willingly in the complete elimination of German power.* Helmuth's scepticism about the chances of avoiding this and

* This is well illustrated by the view expressed in 1954 by the distinguished German historian Gerhard Ritter, who had been himself imprisoned for en-gaging in anti-Nazi activities: 'The Tehran agreement was to sacrifice Ger-many to the friendship which Churchill and Roosevelt hoped for from Russia. To attain that end Germany was robbed of her eastern provinces, divided up into occupation zones, completely destroyed as a power factor and, with half her territory gone, left to the mercy of Russia. Today no German can read the

his refusal to give a high priority to keeping Germany intact largely explain why they thought him lacking in patriotism. But their attitude meant that there was in truth no possibility of fruitful co-operation between them and the Allies until the military decision had been reached. Direct Allied contact with them might have brought clearer mutual understanding but it might equally well have heightened mutual exasperation and caused the intermediaries whose use would have been inevitable to become suspected by each side of failing to do justice to its point of view.

Moscow–Tehran negotiations without deep indignation.' (*Carl Goerdeler and the German Resistance*, p. 260). See also Part V of Adam von Trott's 'Observations on the peace programme of American Churches'. (van Roon, p. 368).

26 The Last Weeks of Liberty
October 1943–19 January 1944

IN Berlin the autumn of 1943 was a time of growing difficulties in all directions:

18 October
I visited the army doctor today and will finally be declared fit for active service. At any rate the man was so dreadfully gruff and unfriendly that that is what I deduce. What a nasty atmosphere of distrust and desire for results reigns there!

In September Dr Viktor Bruns, the director of the Institute for Foreign Public Law, had died (a natural death) and Helmuth tried to use the influence of the OKW to secure the appointment of Berthold von Stauffenberg in his place. Another member of the Institute, however, was pressing the claims of a relation of Bruns who was more favourably inclined to the régime. As part of the intrigue against Stauffenberg, a Dutch SS general was induced to denounce Wengler to the Kaiser Wilhelm Society (the Institute's parent body) on the wholly false ground that he had talked in a defeatist way when the Dutchman (who was not a lawyer) called on him for guidance on points of colonial law.

18 October
A horrible denunciation of Wengler has come in, while he is still in Istanbul. It is obviously part of the fight about the directorship of the Institute. Someone is firing at Wengler in order to disqualify me from having any say in this appointment. There can't be a word of truth in the story. All the same, it has been sent us in all seriousness by the SD and I can't bring myself to put it aside and go over to the day's work.

20 October
The trouble over Wengler's affair got worse yesterday. I must speak about it to Stauffenberg who has started off the whole business/*der die ganze Sache angedreht hat*.

22 October
The whole of today suffered somewhat from my having to break off at 12.30 and go with Oxé to the funeral of my most intimate

enemy in the OKW, Counsellor Wagner. He has died at the age of 70+ and I can only say, three years too late. A great deal could have been prevented if that obstinate self-willed old man hadn't been sitting there. We knew him simply as the Poison Dwarf/*Giftzwerg*. He was an outstanding criminal lawyer and looked at everything purely from the standpoint of domestic law. Well, now he is dead and his successor [Waltzog] is a man with whom at any rate I shall be able to work much more easily.

Reichwein was in very good form yesterday evening.... It strikes me that having his family in security has already improved things for him. [Frau Reichwein and her four children, having been bombed out in Berlin, were now living in the attics of the Kreisau Schloss.]

24 October

Early yesterday Oxé and I went to see Bürkner [about Wengler] at Zeppelin [code-name for Zossen, see p. 232].... Everything went very smoothly. We came back straight away and went from the station to Under-Secretary Sack, the head of the army legal department where my friend Dr Kanter from Copenhagen* was waiting for me. We had a talk with him and Sack about Danish affairs which are coming more and more to a head. We agreed on a programme which should allow us to continue the good work.

25 October

After I had gone through my 'In' tray, Oxé came in to tell me that Bürkner, contrary to our agreement of Saturday, had given orders that Wengler was to be suspended from duty. That made me see red (*fuchsteufelswild*) and I told Oxé that I wouldn't stay if this decision was maintained because (*a*) it was unreasonable to expect a man to work if at the critical moment his assistants were taken away and (*b*) what was much more serious, I wasn't prepared to agree to my assistants being dropped like hot irons the moment an attack was made on them, no matter how damn-fool it was.... This business of Wengler is a very dirty affair. Apart from that, it comes at about the most inconvenient moment possible for me since I simply can't go away if there isn't anybody here who has some idea of what everything's about. I have, however, told Oxé that I am going [on leave to Kreisau] and if he can't put the Wengler business right, that's his business, he and Bürkner can stew in their own juice for a fortnight. But it won't really be as easy for me as that. However, I was so angry that Oxé will end up by doing everything he can to get the business settled.

* Above, p. 268.

26 October

I got to bed at 2 and had to get up at 6 sharp because Wengler wanted to see me at 8. We then worked till 10 on Wengler's case which gets worse and worse. The whole thing is a mean trick.

27 October

I've really nothing to report except work, work, and still more work – each case more serious and difficult than the next. I'm glad to say that the Wengler business is now being got on to sensible lines. He will himself apply for investigation and we will press for proceedings to be put through quickly. In this way I hope that the complete hollowness of the denunciation will be proved in a few weeks. In the meantime a quite passable man has been appointed to represent him and, while I'm away, Wengler will sit around in the office under the excuse of completing his report on his travels. In this way we ought to get by.

As Helmuth's letter of 13 November was to show, the Wengler case continued to give trouble. One of the difficulties was that the Dutch SS general who had laid the information and who was the only hostile witness had gone off to the eastern front and endeavours to get him back to Berlin to give evidence were fruitless. Meanwhile the Nazi head of the Kaiser Wilhelm Society, Dr Teschow, was able to secure the rejection of Canaris's recommendation that Berthold von Stauffenberg should be made head of the Institute.

27 October

Yesterday afternoon and evening we discussed several matters in the Institute [probably connected with prisoners-of-war]. In this way I hope to have put at least two important matters on to a basis which will enable me to sleep peacefully as far as they are concerned. What I find exhausting about such a meeting is that it always turns out to be me who has to ensure that a practical result emerges, that after a long day I have to show myself capable of tackling four different problems at a theoretical level while for each problem a man sits opposite me who had been able to concentrate on it for days at a stretch. It is rather like playing chess with four people at once!

6 November

How lovely those seven short days are to look back on! Whether there will be anything to match them in the future is impossible to tell but one must be grateful for the past. The only consolation is that from all points of view my return was absolutely necessary. Oxé has made rather a mess of Wengler's business which I, however, can clear up, while there are a lot of other things to settle in the office. In addition Adam has come back [from Sweden, p. 269] with news which he wants to discuss with me first of all, and the extensive activities of Newman and Co are getting a bit out of hand.

[Newman, also known as the 'Ersatz Uncle', was Julius Leber, a former SPD member of the *Reichstag* aged fifty-one who was beginning to play an increasing part in discussions involving the workers.[1] After having been kept for many years in concentration camps, he was now running a coal-merchant's business in Berlin.]

7 November.

Mierendorff came yesterday afternoon. My leave proves to have been thoroughly inopportune, since they have rather rushed ahead and in some respects got out of hand. I must now see how I can best recover some control. This will create considerable difficulties. But fundamentally I am glad that all of a sudden matters have gathered such an impetus. [The entry for 11 November suggests that this refers to post-war plans for trade unions.] They now want to train me as a soldier. Eight weeks' basic training. As far as I personally am concerned, I've not the least objection but while I'm away all my work will go to pieces.

9 November

I don't know if you can imagine what it feels like to have more and more paper flooding on top of one every hour and be quite unable to get it in hand. I sit here at my desk literally submerged by paper, with files on all the tables, book-cases and other flat surfaces. They must all be worked through and the size of the pile means that I spend most of my time settling the priority of the individual cases. Meanwhile the telephone rings incessantly with calls from the capitals of all the occupied countries and all departments here. I will get on top of it in time but it is fearful.

To add to all this my private preoccupations are very time-consuming. Yesterday Haubach was there till 3.30, Mierendorff from 6.30 to 9 and then Peter and Adam. We are going through a fundamentally dangerous time in which some people hope to make the boat more seaworthy by sacrificing principles but forget in doing so that they prevent it being steered.

I have a totally unexpected opportunity of writing to you from the basement of the OKW. I didn't write yesterday because it was impossible. I had to spend the whole morning in clearing up and preparing myself for the meeting fixed with Bürkner in the afternoon. There was a vast mass of different matters concerning Norway, Denmark, Holland, France, Italy, the Balkans, Poland, Russia, Turkey, Sweden and Spain. As you see, a Grand Tour of Europe! ... I started on my exposé to Bürkner at 2.45, after an hour we went to

Canaris, from whom we returned after another hour for a further ninety minutes with Bürkner by himself. It was incredibly strenuous but very fruitful because both Bürkner and Canaris had time to spare and we really made progress.

Considerable dangers are in fact threatening. Mierendorff and Leber have gone off on lines which are not dissimilar to those of the Uncle [Leuschner]. Great efforts will be needed to get them back again on to the old track.

13 November

I've told Bürkner that I can't possibly keep up the present burden of work indefinitely and that above all I want to have Wengler back. That finally got something done and yesterday the Berlin Garrison Court took over the investigation. I hope that progress will now be made.

Yesterday I had another visit from SD experts who wanted guidance from me about international law in a few questions. This new and intimate relationship strikes me as highly comic and at times rouses my worst suspicions. But the chaps continue to make a really good impression on me and the practical results are very satisfying. Naturally all my outfit laughs about it and Canaris beams. I hope it will go on like this.

14 November

My desk is clear again! That has lifted a weight from my heart! ... I don't think I shall succeed in getting Mierendorff back on the right line. He is too deeply committed. It hurts me, partly for personal reasons, and also because of the subject matter. For the fact that this deviation was possible shows that things aren't as ripe as they should be and that is regrettable and fraught with pain and grief for the future. Yet facts remain facts, even if they are unpleasant.

The day began splendidly with your two notes which arrived together and pleased me a lot. I took them straight into the office with me and lapped them up there.

15 November

Mierendorff told me that he intended to marry shortly. I find it hard to believe but clearly he has had enough of a bachelor existence. ... I can't get away till Friday at the earliest since Canaris is having a meeting with Steengracht* and Papen then, to which I am being brought in. That is so-to-speak inevitable, as I appear to be the only

---

* Steengracht, Gustav Adolf Baron von Moyland (b. 1903), member of Ribbentrop's personal staff 1940–3; succeeded Weizsäcker as *Staatssekretär* 1943–5; brigadier-general in SA; condemned to seven years' imprisonment at Nuremberg 1949. He and still more his wife were personal friends of the Moltkes.

person who knows precisely what is up....* My evening was very nice. Haubach was there alone and showed himself at his best. Remarkable how this man has developed recently. I hope it will continue like that.

24 November

Here I sit in the office shelter.... Between that first sentence and now several hours have passed. I have in the interval visited Hans Carl's house [Hans Carl von Hülsen was the son of Helmuth's aunt 'Leno'] which is completely in pieces. A plane with a full load of bombs crashed on it. It is a heap of ruins which is still burning. That makes it out of the question for anyone to be still living underneath. ... The centre of the city is nothing but ruins. There isn't a single house left standing in the Tirpitz Embankment, and the same goes for the Bendlerstrasse [which, however, was sufficiently repaired in the next eight months to be a centre of activity on 20 July].... I have rescued a little from the Derfflingerstrasse. [His flat, where he was no longer sleeping, had been destroyed.]

26 November

Unfortunately my room in the office is still not functioning, since our office-managers, chiefs, etc., have completely given up. Instead of someone coming round and taking the trouble to see that we get new offices, telephones, typewriters, cupboards etc., they all stay blissfully aloof outside the city and, if they come in at all, only do so to say that we should do whatever we think best.... Yesterday first thing I was out there with Bürkner and Canaris.... The expedition cost me practically the whole day. We only got back at 4, as it is a crazy trip with continual changes, since only the right-hand line is working between two stations and only the left-hand one between the next two.... Inside the city there is still no water, electricity or gas, here [in Lichterfeld] only gas is off. In addition there is no bread in the city and practically no food at all. Meals are ghastly: cabbage and water without potatoes.

27 November

Ribbentrop and Goebbels – for whom I certainly have no love – concern themselves with everything – visit their wounded and bombed out, inspect the sections of their offices which have been hit and see to it that things are set working again. Ribbi in particular refuses to go back to East Prussia but stays firmly in Berlin.

Stay where you are and don't worry even if you don't hear anything from me. Every evening when the attacks start and we have gone down to the cellar I reflect with much tenderness that your two

---

* Presumably about the Danube boats.

little sons are now snoring sweetly and that you are sitting at your writing-table. And that is enormously comforting.

28 November

At lunch-time yesterday Carlo [Mierendorff, who in this single instance is not called by his cover-name Friedrich] and Julius [Leber] were there. C went off before we had really come to grips and the result of the ensuing conversation was unusually deplorable. It spells the end of a hope and the burning-down of the Derfflinger-strasse now seems to me to be symbolically appropriate. If only the whole formula to which Julius has allowed himself to get committed wasn't so stupid, it would be easier to take.

29 November

You ask me whether one can stand all this. It isn't really so diffi-cult. What is much more difficult is to avoid hardening oneself. I catch myself doing that all the time. It was most noticeable when I saw the remains of Editha and Hans Carl. I overcame my emotion and my grief and then it was all easy. But it is a false reaction. One must overcome the protection of indifference, one must not allow oneself to get hard but must bear it. In order to bear death and grief one is inclined to kill the humanity in oneself, and that is a much greater danger than not being able to bear it.

Yesterday I saw a striking sight. One of the heaps of ruins which I passed had apparently contained a shop selling carnival costumes. Children between four and fourteen had got hold of these, had put on gay caps, held streamers and lanterns in their hands, threw confetti and dragged long paper chains behind them and in this attire were wandering through the ruins. An uncanny sight, an apocalyptic sight!

30 November

Yesterday afternoon I went out to see Konrad [Preysing, whose Palace had been bombed and who was now living in a monastery eight miles north-west of Berlin]. Unfortunately he was pretty ex-hausted and was inclined as a result to write Berlin off. Indeed, he already had written it off. That rather disillusioned me. His flock seems rather to have scattered and he doesn't seem to know quite how he is going to collect them together again. He is too far away from events, for it takes an hour in the train to reach him. Altogether not very satisfactory. I believe, however, it is largely a physical matter because he has a weak heart and that is the real explanation. [Mieren-dorff] came in the evening. My attacks over the past few weeks on the line he was taking have finally borne fruit and he has seen the seriousness of the situation. He was very much taken up with it yesterday and I was correspondingly cheerful. In any case I have at last the impression that I can again – or should I say 'still' – achieve something and so I am once more full of hope in this field.

Given the severity of the air attacks it was almost inevitable that sooner or later one of Helmuth's friends would be a victim. And in fact Carlo Mierendorff was killed on the night of 4 December in Leipzig, where he had gone to visit an aunt. Adolf Reichwein wrote to a common friend, 'O what a different face the future now wears for us after this death! And what a big heritage it is of which we must try to be worthy!' It must be a consolation in retrospect that the man to be taken was one who had already borne his full share of suffering at Nazi hands.

5 December

Peter, Marion [Yorck], Fritzi [von der Schulenburg] and I went to church and a sermon by Lilje.* The sermon, on the horrors of history and the gravity of history, was very good. A great Advent sermon, about the coming of the Lord at the end of all history. Yet, although this sermon had a great and rousing intellectual message, I must confess I find going to church at Gräditz more satisfying because the feeling of community is that much warmer. That has made me more than ever convinced that, no matter how good a sermon is, the decisive thing is the communal spirit among the congregation and that in my view is just what tends to be lacking in a city congregation.

Fritzi came back for lunch, at which we ate your chickens, which were very delicious. Fritzi was nice and seems to be on his way back to us.† He is still sitting here at 7 o'clock and is debating with Reichwein, who has in the meantime joined us, questions of primary schools, while I sit at the writing desk and merely interject something from time to time. They have just got on to Pestalozzi. I am waiting anxiously to see ... whether we can tie Fritzi more closely to us again.

The visit which Helmuth is known to have paid with Freya to Stuttgart to see Bishop Wurm probably occurred at this point.

28 December

[On getting back to Berlin after Christmas at Kreisau]
I went at once to our new office, 10 minutes' bicycle ride from

*Lilje, Pastor (b. 1899), secretary of the Lutheran Council, a body which resisted Nazi claims but was more co-operative than the Confessing Church. After the war Lilje became Bishop of Hanover and head of the United Evangelical Churches of Germany (1948–69).

† Schulenburg had spent most of the time between July and November 1943 in Paris where, under the pretext of overhauling the German administration, he got power concentrated in the hands of Stülpnagel in preparation for a *Staatsstreich*.

Peter [i.e. the Yorck house] and princely, in a school [in Dahlem]. I have a whole class-room to myself. Otherwise nothing new here. How is Caspar getting on and how is the little one? [Caspar had been ill over Christmas with pneumonia in a Breslau hospital. Konrad had had it as well but could be nursed at home.] How lovely it was in spite of all your adversities! How pleasant for me to think that it can, I hope, always stay like that!

29 December

I have practically no work since all the incoming papers which were waiting for me were allowed to go out over Christmas [to Zossen]. Peter and Marion are in Gross Behnitz [with the Borsigs] and I have got hold of a soldier to sleep here because one is helpless in dealing with even the smallest fire-bombs if one is alone. The parcels from Stockholm are here with heavenly toys. I've looked at them and packed them up again so that they can go on to you by post as soon as possible. I hope that that will work. [These were toys which Helmuth had ordered during his last visit to Stockholm.]

How are things going with the various sons? I think of you often. I hope you're not being worried over the young master [Konrad].

31 December 1943

Yesterday evening the elder Stauffenberg brother was there. A good man, better than my Stauffi, more manly and with more character.

The first question which these two short sentences raise is who they refer to. Claus von Stauffenberg was two years younger than the twin brothers Berthold and Alexander, of whom Berthold was the elder. Helmuth does seem to have met Alexander in 1941, but on the whole the most likely conclusion is that 'elder' is a mistake and that the reference is in fact to Claus. 'There' refers to a party with Peter Yorck, who was a cousin of the Stauffenbergs. Helmuth had long ago asked Hans Christoph Stauffenberg whether any use could be made of Claus and received a discouraging answer.* 'Much later' (probably in the autumn of 1943), he told Hans Christoph. 'In the meantime something has been found for your cousin Claus to do.'

But the natural, though not the necessary, interpretation of these sentences (which are the only reference to Claus in the letters) is that Helmuth was now meeting him for the first time. On the other hand Claus had undoubtedly been to meetings at the Hortensienstrasse between his arrival in September and Christmas. Both Countess Yorck and Dr Gerstenmaier had taken it for granted that, in spite of Helmuth's frequent absences, the two men had met on at least one such

---

* Above, p. 158.

occasion. When asked to confirm this categorically, however,[2] they are not now able to go beyond an imprecise belief, while Dr van Husen had already disclaimed having any clear memory on the matter.[3] Helmuth undoubtedly knew about Claus's activities which caused him misgiving, for he said half-jokingly to Adam von Trott (who repeated the remark to Mrs Bielenberg), 'I won't let you meet Stauffenberg!'[4] At Christmas, or possibly earlier, he described to Freya how Werner von Haeften, having met Stauffenberg, was so impressed by him as to ask leave to transfer from Helmuth's section to his. Stauffenberg, for his part, described Helmuth as an uncongenial person.[5] While the evidence is thus inadequate to allow any firm conclusions to be drawn as to the number and timing of their encounters, the assumption that they worked fairly closely together during the autumn of 1943 deserves to be treated with rather more scepticism than hitherto.

After losing an eye, a hand and two fingers of the remaining hand in Tunisia in April 1943, Claus von Stauffenberg was appointed, in August, Chief of Staff to General Olbricht, the head of the General Army Office/*Allgemeines Heeresamt* AHA,* the most important part of the Replacement Army/*Ersatzheer* under General Fromm, a post which he took up on 1 October. It was a job for which Stauffenberg's reputation as an outstanding staff officer made him very suitable, but there is little doubt that he was manœuvred into it by Tresckow and Olbricht, both determined conspirators, in the conviction that a new centre could thereby be created to replace Oster's office in the *Abwehr*, put out of action by the SD in the preceding April. Stauffenberg had already promised his uncle Nicholas von Uexküll that he would join the conspiracy and repeated this promise to Olbricht in August. On taking up his appointment, and even before, he had overhauled and brought up-to-date the plans for a *Staatsstreich* drawn up under the cover of being intended to deal with a rising of foreign workers or the SS, for which the code-word was 'Valkyrie'. The original intention was that these should be put into operation in the course of the autumn but this was frustrated by inability to bring about the assassination, more and more seen as the essential preliminary to the *Staatsstreich*. Stauffenberg's position as Chief of Staff to Olbricht did not carry with it regular access to Hitler, and even if it had the view still prevailed at this stage that the assassination must be carried out by someone other than the man directing the *Staatsstreich*.

These preparations are bound to have aroused renewed discussion between Helmuth and his friends as to whether assassination was justified. Moreover, with Valkyrie overhauled and the assassination hanging fire, Stauffenberg began to turn his attention to other more political

* The AHA is not to be confused with Reinecke's *Allgemeines Wehrmacht-amt* AWA, above, p. 170.

aspects of the plans. The remarks already quoted from Helmuth's letters between 6 and 30 November probably relate, as suggested, to the vexed problem of trade union organisation but the possibility cannot be excluded that broader questions raised by Stauffenberg's activities were involved as well. Certainly there is an ironic piquancy in the way Helmuth continued his letter of 31 December:

I have the feeling that things have come everywhere to a halt. Everywhere one gets the impression of hard frost. Such periods keep on recurring and have proved themselves to be as deceptive as the periods in which everything seems to unfold and develop, maybe to press forward a bit violently. So I don't take this apparent halt very tragically.

I'm afraid poor Falkenhausen has some very unpleasant difficulties. Princess Ruspoli has been arrested and his Chief of Staff, Harbou has taken his own life.* I am enormously sorry. I only hope that he survives the crisis and that is what he looks like doing at the moment. All the same the whole affair is the kind of thing that is better not talked about so as to prevent it getting exaggerated over the jungle telegraph.

What a year lies ahead of us! If we survive it, all other years will pale into comparison beside it. We went to church early yesterday and began the year with a powerful sermon by Lilje on Joel 2, v. 21. [Fear not, O Land; be glad and rejoice: for the Lord will do great things.] I believe it was the best sermon I have ever heard and it provided such a good foundation for 1944. My dear, we can only hope that we shall have the strength to measure up to the task which this year will set us. And how can we do that unless, amid all the evil which will come upon us, amid all the suffering, amid all the pain which we shall have to endure, we know that we are in God's hands? That, my dear, you must never forget. [Lilje later said that he had noticed Helmuth as 'the most impressive face in the congregation'.[6]]

Our chat on the telephone [which was therefore working again] brought me a bit of good news – that Caspar was home. How splendid that he is back and that Konrad has recovered. I hope that it will stay like that and I hope that in these days you can celebrate a lovely Christmas with your sons.

2 January

Adam came to Peter at 12 and Julius [Leber] joined us and we have talked till now – 6.30. He is a convincingly good man who, now

* Above, pp. 261–2. Princess Ruspoli was accused of having used her influence with Falkenhausen to secure improper benefits for Belgians. Harbou was said to have committed suicide to cover his chief who did succeed in keeping his post until after 20 July.

that Carlo has gone, at any rate keeps a firm grip on the purely practical and attaches a good deal less importance to things of the mind than I do.

4 January

I am keen to see how long we shall be able to go on living the relatively orderly life which we lead. Hans [Deichmann, his brother-in-law who had been on leave] was quite astonished how everything still worked, and said that it had not been like that in Italy for a long time. There trains have stopped running and if you don't have a car you are completely immobile. There are relatively few telephones which work.... Well, all that has still to come. But the knowledge makes one all the more thankful for what there still is – that I can sit here in a heated room alone at a clean desk and write to you, that light still comes through the panes [instead of the windows being boarded up after the glass had been shattered by bombing].

6 January

Yesterday I finished reading through all the accumulated business and now know what has to be done. There are really four big complexes: the handling of the bandits and irregulars in the Balkans, Danish questions, Italian questions and the Turkish affairs resulting from my visit to Constantinople. There are also one or two matters concerned with the law about prisoners-of-war and internees. In any case they are all things which should prove capable of being carried a good way forward in the next fourteen days.

The present plans are that I go to Breslau on the afternoon of the 21st, spend the night there and on the morning of the 22nd attend the meeting of the Arbitration Court [in which he was representing Peter Yorck in a private case]. Then I will come home, i.e. with luck by 3, perhaps not till evening. In the night of Monday/Tuesday (24/25th) I will be picked up by Oxé and go on to Vienna, Tuesday to Wednesday to Agram [Zagreb], Thursday to Friday to Klagenfurt, Friday during the day to Munich, and in the night of Saturday/Sunday back to Berlin. In February I am thinking of putting in a trip to the west and in March travelling either to Sweden and Norway or to Turkey.... Naturally it seems comic to make plans like this when a few hours later one may not know where one is going to sleep, even supposing one is still alive.

7 January

The whole world hums with rumours about the forthcoming invasion. I long to see whether it will really take place. I still have a feeling that we shall have to wait for some time yet. That is partly a question of nerves. All such operations only make sense if they are conducted with such overwhelming strength that from the start there can be no doubt as to the result. As long as that isn't the case, such things shouldn't be attempted. [These remarks should be compared with those in the Istanbul memorandum, see p. 276.]

How are things with you? I wonder if you are sitting with Asta [his sister] and have finished looking after your two sons upstairs. I hope the scene is as peaceful as I imagine it. This is a continual consolation for me. O that this peace will endure for you for a little while longer!

9 January (Sunday)

At 10 I cycled to Julius and stayed with him till 1. It was a useful and on the whole a satisfying morning. But I must make a fresh effort to get this man to think as we do. He is a far coarser man than Carlo and much less congenial to me. So the balance which we need for stability won't come automatically. But all the same I am very hopeful.

11 January

I want to answer your question about Form. Form is absolutely essential and not subsidiary. It is a German fallacy to believe that Content is the only thing which matters. I don't in saying so want to imply that Content doesn't matter. But the Form, and in particular the Dogma, is the only way of telling exactly what the Content is. Otherwise it remains purely mystical. Besides, speaking generally, Form helps one to bridge over periods which have no Content. It can't replace Content but it prevents an untimely admission of absence of Content. Don't misunderstand me, I'm not exalting Form to the skies, I only want to call attention to the fact that it isn't something useless or superfluous. The view that commonly accepted forms can be dispensed with and that you can devise your own instead implies a lack of modesty which is deplorable and stupid.

13 January

A man came from the SD at 9, who stayed till 12.30.

16 January

How do things look now with you? Has your son gone to bed? Did you read to him first? Or do something else? Is Asta better again or are you still worried about her? I only hope that you are at peace with the world, and above all with yourself....

At 4 Eugen Gerstenmaier and I went off to visit Popitz* where we

---

* For Popitz, above, p. 206. He was at this time under serious suspicion because of an interview which he had had with Himmler the previous August in connection with the negotiations through Langbehn (above, p. 226). He had also made himself suspect to Beck and Goerdeler by this initiative, a suspicion

stayed till 8. I was very well entertained. He is a clever man, a very able man and a brilliant talker. I had the impression that he was fairly well satisfied too. Whether anything concrete will come of it I don't know, but it may....

The prospect of seeing you again gives me immense pleasure. I hope it will come off.

Those were the last words of any significance which Helmuth wrote as a free man. For on 19 January the SD appeared in his office with a warrant for his arrest. His assistant Wengler had been arrested two days previously, on the charge for which he was already under suspicion.

---

which he intensified by moves he made in 1943–4 to get Goerdeler replaced by Field-Marshal von Witzleben as chancellor-designate.

27 The Spy

A T its upper end, the valley of the River Inn broadens out into the basin of the Engadine. In the centre of this, the two lakes of Sils and Silvaplana gleam in summer like jewels in a green setting, with the delicate peninsula of Chasté, where Nietzsche passed some of his last lucid hours, pushing out like a finger into the former. Between the two lakes and at the foot of high meadows sloping down from the Bernina peaks lies the little village of Sils Maria. In this idyllic and peaceful setting on a summer's day in 1943, Bianca Segantini, the daughter of a famous Swiss nineteenth-century artist, entertained two guests from Germany.

The husband was a doctor Paul Reckzeh, whom she had known as a boy when he came with his parents to stay in Sils. Now he had rung up to say that he had come to Switzerland for medical treatment and ethnological research. He would much like to see again an old friend for whom he had a high regard and to introduce his wife. On arrival, the pair brushed aside the suggestion that their talk should avoid politics and made a critical attitude to the Third *Reich* exceedingly plain. Indeed their hostess was moved to the quick by the young wife's lament that she knew nobody in Berlin to whom she could confide, and offered to introduce her to a Fräulein von Thadden, the former headmistress (until evicted by the Nazis) of a progressive girls' boarding-school and a frequent visitor to Sils before the war. Next day Dr Reckzeh rang up to express his gratitude for the hospitality and to ask for a written introduction to Fräulein von Thadden, since German conditions were such that without this evidence a verbal message might not be acceptable.

When Dr Reckzeh visited Fräulein von Thadden early in September, she was just about to hold, in a borrowed flat, a party designed both to celebrate her sister's birthday and to repay hospitality which had been offered to her, particularly by Frau Solf, widow of a distinguished Orientalist who had been for seven years the Kaiser's Secretary for Colonies and for forty days under Prince Max of Baden the last Imperial Foreign Secretary. Frau Solf had a salon at which politics were frequently discussed, from a standpoint uncomplimentary to the Nazis. For this reason, and because the discussion served little practical purpose, many members of the *Widerstand* (including Helmuth) avoided the gatherings.

Fräulein von Thadden had invited to her party a number of Frau Solf's circle. There were among others Helmuth's friend Kiep, another member of the AA, a retired diplomat and his daughter. In a gesture of sympathy to the young anti-Nazi recommended to her by her close friend in Switzerland, Fräulein von Thadden invited Dr Reckzeh to come too (his wife had disappeared from the picture). It was the day after Italy's capitulation and naturally the talk turned on the possibility of the same thing happening in Germany. The general view was that the war was irrevocably lost and that the time would soon come when Hitler would have to be got rid of and replaced by men with whom the Allies would be willing to negotiate. Goerdeler's name was mentioned. Before leaving, Dr Reckzeh said that he would soon be returning to Switzerland and offered to take letters to people living there. One of the diplomats replied that he could use the post but Fräulein von Thadden wrote a note to Dr Siegmund-Schultze, a relation who was prominent in the World Council of Churches. Next day she regretted her action, went to the doctor's house to recover the letter and was relieved to be told by his father that he too had decided it might be dangerous and destroyed it.

A few days later an official called Plaas, who was sympathetic to the *Widerstand* and worked in an office responsible for listening in to telephone conversations, received from the SD a request for a watch to be kept on the telephone of Frau Solf and a number of her friends, including Goerdeler (although the latter in fact had for some time avoided her house). The official passed on the information to a Captain Gehre, who worked in Department Z of the *Abwehr*. Gehre told Helmuth, who told Kiep. The choice of those to be watched strongly suggested that Reckzeh must have been a spy; he had in fact been deliberately sent to Switzerland by the SD to pick up trails leading back to *Widerstand* circles in Germany.*

The SD often made a practice of leaving suspects at liberty in the hope that they would thus get further information. But Frau Solf and most of her friends at this stage made a serious, though natural, mistake. They refused all further approaches from Dr Reckzeh and cut down to a minimum their use of the telephone. As it happened Dr Siegmund-Schultze (who knew nothing of Reckzeh's connection with Fräulein von Thadden) had reached his own conclusions as to that gentleman's character and, when the doctor called again in the autumn, told him so to his face. The SD realised that the group had been warned and were unlikely, if left at liberty, to provide any more information. Between 10 and 12 January 1944 therefore they arrested Kiep, Frau Solf and her daughter, Fräulein von Thadden and a number of others.[1]

Naturally one of the points in which they were most interested was

* Dr Reckzeh was believed in 1968 to be living in East Berlin.

the route by which warning had been received. Under incessant questioning, not necessarily accompanied by physical torture, somebody mentioned Helmuth's name.* This was indeed grist to the SD mill. For some time they had been looking for a plausible pretext on which to get rid of a man who had put so many spokes in their wheels and who was an influential figure inside the very institution, the *Abwehr*, which it was one of their major ambitions to supersede. Now they could charge him with an undeniable offence. Admittedly the offence was a trivial one but it was enough to justify them in putting Helmuth behind bars and that, at the time, was their principal objective. It needs to be emphasised that they knew nothing about the activities which have filled so many pages of this book. Seventy-three other people are said[2] to have been arrested at the same time for activities brought to light by Dr Reckzeh.

* Plaas, the man who provided the information about the telephone-tapping, was arrested in March and executed at Ravensbrück on 19 July. (Krebs *F. D. Graf von der Schulenburg*, p. 262.) Gehre, the man who passed the information on, found the SD so hard on his heels in March that he went underground, was caught after 20 July and executed in the following winter. Helmuth told Freya that it was not he who disclosed their names.

28 Downfalls

HELMUTH'S arrest had three main consequences:

(a) With himself and Wengler removed, the work of his section in the *Abwehr* came virtually to a halt. In fact it only went on at all because Oxé was allowed to take files into prison and consult him as to how cases should be handled. During the remaining fifteen months of the war, the number and gravity of the Nazi offences against international law undoubtedly increased. To some extent this was due to the fact that, as defeat came to look more inevitable, fanatical Nazis stopped at less and less in their efforts to avert it, reckoning that even if it could not be averted, they would bring down along with themselves as many other people as they could. Thus Helmuth, even if he had remained active, would probably have had increasing difficulty in limiting the cruelty. But it is hard to believe that he would not have achieved some successes which his remaining colleagues found beyond their reach.

(b) When Adam von Trott had been in Istanbul in June 1943, Leverkühn (for whom Adam had at one stage in the past worked) asked him if he could help a young fellow-townsman from Lübeck called Erich Vermehren who was with his wife employed in the *Abwehr* and wanted a transfer to Leverkühn's staff. To obtain a visa, they needed a recommendation from someone in the AA, and this Adam agreed to provide. Shortly afterwards, the couple were able to move to Istanbul. Vermehren was also a friend of Kiep who had nominated him for a Rhodes scholarship which he had been refused because of his 'negative' attitude to Nazism. Shortly after Kiep and Helmuth had been arrested, the Vermehrens were ordered to return to Berlin. In view of all the circumstances, including Helmuth's recent visits, they put the worst possible interpretation on this order, got promptly in touch with British agents and early in February defected. They subsequently denied a story that they had committed the deadliest of sins by taking the *Abwehr* cypher book with them, but this was widely believed in Germany at the time and in addition the publicity which the British gave to their action did no good to their family and friends in Germany. As it happened, two other *Abwehr* agents in Turkey had fled shortly before. At this moment Canaris roused Hitler's wrath by submitting a pessimistic report on German prospects in the east. All these factors combined in helping Himmler, Kaltenbrunner and the SD to take the penultimate stage of their victory over the *Abwehr*. On 18 February Hitler signed a decree placing the main *Abwehr* divisions under Himmler as chief of a unified Intelligence and Sabotage Service, while the Foreign Division in which Helmuth had worked became part of the Command Staff of the Armed Forces/*Wehrmachtführungsstab*. Canaris was removed from his post and given extended leave of absence; at the beginning of July he was made head of the HWK* which by that time must have been an almost complete sinecure. Before he went, he succeeded in appointing as Oster's successor in Department Z a Colonel Hansen who was also sympathetic to the *Widerstand* and continued to pass on valuable information until the whole organisation was finally broken up (and Hansen hanged) after 20 July. But the eclipse of the *Abwehr* as an effective centre of oppositional planning, which had begun with Oster's removal and Dohnanyi's arrest, was now virtually complete. Its place was taken by the General Army Office (AHA) under Olbricht and Claus von Stauffenberg.

(c) Dr Gerstenmaier has assured us[1] that, after Helmuth's arrest, his friends continued their discussions about various aspects of the planning and we know, for example, that the vexed question of denominational schools was discussed in June. Dr van Husen has put it on record that the meetings became even more intensive and frequent.[2] Steltzer, however, claimed that 'our political work as a joint operation ended (especially as regards the choice of Land Commissioners) and what happened thereafter was the responsibility of each individual'.[3] Peter Yorck told a colleague of König's that all the work had come to a halt.[4] What seems probable is that a large part of the time and energies of the group was devoted to the question of co-operation with Claus Stauffenberg.

On the very night of Helmuth's arrest, Stauffenberg called on Yorck† and argued the necessity for Hitler to be assassinated. He met the ethical arguments against such an act by emphasising the horrors which were occurring daily in the death camps and elsewhere, horrors which could only be stopped by a Nazi overthrow. For a long time Yorck remained unconvinced while Steltzer and Rösch were never won round. But other members of the group including Gerstenmaier and Delp were less strong-minded. Stauffenberg's contacts with Trott and Schulenburg, men of his own generation, grew steadily closer. Beck was still generally accepted as shadow head of state and Goerdeler as shadow chancellor but Goerdeler began to be regarded as a security risk and was not kept informed of the planning in detail (while Goerdeler for his part was upset by Stauffenberg's tendency to deal directly with civilians himself). Leuschner was approached with a view to his replacing Goerdeler as shadow chancellor and when he refused (prefer-ring to devote himself to trade union reorganisation) a demand sprang up for Leber to take on the post. Goerdeler was felt to represent the past whereas Leber would represent the future.

Throughout the spring, however, the conspirators were baffled by their inability to get access to Hitler, and so to have an opportunity of assassinating him. But at the end of May a dramatic change occurred in this respect when Fromm, Olbricht's superior as Commander-in-Chief of the Replacement Army, decided (without any intention of aiding the conspiracy) to promote Stauffenberg to be his own Chief of Staff. For the person holding that post was required periodically to attend Hitler's daily war conferences; the conspirators thus gained what they had long been seeking, assured access for one of their own number. Even so, Stauffenberg hesitated at first to take on himself the role of executioner. His doubts arose not from his mutilated condition but from the diffi-culty (which was to prove only too real) of exploding a bomb in East Prussia or Bavaria and almost simultaneously directing a military take-over from Berlin.

But as the summer went on and 1 July, the date on which he fully assumed the new post, drew near, two developments caused him to overcome his hesitations. One resulted from discussions among Hel-muth's friends about the question of working with Communists. Reich-wein in particular argued that contact ought to be established both as a counter-balance to the aspirations of people like Goerdeler and Popitz as well as to make it more likely that a new government would secure wholehearted working-class support. Most members of the group agreed with the position taken in Point 9 of the Istanbul memorandum* that the avoidance of 'National Communism' in Germany required action to rally the strong pro-Russian circles 'in a common constructive effort'. Stauffenberg had some sympathy with this attitude but it is not clear how far he approved the action which was actually taken.[5] For at a meeting in Yorck's house on 21 June Leber, who had previously been against acceding to repeated Communist approaches, reported an over-ture from two Communists with whom he had spent five years in a concentration camp. He felt that with them he could disregard the suspicions voiced by Lukaschek and Husen that Communists were apt only to get out of prison by agreeing to become spies. Although Leuschner and Jakob Kaiser (who were not present) had also been doubtful, it was decided to take the risk and a meeting took place next day at the house of a doctor. It had been agreed that there should only be two people present on each side but the man who had been acting as intermediary brought a third Communist. One of the Communists, again contrary to agreement, greeted Leber by name. The views on

* Above, p. 277.

policy, as expressed by the representatives of the clandestine Central Committee, were so moderate as to make Leber suspicious and he refused to give any details of plans for a *Staatsstreich*. He also on reflection decided against attending a further meeting arranged for 4 July but Reichwein went, only to be arrested together with the Communists. Two of these, Saefkow and Bästlein, came in good faith but the third, Rambow, was a spy. Leber was arrested next morning. The number of Communists seized as a result of the incident was so large as to make it questionable whether the leak to the Gestapo was a calculated Communist move to weaken the non-Communist *Widerstand*.

Stauffenberg felt not merely a personal obligation towards Leber but also a need for his presence in the new government and was determined to rescue him. Moreover Leber was inconveniently close to the centre of the conspiracy and it was impossible to tell what the Gestapo might succeed in extracting from him. The evidence now suggests that the SD knew a good deal already and that Himmler may have been waiting to see whether the attempt was successful before deciding his attitude towards it. But the conspirators could not tell this and the decision to arrest Goerdeler, of which the victim heard on 18 July, must have suggested to them that their time was limited.

But undoubtedly the factor which more than any other led them to decide on action was the war situation. A Russian offensive opened on 22 June and led to the capture of more prisoners than at Stalingrad; it left gaping holes in the German line. In the west, the Allies had not merely succeeded in getting ashore but were pressing steadily forward and the geographical shape of Normandy meant that, once the Americans got to Avranches (which in fact they reached on 31 July), a breakout making the whole German position in France untenable could not be prevented. Lieutenant-Colonel Cesar von Hofacker, the cousin of the Stauffenbergs who acted as liaison between the conspirators and Stülpnagel's staff, made this clear on a visit to Berlin on 16 July.

The *Widerstand* could not foresee that, after the breakthrough, the Germans would in fact succeed in halting the Anglo-American onrush at their western frontier, thus prolonging resistance for another winter. They had to assume that defeat in the field would occur in a few weeks – and military historians are still arguing whether better Allied generalship, and better luck, might not have brought this about. Therefore this was the last moment for action if the world was not to say that the entire German people had backed Hitler to the bitter end. In the eyes of Stauffenberg and those who endorsed his action, the last chance had arrived for saving any shreds of their country's reputation and thereby mitigating the full harshness of defeat. Berthold von Stauffenberg said to his wife on 14 July, 'The most frightful thing is to know that the attempt cannot succeed and that we must do it all the same for our country and children.' His brother Claus said, 'It is time something was done. Of course anyone who tries to do anything must realise that he will be regarded in German history as a traitor. Yet if he leaves the deed undone he would be a traitor to his own conscience.' General Tresckow, when asked whether there was any sense in making an attempt once the Normandy invasion had succeeded, replied that 'the attempt on Hitler's life must be made no matter what it costs. If it fails, the *Staattsstreich* must still be attempted for the only thing which matters now is not the practical outcome but the demonstration in the eyes of the world and of history that there were Germans who were prepared to risk the decisive throw.'

Such motives must command respect, especially in countries whose leaders and responsible officials frequently answered German approaches by saying that, if the *Widerstand* wanted to be taken seriously, they must first show themselves capable of action. It is indisputable that by their action Stauffenberg and those who supported him proved to the world the existence of 'another Germany'. All the same, when the inconvenient question is asked as to what practical good it did to any Germany in the long run, a positive answer is not easy to frame.

Here however the question to be answered is what attitude Helmuth would have taken towards the *Attentat* of 20 July if he had remained at liberty. Would he have stuck to his disapproval in principle or would he have been won over, as Yorck and Hans Berndt von Haeften were, by the need to rescue the good name of his country? This question has to be asked although it is clearly insusceptible of a definite answer, especially as the views of persons in prison and facing death are different from those which they would have held as free men.

After the failure of the attempt but before the SD suspected that Helmuth was connected with it, so that free conversation was still possible, Freya went to see him in prison and his first remark to her was, 'If I had been at liberty, this wouldn't have happened.' During his trial he laid emphasis on his consistent opposition to the killing of Hitler, but this was such an obvious line of defence that it is not conclusive evidence. His last letter to his sons, written in October, is better evidence, and in it he said that he had 'never wished for or contributed to acts of violence like that of 20 July but on the contrary have fought preparations for them because I disapproved of such measures on many grounds and above all believed that they would not get rid of the fundamental trouble which was spiritual'. He was not therefore to be lumped together with the men of the 20 July. In his last letter to his wife, he commented on how Providence had withdrawn him from the stage 'at the very moment when the danger became acute that I might be drawn into active preparation for a rising'.* But to interpret this as indicating a belief that he would have been induced to approve an *Attentat* (as distinct from a coup/*Staatsstreich*) is placing some strain on words: the more natural interpretation surely is that contact with Stauffenberg would have impaired the consistency of his defence. When they were both in Tegel prison after their trial, Dr Gerstenmaier managed to have an hour's talk with him[6] and went again over the theological, moral and political arguments which had led a number of the group to support Stauffenberg. He appealed to Helmuth to make his peace with them over this difference of opinion by accepting their point of view before he died. Helmuth readily emphasised in reply his feeling of community with them and did not seek to argue further. But he did not explicitly recant his previous view and one could hardly have expected him in such circumstances to have asseverated it.

The possibility certainly cannot be excluded that, had he remained at liberty, he would have given his approval to Stauffenberg's intentions. His remark to Falkenhausen ten months earlier,† if correctly remembered, can be taken to support this. But the line which one might expect to come more naturally to him, taking all the evidence, was different. It was that, with the successful landing of the Western Allies in Normandy, the situation had at last been created for which the *Widerstand* had been waiting all through the war, with invincible might being put into the hands of the deliverer of just men long oppressed. Certainly, if he had followed the line of the Istanbul document, he would have urged his friends to let Hitler be, to concentrate on co-operating with the British and Americans, on having the front opened to facilitate their arrival in Germany and perhaps on getting the standard of revolt raised in South Germany or Austria. The moment would have arrived for bringing about the 'concerted defeat'/*Gesteuerte Niederlage* which has been, not unfairly, described as his objective.[7]

The *Attentat* had hitherto been seen to be necessary as the one thing which would induce the Generals to join in a *Staatsstreich*. But the imminent prospect of defeat in the field, which loomed in July 1944 as it had never done before, could have the same effect. Supposing that Hitler had been left unmolested in that month, it is hard to believe that he would have been allowed to go on, as he did, controlling German policy till enemy forces took Berlin. Once the plot had failed, and a terrible revenge had been taken, nobody of course was going to try again. But, if the numerous participants in it had remained alive and at their posts, they would surely have been able to act effectively once the German front in France had collapsed. The picture as seen by the public on 20 August, with the Allies at the gates of Paris and the Germans in headlong flight, was different from that on 20 July. The

* Below, p. 327. † Above, p. 264.

events of that day, although intended to shorten the war, may have had the effect of prolonging it.*

Yet even if this had been the line which Helmuth had taken, it seems unlikely that he would have succeeded in restraining or diverting Stauffenberg. He might well have caused deeper divisions among the German people after hostilities were over than the unsuccessful attempt to kill the Führer did. For surrender in defiance of superior authority, no matter what the circumstances, has a smack of treachery about it and does not call for the personal courage involved in assassination. And he might equally well have brought upon his colleagues an acute crisis of conscience. For the main object of premature surrender was to deliver Germany over to the Western Allies and keep it out of the hands of the Russians. But the Western Allies would almost certainly have continued to insist, as they did to Stauffenberg's emissary Otto John and again in 1945, not merely on unconditional surrender but on unconditional surrender on all fronts at the same time. Yet, once the German generals in the west had got to the point of asking for an armistice, it would not have been easy for them, on finding out the terms, to start fighting effectively again.

In the cold light of retrospect, there may seem to have been two courses which those opposed to Hitler could have pursued with advantage to their country and to themselves. The first was to bring about a change of régime early enough in the war to affect its outcome; this would have been achieved if either of the attempts made in March 1943 had succeeded. An effective intervention of this kind, however, would have been bound to leave questions as to whether Germany might not have fared better if fighting had continued; there would have been no demonstration that overweening ambition does not pay. Once the turning-point of the war had been clearly passed, however, and the Anglo-American–Russian coalition had an outright victory within its grasp irrespective of what happened inside Germany, the obvious practical course for the *Widerstand* was to leave the overthrow of Hitler to that coalition and to conserve efforts and numbers for the post-Hitler situation. An attempt to intervene after the turning-point meant unnecessary loss of valuable lives if it failed while, if it succeeded, it would have been almost bound to leave its authors at cross-purposes with their conquerors. For the former would have considered themselves to have a claim on the latter for gratitude which the latter would have been unprepared to acknowledge – or at any rate acknowledge in the ways that the former expected.

* On the other hand the decision to arrest Goerdeler (above, p. 302) might have marked the start of a general round-up of conspirators. But a view on this depends on the view taken of Himmler's position at this time (above, p. 226).

But this analysis leaves out of account the moral and human issues. It can be argued that the ruling classes of Germany – or former ruling classes – had to atone for their disloyalty to the Weimar Republic and for their failure to keep Hitler from power. The fact that the debt was largely paid by those who were least to blame is more a commentary on life than a refutation of this view. But in addition the whole nature of opposition has to be considered. To have sat still up to the end of hostilities would have involved not merely an insensitiveness to sin and suffering but also a lack of drive which would probably have resulted in there being at the end of the war merely a number of discordant cliques, an unpromising foundation for a new state. Men of spirit cannot be expected to observe evil without wanting to do something about it. The only way to hold the *Widerstand* together was for them to plan and, though the planning of the civilians had of necessity to be confined to paper, the soldiers when they found themselves in a position to act could not be expected to hold back from trying to create a situation where the paper plans could be realised. Thus human nature was at cross-purposes with prudent calculation.

It is perhaps not fanciful to see Helmuth himself as torn by this dilemma. He had trained himself to look beyond the immediate objective and think what would happen afterwards. His capacity for analysis led him to see clearly the objections to behaving in the very way for which the Nazis were denounced, the danger of making Hitler into a martyr, the importance of demonstrating the consequences of National Socialism so as finally to strip it of its attractions for the German people. All these considerations pointed in favour of waiting, of allowing defeat to happen. Like his South African great-grandfather,* he could have said, 'Steady, Willie, take your time.' But on the other hand it did not come easily to him to stand inactively by when things were wrong. His capacity for feeling was deep and his awareness of the suffering continually being inflicted was acute.† His wartime career can be seen as a continual search for a course which would satisfy both needs at once, a task so difficult that it is not surprising for the views he expressed to have varied along with the varying picture of events.

* Above, p. 12.   † Above, pp. 171–6.

29 Imprisonment

On arrest Helmuth was taken to the RSHA offices in the Prinz-Albrechtstrasse at the south end of the Wilhelmstrasse (appropriately enough, the site is today occupied by the Berlin Wall and the East German Ministry for State Security). This was the principal city centre for interrogation. The SD have probably acquired a false image of being as stupid as they were brutal and clumsy in their brutality. In fact some of the cleverest upholders of the régime had found their way into the service and they were often smooth, superficially affable, almost gentlemanly – though none the less sinister on that account. They had no respect for human life but could recognise intelligence and courage when they encountered it. They showed discrimination in their choice of methods and interrogations could be conducted in soft leather chairs just as much as under arc lamps. Helmuth was never tortured, partly out of respect to the Field-Marshal's heir (the reason given by Heinrich Müller, the head of the Gestapo) but partly because their estimate of his character led them to think that it would be ineffective. In the autumn, however, he believed that drugs were being put in his food to make him talk.

His first interrogation (by Müller) took place on 25 January, after which he was taken to his office in the HWK to allow him to produce papers. A further interrogation took place at the Kurfürstendamm office of the Gestapo on 6 February, at which his colleagues Oxé and Jaenicke* were brought in. Much of it concerned the Danube steamers which had been the pretext for the Istanbul visit (maybe the Gestapo were looking for evidence that they were only a pretext). The worst strain at this stage was caused by the Allied air-raids, which were occurring almost nightly. The warders in the Prinz-Albrechtstrasse retired to the shelters, but left the prisoners in their cells after manacling them to obstruct escape in the event of a hit. In one raid a land-mine dropped in the street outside but failed to explode. This inclined Helmuth to believe that Providence was sparing his life for some later purpose and brought the SD to realise that, if their object was to get information from the prisoners, Central Berlin was not a very sensible place in which to hold them. Accordingly on 7 February Helmuth was taken

* As Jaenicke had been taken for active service, he must have been brought back for this meeting.

along with Kiep, Albrecht von Bernstorff* and Dr Hilger van Scher-
penberg (all members of the 'Solf Circle'), to Ravensbrück, forty-five
miles north of Berlin.

Ravensbrück was properly speaking a concentration camp for women
but a newly completed wing (with very imperfect sound-proofing) was
being used to house evacuated political prisoners. Helmuth was put into
a cell next to the sculptress Marie Louise ('Puppi') Sarré, the sister-in-
law of his friend Eddie Waetjen, who had been arrested the previous
autumn for knowing a little – when anything was too much – about the
dealings between Himmler and Langbehn. Albrecht von Bernstorff,
who had the cell beyond Puppi's, was also suspected – wrongly – of
being connected with the Langbehn negotiations and was badly mal-
treated. On the floor below was Isa Vermehren, the sister of Erich and
friend of Helmuth's brother Willo, who was arrested with her parents
and another of her brothers in February not because she had done anything wrong but because the authorities wanted to give anyone who
might be thinking of going over to the enemy an object-lesson in what
would happen to their relatives. Another inmate of Ravensbrück was
Falkenhausen's friend Princess Mary Ruspoli.† To her Helmuth gave a
copy of Kipling's 'If' which he admired, to Puppi a copy of Curtis'
Civitas Dei. Some of the cells had much more light and view than the
others and a good deal of manœuvring went on to secure a good one.

On 23 February and again on 28–29 he was taken back to Berlin
for further interrogations, the second one, at night, lasted for twelve
hours and at the end he was forced to take up a hostile position to an
official colleague. On 14 March he wrote to Leo Lange, the assistant of
Müller's who was in charge of the investigation, protesting against his
continued detention when no serious offence had been proved against
him and asking to be released. On 24 March Lange came to see him
with his colleague Walther Huppenkothen.‡ They told him that there
could be no question of release, that his case was regarded as much
more serious than it had been and that a charge of treason might be
brought. On 26 March he wrote to Huppenkothen saying it was very
unpleasant not being able to discuss matters with colleagues in the office.
He got no reply but from then until August no further action was taken
against him.

During most of the time at Ravensbrück, therefore, he was, in effect,
in preventive detention. In common with the other prisoners he was

* Bernstorff, Albrecht von (1890–1945), nephew of German Ambassador in
Washington during the First World War; Counsellor of Legation in Lon-
don; resigned in protest against Nazi methods 1933; became a banker.
† Above, pp. 262, 292.
‡ Huppenkothen was to play a key role in interrogations of members of the
Abwehr after 20 July and our knowledge of what happened to them derives
in part from evidence which he in turn gave in his trials in 1951–5.

allowed to wear his own clothes, to have his own books and papers, to write letters and to take an hour's exercise in the courtyard daily. Here he would meet and could talk to other prisoners, though, as they were only let out in batches, the question of who would be one's fellows on a particular day was always a matter of advance speculation. Helmuth and a Communist called Sepp were the two most in demand. At Easter he went for a walk of ten kilometres with some of the camp interrogators and a secretary, visiting an inn on the way from which he managed to have a telephone conversation with Peter Yorck. Oxé, who proved a good friend in need,* came to see him with papers from the office as did one of the secretaries, Fräulein Thiel. Kanter, his contact in Copenhagen, continued for some time to get letters from him – without any address. Perhaps the most surprising thing is that he was allowed to go on receiving *Hansard*; no doubt the Gestapo were at a loss to understand how someone in their clutches could possibly still be interested in the debates of the British Parliament. As late as 10 August, he was delighted to find in a House of Lords report the statement that:

> it has once been said that no man with any capacity for going to gaol would ever think of going to sea, because in gaol the quarters were much more comfortable, the food much better and the company more congenial, in addition to which he did not run the risk of being drowned.†

Freya and he wrote to one another daily and the letters, though of course read (and therefore confined to family matters and generalities), were allowed to go through. She came to see him once a month bringing such food as eggs, jelly, cakes and tea to supplement the prison diet, and also the Kreisau account books. She went not to Ravensbrück itself but to the RSHA out-of-town office at Drögen, to which Helmuth was brought by car, complete with his teapot in which they were allowed to make themselves tea. On the way back, they would drop Freya at the station. She thus came to know many of the officials quite well. Their policy was to be so kind and complimentary that on one occasion she said to Helmuth, 'really these are quite nice people' and got the reply, 'Except that they tear off finger-nails!' He and Freya were allowed to

---

* Oxé was killed in Czechoslovakia soon after the war ended.

† Lord Winster on 16 December 1943. Parliamentary Debates, Lords, Vol. CXXX, col. 414, quoting Boswell: *Journal of a Tour to the Hebrides with Samuel Johnson 1773*:

'31 August; Why, Sir, no man will be a sailor who has contrivance enough to get himself into jail: for being in a ship is being in a jail, with the chance of being drowned.

'23 September: The man in a jail has more room, better food and commonly better company, and is in safety.'

L

sit together and talk without being closely supervised; once the room which they usually used was not available and they were taken up to Lange's bedroom, whereupon Helmuth called by signs for special caution. The officials got to know them and their family circumstances so well that one of them said to Freya, 'It's terrible to see what bad luck you've had with your geese this year.' Perhaps because of this intimacy, perhaps because the SD had their hands too full and did not realise Helmuth's significance, Freya was never interrogated and Kreisau was never searched (though, if it had been, the police would have been unlikely to think of looking in her bee-hives, where Helmuth's letters were being used to line the cells! – the documents were hidden in the rafters of the Schloss). In spite of inevitable misgivings, both he and she were in relatively good spirits. The security authorities had not been able to find anything against him, he had done nothing which he regarded as criminal and there was a good hope that he would come through.

The members of the Solf–Thadden group were tried by the People's Court at the beginning of July. Elisabeth von Thadden and Otto Kiep were condemned to death, some of the others to imprisonment, some were acquitted. Frau Solf and her daughter were saved by Japanese intervention, in return for what her husband had done to improve German relations with that country. Helmuth was not brought to court and, once their trial was over, his release seemed imminent. A high Gestapo official paid a visit to discuss his future; there could be no question of his return to the *Abwehr* although his former colleagues wanted him to be sent back to them or allowed to work under observation at Kreisau. The probability was that he would be sent to work in a munition factory. On 17 July his brother Jowo, at that time an officer on Steltzer's staff, was allowed to talk to him for two hours while two warders sat at the other end of the room and paid not the slightest attention. In the course of the conversation Jowo, who had been briefed by Peter Yorck, made clear that action against Hitler was imminent and suggested what Helmuth was to answer if interrogated.

On 20 July Peter Yorck was called into the Home Army Headquarters in the Bendlerstrasse in the early afternoon. Between 5 and 5.30 he called Gerstenmaier to come there, though the latter did not succeed in arriving until 8. Hans Berndt von Haeften's younger brother Werner, who had worked in Helmuth's section in the previous year, acted as Claus von Stauffenberg's adjutant and attended him throughout the day. Haeften was one of the five men shot on the spot, Yorck was arrested and tried with seven other officers on 8 August, being executed immediately. Gerstenmaier was also arrested in the Bendlerstrasse and for some time mistaken for Gisevius, who had also been there but managed to escape; as a civilian, however, he was not tried with the officers.

At first the Nazi authorities were inclined to think that the whole affair had been the work of a few army officers: Hitler, in his broadcast in the early hours of 21 July, spoke of 'an extremely small clique of ambitious, unscrupulous and at the same time criminally stupid officers'. But the investigating commission which was set up by Kaltenbrunner on Hitler's orders soon began to uncover incriminating evidence against a great number of senior people in many walks of life. In all 7,000 are said to have been arrested* (but 5,000 of these were Weimar politicians and party functionaries who were rounded up as a precaution on 22 August although they did not have any direct connection with the events of the previous month). The scale of the conspiracy, and the light it threw on the real attitude towards the régime of many leading officers and officials, made the rulers of the Third *Reich* both angry and alarmed. After much publicity had been given to the trial and executions on 8 August, the curtain was drawn firmly on both discoveries and punishments.

Yorck, before he died, was able to tell Poelchau that the SD were not yet on the Kreisau trail. Freya paid her normal visit to Helmuth at Drögen at the beginning of August. In the course of this, they agreed that, if he wrote a letter instructing her to plough the Kreisau meadows 100 per cent, it would mean everything had been discovered and his case was hopeless; 50 per cent would mean a good chance of escape, nil per cent nothing discovered. In the circumstances it was almost inevitable that Helmuth's name should crop up. Curiously enough, the first mention of it in the daily report of the investigations which were sent to Bormann and Hitler, on 10 August, was in connection with the proposed appointment of Rehrl as *Landesverweser* for Salzburg, but his name is also said to have come up in connection with Haubach.[1] By 25 August a considerable dossier had been collected, and Freya got a letter telling her to plough 75 per cent of the meadows.

This, as well as the mere occurrence of the attempt, affected Helmuth's treatment in Ravensbrück. When Freya, who had ceased to receive letters in mid-August, went to Drögen at the end of the month, they said 'It's a good thing you've come. You can't see him but leave the food and you can take his things away.' They handed her a suitcase containing his own clothes and packed inside it, along with other books, the diary he had kept since his arrest. Thereafter he had to wear the blue-and-white-striped pyjamas which were regulation dress for inmates of concentration camps. After one prisoner had succeeded in committing suicide, all ties, collars and braces were taken away.

* The chief people connected with Kreisau to escape arrest were Einsiedel, Trotha, Gablentz, Peters, König (by going into hiding) and last but not least Poelchau.

Very few people had enough inherent dignity to retain it in this attire. But Moltke did, his aristocratic bearing was as unmistakable in his striped prison dress as in his English suit.[2]

His bearing in these weeks was immeasurably impressive. The friendly interest which he took in all our affairs remained as keen and warm as ever. He always hid the deep scepticism of his nature behind an untroubled and rather ironic laugh. 'Hoping is not my métier,' he once said in a casual way.... 'How can I start telling lies,' he once said to me, 'and thereby destroy and betray retrospectively the things which I regard as right and necessary?'[3]

His cell was changed to a much worse one where he found himself next to General Halder. They used to chat through the ventilator, among other things about the probable Russian strategy: both thought that the main Russian thrust westwards was likely to be north of the Czech frontier so that the Kreisau area would be relatively undisturbed.

Freya went to Drögen without a pass on 28 September in the hope of seeing him, taking a suit with her in a case. She was again greeted by the staff almost as an old friend, 'What a good thing you've come! Your husband has just been taken to Berlin, and will need a suit.' She travelled back with the man who had been sympathetic over the geese. As he helped her put her case on the rack, she said to him, hoping against hope, 'This transfer to Berlin, it isn't serious, is it?' to which he replied, 'Well, yes, I'm afraid it is rather serious.' On arrival she went straight to the Lehrter Street prison where she understood Helmuth to be; a man at the reception post, who won some renown for the help he gave to prisoners' relatives, told her that the prison was too badly bombed to hold any more, and that Helmuth had been taken to Tegel (a civilian prison). She rang up Poelchau, the chaplain at Tegel, who did not yet know of Helmuth's arrival but told her to come to see him next morning. When she did and was waiting in the prison, Reichwein's wife (whose husband had also been transferred temporarily to Tegel) came in and said, 'I've just seen Helmuth coming into prison.' Freya went out and saw him being put into a car; each knew that the other had noticed but made no sign. Poelchau went to see him the same evening and found him with a letter for Freya already written. From then on, through Poelchau's good offices, they wrote to one another daily.

At one stage in his journeys, Helmuth was left alone for a moment with Steltzer and some others. 'Make no mistake about it,' he took the opportunity to say, 'if you have merely done what you have reported, you will be hanged.'[4] But the authorities did not find the task of drawing up an indictment against him straightforward. Having been in custody since January, he clearly could not have been directly involved in planning the July attempt. He had not been caught in contact with

Communists, as had Reichwein, who was tried and hanged in October. Moreover he was able to show without much difficulty that there had been lasting differences of view between himself and the Goerdeler group. He could also argue that he himself had steadily opposed assassination. All concerned in the Kreisau meetings concerted to make them look as theoretical and accidental as possible. His activities outside Germany did not come to light, though there was a bare reference to his trip to Norway with Bonhoeffer. None of the Kreisau documents ever fell into the hands of the authorities, nor did his letters to Freya. The task of preparing the prosecution against himself, Delp, Gerstenmaier (who, after some uncertainty, had been put into the same group), Steltzer and Haubach was entrusted to Neuhaus, a theological student who had lost his faith. It would seem that he and his colleagues could not make Helmuth out and thought him a queer fish. Helmuth encouraged such thoughts as offering a possible means of escape from death.

Gerstenmaier maintained in these months that, if one was to survive, one must believe in one's survival. Helmuth was too clear-sighted, and his inclination to pessimism too habitual, for him to go so far. But those who have portrayed him as awaiting his end without hope or illusions have gone too far. If martyrs are people who sit back with meekness to await what is in store for them, he was no martyr for he fought to keep alive by organising the best possible defence for himself and his colleagues. Having for so long been doubtful about life, he now wanted to live. He, and Freya with him, believed implicitly that in their course so far they had been guided by a divine Providence and thought that the same Providence might well have new tasks for him in the new Germany which was at last coming into sight. At one stage he toyed with the idea that the authorities might keep him alive in order to take advantage of his English contacts. What is true, however, is that, despite some moments of spiritual crisis known only to Poelchau, he was prepared for death as well as for life. And in the long run the Nazis were probably determined to kill him, no matter how difficult it might be to find a formal justification. When Freya went to see 'Gestapo' Müller, one of the things he said to her was, 'We're not going to make the same mistake as in 1918 and leave our internal enemies alive.' They sensed – and rightly – that Helmuth embodied many of the influences which had stood between them and success – humanity, high principle, consistency, clear thinking. If they were in fact doomed themselves, they would wreak as much vengeance as they could manage in the process of collapsing. The same explanation applies to their implacable attitude towards Delp as a representative of the Jesuit order.

Paradoxically this may help to explain the fact, at first sight surprising, that Freya remained at liberty throughout and was never even interrogated, that no attempt was made to take away the children, that Kreisau was never searched. All these things happened to the wives and children of the men involved in the attempted *Staatsstreich*, partly in a search for evidence, partly out of vengeance. But the SD had had Helmuth and Freya under close observation for nine months, they may well have been satisfied that Helmuth had not been engaged in a violent attempt to overturn the state and was therefore not a major security risk. They had a great deal of work on their hands in conditions of ever-increasing chaos. Respect for the Moltke name was undoubtedly in-creased by respect for the way its bearer behaved. They probably took a decision to kill him himself and call the account with his family closed.

Freya divided her time between Kreisau and Berlin, staying in Lichterfelde with Carl Dietrich von Trotha or in Tegel with Poelchau, where she always found peace and had the feeling of being close to her husband. The governor and warders must have had a shrewd idea what the chaplain was doing, not only for Helmuth but for the other prisoners as well. Indeed one official commented on the fact that he always looked much thinner coming out of prison than he did going in. But the fact that they all belonged to the regular prison service, and were under the Ministry of Justice instead of being committed Nazis, may have made them anxious to bend the rules for political prisoners, especially with collapse in sight. Freya saw Helmuth twice in Novem-ber and December in the governor's office, having argued that she needed to consult him about Kreisau. He kept her busy holding inter-views and passing messages in connection with the defence. Thus she wrote to Himmler, saw Müller and got messages through to Steltzer, Haubach, Reisert and others.

But all to no avail. The trial, after being twice postponed, was held on 9 and 10 January. The original charge of conspiracy to overthrow the government had pretty well collapsed for lack of evidence, though there remained the subsidiary charge of knowing that such a conspiracy was on foot (but not its exact date) and failing to report it. (This of itself was enough to send some people to the scaffold, including a Catholic priest who only learnt of it in the confessional.) There were the unde-niable charges of having been hostile to National Socialism and of having discussed what was to happen after the defeat and of having ap-proached individuals with a view to their acting as Land Com-missioners. Along with Helmuth appeared Gerstenmaier, Steltzer, Haubach, Delp, Sperr, Reisert and Fugger.

Helmuth had had a painful attack of sciatica while he was at Tegel and for some time could neither walk nor stand. On the doctor's orders, his handcuffs had been removed. He was much better by the time that the trial came on but was nervous about the kind of figure he would make. All the accused had to stand while they were being interrogated and he did not know if he would be able to do so. Accordingly Freya went to see the judge, Freisler, and explained the position; she was received with much politeness and assured that a chair would be provided so that he was in fact able to sit for most of the time.[5]

30 Trial and Death

THE trial was held in a commandeered building in the Bellevue Strasse, between the Wilhelmstrasse and the Tiergarten in the centre of Berlin.[1] The People's Court, over which Roland Freisler had presided since 1942, had been set up in 1934. Freisler had been a prisoner-of-war in Russia during 1914–18 and is believed to have been a Communist in Kassel in 1918 before becoming a Nazi in 1925. He had been an under-secretary in the Ministry of Justice and is said to have regarded his appointment to the Court as a set-back to his career which he was determined to overcome by making a name for himself in the post! His methods of procedure were reputedly modelled on those used by Andrei Vishinski during the Russian purge trials of 1937–8. Accounts make it sound as though he had missed his vocation and would have won a considerable name for himself on the stage. He possessed the lawyer's ability to master a brief but did not hesitate to combine the role of prosecutor with that of judge. Delp said of him, 'Freisler is clever, nervous, vain and arrogant. He is performing all the time in such a way that the player opposite to him is forced into a position of inferiority.... All the questions were neatly prepared and woe betide you if the answers you gave were not what Freisler expected.'

After the verdict Helmuth was not taken straight to execution at Plötzensee, as had happened to some people, but back to Tegel. He was therefore able to describe the proceedings to Freya in two final letters which Poelchau conveyed. They have been printed already[2] but never in a context which will show how completely they are a culmination to his life. The suggestion has been put forward that they were written in the awareness that they might fall into the hands of the SD and accordingly laid exaggerated emphasis on the claim that 'we are to be hanged for thinking together'. The final paragraph of the first letter, however, is enough to show that no overlooking SD eye was in mind. What has been said already about the limited nature of the evidence available to the Nazis against Helmuth should make clear that, in speaking like this, he is only talking about what went on in the trial. He would never have claimed that his activities against the Third *Reich* had been confined to thinking! Thinking was what he wanted his enemies to condemn him for, and managed his defence with that end in view. He was not wholly successful, for someone wrote on his sentence, 'He did more than think.'

10 January 1945

What a stroke of luck! I have been brought back here to Tegel once again, so that the dice, although it is already determined how they shall fall, are once more balancing on edge, so to speak. So I can still write a report in peace and quiet.

To take the end first; at about 3 o'clock Schulze,* who did not make an unfavourable impression, read out the proposed sentences: in the case of Moltke, death and confiscation of property. Delp, the same; Gerstenmaier, death; Reisert and Sperr, the same; Fugger, 3 years' penal servitude; Steltzer and Haubach to be dealt with separately. Next came counsel for the defence, all of them really very decent, no monkey-tricks. Then the last statements of the accused, when I was the only one to refrain from speaking. I noticed from Eugen's statement that he was getting a bit rattled.

Now for the course of the trial. All these details are, naturally, official secrets.

It took place in a small hall, which was full to bursting. Looked as though it had once been a schoolroom. After a long introduction from Freisler concerned with formalities – that the trial was secret, veto on reporting it, &c. – Schulze read out the indictment, and again only the short text, as in the warrant for arrest. Then they called on Delp, whose two policemen stepped up alongside him. The procedure was as follows: Friesler, whom Hercher† has very accurately described as talented, with some genius in him, and unintelligent, and all three in the highest degree, outlined one's career, one confirmed or supplemented what he said, and then he got down to the facts which interested him. Here he picked out just those that suited his book, and left out whole sections. In Delp's case he started off by asking how he got to know Peter and me, what the first conversations in Berlin had been about, and so came to the Kreisau meeting of autumn '42. Here again a lecture by Freisler, into which one might insert answers, objections, or even fresh facts; however, if this looked like breaking the thread of his argument, he got impatient, made out that he didn't believe it, or bellowed at one. The build-up for Kreisau as follows: first there had been general discussions more on matters of principle, then what was to be done in the case of defeat had been discussed, and finally the choice of Land Commissioners. The first phase might have been tolerable, though it was considered surprising that all these conversations should have taken place without the participation of a single National Socialist, but

* The Public Prosecutor.
† Helmuth's counsel.

instead with ecclesiastics, and only people who subsequently were implicated in the 20 July affair. The second phase, however, was in itself utter defeatism of the very blackest kind. And the third, open preparation for high treason. Then came the conversations at Munich. These were all made out to be much less serious than the indictment suggested, but a hail of brickbats assailed the Catholic clergy and the Jesuits: assent to tyrannicide – Mariano* – illegitimate children, anti-German attitude, &c., &c. All this bawled out but only with moderate violence. Even the fact that Delp had absented himself from the discussions held at his quarters was thrown in his teeth as being 'typically Jesuitical'. 'By that very action you yourself showed that you knew perfectly well that high treason was afoot, out of which such a holy, consecrated fellow would naturally be only too anxious to keep his tonsured pate. So off he goes to church, to pray the while, that the plot may develop along lines pleasing to God.' Next came Delp's visit to Stauffenberg. And finally Sperr's statement, on 21 July, that Stauffenberg had made overtures to him about a *coup d'état*. These two last points passed off quietly. It was noticeable, however, throughout the hearing that my name was brought in by Freisler in every other sentence like 'the Moltke circle', 'Moltke's plans', 'also belonging to Moltke', &c.

The following were laid down as fundamental principles of the law: 'That the People's Court regards as being already tantamount to treason any failure to report defeatist utterances such as Moltke's, especially when emanating from a man of his consequence and position. – As being already tantamount to preparation for high treason to broach matters of high policy with people who are in no way competent to deal with them, particularly when they do not even belong, in any active capacity, to the Party. – As being already tantamount to preparation for high treason for anyone to presume to form an opinion about a matter that it is the Führer's business to decide. – As being tantamount to preparation for high treason for anyone, even while himself holding aloof from all violent action, to prepare measures for the event when a third party, namely the enemy, shall have overthrown the Government by force, for by so doing he is counting on the force of the enemy.' And so on and so forth. The only conclusion to be drawn from it all being that it is tantamount to high treason if one does not suit Herr Freisler.

Next it was Sperr's turn. He more or less got out of the Kreisau business – it must be admitted somewhat at my expense. However, he was reproached as follows. 'Why didn't you report it? Don't

---

* Mariano, Juan (1536–1624), Jesuit author of *De rege et regis institutiore* where he defended the killing of tyrants. 'Illegitimate children, anti-German attitude' were other charges made by the Nazis to discredit the Jesuits.

you see how important that would have been? The Moltke circle was, up to a point, the moving spirit of the "counts group", which in turn had charge of the political preparation for the 20 July plot: for the real motive power behind 20 July lay in these young men and not at all in Herr Goerdeler!' Taking it by and large, Sperr's treatment was friendly.

Next Reisert. He was treated in a very friendly fashion. He had had three conversations with me, and it was chiefly held against him that he had not immediately noticed after the first that I was an arch-traitor and rank defeatist, but had gone on and had two further talks with me. Above all he was charged with not having denounced me.

Finally Fugger. He made an excellent impression. For some time he had been under the weather, but had now pulled himself together, was discreet, sure of himself, did not incriminate any of us, spoke good, broad Bavarian, and never pleased me so well as yesterday; not a trace of nerves, although he had been scared stiff all the time he was here. He at once admitted that, after what had been said to him that day in court, he realised he ought to have reported matters, and was dismissed with such good grace that yesterday evening I really thought he would be acquitted.

However, the name of Moltke kept cropping up all through the other examinations. It ran through everything like a scarlet thread, and, in view of the aforementioned 'legal principles' of the People's Court, it was clear that I was to be done away with.

At this point, a brief explanation of the picture.

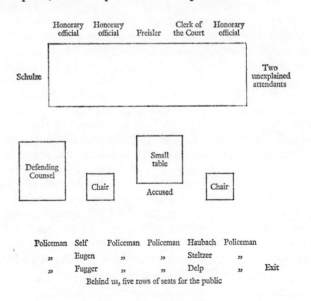

The whole trial was microphonically recorded on steel tapes for the archives. So, later on, should you feel inclined, you will be able some time to have them played over to you. One stepped up to the table, one's two policemen with one, and they sat on chairs one on the right and the other on the left. A chair was at once provided for Reisert, as also for me, without our having to ask.* Schulze, Freisler and the Clerk of the Court in red robes. One incident was typical. For some reason a copy of the Penal Code was needed, since Freisler wanted to read out an extract from it. However, it turned out that there was not one anywhere to be found.

And now for the second day. That was where my turn came. We started off quite mildly but very fast, practically breakneck. Thank goodness I'm quick in the uptake and could take Freisler's pace in my stride; which incidentally obviously pleased us both. But if he carried on like that with someone not particularly quick-witted, the victim would have been condemned before he so much as noticed that Freisler had passed beyond the preliminary account of his career. Up to and including the conversation with Goerdeler and my position with regard to it, everything went quite smoothly and without much fuss.

At this point I objected that the police and the security authorities had known all about it. This gave Freisler paroxysm No. 1. Everything that Delp had previously experienced was mere child's play by comparison. A hurricane was let loose, he banged on the table, went the colour of his robe, and roared out, 'I won't stand that; I won't listen to that sort of thing.' And so it went on the whole time. As I knew in any case how it would turn out, it all made no odds to me; I looked him icily straight in the eye, which he obviously didn't care about, and all of a sudden could not keep myself from smiling. This spread to the officials sitting to the right of Freisler, and to Schulze. I wish you could have seen Schulze's expression. If a man were to jump off the bridge over the crocodiles' pond at the Zoo, I don't think the uproar could be greater. Well, anyhow that exhausted the subject.

Next, however, came Kreisau. And there he did not waste much time over the preliminaries, but made a bee-line for two things: (a) defeatism, and (b) the selection of Land Commissioners. Both gave rise to fresh paroxysms as violent as before, and, when I submitted in defence that it all had come about as an offshoot of my official duties, a third paroxysm. 'All Adolf Hitler's officials set about their work on the assumption of victory, and that applies just as much in the High Command as anywhere else. I simply won't listen to that kind of thing – and even were it not the case, it's clearly the

* Above, p. 314.

duty of every single man for his own part to promote confidence in victory.' And so on in long tirades.

But now came the crux of the whole thing. 'And who was present? A Jesuit father! Of all people, a Jesuit father! And a protestant minister, and three others who were later condemned to death for complicity in the 20 July plot! And not a single National Socialist! No, not one! Well, all I can say is, now the cat is out of the bag! A Jesuit father, and with him, of all people, you discuss the question of civil disobedience! And the Provincial head of the Jesuits, you know him too! He even came to Kreisau once! A Provincial of the Jesuits, one of the highest officials of Germany's most dangerous enemies, he visits Graf Moltke in Kreisau! And you're not ashamed of it, even though no decent German would touch a Jesuit with a barge-pole! People who have been excluded from all military service, because of their attitude! If I know there's a Provincial of the Jesuits in a town, it's almost enough to keep me out of that town altogether! And the other reverend gentleman! What was he after there? Such people should confine their attentions to the hereafter, and leave us here in peace! And you went visiting bishops! Looking for something you'd lost, I suppose! Where do you get your orders from? You get your orders from the Führer, and the National Socialist Party. That goes for you as much as for any other German, and anyone who takes his orders, no matter under what camouflage, from the guardians of the other world is taking them from the enemy, and will be dealt with accordingly!' And so it went on, but in a key which made the earlier paroxysms appear as the gentle rustling of a breeze.

The upshot of the examination 'against me' – since it would be absurd to talk of 'my examination' – the whole Kreisau meeting, and all subsidiary discussions arising therefrom, constituted preparation for high treason.

Really, after this climax, the only thing I need tell you is that the end came in about five minutes. What we did in Fulda and Munich was, on the whole, passed over, Freisler being of the opinion that we could make what we liked of that. And then he asked, 'Have you anything more to say?' To which, unfortunately after some hesitation, I replied, 'No,' and so was through.

To sum up the effect of all this I rather think that if the others, whose names have come to light – though not during the trial because, when we saw how matters were going, we all took care not to mention any other names – have not yet been arrested they are probably regarded as a negligible quantity. However, should they be arrested later, and then prove to have had knowledge amounting to more than mere social chatter on these matters, especially on anything connecting them with a possible defeat, then they must expect the death penalty.

Taking it all in all, this emphasis on the religious aspect of the case corresponds with the real inwardness of the matter, and shows that Freisler is, after all, a good judge from the political angle. This gives us the inestimable advantage of being killed for something which (*a*) we really have done, and which (*b*) is worth while. But that I should die as a martyr for St Ignatius Loyola* – which is, what it ultimately amounts to, since all the rest was a side-issue by comparison – really is comical, and I already tremble at the thought of Papi's paternal indignation, since he was always so anti-Catholic. The rest he will approve, but that! Even Mami won't be wholly in agreement.

(Something else for the record has just occurred to me. He asked me, 'Now do you appreciate that you are guilty?' I in effect said 'No.' Whereupon Freisler: 'Look here, if you still can't see it, if it still has to be drummed into you, then that shows that you are living in a world of your own, and by your own act have cut yourself off from the fighting community of the people.')

The best thing about a judgment on such lines is this. It is established that we did not wish to use force; it is further established that we did not take a single step towards setting up any sort of organisation, nor question anyone as to his readiness to take over any particular post; though the indictment stated otherwise. We merely thought, and really it was only Delp, Gerstenmaier and I, since the others counted as associates, and Peter and Adam as maintaining connexion with Schulenburg, &c. And in face of the thoughts of these three isolated men, their mere thoughts, National Socialism gets in such a panic that it wants to root out everything they may have infected. There's a compliment for you! This trial sets us poles apart from the Goerdeler mess/*Goerdeler Mist*, right apart from all practical activity; we are to be hanged for thinking together. Freisler is right, a thousand times right, and if we are to die I am all in favour of our dying on this issue.

I am of the opinion – and now I am coming to what has got to be done – that this affair, properly presented, is really somewhat better than the celebrated Huber case.† For even less actually happened. We did not so much as produce a leaflet. It is only a question of men's thoughts without even the intention to resort to violence. The submissions we all made in our defence, that the police knew, that the whole thing arose out of official business, that Eugen didn't catch on, that Delp was never actually present, these must be brushed aside, as Freisler rightly brushed them aside. So then all that is left is

*The founder of the Jesuit Order.   † Above, p. 213

a single idea: how Christianity can prove a sheet-anchor in time of chaos. And just for this idea five heads (and later it may well be Steltzer's, Haubach's and even possibly Husen's as well) look like being forfeited tomorrow. But for various reasons – because the emphasis during the trial lay on the trio Delp, Eugen, Moltke, and the others were only involved through having been 'infected', because no member of any other faction was involved, no representative of the working class, no one having the care of any worldly interest – because he made it clear that I was opposed in principle to large estates, that I had no class interests at heart, no personal interests at all, not even those of my wartime job, but stood for the cause of all mankind – for all these reasons Freisler has unwittingly done us great service, in so far as it may prove possible to spread this story and make full use of it. And indeed, in my view, this should be done both at home and abroad. For our case histories provide documentary proof that it is neither plots nor plans but the very spirit of man that is to be hunted down. Long live Freisler!

To make use of this story is not your task. Since we are to die in the main for St Ignatius, let his followers make that their concern. You, however, must see that this account gets to them, and if they choose to call in people from Wurm,* well and good; the best man would probably be Pressel.† I'll talk it over with Poelchau tomorrow. If it comes out that you have received this letter and passed it on, then you too will be put to death. Tattenbach‡ must obviously take that on himself, and in case of need say that he received it from Delp with his last lot of washing. Do not part with this version but only a copy of it and the latter must at once be transposed so that it could have come from Delp and been written by him in the first person.

So much for that. The rest follows separately.

Tegel, 10 January 1945

My dear, first and foremost I must say that obviously the last twenty-four hours of one's life are no different from any others. I had always imagined that one would have no feeling but shock, that one would tell oneself, 'This is your last sunset, now the clock will only go round twice more, now you're going to bed for the last time.' But there's no question of any of that. Am I really a little intoxicated? I certainly can't deny that at present I'm in the best of spirits. Only I beg our Heavenly Father that he will keep me in them, for so to die is surely easier for the flesh. How good God has been to me! Even at

* Bishop of Württemberg, above, p. 196.
† Bishop Wurm's adviser on Church matters, p. 374.
‡ A younger Jesuit who had been looking after Delp's interests.

the risk of sounding hysterical I'm so full of gratitude that there's really room for nothing else. He guided me so surely and clearly through those two days. The whole assembly could have bellowed, like Herr Freisler, and all the walls have rocked and it would have made no odds to me. It was exactly as it says in Isaiah 43, verse 2: 'When thou passest through the waters I will be with thee; and through the rivers, they shall not overflow thee: when thou walkest through the fire, thou shalt not be burned; neither shall the flame kindle upon thee' ... that is to say upon thy soul. When I was called on to make my final statement I was in such spirits that I almost said, 'I have only this to say in my own justification,

> Nehmen Sie den Leib,
> Gut, Ehr, Kind und Weib,
> Lass fahren dahin, Sie haben's kein Gewinn,
> Das Reich muss uns doch bleiben!'*

But that would only have been damaging for the others; so I only said, 'I have nothing I wish to say, Herr Präsident.'

Now there is still a hard bit of road ahead of me and I can only pray that God will continue as good to me as He has been up till now. Eugen had written down for us for this evening Luke 5, verses 1–11. He meant it differently but it remains true that today there was for me a miraculous draught of fishes, and this evening I am justified in saying 'Depart from me, for I am a sinful man, O Lord.' And yesterday, my dear, we read this beautiful passage: 'But we have this treasure in earthen vessels, that the excellency of the power may be of God, and not of us. We are troubled on every side, yet not distressed; we are perplexed, but not in despair; persecuted, but not forsaken; cast down, but not destroyed; always bearing about in the body the dying of the Lord Jesus, that the life also of Jesus might be made manifest in our body.' Thanks be, my dear, before all else to God. Thanks also to yourself for your intercessions, thanks to all those others who have prayed for us and for me. That I, your husband, your weak, faint-hearted, 'complicated', very average husband, should have been allowed to experience all this! Were I now to be reprieved – which I swear is neither more nor less likely than it was a week ago – I must say that I should have to find my way all over again, so tremendous has been the demonstration of God's presence and omnipotence. He shows them to us and shows them quite unmistakably, precisely when He does what we don't like. Anything else is nonsense.

---

* 'Slay my body, take my property and my honour, wreak your will on my wife and child, do your worst, you still have no victory, the City of God remaineth.' (Quotation from a poem by Luther.)

So then, my dear, I have only one thing to say: may God be as good to you as to me, then even your husband's death will not matter. He can demonstrate His omnipotence at any time, perhaps when you are making pancakes for the boys or cleaning them up. I ought to take leave of you – I can't do it. I ought to deplore and lament your daily toil – I can't do it. I ought to think of the burdens which now fall on you – I can't do it. I can only tell you one thing: if you get the feeling of absolute security, should the Lord vouchsafe it to you, which you would not have had without this time and its outcome, then I am bequeathing you a treasure which no man can take away, against which even my life cannot weigh in the balance. These Romans, these wretched creatures Schulze and Freisler and whatever the whole pack are called, they won't begin to know how little they can take from you!

I'll write more tomorrow, but as one never knows what will happen I want at any rate to have touched on all subjects in the letter. Of course, I don't know whether I shall now be executed tomorrow. It may be that I shall be interrogated again, or beaten up or held in reserve. So please go on tapping on doors, as that perhaps will deter them from too savage a beating. Even if I do know after today's experience that God can also turn this beating to nought, even should I not have a whole bone in my body before I am hanged, even if at the moment I have no fear of it, still I should prefer to avoid it. So good-night, be comforted and undismayed.

Hercher, who really is a good fellow, was rather shocked at my good spirits; from which you can see that they couldn't be suppressed.

11 January 1945

My dear, I just want to chat with you for a little. I've really nothing to say. We've discussed in detail the material consequences. You'll get by somehow or other and if someone else is installed in Kreisau you'll get over that too. Just don't let anything trouble you. It really isn't worth it. I'm definitely in favour of ensuring that the Russians know of my death. Perhaps that will make it possible for you to stay in Kreisau. To wander around in what is left of Germany is in any case a dreadful prospect. If against all expectations the Third *Reich* does last, which in my wildest dreams I cannot imagine, then you must see how you can keep the boys from the poison. I should then naturally have no objection if you too were to leave Germany. Do whatever you think is right and don't consider yourself bound one way or the other by any wish of mine. I have said to you again and again 'the dead hand cannot govern'....

With untroubled joy I think of you and the boys, of Kreisau and everybody there; for the moment the parting does not seem at all grievous. That may still come, but at present it doesn't trouble me. I am not in any way burdened with thoughts of parting. Where this comes from I don't know. But there's not a trace of the feeling which overwhelmed me after your first visit in October, no it was in November. Now my inner voice says that (a) God can guide me back today just as well as yesterday, and (b) if He calls me to Himself I can take it all with me. I haven't at all the feeling which sometimes swept over me: oh, I would love to see it all just once more! At the same time I don't feel in the least 'other-worldly'. As you see, I am happily chatting with you instead of turning to the good God. There is a hymn which says, 'Then he for death is ready who living clings to Thee.' That's exactly how I feel. As I am alive today I must 'living cling to Him'; He does not ask for more. Is that Pharisaical? I don't know. But I think I know that I am living now in His grace and forgiveness and have nothing deriving from myself and can of mine own self do nothing.

I am chatting, my dear, just as things come into my head, so now here is something quite different. In the final count the following was the really dramatic thing about the trial: in the course of the proceedings all factual charges proved to be untenable and were dropped. Nothing remained except this (which, however, strikes such terror into the Third *Reich* that it has to put five men to death, ultimately the number will be seven). It was established that a private individual, namely your husband, had discussed with two eccelesiastics, both Protestants, with a Provincial of the Jesuits and with several bishops, matters 'which are the exclusive concern of the Führer', and without the intention of taking any active steps, as was also established. The discussions had nothing to do with organising any opposition or the reconstruction of the *Reich*. All that dropped out in the course of the trial, and Schulze expressly said so in his speech for the prosecution ('this case differs radically from all other cases in that there was no mention in the discussions of violence or of organised opposition'). What was discussed concerned the demands in practice of the Christian ethic, nothing more. And for that alone we are sentenced. In one of his tirades Freisler said to me, 'Only in one respect are we and Christianity alike; we demand the whole man!' I don't know whether the others sitting there took it all in, for it was a sort of dialogue – a spiritual dialogue between Freisler and me, since I did not get the chance actually to say much – during which we got to know each other through and through. Of the whole gang Freisler was the only one who thoroughly understood me, and also the only one of the lot who knew why he had to do away with me. Nothing was said about 'a tortuous character' or 'complicated thinking' or 'ideology', just that 'the mask was off'. But only for Herr Freisler. We were, so to speak, talking to each other in a vacuum. He made not a single joke at my expense as he did with Delp and Eugen. No, here it was all grim earnest. 'Who do you take your orders from? From the Other World or from Adolf Hitler?' 'Who commands your loyalty and your faith?' Rhetorical questions of course. Anyhow Freisler is the first National Socialist who has grasped what I am, and dear Müller is a simpleton by comparison.

My dear, your very dear letter just arrived. The first letter, my dear, in which you have not grasped my state of mind and my condition. No, I am not busy with the good God or with my death. He has the inexpressible grace to come to me and to be busy with me. Is that presumptuous? Perhaps – but He will be forgiving me so much this night that finally I dare to beg forgiveness of this last presumption also. But I hope it is not presumptuous as I am not extolling the earthen vessel, no, I am extolling the precious treasure which is making use of this earthen vessel, this utterly unworthy lodging. No, my dear, I am reading exactly those passages from the Bible which I should have read even if there had been no trial, namely Joshua 19–21, Job 10–12, Ezekiel 34–6, Mark 13–15 and the rest of our Second Epistle to the Corinthians, apart from those short passages which I wrote out for you.... So far I have only read the Joshua and our passage from Corinthians, which ends with the beautiful, familiar sentence, so often heard from my childhood up: 'The grace of Our Lord Jesus Christ and the love of God and the fellowship of the Holy Spirit be with you all. Amen.' My dear, I feel as though I had been given absolute authority to say this to you and the little sons. And am I not fully entitled to read the 118th psalm appointed for this morning? Eugen had meant it for other circumstances, but it has become far more true than we had ever thought possible.

So then, my dear, you are getting your letter back in spite of your request. I take you across with me and for that need nothing, neither sign nor symbol. It is not just as though I had been promised I should never lose you; no, it is far more. I know it.

A long pause, during which Buchholz was here, also I had some coffee, rolls and cake. Now I go on chatting. The decisive phrase in the trial was, 'Herr Graf, we National Socialists and Christianity have one thing in common and one only: we demand the whole man.' Was he clear what he said there? Just think how wonderfully God prepared this His unworthy vessel. At the very moment when the danger arose that I might be drawn into active preparations for a rising – Stauffenberg came to see Peter on the evening of the 19th [January 1944] – I was taken away, which means that I was and remain free of all connection with the use of violence. Then He endued me with this socialistic leaning which frees me as a great landowner from any suspicion of looking after my own interests. Then He humbled me as I have never been humbled before, so that I must lose all pride, so that at last after thirty-eight years I understand my sinfulness, so that I learn to pray for His forgiveness and trust in His grace. Then He lets me come here so that I may see you standing firm and can be free of thoughts of you and the boys, that is to say of worries about you. He gives me time and opportunity to arrange everything that can be arranged, so that all earthly cares may fall away. Then he lets me experience to their utmost depths the agony of parting, the terror of death and the fear of hell, so that all these are behind me. Then He endows me with Faith, Hope and Charity in such measure that it is really overwhelming. Then He gives me the chance to talk with Eugen and Delp and clear up certain points. Then He lets Rösch and König escape, so that the trial did not amount to an indictment of Jesuits and at the last moment Delp was joined to us. Then He lets Haubach and Steltzer, whose cases might have introduced irrelevant matters, be dealt with separately, and finally sets Eugen, Delp and me to all intents and purposes alone. Then He induces in Eugen and Delp, because of the very human hopes they cherish, a weakness which makes their cases seem only secondary, and so the denominational aspect is removed. Then your husband is picked out and, as a Protestant, attacked and condemned primarily because of his friendship with Catholics, and therefore stands before Freisler not as a Protestant, not as a great landowner, not as a nobleman, not as a Prussian, not as a German – all that was specifically excluded at an earlier stage, as for instance in Sperr's statement, 'I thought what an astonishing sort of Prussian' – no, as a Christian and as nothing else. 'The mask is off,' said Herr Freisler. Yes, every other category was wiped out – 'a man', said Schulze, 'whom others of his rank would naturally keep at arm's length'. For what a mighty task your husband was chosen! All the trouble that God took with him, the endless short cuts, the intricate tacking, the purport of it all is suddenly revealed within a single hour on 10 January 1945. As a result everything that was obscure acquires meaning. Mami and Papi, the brothers and sister, the little sons, Kreisau and its troubles, the Labour camp and my hatred of flag-wagging and refusal to join the Party or any of its offshoots, Curtis and the journeys to England, Adam and Peter and Carlo, all of it at last became intelligible in a single hour. For this one hour God gave himself all that trouble.

And now, my dear, I come to you. I have not dealt with you elsewhere because you, my dear, are in a different position from all the others. You are not part of the means God used to make me what I am, rather you are I myself. You are my 13th chapter of the first Epistle to the Corinthians. Without this chapter no man is really a man. Without you I would have taken love as a gift, for instance I accepted it from Mami, gratefully, happily, as one is thankful for the sun which warms one. But without you, my dear, I would have 'had not Charity'. I do not say that I love you, that would not be correct. Rather you are that part of me which would be missing if I were alone. It is good that I lack this; for if I had, as you have, this greatest of all gifts, then I could not have looked on the miseries which I have had to see, and much else besides. Only in union do we two constitute a human being. We are, as I wrote to you symbolically a few days ago, one creative thought. That is true, literally true. And so, my dear, I am certain that you will not lose me on the earth, not for a moment. And we have been allowed finally to symbolise this fact through our shared Holy Communion, which will have been my last.

I just wept a little, not because I was sad or melancholy, not because I wanted to turn back, but from intensity of gratitude at this proof of God's presence. It is not given us to see Him face to face, but we must needs be overwhelmed when we suddenly realise that He has gone before us our whole lives through, as a pillar of cloud by day and of fire by night, and that in a flash He suddenly lets us see it. Now nothing more can happen.

My dear, this last week and above all yesterday have certainly overtaken several of my farewell letters. They will read like cold coffee. I leave it to you whether you want to forward them in spite of this and whether you want to add anything to them in writing or by word of mouth. Naturally I hope that one day the little sons will understand this letter, but I know this is a question of grace and not of any external influence. Since God has the unbelievable grace to be in me I can take with me not only you and the boys, but all those whom I love, and numberless others who are not so near to me. You can tell them that.

One thing more. This letter is in many respects a completion of my report written yesterday, which is far more prosaic. The two in conjunction must be made into an object-lesson, but it must be put together as though Delp had told it about me. I must remain the chief character, not because I am nor because I want to be, but because otherwise the story loses its thread. I have simply been the vessel for which God has taken such endless trouble.

My dear, my life is finished, and I can say of myself 'He died in fullness of years and of life's experience.' This in no way alters the fact that I would gladly go on living, that I would gladly accompany you further on life's journey. But then I should need a new task from

God, since the one for which he created me stands completed. If He is willing to give me another task then it will be made clear to us. So keep going with your efforts to save my life, if I should survive today. Perhaps there may be another task.

I will stop, since there is no more to say. I have named nobody whom you are to salute or embrace for me. You yourself know to whom such requests would apply. All the texts we love are held in my heart as they are in your heart. But I end by saying to you by strength of the treasure which is in me, and which fills this humble earthen vessel:

> The grace of Our Lord Jesus Christ and the
> love of God and the fellowship of the Holy
> Spirit be with you all. Amen.

Freya was allowed to see Helmuth once again. Gerstenmaier, besides the interview already mentioned,* was able once to look through the door into his cell and recognised the book which he was reading as Lilje's *Commentary* on the Book of Revelation. And Lilje, who was in the prison himself on an exaggerated charge, has added his own testimony: 'Right to the end he was completely free in soul, friendly, helpful, considerate, a truly free and noble man amid all the trappings of horror.'[3]

On 23 January Poelchau went to see Helmuth as usual at about eleven o'clock and effected an exchange of letters. But when he glanced into the cell at one o'clock, it was empty for Helmuth had been taken off to Plötzensee, two and a half miles away. Poelchau immediately called up Buchholz, but learnt that Helmuth, although expected at any moment, had not arrived. Buchholz went over at once to the death cell and was able to report to Freya later that Helmuth went on his last journey 'steadfast and calm – even with joy'.

Ten people were executed at Plötzensee on that day, of whom only Helmuth and Haubach belonged to the Kreisau group. Among the other eight was Erwin Planck, with whom he had had supper in Brussels in June 1943.†

Barely ten days later, on 3 February, Freisler had just pronounced a sentence of death and was turning to the case of Fabian von Schlabren-dorff (the man who, though the SD still did not know it, had smuggled the bomb on to Hitler's aircraft on 13 March 1943). At that moment, an air-raid alarm sounded; the court-room was emptied and Freisler with everybody else took refuge in the basement. The building received a direct hit and a beam fell on him, fracturing his skull. The attendants went out to get a doctor, and brought in one whom they came across in the street outside. He happened to be Rolf Schleicher, whose brother

* Above, p. 304.   † Above, p. 262.

Rüdiger (an official in the Legal Department of the Air Ministry and brother-in-law of Dietrich Bonhoeffer) had been on the previous day condemned to death by Freisler.*

Helmuth was, as has been said earlier,† a liberally minded individualist in an authoritarian society – and an authoritarian society suffering from acute paranoia. To be at odds with one's surroundings is bound to be a painful experience and anyone who in consequence finds himself struggling against the tide is lucky if he achieves results which are both positive and practical.

> Patience is more oft the exercise
> Of Saints, the trial of their fortitude,
> Making them each his own Deliverer
> And Victor over all
> That tyranny or fortune can inflict.‡

In a farewell letter to his sons Helmuth wrote:

Throughout my life from my schooldays onwards I have fought against a spirit of narrowness and subservience, of arrogance and intolerance, against the absolutely merciless consistency which is deeply engrained in the Germans and has found its expression in the National Socialist state. I have made it my aim to get this spirit overcome with its evil accompaniments, such as excessive nationalism, racial persecution, lack of faith and materialism. In this sense and seen from their own standpoint the National Socialists are right in putting me to death.

His death cannot therefore be regarded as an accident but as the logical culmination of his life, a tragedy in the most authentic sense of that term. And, grievous as it was for his family and friends to lose him just as all that he stood for seemed to be coming into its own, one cannot be sure how happy or effective he would have been in post-war Germany. Some of the fundamental reasons for its success – the reconciliation between Christians, the healing of the gulf between the workers and the rest of the population, the say given to the workers in

---

* Of the persons mentioned in this book Beck, Bernstorff, Bonhoeffer, Canaris, Delbrück, Delp, Dohnanyi, Goerdeler, Görschen, Guttenberg, Hans Berndt and Werner von Haeften, Ernst von Harnack, Hassell, Haubach, Albrecht Haushofer, Kiep, Langbehn, Leber, Lehndorff, Leuschner, Maass, Oster, Popitz, Reichwein, Sack, Schulenburg, Sperr, Berthold and Claus von Stauffenberg, Tresckow, Trott, Nicholas von Uexküll and Yorck were all executed, many of them after great suffering, quite a few in the very last days of the war.

† Above, p. 24.

‡ Milton, *Samson Agonistes*, lines 1287–92.

industry – are due to the putting into practice of principles which he, along with other people, regarded as essential. But there is much in the Federal (not to mention the Democratic) Republic which runs counter to his ideas and with which he would have been out of sympathy.

Helmuth, however, believed that Fascism in general and National Socialism in particular were not isolated phenomena but only particular and initial examples of a trend to which mass industrialised society was prone. Today it seems possible that he was right, that the answers which were found after 1945 and which seemed to be successful owed that success to the power situation left by the war and that, now the dominance of the victors is waning, the dangers which he emphasised are rising again, reinforced by the effects of further technological development. Intolerant right-wing governments are established in a number of countries. Traditional spiritual and moral values are losing their authority without new ones being convincingly formulated, states are becoming too big to be human, and man as ruled is becoming more and more estranged from man as ruler. The obsession with economic growth (among communists as well as capitalists) is threatening to make life unbearable – if not actually unliveable – while science has invested with fatal possibilities the division of the world into sovereign states recognising in the last resort no means of settling disputes other than violence. Helmuth had the insight thirty years ago to identify these as the problems of the century and the relevance of his diagnoses is even more visible today than it was then.

If he had survived to bear responsibility after 1945, he would probably have come to realise that these tendencies are caused by forces even more deeply rooted than he imagined. For they rest on characteristics of human nature which are not easily sublimated and which, if unskilfully repressed, can burst out again with redoubled vigour. But, if this makes remedies harder to apply, human nature still possesses other higher characteristics and capabilities. And, though Helmuth may have been inclined to pessimism as a shield against disillusion, he never lost faith in the need to make those higher qualities prevail. But the fight that he fought is never won for long. The tides of history are not easily turned and, if the feat can be achieved at all, it is only by the will of numerous individuals sustained over several generations. Those in the present and future must live up to the examples set by those in the past.

But, if that is to happen, those now dead who provide the examples must not be sanctified. Much as we may admire them, we must not exaggerate their dimensions or credit them with abnormal qualities since we should thereby be providing ourselves with an excuse for inaction. Helmuth had weaknesses as well as strengths; like the rest of us, he was not always consistent and he was not always right. If his spiritual stature grew until in the end it was as outstanding as his physical one, that was because he had the strength of mind and character to persevere in the face of evil, adversity and suffering. What he did, others can do. The situation is still as he described it in writing to Freya on 16 November 1941:

What vast problems we face and what a small chance there is of finding a giant to solve them for us! Is it conceivable that a group of ordinary men can manage it? Or is such a group more likely to do it than a giant?

APPENDIX

The Last Months in Kreisau

*AN ACCOUNT WRITTEN BY FREYA VON MOLTKE
IN 1961 AND TRANSLATED BY J.F.*

APPENDIX

The Last Months in Kreisau

AN ACCOUNT WRITTEN BY FREYA VON MOLTKE

O N 25 January 1945 Marion (Yorck) and I travelled from Berlin to Kreisau.* Edith and Henssel took us to the train. They brought some delicious bread and butter for us and Marion had a bottle of old Malaga. The bottle was wrapped in a paper napkin; it looked as though it were coffee with milk. Marion and I sat close together on a double seat in the 3rd class. We travelled on and on endlessly, and got no rest. We were travelling against the tide of refugees and therefore needed exactly twenty-four hours to get to Kreisau, but in memory it remains a good journey. I think we were reasonably cheerful. So far nobody in Kreisau knew of Helmuth's death. Asta had Wend (her husband) there and with him were eight or nine soldiers, a complete anti-aircraft unit. Frau Pick (Helmuth's former housekeeper in Berlin) was in her element cooking for all these men. Marion went straight on to Nimptsch where Muto (Peter Yorck's sister) was in practice, though just then she was in bed with diphtheria. Telling Caspar was very hard for me. He was lying in my bed, where he had been sleeping; I sat on the edge. But we got through it, and when next morning he found me sorrowful he said, 'About Pa? Still?' This was really a great relief.

Everything was in confusion. The Russians were pressing westwards at high speed. For several weeks we had had the Berghaus and the Schloss and the whole village full of refugees from across the Oder. In the Berghaus some were living in the sitting-rooms. Their cart stood unloaded in our little yard and down the hill the whole farmyard was full of other people's vehicles. Something had to be done, but everyone was undecided. Looking back the days seem like weeks, until the old inhabitants of the Schloss, the children, Zeumer's daughters who, like Asta, were expecting babies, and Asta herself, all departed in the ambulance-train from Schweidnitz – heading west. This must have been during the first days of February. Wend and his 'merry men' as

---

* Before Freya left Berlin she had to visit Schultze (the public prosecutor) to get a death certificate. She took the opportunity to give him a piece of her mind, ending up by saying 'I hope that before you die you will have a better understanding of Helmuth von Moltke.'

Frau Pick called them had already gone. The purpose of his little team was that they had with them some especially valuable 'apparatus' which they were to 'protect'. This commission gave them a brilliant excuse over and over again for making themselves scarce. Anyhow, they couldn't stay on with us.

Snow was lying and we drove in two sleighs to Schweidnitz to see off the travellers who were to go by ambulance-train. Asta was sitting in the first sleigh 'back to the engine', and I was in the second 'facing the engine' and even now I can see her still, sad face. All the time it kept reappearing, filled with silent sorrow. What was going to become of us all? Then the first sleigh drew ahead; Asta's face vanished. Ten minutes later we caught them up, and there was her face again with the same expression. Then they all departed. Later, in April when post once more came through from the West, I suddenly got a postcard from Asta. She had gone first to some Wendland relations in Mecklenburg and was just going on from there to Holstein, so as to have her baby with Aunt Leno.

A few days later, after this batch of women and children had gone, Zeumer rang me up early one morning in the Berghaus from the Hof. 'Now it's come to the crunch,' he said, 'we must evacuate our village.' Women and children and old people were to cross into Czechoslovakia, orders from the Party! From the start I was determined to stay. What would become of us on country roads in the middle of winter? Nor were the Russians there yet; also Helmuth had advised me to stay as long as possible. In Ravensbrück he had discussed our situation through the ventilator with General Halder, who was confined to the next cell. They both considered our mountain country safe, believing that the Russians would leave it 'on their left' in their drive to reach Berlin. Romai Reichwein and her children, who were still living in the Schloss, also wanted to stay.

But in the Hof below and along the village street there assembled that morning the unhappy cavalcade. Frau Zeumer went with them, while Zeumer and I stood in the Hof beside the gathering rows of carts. We only kept the horses for the milk-float and a pair of young foals – all the other horses went too. Women and children had already driven off in carts with trailers. But snow was lying on the passes over the Eule, the roads were full of refugees, the trailers might skid – we daren't overload them. Our funny old gardeners, the Stäsches, who had lived beside us on the hill-top, had already gone. Stäsche himself with his distorted, weary face, hardly able to speak and very lame, kept on assuring me that he didn't want to be pole-axed.

That morning Schwester* and her children were still there. I had advised her not to be in any hurry to go with the others. Next morning

* Above, p. 15.

when I went to the village she and all the children in her charge were gone. She had obtained a special army truck and had seized the opportunity. She became separated from the other Kreisauers, reached Bavaria quite quickly and all in all had not too bad a time in those frantic days.

But the life and soul of the village went with her. It hurt me afresh each time during the ensuing months that I passed the empty playground. How often had I gone to see her with or without Helmuth, sat in one of the basket-chairs in her room and discussed the troubles of the village. I can still hear Helmuth asking 'Little Schwester' how are things in the village. She knew everything. With love and great understanding she influenced the grown-ups, and with strict hand and shrill voice she controlled the village children, who all, every one of them, passed through her school. The Field-Marshal had founded the school, it had been supported by the farm until the great crisis occurred. Then it was taken over by the village and thereafter the estate participated only as the largest taxpayer. Schwester was closely linked with everyone, especially with the Moltkes. She had arrived before Jowo was born. When we went to see her we mostly chatted for quite a time and meanwhile the children fretted at the door and wanted to come to 'Mamma' for she maintained herself and her household by taking care of children, who were sent to her by the welfare office – and only with difficulty could she deter them from bursting into the room. In any case she always had one on her lap. In her room things always lay around in heaps. 'Looks nice in here, doesn't it?' she would say sarcastically, flicking her blue deaconess's apron over the table – and we'd settle ourselves in the basket-chairs. Now she was gone and the playground stayed empty.

However, I hadn't much time to brood over it, for almost on the heels of the departure of our villagers Davy Moltke arrived with the evacuees from Wernersdorf. Wernersdorf had been occupied by the Russians, so they'd really had to get out – Davy came with her entire retinue, there were also a number from the Yorck household with her. Soon after Davy and her trekkers Marion and Muto arrived back from Nimptsch. I ran into them on foot near the farm at Nieder Gräditz, a car having dropped them not far away. I was so relieved and happy to see them. Now the village was taken over by German troops. They had come from Prussia and were determined to leave as little as possible for the Russians. Nobody ever came up to the Berghaus – it was too far off the beaten track and looked from a distance thoroughly insignificant. But down in the Hof the waters were rougher. After another week the Wernersdorf trekkers decided to go on into the county of Glatz.

We too were constantly tormented by the question 'Ought we to leave as well?' The Russian front was just over six miles away. The

Russians were firing cannon and by day the noise was disturbing and seemed to be coming nearer. But we were in touch with our German garrison. A major and a lieutenant sat in the Blue House on the road to Gräditz, and in the Schloss a feeding unit was installed on which the front made calls. Food supplies for the troops at the front were stored in all our barns at the Hof. The distribution teams in their Russian-type carts with Russian ponies came dashing down the street and collected their supplies from the Hof. In the cellars and in the former kitchen of the Schloss hung whole deer, sheep and pigs, and sausages in piles. In the hall shoes and clothing were stored. Out of respect for the Field-Marshal the Schloss was not garrisoned. The children loved the food teams because there there were sweets. Zeumer too was delighted because the high-ups of the unit lodged in his house, so he fed on the fat of the land. These people were all well fed, plump – and Nazis, who still talked victory, and later, several days later, insisted that in any case the fight would go on.

We re-buried the Field-Marshal in Helmuth's and my empty grave, him and his wife. His poor sister had to remain by herself in the chapel, where all three coffins had stood side by side. We tried to let down her coffin on top of Papi's, but it wouldn't fit in. Eight NCOs in steel helmets were drafted to carry the coffins down the slope. It was quite dignified and at the same time so hopeless. We often went to the Blue House to ask about the war situation, and to take advantage of the help which our connection with the army gave us against the Party. One day another inhabitant of the Blue House sought us out. He wanted to know whether we were staying or whether we intended to leave. He was determined to stay. He was an old opponent of the Nazis, and through his daughter had made contact with two Russian workmen, who were in reality Russian officers and spies. From these two Russians he had obtained a pass.

Those men who had not long since been called up stayed on in the village. Some of the women, too, seeing that everything remained unchanged and the front came no nearer, returned to Kreisau on the sly from Czechoslovakia for shorter or longer periods. Our people were sitting in a village in the Bohemian plain not far from Prague. Some of the farmers' wives came back for good. However, at the Hof there were only Poles still working. Romai continued to live on the top floor in the Schloss, but each evening 'come hell or high water' she came up to the Berghaus to hear the English news. We tried to prepare our eventual retreat in the light of all possibilities. We deposited a cartload of potatoes, flour, and one or two trunks at Michelsdorf in the mountains near the Weistritz dam. This meant a long bicycle ride into the mountains. The villages of the Eulengebirge had not yet been evacuated, but were in constant dread of that happening today or tomorrow or the day after.

On such expeditions we used to enjoy the beauty of the countryside to the full. Individual Russian planes would come over and drop bombs. Mostly they were attacking the aerodrome at Weizenrodau. One saw our planes take off from there, also dropping bombs. It looked like a game, not like something really dangerous. And so one morning, just as though nothing was happening, Marion, Muto and I gaily pedalled from Ludwigsdorf to Leutmannsdorf, just after several bombs had fallen there and a number of people had been killed. I saw the body of a woman lying on a dungheap by the upper mill, and when we came to the pastor's we found there a child badly wounded in the head lying at death's door. Beautiful the dying child looked, and full of knowledge; the rattle was in its throat, the mother wept, the pastor comforted her. Marion was deeply moved. We had wanted to ask the pastor for addresses deeper in the mountains where we and the six children might in certain circumstances find a refuge. Frau Pick was very scared and wanted to leave. After her Berlin experiences she couldn't stand bombs any more and she claimed to know for certain which bang came from a gun and which from a bomb. She wanted to go, go, go and if I spoke of going she wanted to stay, stay, stay. All this passed over the children's heads. They played, ate, slept, and hadn't a care in the world. But as I look back it seems to me that it all passed over my head too. It went on from day to day but it was all like a dream.

Next came several severe warnings from the local Party leadership in Gräditz that I must leave Kreisau directly, and finally the order to leave Kreisau within two days, otherwise we should be escorted from place to place by the police. I cycled to Gräditz to the Party office. It was situated next door to our butcher's, where once Herr Suhr, and later a young butcher, had sold us meat, until they were both condemned to long terms of imprisonment for slaughtering for the black market – neither of them was Nazi. It was opposite the brickworks which ultimately became a camp for Jews. The whole place was in chaos and the local Party boss wasn't a bit pleased to see me. The whole Moltke case was extremely disagreeable to him. He assured me in a really friendly way that to have six children in his 'territory' was quite impossible, but Wierischau was not part of his territory, so he didn't mind what happened there, and was quite ready to allow me a week's grace. So a week later all the children and Romai moved into two rooms in the grange at Wierischau which was standing empty. This really didn't go badly. They lived there very contentedly, often coming to see me at the Berghaus, where also we celebrated Easter. Marion and Muto wanted to see their family again, who meanwhile had moved to Mecklenburg. Then I lost my nerve and decided after all to take the children away. Romai had a short time before discovered an empty cottage in Pommerndorf above Hohenelbe in the Riesengebirge about 3,000 feet above sea-level. But it stood on the Czech side of the range. Thither we decided to go, and after Easter really went. Two cartloads of things, the six children, Fräulein Hirsch – the forester's daughter – Aunt Leno's Bertha, Frau Pick, Romai and I. Two of our Poles were the coachmen. All the time I had the feeling that this effort was unnecessary, but hadn't the nerve to stay put. I remember that I said to Marion and Muto, before they went off, that I must 'bite the apple', and bite we did. The first day we got as far as Michelsdorf, the second to Friedland, the third to Trautenau. The children stayed there with Frau Pick and Romai in the hotel, and followed me, the Poles, Fräulein Hirsch and Bertha by train to Hohenelbe next day. Here everything was still running in orderly fashion, and this region lying in Czechoslovakia, protected by mountains, had in all respects been spared the onslaught of war. The trek was lovely. Spring had come, the weather was dry and sunny. Slowly and steadily our two heavily laden carts rolled up hill and down dale. I remember a particularly beautiful stretch between Friedland and Schönberg, a lovely road over a pass. The children remained at the inn below and had potato soup. Fräulein Hirsch and I in one cart with the four horses went on ahead. Then the horses went back and fetched the children and the other cart to which a trailer had been attached for any child who might be tired. Fräulein Hirsch and I waited in the wood at the top. That hour in the wood while Fräulein Hirsch slept is unforgettable to me. Away beyond the pass spread the view of the Riesengebirge. It embraced the very heart of the Silesian mountains and had the whole beauty of this landscape, a special combination of gentleness and strength in colour and form, of great distances and charming foreground. As usual the children were quite unaffected and enjoyed the whole thing as an exciting adventure. We had great difficulty in getting the heavy carts up the steep hill above Hohenelbe. We found the little house high up in the mountains, one of a group of about ten on a great grassy slope. We lived split up between three cottages; Fräulein Hirsch and Bertha rather nearer civilisation in the house of the mayor of Pommerndorf, separated from us by twenty minutes' walk along a lovely woodland track. The elder children were soon going to the local school under a Nazi teacher. He had, however, by this time seen the light sufficiently to treat our children well. We added to our stores because there was still plenty to eat in Bohemia, although we had brought provisions with us.

After three weeks I left the children so as to have a look at Kreisau. I set off by bicycle. Actually I had only intended to cycle as far as Trautenau, that is to say out of the mountains and then parallel with them north-eastwards, about three hours' ride. One has the mountain-range on the left in full splendour. I rode through the landscape in all its spring greenery, well farmed, looking like Austria. Arriving in Trautenau between midday and one o'clock, I discovered that the next train was not due to leave until the following morning. It was still early and I was full of beans. So I decided to see how far in the direction of Kreisau I could get. I now knew the whole area well and its perfect spring beauty delighted me. After Friedland I began to tire, and Helmuth's bicycle, on which so far I had ridden very comfortably, suddenly became uncomfortable. But I knew that from the top of the Reinsbach valley, the so-called Valley of Silesia, it was downhill all the way to Kreisau. So on I went, on and on, saw my friend the Eule from behind, then passed into its shadow, rode down the long Wüstewaltersdorf valley, skirted Kynau and the Weistritz dam, and coasted down the beautiful lakeside road to Oberweistritz. The daylight now began slowly to fade, but my joy that I should soon see the Mühlberg and the Kapellenberg on the skyline, the growing joy at coming home lent me wings. The spring evening was heavenly. I left the hills and rode towards Ludwigsdorf. The Kappellenberg surfaced with its spruce trees, the Mühlberg with its fuzz of accacias, and once I had breasted the little ridge at Ludwigsdorf there lay Wierischau, there lay Kreisau before me, there the Berghaus beckoned under its big accacia. It was simply lovely to get home. Muto and Marion were back from Mecklenburg, hadn't expected to see me and received me with joy. There was the house, my room, my bed. It was about 7.30, I'd started at 9.30 and it must be over sixty miles through the mountains. That evening I felt that on this journey home all the happiness and all the riches of our life in Kreisau once more came together in me.

I stayed in Kreisau three or four days. I have especially happy memories of them. Then I set out again and went back to the children. That must have been in the last days of April, with the Third *Reich* sinking rapidly to its end. The Russians were fighting in Berlin, Hitler was besieged in the *Reich* chancellery. We sat on our mountain top and tried to get news. We had no radio. So then Romai and I went up still higher to the châlet of her old friend, thanks to whom she had found our little house. Just as we arrived it was being announced that the Russians had captured Berlin. It was thought that Hitler had taken his own life in the chancellery. The people up there said, 'can one believe it?' But I knew at once and for sure: that's how it is. The Third *Reich* was finished! Now the Russians would take over Kreisau. I had the feeling that in that case I must be there. Once more I left the children with Romai and Frau Pick. This time Fräulein Hirsch came back with me. Again we cycled, but stayed overnight on the way. In Kreisau I waited with Marion and Muto for the Russians. German men were uneasy. We had never had any out-and-out Nazis in the village, but the half-Nazis were scared. They asked me what they should do. 'Stay,' I said. Then Zeumer had a good idea. 'Now, before it is completely finished,' he said, 'we must get the evacuees back. If we wait it may be too late.' He was worried about his wife. 'I'll go over and fetch everybody back.' And this he did, and so left Kreisau. Even the Poles, whom we had had with their families for years working on the farm, now became uneasy. 'If you are staying,' said one of them, 'then we'll stay too.' One day at this time I was walking through the village when down the cherry avenue came a motor-bike ridden by a Russian soldier; behind him sat a civilian, and the front of the bike was decked with a spray of lilac. The soldier stopped when he saw me. The passenger, obviously a Pole, asked me in broken German whether the bridge across the Peile was still intact, and when I said 'Yes' they drove across the bridge to the station and then back again. A few hours later the Russian army began to roll through Kreisau – objective the mountains and Czechoslovakia. It was an amazing spectacle. Primitive-looking material, carts piled high with booty, wretched mechanisation, but the men defiant, healthy, strong – triumphant. A torrent of vitality poured through the little, remote village of Kreisau, whose bridge by being intact had suddenly become significant. Marion, Muto and I did not want to miss this performance, but we soon gave up because the Russian soldiers chased after all women, and we had been standing openly right and left of the entrance to the Kreisau farmyard, beside the piers below the two gladiators, and that was not sensible. We fled, and during the coming days learnt the art of concealment. We also did not sleep at the Berghaus, but in the little barn of our neighbour on the Berghaus hill, or else in old people's houses. These days were the only time when we felt really insecure. But after the army had passed through everything quietened down and after some days we even ventured to walk into Schweidnitz. There we hoped to get protection from the commanding officer against assault. We actually forced our way in to him, and asked if he knew how the Russians were behaving all around. He had no idea what we wanted, merely remarked quite amiably that 'every man needs a woman – that's the way it goes'.

Even before we went to Schweidnitz the evacuees actually came back, fit and well, with all their horses and chattels, quite uninjured by the Russian army driving on in the opposite direction to take over Czechoslovakia. The Russians only encouraged them to go back to their villages. Zeumer had urged speedy departure, had guided the column along side-roads and crossed the Czech–German frontier before the Czechs themselves had anything to say. It was not a reassembly of the whole village, but many farmers' families were back again and all our women from the Hof.

I was fretting about the children and wanted to collect my own little bunch of evacuees. Zeumer gave me a horse, an old, light cart and a young man along with them who was a baker and knew as little about

horses as I did, but was full of good-will. A semi-invalid with acute
rheumatism of the joints, he had not been a soldier. A Russian had
written out for me in Russian on a piece of paper, 'This woman is on
the way to fetch her children home.' Nothing more, above all no official
stamp. I can't recall whether it was signed. Once more I took the well-
known road over the mountains. I had two hurdles to surmount, only
two, although by now there were returning Russian soldiers to be encountered along the road. I remember that a young tough accosted my
cart, rummaged through my rucksack and examined everything, but
only took away a good pocket-knife. The first hurdle was a Pole, who
came towards us leading a gang of people. He coveted my horse. Then
it wasn't good enough for him. He gave it a thwack and let us go on.
The second hurdle was two Russians, who stopped us and seemed to
want to know what we were doing. I held out my scrap of paper to
them. The senior of the two took a dim view of it, but the less important one reasoned with him. I didn't understand a word, but it
sounded like 'Oh let her carry on!' and he did just that. And so with
my Willy I eventually reached the children. There I found all the
grown-ups looking pale. Something really horrible had happened. The
Germans had collected in a camp over 3,000 feet up in the Riesengebirge the so-called Wlassow Russians. These were Russians who were
prepared to fight against Communism, and who were training there.
These Russians were scared of their advancing compatriots, and at the
last moment the Germans had dissolved the camp and allowed the
inmates to escape armed. The most important thing for these men was,
of course, to get rid of their German uniforms and acquire civilian
clothes. A few days before my return Renate Reichwein (a daughter)
had, as every morning, gone to fetch milk from the farmer next door,
who was also our landlord. The farmyard was quite isolated, separated
from our hillside by a belt of woodland. Renate found the kitchen
empty, and looked for the farmer's wife in the house and in the stable.
There lay all four members of the family murdered. Russians looking
for clothes had killed them all. They had fought shy of the group of
houses where we were living. It was just before Whitsun. The weather
was marvellous. Romai suggested postponing the return journey until
after Whitsun. But I didn't want to put it off for a single day. Once
again we got ourselves a certificate. This time it was in Czech and
written by a schoolmistress there, and it had more on it. In this sense:
'These women, whose husbands were condemned to death and executed
by the National Socialist Régime, are returning with their children to
their native village, Kreisau in Silesia.' And again the certificate did us
good service. The trek back was not easy. We only took one cart and
the dog-cart. We left a lot of luggage in the mountains. We had only
three horses. One pair had been quartered all the time at a farm in the

valley. They were well fed and in good condition, but the cart was piled high with our luggage and provisions under a tarpaulin, so that the horses had a hard time. One wheel of the cart broke in pieces, and what's more on the Czech side of the frontier. I fetched the blacksmith, who actually made the cart road-worthy with an old wheel, without our having to unload everything – we had managed to shove wood blocks under the broken wheel on both sides. He shook his head over us. 'Strange people you be!' Obviously not peasants, knowing nothing about horses or carts, no sensible man in charge. He wasn't used to such travellers. But the Sudeten Germans were friendly and we all stood up well to the fatigue. We slept the first night in the hay at the farm of a Sudeten German. Next morning we reached the frontier. On both sides of the road German military vehicles lay abandoned in the ditches; one could pick up bundles of German money in the bushes. We didn't touch anything, just drove on. Slowly we advanced. On Whit Saturday we reached the convent of Grüssau. We stayed there overnight and on Whit Sunday heard High Mass in the beautiful great Baroque church. It was full and very splendid. Then off we went once more. On a slope beyond Grüssau, as the horses were exhausted, I put a rock behind one of the wheels and the fourth finger of my right hand was crushed. It was not so very bad, but all the same the horses had to pull forward to release my finger; and it has been crooked ever since. Soon after that our much loved little dog, Flitz, a black Aberdeen terrier, who had mostly kept up with us so slow was our progress, lagged behind and was run over by a Russian lorry. Fräulein Hirsch stayed behind with the bicycle long enough to bury the little creature. These, however, were our only mishaps, and it still seems to me a miracle that those five women, six children and half a man really got back to Kreisau safe and sound. I had a little spasm of pride as I drove downhill from Ludwigsdorf to Wierischau that I had brought safely back to Zeumer his team for the milk-cart, which after Easter he had torn out of his heart to give us.

And so the summer began. At first we noticed little of the Russians. To begin with we had only a small garrison and they left us more or less in peace. At first they wanted to make me mayor, but I was unwilling, and we got instead a good Kreisau man who turned out very well. As soon as possible we got down to work. We tilled the fields again. We had a modicum of labour, we had our horses, we had machines, we had cows. It was not our own herd. At the beginning of February these had been commandeered by the Party and driven off to the abattoir at Waldenburg. Zeumer had resisted, but was severely threatened and had to let the cattle go. But, during the chaos caused by evacuating the villages into Czechoslovakia, a lot of cattle had simply been let loose and were standing about in the meadows bellowing – because they hadn't been milked. They couldn't be left in the lurch and so very soon our beautiful, great, old byre stood brim-full with this motley collection. They were still there when the war ended. In some ways it was difficult, but we got going and paid our people with provisions. We all had enough to eat and now and again we killed a cow for the whole village. I bicycled into Schweidnitz and sought out our former schoolmistress, Fräulein Seiler, who was the daughter of the photographer. We took her in with us in the Berghaus and opened up the school again. Romai and her children also moved into the Berghaus. In February we had emptied the sitting-rooms downstairs for the first batch of refugees. The Reichweins took these over. A full, well-used house was more easily kept from the Russians. And one day Liesbeth also came back from Striegau. Brought up by Schwester, she had been house-cum-nursemaid with us. When we left she decided to go to her mother. Now she came back. Muto and Marion made a great reconnaissance on foot to Kauern and Klein Öls, dragging a light trailer behind them with their rucksacks. Later they undertook as a priority to leave Silesia and look up their relations in Mecklenburg. But they kept coming back to the Berghaus at intervals.

In the village, in the Hof, in the Berghaus everyone was living a more or less ordered working life. The children were in splendid form. The household was running; I spent a lot of time in the Hof, the village, and going about the neighbourhood, and drove across the fields with Zeumer as in the past. At first the Russians still tried occasionally to get into the house of an evening, but our front door stood up to the assault, and we were careful each night to shut all the window shutters and doors. But it was not a bit pleasant when a Russian hammered like mad on the door or rattled the latch. It was, however, well known that such enterprises would not be supported by the authorities, while if one managed to summon outside help – even Germans – then the Russians would run away. So I sat upstairs with the fire-alarm, so as to summon Raschke, our neighbour, in case of need – but it never came to that.

The Russians stole also – but only now and again – once chickens from me. I caught the Russian in the act. If you stood up to them fearlessly they were always reasonable, even friendly – only if one showed fright they got wild and couldn't cope with it. The chickens – we only had fifteen or so left – laid zealously and were very valuable to us. They now lived with us at the Berghaus. Following in Mami Moltke's footsteps I had left them in the Hof in the care of old Rose, who invariably cosseted the newly hatched chicks for some days in her bed. Frau Zeumer despised our lackadaisical attitude to the poultry. That was not suitable for a Silesian countrywoman! And indeed many eggs went astray between the Hof and the Berghaus. But it satisfied me so long as Rose appeared each week in the Berghaus with a big white enamel basin full of eggs and drank coffee with Mamsell. Now the flock had diminished from around fifty to about fifteen and this residue was safer close to us. So that the cry 'There's a Russian in the hen-house' sounded far from agreeable. I can still see the Russian's cheerful face as he pushed one hen after another into a sack. 'Not all of them,' I cried in panic. Laughing he shook his head, held up six fingers and then vanished with his booty.

Defending the bicycles was difficult. They all wanted them and they were very important to us. I caught one Russian just as he was riding my last reserve bike out of the Berghaus yard. I tried to explain to him how important a bike was for us. He understood me quite well. He would return the bike that evening, he promised. That was the stock answer and everyone knew it was a lie. So then I laughed and he laughed and he left me the bike.

During the summer the Schloss was occupied by a whole (Russian) company. They were to control our harvest. Fräulein Hirsch was once more installed in the basement of the Schloss. She had already lived there during the war years with her father, who later died. Old Hirsch had come to Kreisau as a forester on pension. In exchange for free lodging he regularly walked through the various woods and kept in order the Kapellenberg and the Field-Marshal's mausoleum (where the family burial ground was as well). He also worked for the lessees of the shooting. In the years when he was trying to save Kreisau from compulsory auction Helmuth had let the shooting to a group of doctors in Schweidnitz, and this arrangement lasted until the end. After Hirsch's death his daughter had kept on the dwelling in the basement of the Schloss, and had taken over the care of the Field-Marshal's room as well as the Kapellenberg. The room in which the Field-Marshal had lived, behind the great white and gold dining room, had been left unchanged after his death. From his wig-stand of pink porcelain and the small wash-basin to his felt slippers and the great black mantel of the Knights of Malta, made of moiré silk, which hung in the wardrobe, from his crested helmet to a family tree of the Moltkes which covered a whole wall, everything was still there. There were often pilgrims who visited the Kapellenberg and then asked to see the room, over and over again they were deeply impressed by the modesty of this room, and most particularly during the Nazi period. 'That the room of a field-marshal!' Mostly the aunts had acted as guides when they were in residence at the Schloss – always in summer and sometimes in winter. But when they were not there the Hirsch family came to the rescue. When during the war the Schloss filled up with refugees, families from Berlin who wanted to get away from the bombing, Fräulein Hirsch became a sort of custodian there. She was delighted to do it and was a great help to me. She was a real good soul. She was on terms of friendship with the better 'ladies' of the village, and she stuck to us through thick and thin. At this period after the evacuation she had set up in the basement of the Schloss with Aunt Leno's famous Bertha. Bertha was also typically Silesian, efficient, spruce and hard-working. Heart and brain were in the right place. When Aunt Leno and her grandchildren left in the ambulance-train she had decided to stay 'with the things' and to keep guard for Aunt Leno. Now with the Russian company in the Schloss the two women found work and food. Fräulein Hirsch helped in the kitchen, Bertha did sewing, mostly bust-bodices. These were in great demand by the Russian women – and of them there were all shapes and sizes. I visited Fräulein Hirsch and Bertha every few days, and brought myself up to date on the latest Russian gossip. What they ate, how much better the captain lived – he got his potatoes fried only in the best butter – the women's tales, what an awful state the lavatories were in – they were soon abandoned and the whole personnel, including the captain, used two huts outside. The two old girls were overflowing with it all, and they wanted my advice. Fräulein Hirsch was diffident, even if she basically knew what she wanted, but Bertha refused to countenance anything and for that reason was generally respected.

Soon after the occupation we were ordered to hand in our radios. I could not make up my mind to give mine up just like that without more ado. It was our only link with the world, and we had it on every evening, when we listened to the BBC news. Heavy penalties were fixed for those not complying with the order to hand over, but we didn't take that too seriously. Zeumer had two radios and he, who rightly did not want to take any risks, offered me his second radio to hand in. And that was what we did. We left our radio standing in the sitting-room covered with a cloth. Left so openly, we thought it would be least likely to be noticed, and this proved to be the case. All summer we listened each evening as quietly as possible to the English news. In the end we became quite well known among the Germans in the area as being better informed than other people. Often people who wanted to know what was happening in the outside world, and to be advised what they should do, came to us, especially when it became clear that the area was to become Polish. This first became certain after the Potsdam Agreement. Kreisau lies between the two rivers Neisse, the Glatzer Neisse and the Görlitzer Neisse, and even at the time when the Polish take-over, which the Russians tolerated, was clearly foreseeable, it remained undecided whether this region was really to become Polish. In the meantime the Poles wanted to create *faits accomplis*. First the authorities in Schweidnitz became Polish. When we had to do with them they were, generally speaking, not unfriendly. One day a German appeared who had been deputed by the Poles to manage Kreisau. He came from the east and had worked together with them there. He was certainly not a bad man. He left Zeumer in his position, was friendly and forthcoming with me, discussed all questions of management with me, saw to it that our household had bread, butter and milk, and when he was no longer allowed to supply us with milk procured a goat for us. Zeumer, who was always difficult, self-willed and uncouth, along with many other good qualities, and whom Helmuth had always known how to handle, got absolutely furious over this man. He had to move out of his house and leave it to him, but was installed very comfortably in the manor of Nieder Gräditz in one of our nice new workers' flats. Of course, he had now become the second man in the business and that was hard on him, even if he was intelligent enough to see that he was doing comparatively well out of it. It was in the interests of this manager to let everything continue to run along the existing rails for the time being, and so we all carried on not too badly. But now came the last of Zeumer's and my drives together over the fields – in unusually dramatic fashion.

Zeumer in his gig, a little light two-wheeled cart to which one horse was harnessed, was a familiar sight to everyone in Kreisau. It looked a dangerous vehicle. The seat, constantly repaired, was perched high above the quite unprotected wheels, and in this contraption one drove on more or less regardless, horse, cart and passenger across slopes, through ditches, up hill and down dale, across plough and meadow. Since the outbreak of the war I'd driven round the various works with Zeumer, mostly between one work break and the next, sometimes quite early, sometimes during the midday break. Sometimes we would stay quite a time in one area, sometimes we covered a large part of the estate. Asta, who to avoid any other war-work had for some time in the early days driven the tractor at Kreisau, always said that it only needed something to go wrong and Zeumer and his little cart would appear over the horizon. In his own particular way he was a very good manager. This enabled me to give Helmuth precise, daily reports on the state of the various activities and the situation on the estate, and so he could keep in close touch with Kreisau all the year round. In the whole five years I never once fell from this vehicle. I remember Carl Berndt being amazed about it. Now one day in this summer when we were driving round together, the pony stumbled coming downhill along the cherry avenue. It took fright, broke loose, the shaft shot upwards and the cart fell over backwards. Zeumer and I both went flying. I didn't hurt myself at all, but lay still for a while, actually only because I was so comfortable and because my head was buzzing. Worried people came running, as well as Zeumer who had also not been hurt. I stood up, reassured everyone, went home and lay down for a while. And never again did either Zeumer or I have a chance to drive across the fields. On our last drive, although we didn't know it was the last, we both came a cropper.

On the smallholdings too, Poles appeared, took over the farmyards, lay in the farmers' beds, and let the Germans work for them. This happened at one farm after another. Many of these Poles came from the eastern areas which had been transferred to Russia. Some German farmers were treated like slaves, others reconciled themselves with 'their' Poles, and almost all wanted in spite of everything to stay in their own homes for as long as possible. But in August the evacuation of the villages began. We heard about it from other regions. With us it stayed quiet for some time yet.

After Marion and Muto, Romai was the next to leave us, to attempt a trip to Berlin. She was away for some time and came back one day with wonderful written statements for us, on which the Municipal Council of Berlin – then still occupied only by the Russians – had declared in five languages, German, Russian, Polish, English and French, with official stamp and signature, that our husbands had been murdered and that we were victims of Fascism and therefore should be well treated. She had had a look round Berlin, but for the time being there was no question of her wanting to leave Kreisau. As usual she'd had various adventures on the way, had accepted a lift from a Russian lorry and, when one of the men got fresh with her and she in consequence bit him in the thumb, had been thrown off the moving lorry. Luckily what with one thing and another there had been so much shouting and noise in the back of the lorry that the driver had braked and they were going quite slowly – so really nothing had happened to her. The lorry simply drove on. All the same . . . !

At the beginning of July something exciting for us occurred: the Western Allies moved into Berlin, took over their particular sectors and began to administer Berlin together with the Russians, so as to be able to set up there the Control Commission for the whole of Germany. The Americans and English had not long been in Berlin when Marion and Muto also showed up there, arriving from Kreisau. On their very first evening they visited some friends. After supper the doorbell rang and there stood an English officer. Why he had come to just that house I don't know. Anyhow his object was to inquire if the inhabitants of the house had any information about Helmuth Moltke's wife and children in Silesia. When Muto and Marion said, 'We've arrived from there today,' he could hardly believe it. He had been commissioned by our English friends and this was his first attempt to find out something. Only next morning, when the two women called on him in his office and confirmed all their statements, did he really believe it to be true – and thus contact with our English friends was re-established.

Meanwhile our Russian company in Kreisau had got used to us and we to them. We knew one another by sight, but the Russians generally speaking did not talk to us. All the same they knew exactly who we were. One of the soldiers once said to Fräulein Hirsch that we were being left in peace only because of our husbands. Most women in every class, and above all those previously in the top class, had to work in the fields. A friendly soldier, who also found our cucumbers attractive, arrived one day with his girl-friend – also in uniform – and demanded to see the 'Contessa'. I had met him at the front door with bare legs in rubber boots – I had just been watering the said cucumbers, and my hair was tied up with a head-scarf, having just been washed. He absolutely refused to believe that I was the 'Contessa'. He simply laughed in my face. I called to Frau Pick to come to the rescue, would she please tell the man who I was. He didn't believe her either. In the end I fetched my passport. That convinced him. Later he came again and yet again, whether for the cucumbers or me remained obscure.

A couple of Russians had seen our pretty Liesbeth working in the fields and came up after her. Liesbeth hid in the attic under some large laundry-baskets when they rang our doorbell. They were two very nice lads. I negotiated with them. She wasn't available and they couldn't see her: but they besought me, they only just wanted to *see* Liesbeth. Would they promise to go away afterwards. Yes, that they'd solemnly promise. All right, I'd fetch her. And she came after I'd reasoned with her, slowly, and on the stairs some way from the bottom she remained standing like a princess. The Russians beamed, gazed at her a while, exchanged a few words and then dutifully departed. We were delighted that all had gone so well, and shut the door behind them. It must have been between seven and eight o'clock in the evening. Up I was going to my room when down the stairs towards me, in fits of laughter, comes one of the boys, and still laughing leaves the house a second time. He'd just shown what he could do if he chose! Outside he had swarmed up one of the iron stanchions which supported the ugly but useful corrugated iron porch. He had then climbed through the open window of the children's room and came down through the house. Konrad who had already gone up to bed, remembers to this day the Russian who went through his room. 'No,' he still says, 'I was not scared.' Every Russian had always been friendly to the children, and always admired Konrad's lovely short curls which covered his head in great soft light-brown waves. These they had to stroke, and so for the children the Russians were not people of whom one was afraid. The two lads returned several times. In the end they even sat with Liesbeth in the kitchen and played Black Peter with her and Frau Pick. For this one of them wore a top-hat which he had found in the house and which he considered half-beautiful, half-comic. I made him a present of it. But someone must have forbidden them to visit us, for after a bit they came no more. Perhaps they were posted away, as they did not belong to the company at the Schloss.

When Romai got back from Berlin and the terms of the Potsdam

Agreement became known – our radio still gave us the news each evening – the time seemed to have come for me also to go to Berlin so as to write letters from there, to talk to our friends and take counsel for the future. However well things had gone for us so far, as time passed it looked more and more certain that we should have to leave. We were completely cut off from the west. To be sure I had from time to time entrusted news for my mother to people who were trying to get through to West Germany from Silesia. But we had heard nothing. There was no post and trains ran very irregularly.

But before I left I had a significant experience. During the summer the Poles had set up a sort of militia. In the main they openly recruited it from people who had done forced labour in Germany. They were men who had suffered much in Germany and hate was written all over their faces. They were an entirely different type from the Poles who were taking over the land all round us. Most of them were also active Communists. They were the ones who beat people up, imprisoned them, cheated them. The Germans complained bitterly about the Militia, and Poles too sometimes. So, then, a militiaman arrived on our doorstep one day, and in a rough and insolent tone demanded to see our papers. What it was about him that so annoyed me I don't know, probably only his offensive manner. I said that I didn't let myself be spoken to like that in my own house, and what authority had he to see our papers. If he couldn't behave decently I'd show him absolutely nothing, on the contrary I'd lay a complaint against him. He was livid and threatened me with his revolver. But I knew perfectly well that he wouldn't shoot and said, 'Get out of my house!' Frau Pick's horrified murmur under her breath, 'Gräfin Moltke!' still sounds in my ears. Standing in the kitchen door she had witnessed this scene. The man put away his revolver, gave me a swingeing box on the ear and departed.

At that time we none of us knew for certain exactly how our relations stood to Russians and Poles, or which was the boss, and we all preferred to recognise the Russians rather than the Poles. Actually the Poles took over the general administration of the country, while the Russians were just the occupying military power.

With one red and one pale cheek I hurried off at once to the Schloss to the Russian captain. I should be most uneasy to leave the children exposed to acts of tyranny by the Poles. I had to go to Berlin on matters to do with my husband, I told the somewhat astonished captain. This – showing my cheek – had happened to me. Might I put the children and our house under his protection while I was away, in case more Poles should come? To this the captain agreed without further ado, and I was really relieved and calmed. The Russians didn't like the Poles, gave the Germans the benefit of every doubt, and treated the Poles badly. And indeed Russian protection soon proved to be effective.

Far the best way of getting to Berlin was from Waldenburg, because the first coal trains to reach Berlin after the end of the war were from the Waldenburg coalfield. As soon as a coal train was coupled together, away it went. Here and there a few empty goods-wagons would be joined on because troops had to be moved, or perhaps for the many women and children who always wanted to go too. The crews on these trains were still Germans. When Frau Raschke, the wife of our neighbour and a smallholder, heard that I wanted to go to Berlin she asked to come too. Her mother was in Berlin and she would like to see her. It was all right with me. I left the children well protected in the Berghaus and set off with Frau Raschke. In Waldenburg we actually managed to install ourselves in a cattle-truck, and late that afternoon our train set off. But about halfway we were all turned out of the truck: it had been attached for the transport of some Russians. There we stood in the middle of the night, and there was nothing else for us to do but climb up on to the coal. That was not too bad for us, but in the truck had been families with small children, prams and luggage: they all had to climb up on top of the coal. However, it was a warm August night, clear and starlit and with wonderful air, we weren't cold. We two found a place up in front, fairly high up on a heap of coal. Towards dawn we grew sleepy, and that was dangerous because one could easily fall off the coal in one's sleep. Frau Raschke kept on calling, 'Don't go to sleep, Frau Gräfin!' But it was quite exciting enough not to go to sleep. There was a guard of Russians in charge of the train. Whenever the train stopped all sorts of thieves immediately sprang aboard. The coal and the passengers' luggage were both at that time worth gold. The thieves waited on the platforms for the trains and then made a killing. We often heard them rummaging about in our vicinity. Then the people on the coal all yelled and shouted, and the Russian guard in reply fired several times in the air. This didn't seem to make much impression on the robbers, because the groping around soon began again and the whole process started afresh. That kept us awake. We travelled on through the dawn, and around seven in the morning found ourselves in Nieder Schöneweide, a suburb of Berlin. But from there one could take the city railway – and it was running.

In Berlin I lived in the Hortensienstrasse, in Peter and Marion's dear little house. After Peter's death the SS took over the house with all its contents. When Marion after her release from prison rang the bell the door was opened to her by a woman wearing her clothes and decked with her jewellery. However, it all turned out quite well in the end. True the house had been damaged by bombs but it was still habitable. The SS inhabitants had left everything in place, the Russian tide had flowed over it and away, and then an elderly plumber and his wife, who had worked for the Yorcks, immediately took possession. Thus it came about that everything seemed unchanged. Many of the household utensils had been stolen, but all the rest was still there. To be sure other people were living in the house, but at once it became, as it had been ever since our flat was burnt out, a real home in Berlin. Marion and Muto were away and I slept in the sitting-room. Now I wrote again to my mother, for the first time to my brother Carl in Switzerland, to Lionel Curtis in England and to Dorothy Thompson in the United States. I sought out those German friends who I thought were in Berlin, got in touch with the English and Americans and asked them to forward my letters. In this way I came in contact with Allen Dulles's Intelligence Unit which was in Dahlem, and made the acquaintance of Dulles himself, of several friendly officers and of Gero von Schulze-Gävernitz. They all knew about us, wished to be informed about conditions in Silesia, and were very dubious when I said I wanted to return there. I also had a message for a Communist who was one of the leaders of the party in Berlin. In one of the villages near Kreisau, Faulbrück, an old Communist had lived throughout the Nazi period. One day this man sought me out and during the ensuing months we had kept in touch. Now he wanted to know from the Berlin Communists how the people in Silesia should behave towards the Poles and Russians, whether they should stay or whether they should leave. I went to the party offices of the KPD (German Communist Party) near the Spittelmarkt, where they made great play with 'mate' and 'comrade'. I had to wait some time and then the man received me and gave me rather vague information. Vague because the Party was not yet clear how it would behave, and the evacuation of Silesia was only just beginning. He didn't say much except that the Communists should behave like everyone else.

To be on the safe side I registered the children and myself with the police as being resident at No. 50 Hortensienstrasse. Then I was ready for the journey back. However, a Swede had told me that in certain circumstances the Reichwein children could soon, if they wished, go to Sweden. So I wanted to wait for a definite decision. I allowed a day or two for that. I had a longing for the Poelchaus' flat in Tegel. I didn't expect to find the Poelchaus in Berlin, they had intended to wait for the end (of the war) with their friends the Truchsess, in Northern Bavaria. Truchsess himself had also been confined in Tegel and Harald had made friends with him. I just wanted to look again at the dwelling which had become so dear to me in the months before Helmuth's death, where I had seemed almost to live 'with' Helmuth. It was still rather troublesome to get there, but the Underground ran part of the way and then one could take a tram. Inside the house I climbed the stairs; the Poelchaus lived on the top floor. I rang and waited. It was Gertie Siemsen, a friend of the Poelchaus, who opened the door. She was living there with her baby born early in March. She said at once: 'Do you know who's lodging with me? Your brother-in-law, Wend!' Today one can hardly imagine how amazing it was that we should find one another. Naturally I had heard and seen nothing of him since the end of February when he drove off from Schweidnitz, waving from his army truck, while I stood there on the sidewalk. It was now the end of August. Soon afterwards he had been run into and injured by a German army truck, could not walk and landed up in a hospital in the Lausitz. There the Russians caught up with him, and had only recently discharged him from hospital, they were not interested in men who were not fit. He had travelled to Berlin and was now trying to get through to Asta 'in the west'. So far Asta knew nothing of his whereabouts. We were both very glad and very relieved to see one another. Wend possessed nothing, and I also had nothing which was any good to him, but a pair of stockings from Muto or Marion came in most useful! We spent my last day together and next morning he took me and my good Frau Raschke to Nieder Schöneweide, whence the empty coal-trucks were to start out for Waldenburg.

The Americans had provided me with U.S. army rations. They were rather troubled that I really wanted to go back to Silesia. The Germans assured me that I wouldn't make it, because the Oder and the Görlitzer Neisse were now an inter-state frontier and the Poles were chucking the Germans out, and certainly would not let any more in. This news was not at all encouraging, but my children exerted a powerful pull on me and Frau Raschke felt the same.

So started the most adventurous journey that I have so far experienced, and it was typical of the conditions at that time, and of people in general, in that it was full of pleasant and unpleasant experiences. For this reason it is worth the telling.

The journey lasted three days and three nights. At first it went like a charm, open empty coal-trucks and fine warm weather. We stopped here and there, to be sure, but not for too long. So around midday we crossed the frontier. We simply drove across. But a few miles further on the train stopped at a station. Polish militiamen came aboard and turned all Germans off the train, except German soldiers who were being demobilised to Silesia from the west; curiously enough they were allowed at the time to make their way home. A great crowd of people gathered in the station lamenting, and were then driven back like a herd of cattle by Poles wielding long whips: back to the German frontier. We were among them. I wondered how I could get myself noticed. I kept calling out to one of the whips 'I have international papers' – over and over again. It wasn't quite exact but it worked. He took notice and directed me to a young lieutenant of the militia who had a sort of office close by. So then at least we were out of the herd. I saw at once that the lieutenant had that expression, full of hatred, characteristic of so many of these militiamen. I showed him Romai's beautiful papers and a further certificate from the Berlin magistrates which I had procured, to the effect that I had been to Berlin on business connected with my husband, and must now go back to my children in Silesia. The militiaman went through them all, amused himself hugely and scornfully over the fallen countess, considered a little and then said, good, I could go on, but this woman – indicating Frau Raschke – she must go back. Good Frau Raschke at once raised a great despairing cry: 'Don't leave me in the lurch, don't leave me in the lurch, I must come with you!' Great outcry! So then I said we both had to go to Silesia. If we wanted to stay together, he replied, then we must both go back. So then, more or less in despair, I opened my rucksack and tried to bargain: food they didn't want – had plenty of their own – but six American cigarettes which were part of the rations did the trick. I also offered him a hideous yellow waterproof cape made of plastic, and I clearly remember how an elderly Pole in the group took the cape, folded it carefully and behind the officer's back stuffed it in my rucksack again. We really could go; it was hard to believe it. As fast as we could we went back to the train, climbed into a truck and sat there, worn out and as quiet as mice. Hardly were we installed when there came another Polish round-up and out we went once more – our protests were in vain. But the lieutenant was standing on the platform, recognised us and let us get in again. After a bit, with a great jerk, the train really set off eastwards. It was a marvellous feeling. We really thought it was all over, but it wasn't so easy. In the closed goods-van there were, in addition to ourselves and various other people, two of the demobbed soldiers. One was a bank clerk from the Waldenburg district and the other a farmer from Upper Silesia. He could speak Polish. We actually started off and went quite a distance, but then stopped again. We noticed that we did another stretch, and during the night whenever we stopped there came ghostly creatures into our truck, groping for things and shining lights in our faces. The farmer would call out in Polish 'We're Poles', and then it was all right. The two soldiers had joined up with us and the four of us travelled together. Frau Raschke and I were in any case so exhausted that we lay down on the floor of the truck, laid our heads on our rucksacks and slept peacefully. Next morning we discovered that we were only in Sorau. This is just north of Sagan, some two and a half hours by fast train from Berlin in the old days. We had been standing there for some hours. You had the feeling on this single track – formerly there had been four lines in places, but the Russians had dismantled all the tracks in the first months – that one goods train was piling up behind another, and that we should stand there for days on end. We, the two soldiers, Frau Raschke and I, thought that we would

N

probably make better progress by road and decided to get out. As we marched off along the country road from Sorau to Sagan we were over-taken by a whole column of empty carts with Russian or Polish ponies between the shafts. By this time we were quite accustomed to these typically eastern vehicles. First the German troops had used them, then the Russians and now the Poles: in contrast to our heavy farm-carts they are quite light vehicles, pulled by light-weight horses. They don't get stuck in the sand so easily, and on our country roads – when un-loaded – they seemed almost to dance along in time with the rhythm of their trotting ponies. We let the whole column pass us, until almost at the end we plucked up courage to thumb a lift from one of the last carts. The Polish driver stopped at once; without saying or asking much he let the four of us come aboard, and we drove quickly and happily as far as Sagan station, where in fact all these carts were to be loaded. In every sense we had been lucky because on foot we should probably have been picked up by the Poles and drafted into labour gangs which they were setting up everywhere for clearing-up operations; we passed one such trap. Once caught people sometimes had to work there for weeks on end before they might go on. So we got safely to Sagan station. It was just as hopelessly full of trains as Sorau. Only goods-trains, full of dismantled machinery, old tanks etc, which were to be transported to Russia, and also choc-a-bloc with people. Not many Germans, but a lot of Russians and Poles still coming out of Germany and wanting to get home. They glared at us angrily and drove us off when we tried to get into goods-wagons which were already full. And yet I recall a little Russian or Polish girl who suddenly slipped a bit of bread into my hand. As we wandered aimlessly to and fro on the crowded platform two Russian soldiers, fully armed, made a bee-line for Frau Raschke and me and beckoned us to go with them. This was not a bit nice and our hearts sank. The two soldiers came with us, unquestioned and unhindered. We all went through the barrier. What could we do but follow? Why had they picked on just us in that nameless throng? What could it mean? This worried us as we went down the stairs and through the station and out of the station. They led us a few paces along the station and then in again at another door in the corner of the building. Here was an office and Frau Raschke and I were ordered by signs to clean it. Frau Raschke did it beautifully, I less so but all the same not so badly as to fall foul of the Russians. The two soldiers meanwhile polished away at a motor-cycle, and in about an hour we were finished. The Russians were very pleased, regretted that they could not give us anything for our trouble, but told us which of the many trains would be the first to depart, which was a real help to us. This train too was full of people and machinery. On a flat truck on which a tank was mounted stood a Russian lieutenant, and next to him a young Russian woman. We made discreet signs to the

Russian because up front, in front of the tank was a lovely empty space where all four of us could have sat in comfort. The Russian was inclined to turn us down, but it seemed we had an advocate in the woman. She pleaded with him and in the end he nodded to us and we climbed gratefully aboard. By this time we had grown quite used to the different time-schedule of the east which had moved into Silesia along with the Russians and Poles. Hours mattered nothing any more. Patiently we endured what couldn't be altered. I don't remember now how long it took until the train started, I only recall that at the last moment a Russian soldier jumped up beside us and travelled some way with us. He immediately lay down, wrapped himself in his greatcoat and went to sleep. Later he woke, took from his coat pocket some bread and a crumpled bag of sugar, ate both together and without a word gave us some. We didn't get far before stopping again, often in open country. Then everyone jumped out of the trucks, ran into the fields and looked for potatoes. With stones they would make little hearths alongside the train and boil water in tins and bake potatoes in the embers. We did exactly the same and shared our food. When the train could go on there were two blasts on the whistle, between the whistles the people were given enough time to clear up and get on board and then the train started. But that evening we still did not get to Liegnitz. We had to wait all night on a side line. This time I slept under the tank. I had more room there, but the night was cooler and towards dawn I felt faint and miserably cold. Then up near the engine I saw a lovely big fire. I didn't care any more; I felt ill and wanted to get to the fire. So I went stumbling along the length of the train till I came to the fire. There sat the engine-driver, a Pole, and a solitary, enormously tall Russian soldier. When they saw me slowly approaching they at once pulled a block of wood close to the fire so that I could sit there, and gave me hot potatoes to eat which they had baked, and some tea which the Pole had brewed with water from the engine – and were most kind to me without being able to say a word to me or indeed wanting to. All in all this did me so much good that after a time, warmed inside and out, I was able to go back restored and comfortable to my tank-wagon.

Then it grew light and morning came, and we were still standing in the same place when suddenly with a lot of smoke and whistling there appeared out of nowhere – or so it seemed – a passenger train. Full to bursting, but it stopped and, deciding in a flash, we changed into it. That is to say that we had to clamber on to the roof of a coach, because at the doors people were already hanging on like bunches of grapes. But on top of the coaches it was still quite empty and we had no difficulty climbing up. The sun was shining again; and rattling and whistling, with a great deal of smoke, we drove off through the countryside. We felt like kings up there, but were careful to keep our heads down under the bridges, and about an hour later reached Liegnitz. I hadn't seen the station at Liegnitz since the end of January. It was in a terrible state – a great gaping sewer. We hoped for more good luck in Liegnitz. But nobody there knew when a train would leave or where it would go. To be sure there were one or two engines shunting about the station, but their drivers did not know where they would finally be sent to, and the few trains which did get away did not go in our direction. But from Liegnitz to Kreisau is only another thirty-five miles. If we had to we could do that on foot, but we had again lost a lot of time through waiting about, and were tired and preferred rather to get another night's sleep. We somehow found our way to a house run by church people. We were indeed taken in, but all four had to sleep on the floor and that was the third night in succession we had done so. So we broke off very early next morning and walked as far as Jauer. That took a whole row of hours. We had no difficulties to surmount but I was worn out and also hungry, for although I still had a small reserve out of the American rations they had not been calculated to last us for three days and nights, and I did not want to use it all up in case I should be held up still longer. I lagged a bit behind the others and finally went into a house and asked if I could get something to drink. The farmer's wife had the remains of breakfast still on the table and said I might by all means finish the fried potatoes, and she gave me a cup of a herbal tea to drink with them, which was standing still warm upon the stove. These restored me like manna from heaven. However, when we reached Jauer station we preferred to wait for a train going eastwards to walking any farther. Like the other people we sat on the platform swinging our legs above the rails and waited. It wasn't so very long before another lovely passenger train came in. We could even get straight in and find seats, and it actually went without incident and without much hanging about – for we were now on a secondary line – through Striegau, Königszelt, Schweidnitz, and on its further way to Kamenz stopped like a well-behaved train in Kreisau. So we got there between six and seven in the evening. Everything was wonderfully peaceful. As we walked uphill to the Berghaus Caspar came running to meet me. 'Oh there you are again, Reialie!' he called out joyfully, as though I had only been a few hours away, and the Berghaus seemed to me an island of peace in a stormy sea.

But even there the time had not passed without difficulties. The Poles had returned, four of them, and this time Romai had received them, but first she sent her Roland, who was then just nine years old, to the Russian captain. He had jumped out of a window and run in five minutes to the Schloss; after a further ten minutes four armed Russians had appeared and the Poles had immediately withdrawn. Meanwhile at the Hof the first manager had disappeared and a real genuine Pole had moved in, with whom Zeumer had an even worse time, but who behaved in a not unfriendly way to us: for the future the estate was to be managed as the property of the Polish State.

After my return from Berlin we had another nice experience with our captain in the Schloss. At the beginning of the summer our bombed-out tenant in Wierischau had brought us his delightful young black spaniel, before he himself moved out to join his family. This lovely creature with its silky black curls seemed to the Russians just as beautiful as Konrad with his curly hair, and we soon noticed that they were after the dog. But the children loved him too and so we kept a close watch on him. But finally one day at the end of the summer he disappeared. Where on earth could he be? Roland Reichwein soon found out; there had been barking in the Schloss! Now what should we do? We didn't want to let our dog go too easily, but equally we didn't want to get on the wrong side of the captain. Romai and I went together to the Schloss and asked to speak to the captain. We waited a bit. Then a Russian woman in 'civvies' who worked there and was to act as interpreter led us away. In the upper hall sat the captain, just as one might imagine a Russian Satrap, in the vast golden throne bedizened with black damask, out of which, so it was said, the still vaster and very fat Uncle Ludwig Moltke from Wernersdorf had been unable to get up without assistance. So there sat the Satrap looking stern, for he knew quite well we had come about the dog. But now came our trick and it worked wonders. I asked the interpreter to tell the captain that we should have pleasure in making him a present of the dog. The captain jumped up at once, smiled, was pleased and wanted to know the dog's name. 'Rago,' he repeated carefully. Had he a pedigree, was he trained for hunting? I told him that with luck we might find a pedigree at Wierischau and he agreed to drive over there with me. As he was obviously now in the best of humours, Romai asked if she might perhaps, as it was rumoured that the company would be moving to Schweidnitz, take up to the Berghaus two beds which belonged to her and which she needed. The captain replied in the frankest way that they would be moving out during the next few days, and that everything would be left there exactly as it was. Then Romai could take away whatever she wanted. Thus Rago set the seal on the friendly relations which we had had that summer with 'our captain'. The Russians actually moved out the next day. When we afterwards came into the Schloss it was stripped bare. Apart from two exquisite small eighteenth-century cupboards, which belonged to Wend and Asta – the only two really good things still in the Schloss – there was nothing left! The wind whistled through the empty building.

In Berlin Gero Gävernitz had told me that in his parents' country house near Neurode, whence he had had no news in recent years because he and his family had gone to the United States, there must be people still living whose well-being was important to him. He would like to know how everything was, wanted to send greetings and to advise his friends to leave Silesia. He had asked me if possible to go and see how things were. Neurode does not lie, as does Schweidnitz, in front of the hills, but within the beautiful middle ranges which constitute part of the Sudeten mountains, to which the Eule also belongs. To get there we had to cross our first ridge of hills by a valley lying farther east than we had been on our trek. There was no railway connection; and we couldn't risk going on bicycles. The Russians no longer took the bikes, but the Poles did, and meanwhile all Germans in Silesia had to wear white armbands. We didn't do so, but in consequence risked getting into trouble. Some time after my return from Berlin, when Marion and Muto were once more with us, Marion and I undertook this visit to the Gävernitz's home. This expedition too has remained a very happy memory. It was a long way, farther than we had expected. One day early in September we set out at dawn and, although we did not stop long anywhere, only arrived late in the afternoon. We found an imposing house in a large park; Helmuth had often been a guest there before he married. Poles were installed in the big house, the people for whom Gävernitz was concerned were living in houses round about. They were having a bad time. They had had experiences with Russians and Poles similar to our own. They were delighted by our visit and the link with Gävernitz. We stayed the night there and returned next day by another route. Altogether it was some twenty-eight miles and our feet rebelled at having to walk so far inside two days. In spite of thick shoes they were covered with blisters, but apart from this the trip did us no harm. Hardly were our feet recovered when Romai burst into the house one day to tell us that there were Americans in the village and that they had come to visit us. She was quite worked up, and just as we rushed out of the house up drove a big American touring-car and out got Gävernitz. With him as chauffeur came an American soldier who spoke fluent Polish and Russian. Gävernitz had managed to get himself a permit from the Russians and Poles to travel to Silesia, and had decided to have a look at his house at Neurode himself. They stayed the night with us and drove over next day, but came back the same evening. The Americans wanted to find out as much as possible about conditions in Silesia. In Berlin they had already asked us for a precise account, and we had been working on that in the interval. The systematic evacuation of Silesia had only got into its stride in recent weeks, and was proceeding in a very horrible way. Now Gävernitz wanted to get as true a picture as possible with his own eyes. He asked if we could go with him next day to Breslau where we had connections with both Catholic and Protestant clergy. In Silesia at that time the churches constituted the sole network over which any reliable news could still be spread, and by

which contact between isolated areas could be maintained. Marion and I were delighted to drive by car through the countryside, look at it all for ourselves, and especially to see Breslau. But it was a wretched impression that we got. Behind the front on which the Russians had halted at the end of the war everything was destroyed, shot up and laid waste. To be sure you could see that here too evacuees had returned and were trying to start again among the ruins; but the destruction was terrific, the land was untilled, weeds grew high on the fine ploughland. Now for the first time I saw the difference between the two zones. The city of Breslau was equally shattering; driving in from the south we saw nothing but ruins, and yet the heart of the town was fairly well kept.*
We had a meeting with the people to whom we had been referred, had a look at the shattered town in which only a few shacks seemed to be inhabited, although of course in fact thousands of people were still living there, and in the afternoon drove back again. It was already getting dark when we reached Kreisau. Before we got to the hill where the Berghaus stands we were accosted by some of the villagers. We must be careful, there were Poles up at the Berghaus. They had been there some time already, and had taken up an empty lorry. Russians were also there. This was not exactly pleasant for the Americans. But they realised that we wanted to get there as quickly as possible, and equally were determined not to leave us in the lurch. Gävernitz in his fine American colonel's uniform was anything but a soldier, but that evening he bore himself as a soldier. I can see him now catching his breath at the door of the house. But thereafter he was splendid. The Poles and the Russians were simply pop-eyed to see an American officer in their midst. In sober fact the house was full of Poles poking into everything. The children were all sitting with Frau Pick in the kitchen and were being guarded, that is to say protected, by a Russian soldier with a great moustache, who sat cosily on a kitchen chair with a gun in his hand. Muto and Romai were busy about the house. This is what had happened: the Poles had arrived and said that we had valuables walled up in the basement of the house. These they now wanted to take out and remove. In fact I had, with the help of a Polish mason who worked for us at the Hof – he was by the way the man who had said if I stayed he'd stay too – walled up linen, clothes, silver and books under our cellar steps and under the steps down to the cellar in the Schloss, not only for ourselves but also for those who had already gone, for safety from the German troops as they filtered back, for they were in such a

---

* Gauleiter Hanke 'waged the battle of Breslau without regard for human lives or historic buildings and even had his old friend the mayor, Dr Spielhagen, publicly hanged. Then ... shortly before the surrender of Breslau he flew out of the besieged city in one of the few existing prototype helicopters.' A. Speer, *Inside the Third Reich,* p. 423.

destructive mood. The things under the steps in the Schloss must still be there today, and have long since mouldered away. For the Russians had gaily cooked against this wall all summer and had noticed nothing, though they usually had a quick nose for such tricks. They couldn't have benefited much from the stuff they took away either, for the Moltkes had no treasures, and what they valued wouldn't much have interested the Russians and Poles. However, in the Berghaus the Poles had now broken down the wall and carried everything upstairs, where it lay about higgledy-piggledy. They were apparently somewhat disappointed with what they had found, and in addition were rummaging about among my papers upstairs. This was not so pleasant because the account of conditions in Silesia was lying open in my room, and this they really must not find.

The Americans had come just in the nick of time. They held the Poles at bay and Gävernitz made it clear to them with the help of his interpreter that they had no right to take our belongings from us, they could kindly leave everything where it was and take themselves off. This made an impression, but there was still some arguing and finally Gävernitz's interpreter drove back with them to Schweidnitz to discuss the matter there with their superiors. He came back after an hour or so. Yes, everything was in order, I could keep the lot. My typewriter had caused the greatest difficulty; for that they had fought the longest. The radio by the way they never noticed; standing in its usual place it survived the raid. But now the presence of the American soldiers in uniform had attracted attention in Schweidnitz where it had been unknown to the Poles and the Russians. And sure enough two Russians arrived early next morning and demanded to see the Americans' papers. I was in the room, could naturally understand nothing, but saw clearly from my two friends' expressions that they were ill at ease. The Russians examined everything for some time, there was a lot of discussion, but at last they departed. Hardly were they out of the house before Gävernitz gave me to understand that his licence to travel through Poland had already expired, that he had squared this only by word of mouth with the officials at the frontier, and that in addition the permit had been issued not to him but to another officer. The latter had not been able to undertake the journey. So Gävernitz had seized the good opportunity and was travelling under a false name. If this came out it could mean trouble all round. Off then, as soon as possible! In this way the Schweidnitz Russians would have no chance to get a second look at the papers. Pale and agitated the two men climbed into their beautiful car. I handed over to Gävernitz the first packet of Helmuth's letters which had so long been hidden away from the Nazis in the backs of my bee-hives. From the car Gävernitz once more leaned out to us. 'You must all leave here,' he said, 'and as soon as possible. You're sitting on a volcano!' And with that he was gone. He and his companion reached the frontier without incident, passed straight over and reached Berlin. It had become clear through all that we had experienced that we could not in the long run stay in Silesia. All the same we felt that it was worth holding the position a little longer, especially because we felt ourselves in the same boat with many other villagers. But it was certain that the fools' paradise of this summer could not last through the winter. To be sure in the spring after the Schloss was empty I had had all the available stocks of coal moved up to the Berghaus, but further supplies were not obtainable. So it was more sensible to bring the children away from Kreisau in good time. Romai next got herself and her four children ready. She packed up and made bundles and got things in order and divided her freight, herself assuming incredible burdens. She had already shown tough and inexhaustible energy, after the loss of all her possessions in Berlin through bombing, in building up under difficult and uncomfortable conditions a new and smooth-running household in the Schloss. Now with the same strength and tenacity she took on the removal to Berlin of herself, her children and as many of their belongings as possible. It was planned that after she had got her children well settled she should herself come back again to Kreisau so that I could then bring my children away. We escorted the family to Kreisau station and waited there patiently until a train arrived. With bags and bundles they found places and vanished.

So now our household had already dwindled. I suppose a week or two had passed after Gävernitz's visit when we once more experienced something quite out of the ordinary. We had just been in Schweidnitz selling various objects for Polish currency. German money, which we had, was no more use. But without Polish money we could no longer manage for any length of time. Of course we had plenty to sell. The first to go was a length of silk and a pair of women's shoes which Carl Berndt had sent to me from Greece for safe-keeping. Marion came with me. It's only a full hour on foot to Schweidnitz if you go across the fields. The amazing thing at that time was how quickly and how radically Schweidnitz had changed in the six months since the war. It already had quite a Polish look. And this was only partly due to the new inscriptions and street signs in Polish and to post-war difficulties of all kinds, it also had to do with the different kind of people in the streets and the wholly altered rhythm of life which they had brought with them. I should never have thought it possible that a change could so quickly become complete. We finished our business and, as we thought, very advantageously. Polish money jingled in our purses as we set off home. On our way through the Hof to the Berghaus people called out to us. We had more visitors. This time they were English. I wouldn't believe it but the woman was quite sure. Yes, they had asked the way of her personally and were up there now. We fairly stepped out and sure enough there on our narrow drive stood a small unmistakable English four-seater; what's more it had a British flag up! What a sight in the middle of Silesia, among all those Russians and Poles!

Indoors we found, conversing as best they could with Muto, two equally unmistakable English gentlemen, Mr Hancock and Mr Finch from the British Embassy in Warsaw. How deeply moved I was after all the war years by those English gentlemen with their English shirts, English jackets and their English ways! Another world, yet so well known to me, and they seemed to have dropped out of the clouds into our Berghaus. Their appearance was the answer to my letter from Berlin to Lionel Curtis. He was moving heaven and earth to get us away from Kreisau. He had applied to Bevin, the British Foreign Secretary. Bevin had made inquiries about us, by chance, of Con O'Neill in the Foreign Office, whom Helmuth had known and liked in Berlin, so that after their interview Bevin had asked Montgomery in Berlin to inquire of the Russians and Poles whether the English might fetch us away from Kreisau. The Englishmen had come to tell me all this. They had other business to do in the neighbourhood of Liegnitz and then wanted to get back to Warsaw as quickly as possible. Therefore they only stayed to lunch. They spoke very seriously to us; they didn't know whether the removal would be allowed, they had no way of letting me know the result of the British intervention. I was to wait four weeks. If by then nobody had shown up it would mean that the British effort had failed, and I must promise to leave Kreisau under my own steam. Before they left, the senior of them, Mr Hancock, drew me aside. Like a father he asked me if I had enough Polish money. I explained to him how I could set about obtaining some. But that didn't seem to him good enough. He gave me the equivalent of £50 in zlotys and I gave him a receipt made out to the British Embassy in Warsaw. Later I was able to pay it back from England, but at the time it seemed to me like a fairy-tale. Then our two friends drove away.

Now at last we lost the radio, and it was to the comical Russian with the moustache who had protected the children in the kitchen during the Polish raid. On that occasion he'd had a good look into our larder, and discovered that we had quite a lot of very good home-made jam. So the man came around every few days and as his tribute collected another pot of jam. He seemed to find it excellent, and his consumption was considerable. One day he arrived with a most conspiratorial expression on his face. He had heard from the Poles that each evening we made – in a word – türülürülü. So we must have a radio! 'Upstairs,' he said, and went to look for it. At first we behaved as though we didn't understand, and in the interval considered how we were to get out of it. The Russian made dramatic signs; if the radio wasn't handed over – grrr –

(in his throat) – so better give it up! We knew now that we were not going to be able to stay. But we didn't know which was better, to give in or to dump the thing secretly in the undergrowth. This was not so simple, and we made up our minds while the Russian hunted through the upper part of the house. Yes, better let him have it, whom we already knew and had no fear of. We took it into the kitchen and called him down. He came, saw it – and was enraptured, beaming, happy as a child. When he switched it on and really heard music he could hardly control his delight, but danced ceremoniously round the kitchen. When he had somewhat recovered he told us to put it away again, to hide it until the evening. That evening, after dark, came a different, unknown Russian on a motor-bike. He had brought several blankets with him in which he carefully wrapped up our radio, then strapped it on and vanished. We had got rid of it in the best of all possible ways, quite unofficially as private Russian loot!

And so it came to the last weeks in Kreisau. Marion and Muto went to Berlin again. Then the children and I were alone with Frau Pick and Liesbeth. They were very peaceful, lovely autumn days of calm, sunny, October weather. I felt as though time were once more briefly at a standstill. Nothing disturbed us; we had no news and we were not uneasy. I had a nasty, septic infection of my right forefinger which had to be lanced at the hospital in Schweidnitz. The cut was slow to heal and hampered me, and until my hand was well again I simply could not undertake the journey to Berlin with the children, across that difficult frontier where everything one had might be confiscated. One could only wait, and the waiting was wonderful. What I still did around the Hof I don't know, for I had nothing more to do there. Be that as it may, I had been in the piggery at Nieder Gräditz, and was just coming out of the door when Casparchen came running into the Hof, and called out in his clear child's voice: 'Reialie, come on, we've got to go. The Englishmen are here.'

It was four weeks to the day since the motor from Warsaw had been there. The Englishmen had come with a big car and a small lorry. The lorry was half-full of 'emergency equipment'. The friendly Major Caird and his two soldiers felt themselves to be on a military expedition into enemy territory. I had difficulty in persuading them not to put up tents, but to spend the night peacefully in beds in the house. But in the end they did so, while I packed. There was still a lot of ready-packed stuff standing about the house after the Polish raid. It ran through the village like a forest fire that we were now really going, and although I had been told that I might take only my own most special things with me I took all the same a whole row of other cases as well. But every single object from Kreisau that we still have today we owe to the English. Unfortunately the empty half of the lorry was very quickly filled.

But my conscience still pricks me for having refused to take along for the young postman his giant accordion, which he brought up on a trailer. However, there were too many other things to take which at the time seemed more important. In the first instance only the children and I were supposed to go. But the kind major took pity on Frau Pick. She might come with us.

We left early next morning. The house remained open and inhabited. We drove down the Berghaus hill on the slope facing the Eule. As the car moved forward I asked Caspar, 'When shall we come back again?'

'In a year!' he answered, happy and certain. We drove along the narrow, bumpy road to the station, reached the *Dorfstrasse*, crossed the bridge over the Peile, passed the Kapellenberg, the mill, the school, Schwester's kindergarten, along the wall of the big byre, past the gates to the Hof – there lay the Hof and the Schloss in full view – then on through the village to Gräditz, where we joined the high road to Schweidnitz. Seven hours later we were in Berlin. At the frontier the Poles saluted, opened the barriers and let us pass through without inspection. That is how the universally dreaded Polish–German frontier was for us, thanks to the friendship of the English.

Notes

CHAPTER 1: THE MOLTKE FAMILY

1. This account is based on:
   J. Burke, *History of the Commoners* (1838), Vol. IV, p. 7.
   J. Burke, *Genealogical Dictionary of the Landed Gentry* (1838), sub Burt McIlWraith (ed.), *Field-Marshal von Moltke's Letters to his Wife* (1892), Vol. I.
   Marie von Moltke eine Soldatenfrau (1944).
   F. P. Parker, *Some Account of Colton and the de Westerey Family* (1897).
   Directories of Staffordshire (1818, 1834).
   Land Tax Returns for Colton 1805–21, County Record Office, Stafford.
2. Gordon A. Craig, *The Politics of the Prussian Army, 1660–1945*, pp. 193–216.
   E. Kolb in *Historische Zeitschrift* for 1969, Vol. 209, pp. 318–56.

CHAPTER 3: JAMES ROSE INNES AND HIS DAUGHTER

1. *Milner Papers* (ed. Headlam) (1933), Vol. II, p. 121.
2. The authors are grateful to Professor Wright for putting his draft introduction at their disposal.
3. W. K. Hancock, *Smuts* (1968), Vol. II, p. 260.
4. Letter to Professor Bluntschli, 11 December 1880, *Gesammelte Schriften* (1895), V, p. 193.

CHAPTER 4: EARLY LIFE

1. Prince Louis Ferdinand of Prussia, *Als Kaiserenkel durch die Welt* (1952), pp. 66, 67.
2. Ernst Feder, *Heute sprach ich mit* (1971), p. 322.

CHAPTER 5: TWO IMPORTANT INFLUENCES

1. This account is partly based on information kindly supplied by Frau Alice Herdan-Zuckmayer.
2. V. Sheean, *Dorothy and Red* (1964), p. 4.
3. ibid, p. 98.
4. E. Rosenstock and C. D. von Trotha, *Das Arbeitslager* (1931), p. 28.
5. Sheean, op. cit., p. 33.
6. This account is based on Countess Dorothy's letters which show that previous accounts of the gathering at Kreisau have exaggerated its size and formality.

CHAPTER 6: CRISIS AT KREISAU: MARRIAGE

1. F. J. Furtwängler, *Manner die ich sah und kannte* (1952), p. 217.

CHAPTER 7: THE NAZI MENACE

1. Furtwängler, op. cit., p. 217.
2. E. Mowrer, *Triumph and Turmoil* (1970), p. 226.

CHAPTER 8: LIFE AND DEATH IN NAZI GERMANY
1934–5

1. Helmuth in one of his letters reports having heard this from Ernst von Weizsäcker, the anti-Nazi State Secretary in the *Auswärtiges Amt* (Foreign Office).
2. The comment mentioned by van Roon on p. 27 was in fact to the effect that the loss was much worse for him than for the others because they believed in an after-life whereas he did not.
3. C. Sykes, *Troubled Loyalty* (1968), p. 396.

CHAPTER 9: A LIFELINE TO ENGLAND 1935–8

1. W. K. Hancock, *Survey of British Commonwealth Affairs* (1957), Vol. I, p. 54n.
2. W. Nimocks, *Milner's Young Men The Kindergarten in Edwardian Affairs* (1970), pp. 99, 160.
3. M. Gilbert, *The Roots of Appeasement* (1966), pp. 30–1.
4. K. Slack, *George Bell* (1971), p. 9; also pp. 60–73.
5. Bell Papers, Box 7, German Church, brought to the authors' attention by Dr P. Ludlow.
6. A. L. Rowse, *All Souls and Appeasement* (1961), pp. 95–6.
7. C. Sykes, op. cit., p. 261.

CHAPTER 10: HITLER OFFENDS THE ARMY 1938

1. There is no trace of the document in the public archives. When on 30 March the Foreign Office heard for the first time of a 'trial of Fritsch' (without further details) the official concerned presumed it was 'for his complicity in the alleged monarchist plot'. PRO 21660 F.O. 371 C2515/-62/18. By 13 April a story of the trial appeared in *The Times* and, although the nature of the charge was not mentioned, the correspondent wrote as though he were aware of it.
2. See H-J. Reichardt, 'Resistance in the Labour Movement', in H. Graml, etc., *The German Resistance to Hitler* (1970), pp. 149–92 and T. Mason, 'The Legacy of 1918 for National Socialism', in A. Nicholls and E. Matthias, *German Democracy and the Triumph of Hitler* (1971), pp. 215–39.
3. Letter of Halder to Dr van Roon, Institut für Zeitgeschichte, 9 August 1963.
4. See van Roon, p. 103. Lukaschek's memory in other cases does not seem to have been accurate, p. 376 below.

CHAPTER 11: THE MUNICH CRISIS

1. Cabinet Minutes, quoted in I. Colvin, *The Chamberlain Cabinet* (1970), p. 43.
2. D. MacLachlan, *In The Chair* (1971), p. 233.

CHAPTER 12: THE LAST MONTHS OF PEACE

1. Carl Zuckmayer, *A Part of Myself* (1970), p. 43.
2. L. Curtis: *Civitas Dei* (1950 edition), p. 603, when the exchange of views is attributed to 1938. But Curtis seems to have been, and represents Helmuth as having been, under the impression that the Ides of March fall on the 7th instead of the 15th. The only year in which Hitler's action did fall on the Ides was 1939 which in other respects fits better with Helmuth's known movements.

CHAPTER 13: THE 'ABWEHR'

1. A. Krebs, in his biography of *Fritz-Dietlof Graf von der Schulenburg* (1964), says that 'the notes of the Countess who from 21 September to 20 October was living on one of the Yorck estates, mention a number of visits by her husband to Count Moltke in Kreisau'. But Schulenburg did not reach Breslau until Helmuth had left for Berlin. As Helmuth did not come back to Kreisau until Christmas, and then only for a few days, the visits referred to must have occurred at some other time. The only visit which Freya von Moltke can remember was early in May 1940.
2. H. B. Gisevius, *Wo ist Nebe* (1966), p. 104.

CHAPTER 14: WORK IN THE 'ABWEHR':
SEPTEMBER–DECEMBER 1939

1. For these negotiations and the army's preparations, see:
   J. W. Wheeler-Bennett, *The Nemesis of Power* (2nd edition 1967), pp. 456–79.
   H. Groscurth (ed. Krausnick and Deutsch), *Tagebücher eines Abwehr offiziers 1938–40* (1970).
   H. Deutsch, *The Conspiracy against Hitler in the Twilight War* (1968).
2. For full text, see *International Military Tribunal (Nuremberg)*, Vol. XXXIV, pp. 608–41.
3. See, however, G. van Roon, *Graf Moltke als Völkerrechtler im OKW*. VfZ., Vol. 18 (1970), pp. 12–61.
   H. Sohler, *U-Boot Krieg und Völkerrecht, Beiheft 1 der Marine Rundschau*, September 1956.
4. M. Salewski, *Die Deutsche Seekriegsleitung 1935–45*, Vol. I, 1935–41 (1970), p. 140.
5. Nuremberg Document 2992 (in files of IfZ).
6. A. Hoch, Vfz., Vol. 17 (1969), pp. 383–413.
7. S. P. Best, *The Venlo Incident* (1950).
8. H. Trevor-Roper (ed.), *Hitler's War Directives* (1964), pp. 18–21.
9. Nuremberg Document 1722 (IfZ.).
10. Minute by Counsellor Dr Lohmann, 11 December 1939 (IfZ.).

CHAPTER 15: WAITING FOR THE ATTACK:
JANUARY–APRIL 1940

1. Not, as has sometimes been stated, under Eugen Rosenstock.
2. These articles are likely to have included – *The Times*: 'Paying for the War' by Keynes, 14 and 15 November; 'Reply to critics', 28 November; 'Real Economic Warfare', 30 November; 'The Economic Weapon', 4

December; 'Money in Two Wars', 23 December. *The Economist*: 'The Economic Front', 4, 11, 25 November; 'Germany's Vulnerability, 18 November. *Round Table*: 'War Economics', December issue.
3. Text of original document in *Bundesarchiv* (MA Vol 7/227) communicated to Freya von Moltke by Dr G. van Roon.
4. Groscurth, op. cit., p. 240.

CHAPTER 16: THE CRISIS OF CONFIDENCE: MAY–JUNE 1940

1. By Will Durant.
2. G. Kennan, *Memoirs 1925–50* (1968), p. 121.
3. F. J. Furtwängler, op. cit., p. 218, claims to have attended meetings at the Derfflingerstrasse in the winter of 1939–40 in company with Yorck, Haeften, Schulenburg, Einsiedel, Reichwein and 'Generals of the Army High Command'. But Schulenburg was in Breslau during the winter and Haeften in Bucarest so that the chronology seems to have become blurred in retrospect.
4. For text, see van Roon, p. 295.
5. According to Dr Eduard Waetjen (van Roon, p. 108), education was the principal subject discussed on this occasion. Freya von Moltke and Marion Yorck, however, are sure that the conversation was general and by no means confined to this subject.
6. In the German edition of Dr van Roon's book, the correspondent in these cases was wrongly given as Yorck.
7. van Roon, pp. 310–17.
8. IfZ.

CHAPTER 17: KEEPING A HEAD ABOVE WATER: JULY–DECEMBER 1940

1. The next paragraphs owe much to Dr van Roon's essay, already mentioned in VfZ., Vol. 18 (1970), esp. pp. 41–7.
2. From papers of Admiral Gladisch in the *Bundesarchiv/Militärarchiv* Freiburg, photocopy in IfZ.
3. Quoted in van Roon, op. cit., p. 41. A letter of Helmuth's of 22 July makes it possible, however, that the group concerned with peace terms was a different one, in which he was not ultimately involved – though see p. 141.
4. A letter dated 7 September to Berthold von Stauffenberg of which there is a photostat copy in the IfZ. has led Dr van Roon (*Neuordnung im Widerstand*, p. 334) to state that Helmuth went on a second journey to France and Belgium with Admiral Gladisch in September. But not only is Freya von Moltke positive that no such second journey occurred but the initialled signature on the letter is definitely not Helmuth's. (It is possibly that of Dr Widmann, another assistant of Gladisch.)
5. Letter from Deuel to Dr van Roon, in IfZ.
6. Churchill's actual words were: 'The right to guide the course of world history is the noblest prize of victory. We are still toiling up the hill; we have not yet reached the crest-line of it; we cannot survey the landscape or even imagine what its condition will be when that longed-for morning comes. The task which lies before us immediately is at once more practical, more simple and more stern. I hope – indeed I pray – that we shall not be found unworthy of our victory if after toil and

tribulation it is granted to us. For the rest, we have to gain the victory. That is our task.'
Helmuth would seem to have been working on a German summary of the speech or repeating it from memory.
7. At the instigation of Gablentz. See van Roon, p. 301.
8. Kennan, *Memoirs*, p. 120.

CHAPTER 18: INTERLUDE: JANUARY–22 JUNE 1941

1. For Haushofer, see J. Douglas-Hamilton, *Motive for a Mission* (1971). The meeting on 10 December was probably the occasion 'in the autumn of 1941' on which Haushofer, according to R. Hildebrandt, *Wir sind die Letzten*, p. 130, 'lectured' to 'men round Count Moltke'. Haushofer was never in Kreisau itself nor do Hildebrandt's words necessarily imply that he was.
2. For text, see van Roon, pp. 317–28.
3. A photocopy of Helmuth's minute, dated 29 March 1941, to Bürkner exists in the IfZ. There can be no doubt about its authenticity, but its author may have been wrongly informed.
4. Bürkner deduced from a memorandum of Keitel's about Romania issued on 20 September 1940 that an attack on Russia was being contemplated and told Weizsäcker so next day (*Nuremberg Trials of War Criminals*, Vol. XIV, p. 380). He is unlikely to have told Helmuth so early but the likelihood of Helmuth having had considerable advance warning seems strong.

CHAPTER 19: FRESH IMPETUS: 22 JUNE–DECEMBER 1941

1. Letter in IfZ.
2. T. Steltzer, *Von Deutscher Politik* (1949), p. 72.
3. Baron H. C. von Stauffenberg, in van Roon, p. 269.
4. It is unlikely to have been Hans Christoph because (a) Helmuth had met him in 1938 – above, p. 81, (b) they were now working in the same office, (c) he seems to have had dealings with H.C. in 1940, above, pp. 130, 157.
5. For Mierendorff see the tribute paid to him on his death by Carl Zuckmayer, *Carlo Mierendorff, Porträt eines deutschen Sozialisten* (1947), and (more accessibly) Zuckmayer's autobiography, *A Part of Myself* (1970).
6. See C. Sykes, *Troubled Loyalty* (1968), Chapter 14. Furtwängler came under SD suspicion in 1942 and his *Widerstand* activities had to be somewhat curtailed.
7. Letter from Steltzer in IfZ. Allan Dulles's statement (*Germany's Underground*, p. 91) that Helmuth met him on a course at Rendsburg in the 1920s is therefore incorrect.
8. T. Steltzer, *Sechzig Jahre Zeitgenosse* (1966), p. 149.
9. J. Donohoe, *Hitler's conservative opponents in Bavaria 1930–45* (1961), p. 261.
10. 13–16 March 1942, 25–27 July 1942, 6–7 February 1943.
11. B. Schwerdtfeger, *Konrad Kardinal von Preysing* (1950), p. 108.
L. Lochner (ed.), *The Goebbels Diaries* (1948), 11 March 1942.
12. For the record of his interrogation, see van Roon, op. cit., p. 130.
13. Letter of 9 August 1963 in IfZ.

14. van Roon, *German Resistance to Hitler*, p. 130.
15. G. Kennan, *Memoirs*, pp. 120–22.
16. H. Krausnick, etc., *Die Anatomie des SS Staates* (1965), Vol. II, pp. 261–3; IMT XI 444–62.
17. Text in Krausnick, op. cit., Vol II, pp. 251–8.

CHAPTER 20: STEPS FORWARD: JANUARY–WHITSUN
1942

1. Steltzer, *Sechzig Jahre Zeitgenosse*, p. 150.
2. B. Schwerdtfeger, op. cit., p. 130.
3. Speech of 9 September 1941, 'We are still masters of our fate, we are still captains of our souls.'
4. The statement contained in the German edition of Dr van Roon's book that these included Berggrav has now been established to rest on a confusion with later visits.
5. Steltzer, *Sechzig Jahre Zeitgenosse*, p. 144.
6. IMT Nuremberg XII, p. 270.
7. The week-end in August 1940 (above, p. 129) is not regarded as part of the series.
8. Text in van Roon, pp. 358–61.
9. ibid., pp. 361–4.
10. See, on these matters, VfZ. 5 (1957), pp. 388 ff.; Sykes, op. cit., pp. 377–80; Bethge, *Dietrich Bonhoeffer* (1970), pp. 660–76; Bonhoeffer, *Gesammelte Schriften* (1958), I, pp. 372–413.
11. Bonhoeffer, *Gesammelte Schriften*, I, p. 408 (report by Bell).
12. See E. Gerstenmaier, VfZ. 15 (1967), pp. 236–7.
13. Dr Gerstenmaier regards it as 'highly probable that Helmuth was well-informed about our memorandum of April 1942 even if he had not gone over it word for word'. (Letter to M.B. of 27 September 1971.)

CHAPTER 21: THE TURNING POINT:
WHITSUN–CHRISTMAS 1942

1. Text in van Roon, pp. 329–31.
2. Letter of van Husen to van Roon, 5 July 1964, in IfZ.
3. M. Steinert, *Hitlers Krieg und die Deutschen* (1970), p. 69 quoting an S.S. document in the *Bundesarchiv*.
4. Dr Gerstenmaier had known Helmuth and Peter Yorck since 1939–40 but only distantly. Some confusion has been caused by a letter of 19 June in which Helmuth speaks of meeting 'a man from Wurm'. This has been taken to be Dr Gerstenmaier but was in fact Dr Pressel, the bishop's adviser on Church politics. Helmuth had already met Gerstenmaier on 3 June when he described him as 'the man who is so-to-speak Wurm's representative in Berlin'.
5. van Roon, VfZ., p. 23.
6. ibid, p. 33.
7. Gladisch papers in *Bundesarchiv* Freiburg: copy in IfZ. In 1944 Gladisch and Dr Widmann, another member of the Committee, produced a book on '*Grossfragen des Seekriegsrechts im zweiten Weltkrieg*' which was presumably based on the Committee's activities.
8. On 1 August Helmuth wrote that Delp had called 'on behalf of the three bishops, Faulhaber, Pr[eysing] and Dietz and brought an invitation to the discussion for [Mierendorff] and myself'. It is not clear from this

wording that all three bishops were to be present at 'the discussion'; for security reasons, so big a gathering seems unlikely. In any case Freya von Moltke does not believe that a tripartite discussion of this kind ever took place.

9. Texts in van Roon, op. cit., pp. 332–7.
10. van Roon, German edition, p. 276.
11. VfZ. 15 (1967), p. 235.
12. A. Krebs, *Fritz-Dietlof Graf von der Schulenburg* (1964), p. 265.
13. The authors are most grateful to Domkapitular Walter Adolph for his help in establishing the facts about the origin of the Pastoral Letter.
14. B. Schwerdtfeger, *Konrad Kardinal von Preysing* (1950), p. 129.

CHAPTER 22: ARGUMENT AND FRUSTRATION:
JANUARY–APRIL 1943

1. Letter of 24 January 1943.
2. Hassell, *Vom anderen Deutschland* (1946), p. 295.
3. Dr Gerstenmaier (VfZ. 15 (1967), p. 245) says that Helmuth did not mention Kerensky in response to an exposition of Goerdeler's but muttered it half to himself, that it was taken up by the others and had a bad effect. Helmuth's account, however, written on the day after the event, makes clear that it was a very calculated intervention!
4. Professor H. Mommsen, in suggesting that the use of this 'ominous expression' is 'evidence of the great fear that Germany would experience Bolshevism after her defeat' (*The German Resistance to Hitler*, p. 123), does not seem to have understood this point.
5. Said to Herr von Portatius in 1943. Letter in IfZ.
6. van Roon, p. 174. No indication of date.
7. ibid. The statement ends 'the military authorities ought to make an Armistice and peace in the West.' This suggests a date in the second half of 1943.
8. Said to Dr Gottfried Falkenhausen in Paris, June 1943, below, p. 263.
9. Emphasised by Professor Christiansen-Weniger in a letter to M.B. 12 October 1971. But see also M. Steinert, *Hitlers Krieg und die Deutschen* (1970), Part IV.
10. Reisert was later considered as a possible Minister of Justice, Fugger as Land Commissioner for Bavaria.
11. *Spiegelbild einer Verschwörung*, p. 438 (in general a source of doubtful reliability but one which there is no reason to distrust in this instance). Letter from Reisert in IfZ. (Cf. Note 7 to Chapter 24.)
12. Letter from Frau Borsig in IfZ.
13. Letter from Mr Andersen in IfZ.
14. J. Glenthøj, *Dokumente zur Bonhoeffer Forschung* (1969), p. 265; van Roon p. 387. On the authority of Berggrav's private papers Dr P. Ludlow thinks that the statement about Helmuth's willingness to join in killing Hitler may not have been put on paper by Berggrav immediately and is not therefore beyond question. Berggrav is said in van Roon to have made 'notes on meetings with Steltzer and Moltke on 8 January and 18 March 1943'. Steltzer may well have been in Oslo on 8 January but Helmuth was certainly in Berlin on that date.
15. Photocopy of minute by Ausland VI (d) in IfZ.
16. Dr Robert Mackie DD has stated (Letter to M.B. of 10 October 1971) that he did not meet Helmuth on this (or any other) occasion or convey copies of the Scholls' leaflets to Britain.

17. **Glenthøj**, p. 285. The words 'try to' do not occur in the original. The only way of getting to Britain was in a British military aircraft which flew about twice a week and carried a single passenger. Places were hard to get and there is no evidence of Helmuth having had any contact with the British Embassy. The chances of his being able and allowed to make the double journey within a few days were extremely small. Bishop Bell for example had been kept waiting in Stockholm for a week before he could get off – but Helmuth was presumably unaware of the logistical difficulties.

18. H. Lindgren, *Adam von Trott's Reisen nach Schweden 1942–4*, in VfZ. 18 (1970), pp. 274–91.

19. Texts in van Roon, pp. 364–7.

20. As Helmuth mentioned at the end of the letter to Curtis, he wrote separate letters to M.B. and J.F. These both arrived, through the ordinary post, and signed 'Maria Strindberg', about the end of May. J.F. was visited a few days later by an Intelligence Officer who asked him about the contents of the letter and the identity of the writer. As he had already been under suspicion on account of his links with the Moltkes, suspicion which Curtis helped to remove, J.F. mentioned this visit in writing to tell Curtis about the letter. Curtis replied that he had shown J.F.'s letter to an officer of MI5 and could assure J.F. that 'the enquiries made of you are in no way directed against you. You are simply a valuable source of information about H who is at last beginning to interest people that matter.'

J.F. had, however, got into the habit of destroying letters relating to Helmuth and therefore did not keep the Stockholm letter. M.B. kept a copy of his letter; the original, as far as he can remember, he handed over to interested authorities in London. Most of it consisted of family news but extracts are quoted on pp. 228 and 258. The letters through the post arrived, of course, over three months before the communication through Tracy Strong.

21. H. Höhne, *Kennwort Direktor; Die Geschichte der roten Kapelle* (1970).

22. van Roon (German edition), p. 287.

23. H. B. Gisevius, *Wo ist Nebe* (1966), pp. 236–7.

CHAPTER 23: HARD AT WORK: APRIL–AUGUST 1943

1. He had added questions about prisoners to his other responsibilities at the end of 1942 when his assistant Jaenicke was sent to the front.

2. Wengler, article in *Die Friedenswarte*, 1948.

3. After the war Hans Lukaschek (in a speech quoted in van Roon, p. 172) declared that Helmuth asked him to come to Berlin on 10 August and there told him that Hitler, Göring and Himmler were going on 13 August to the Rastenburg headquarters in East Prussia where they were to be arrested by the Armoured Division which guarded it and which was under the firm control of resolute men. Lukaschek was given a document appointing him Reich Commissioner (?*Landesverweser*) for 'the Eastern Provinces'. The plan, however, came to nothing because Hitler never went to Rastenburg. If this story could be confirmed, it would be interesting evidence of Helmuth's continued readiness to approve and assist in organising a *Staatsstreich*. And Lukaschek did see Helmuth on 9 August. Hitler, however, had gone to Rastenburg on 19 July and (except for a one-day visit to the eastern front on 27 August) stayed there till September. There is no evidence whatever to suggest

that the conspirators ever had control over an Armoured Division at Rastenburg or anywhere else – if they had, history might have been different! In 1943 Lt.-Col. Georg Baron von Boeselager did succeed in organising (largely from Cossacks) a cavalry regiment attached to the Central Army Group on the Russian front and there was some talk of using it for a coup (P. Hoffmann, *Widerstand, Staatsstreich, Attentat,* 1969, pp. 327–8). A passage in Papen's *Memoirs* (1952) (p. 498) suggests that this talk spread to Germany and a garbled version might have provided the original basis for Lukascheck's story. Helmuth was unlikely to have handed anyone a document of appointment as he had no authority to do so (Gerstenmaier, VfZ. 15, p. 244).

Lukaschek also declared (van Roon, German edition, p. 288) that in April 1944, when he was on a visit to Kauern at which he met Freya von Moltke, he was told by Yorck of Claus von Stauffenberg's appointment as Chief of Staff of the Home Army. Freya did meet Lukaschek at Kauern late in April 1944. But Fromm, the GOC of the Home Army, would only seem to have decided to make the appointment at the end of May (Müller, *Oberst i G. Stauffenberg* (1971), p. 396). If it was Stauffenberg's appointment as Chief of Staff of the General Army Office that Lukaschek heard about, he was seven months behind the times! His memory for detail is not impressive.

CHAPTER 24: PLANS

1. Professor Schmid was unaware until informed by M.B. in May 1972 that the 'Fundamental Principles' had contained such a proposal. He himself first formulated the idea soon after 1933. He talked over with Helmuth many problems related to Germany's post-war political reconstruction and he was considerably influenced by Helmuth's ideas. But he is no longer able to be sure whether they ever discussed this particular provision. (Letter to M.B. of 5 June 1972.) Professor Mommsen (*The German Resistance to Hitler*, p. 120) credits Goerdeler with a similar scheme but M.B. has been unable to locate its whereabouts.
2. Hugo Preuss, the man principally responsible for drafting the Weimar Constitution, had also been anxious to base democracy on the active consciousness of citizenship at local level (S. Grassmann, *Hugo Preuss und die deutsche Selbstverwaltung*, 1965).
3. This assumption is supported by Steltzer's post-war views, *Von deutscher Politik* (1949), pp. 131–5.
4. Krebs, *Schulenburg*, p. 241. Douglas-Hamilton, *Motive for a Mission* (1971), p. 216.
5. Macaulay, *History of England* (1849–61), Vol. I, Chap. 10.
6. See B. Scheurig (ed.), *Deutscher Widerstand 1938–44 Fortschritt oder Reaktion* (1969). Graml, Mommsen, etc.; op. cit.
7. *Spiegelbild einer Verschwörung: Die Kaltenbrunner Berichte an Hitler und Bormann über das Attentat vom 20 Juli 1944* (1961), p. 419 (cf. Note 11 to Chapter 22).
8. F. R. Barry, *Secular and Supernatural* (1969), p. 9.

CHAPTER 25: TRAVELS: APRIL–DECEMBER 1943

1. There has been some doubt about the chronology of this visit and Helmuth had indeed been anxious to make it for some months but the establishment of communications with the Cardinal had to be done unobtrusively

and therefore took some time. Helmuth wrote to Freya 'on the way to Warsaw' on 1 May, reached Pulawy late that night and was back in Berlin in time to write again on 4 May. This chronology and other details have been confirmed by Professor Christiansen-Weniger. (Letters of 12 October and 7 November 1971 to M.B.)

2. W. Ritter von Schramm, *Der 20 Juli in Paris* (1953), p. 28.
3. van Roon, p. 210.
4. *Spiegelbild einer Verschwörung* (1961), p. 390.
5. The evidence about the purpose of the meeting comes from a letter of 20 August 1943. The matter under discussion with the Ministry may have concerned one of Helmuth's private legal clients.
6. This account is based on L. Yahil, *The Defence of Danish Jewry – Test of a Democracy*, 1969.
7. Letter of A. Kirk to M.B., 21 May 1971.
8. Told by Wengler to M.B., 29 May 1971.
9. As the OSS archives are still shut, some parts of this narrative are 'best available guesses'.
10. Letter of A. Kirk to M.B., 28 June 1971.
11. Dr Gerstenmaier would seem to have overlooked this statement in arguing (VfZ. 15 (1967), p. 243) that Helmuth was not expecting arrest at the end of 1943 and that a statement to that effect by Dr Pressel was based on confused recollection. On the other hand, Helmuth never gave Freya reason to think that he was anticipating arrest.
12. Sykes, *Troubled Loyalty*, pp. 303–4.
13. ibid., pp. 321–3.
14. Hoffmann, *Widerstand*, etc., p. 278, based on a speech by Brandt.
15. See B. Scheurig, *Freies Deutschland, Das National Komitee und der Bund deutscher Offiziere in der Sowjetunion 1943–5* (1960); *Verrat Hinter Stacheldraht* (a collection of documents on the same subject, 1965).
16. According to a letter from Herr von Portatius in IfZ., Helmuth said during his visit to Béthune (above, p. 258) that contact had been established with Madame Kollontai. Trott is also said to have seen her in 1944, but Sykes (*Troubled Loyalty*, p. 426) believes the story to be false and to rest on confusion with the activities of Peter Kleist in 1943.

CHAPTER 26: THE LAST WEEKS OF LIBERTY: OCTOBER 1943–19 JANUARY 1944

1. This identification is made on the authority of Freya von Moltke.
2. By M.B. in June 1971.
3. Letter in IfZ.
4. Told by Mrs Bielenberg to M.B., April 1970. But Sykes, p. 406, suggests that Adam met Claus in November 1943.
5. Marion Yorck was told this by Schulenburg.
6. Lilje, *Im finstern Tal* (1947), p. 67.

CHAPTER 27: THE SPY

1. The account of Dr Reckzeh's activities and of the fatal tea-party is based on Irmgard von der Lühe, *Elisabeth von Thadden, Ein Schicksal unserer Zeit* (1966). This book differs on several points from other and previous accounts but is more directly concerned with the protagonist

and is borne out by Countess Ballestrem-Solf's account in Eric Boehm, *We Survived* (1949).
2. Reitlinger, *The SS* (1956), p. 304.

CHAPTER 28: DOWNFALLS

1. VfZ. (1967), p. 223.
2. Letter in IfZ.
3. *Von Deutscher Politik* (1949), p. 77.
4. van Roon, p. 270.
5. Müller, p. 419.
6. VfZ. (1967), pp. 233–5.
7. Gisevius, *Wo ist Nebe* (1966), p. 106.

CHAPTER 29: IMPRISONMENT

1. It has been said (e.g. Isa Vermehren, *Reise durch den letzten Akt* (1946), p. 28) that Helmuth's name occurred in one of the lists of prospective office-holders in the Goerdeler government. But there is no mention of this in the reports of the investigating commission and the name does not occur in the various lists printed by Hoffmann (*Widerstand, Staatsstreich, Attentat*, pp. 435–6). Indeed Hoffmann denies (p. 610) that any such lists ever came intact into SD hands. There is a story, deriving from Huppenkothen, that one made out by Oster in 1939 was found in a cupboard at Zossen (Manvell and Fraenkel, *The Canaris Conspiracy* (1969), pp. 190, 240) but even if this was true, Helmuth's name was unlikely to be included in anything so early.
2. I. Vermehren, op. cit., p. 43. The suit was not English. Above, p. 49.
3. ibid., p. 28.
4. Lilje, *Im finstern Tal*, p. 67.
5. This is the origin of the story reproduced in Manvell and Fraenkel, *The July Plot* (1964), p. 247, that Helmuth was too weak a man to stand during his interrogation.

CHAPTER 30: TRIAL AND DEATH

1. Because of bomb damage, the court moved about a good deal. The trial of 8 August had been held in the *Kammergericht* building in Schöneberg, used after the war by the Allied Control Commission.
2. 'A German of the Resistance', *Round Table*, June 1946 and Oxford University Press, 1946–8.
3. H. Lilje, *Im finstern Tal*, p. 62. Lilje gives certain further details which are not corroborated by other sources and have therefore been omitted.

Index

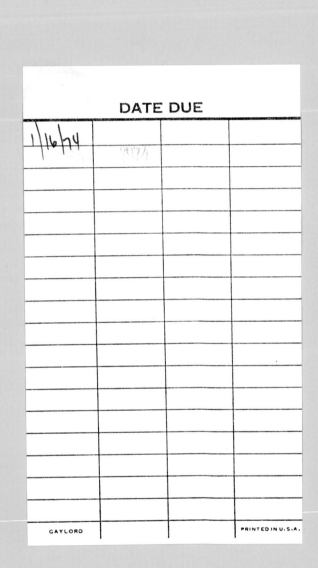

DATE DUE

1/16/74			
GAYLORD			PRINTED IN U.S.A.